KEITH SOMERVILLE

Ivory

Power and Poaching in Africa

HURST & COMPANY, LONDON

First published in the United Kingdom in 2016 by
C. Hurst & Co. (Publishers) Ltd.,
41 Great Russell Street, London, WC1B 3PL
© Keith Somerville, 2016
This updated paperback edition first published in 2019
All rights reserved.

Distributed in the United States, Canada and Latin America by
Oxford University Press, 198 Madison Avenue, New York, NY 10016,
United States of America.

A Cataloguing-in-Publication data record for this book
is available from the British Library.

ISBN: 9781787382220

This book is printed using paper from registered sustainable
and managed sources.

www.hurstpublishers.com

Printed and bound in Great Britain by Bell & Bain Ltd, Glasgow

PREFACE TO THE SECOND EDITION

Since the completion of the manuscript of *Ivory: Power and Poaching* in the summer of 2016 there have been major developments in the international, notably the Chinese, responses to the continued high level of elephant poaching in Africa. These include the failed attempts at the CITES (the Convention on International Trade in Endangered Species of Wild Fauna and Flora) Conference of the Parties in Johannesburg in late September 2016 and then Geneva in August 2019 to change the listing of southern African elephant populations to prevent future trade in ivory, and the unsuccessful attempts attempts by southern African range states to get permission for sales of legal stocks of ivory. This might lead to Botswana, Namibia, South Africa, Zambia and Zimbabwe finding ways to circumvent CITES restrictions or to them deciding to leave CITES. Another major development was the election of a new president in Botswana, which has led to elephants becoming the focus of a political power struggle between the new and old incumbents over hunting and approaches to elephant conservation. The latter has strong implications for the future of wildlife and specifically elephant management in southern Africa, but the former events have done little to change the pace of poaching (thought to be c. 20,000 killed a year) and the extent of the illegal trade.

China has long been identified as the major market for legal and illegal ivory sales, with the legal market and legally-held stocks of ivory being used to launder illegal ivory smuggled into the country through air and sea ports, from Hong Kong (where the trade remains legal until 2021, according to legislation passed there in 2018 on the phasing out of the legal trade) and across land borders from Vietnam, Laos and Myanmar. Under heavy pressure from wildlife NGOs, Western governments and some African elephant range state governments, the government of President Xi Jinping decided that the legal industry was not important enough given the bad image it was creating of China. He announced and legislated for a ban on the domestic trade (though it was never clear whether this was intended as a permanent one or a moratorium). On 31 December 2017, a ban on legal domestic working and sale of ivory came into force. In the run up to the ban 67 factories and shops dealing in ivory were closed and the remaining 105 were shut when the ban came into force, according to the official Chinese news agency Xinhua. The move was welcomed by animal rights NGOs, such as WildAid, which called it "a great moment in the history of elephant conservation". Organizations like the WWF, Born Free and the Environmental Investigation Agency followed suit. But since the ban, while the price of ivory has fallen from around $1322 per kg in 2015 to $660–750 in 2017, the trade does not seem to have diminished in size and there is no clear indication of a fall in poaching. The trade expert Dan Stiles told the *Guardian* in June 2017 that the fall in price did not necessarily mean a drop in demand but there were signs that it was because of a surplus of raw ivory available from poaching and traders and end users were unwilling to pay high prices. He also warned that the closure of legal markets could lead to an increase in illegal selling to cover the gap in supply caused by the ban and to stockpiling ahead of any lift in the ban, which several leading ivory trade researchers told me in confidence was highly likely within the next five to ten years.

The closure of the Chinese factories and shops meant that many Chinese carvers simply relocated to Vietnam and Laos, where illegal ivory was worked and smuggled across porous land borders into China. And there was no let up in the smuggling of ivory into East Asia, as shown by seizures in early 2019—the *South China Morning Post* reporting in April that over seven tonnes of ivory had been discovered by customs officials in the eastern Chinese province of Anhui. The haul was made up of 2,478 tusks, according to customs officials. In March 2019, Vietnamese customs officials had seized nine tonnes of ivory at the port of Da Nang, hidden in a consignment of timber imported from the Republic of Congo, which would have involved the killing of around 1,000 elephants. These are just the largest among the continued reports of seizures of ivory. The size but also the regularity of reporting of seizures in Malaysia, Cambodia and Thailand in addition to Vietnam and China indicate the volume of the continued trade, and reports in the media across African range states show continued, regular arrests of poachers (see the African Sustainable Conservation news website—https://africasustainableconservation.com/ for regular updates on seizures and capture or conviction of poachers and smugglers).

The Chinese ivory ban has also had the effect of increasing the demand and sale, still legal in China, of mammoth ivory dug up from the perma-frost areas of Yakutia and other areas of Siberia. The Phys. org website carried out research into the trade and estimated that Russian exports of mammoth tusks amounted to 72 tonnes in 2017, with over 80 per cent going to China. Chinese buyers were going regularly to Yakutia to buy tusks directly. Good quality mammoth ivory can fetch $1,000 per kg in China and is legal. The trade may fill some of the gap created by the ivory ban but could also provide cover for sales of poached ivory.

The Chinese ban was followed by the enactment of legislation by the British government in December 2018 to enforce a total ban on the sale, import or export of ivory or items containing ivory from a date to be set in 2019. Some items (of an antique nature and those containing less than 10% ivory) would be exempt but the regulations were much stricter than before and particularly aimed at stemming legal exports of antique ivory that could be bused to launder illegal ivory. The measure is unlikely to have a huge effect on the market and is largely symbolic.

Amid all these attempts to ban the trade, poaching continues with tusks taken from illegally killed elephants across the range states. In Tanzania, the level of poaching has dropped from the catastrophic level of recent years, with a population of 142,000 falling to 55,000 between 2005 and 2015, with the Selous Game Reserve numbers falling dramatically from 70,000 to 13,000 and a similar decline observable in Ruaha National Park. In 2018, the Tanzanian Wildlife Research Institute (TAWIRI) said that poaching levels had falling since 2015. While this may have been partly a result of improved anti-poaching measures, it was also clearly a product of there being far fewer elephants to kill. Poaching has continued to be a problem, too, in the Democratic Republic of Congo, where an almost perpetual state of war makes law enforcement nearly impossible, and Gabon, the home to the largest numbers of forest elephants, and Mozambique. Minor increases in poaching, though not at a level to affect the substantial southern Africa populations, have also occurred in South Africa's Kruger and in northern Botswana.

The Botswana elephant battle

Since the first edition of this book was published, Botswana has become the location for an important and politically charged battle over elephant conservation. At the centre of this long-running and increasingly bitter controversy are several factors:

- Vastly different estimates of elephant numbers, and elephant poaching levels.
- Competing approaches to the conservation of wildlife and habitats.
- Major political divisions within Botswana since the change in president in April 2018.
- Conflicts between eco-tourism and anti-sustainable-use lobbies on the one side, and the interests of rural people and their elected representatives on the other side.
- Western animal advocacy campaigners' sentiments, whose approach appears to be that a focus on individual animals or species at any one time is more important than the people and their livelihoods in the countries where these animals exist, the habitats that need to be protected by the most sustainable and locally-supported means and the long-term future of wildlife ranges that include or are adjacent to human settlements.

The controversy kicked off in September 2018, when Mike Chase (the veteran elephant researcher and founder of the advocacy group Elephants Without Borders) told the BBC that the carcasses of 87 elephants had been found between the Okavango and the Chobe River in Botswana, and that many had been poached. There was no verifiable evidence of how many had been poached or of the exact age of the carcasses; most carcasses had been seen from the air and only a minority had been inspected on the ground. The BBC ran with the story, uncritically reported Chase's claim that "the scale of poaching deaths is the largest seen in Africa". This was followed by the assertion that the discovery of the elephant bodies indicated a massive rise in poaching and that it resulted from "Botswana's anti-poaching unit being disarmed"—a story that is not supported by the evidence. The unit had not been disarmed but had been stripped of the military-grade, automatic weapons that had been supplied to them by the Khama government in contravention of its own firearms laws. They retained their normal semi-automatic weapons and were still supported by heavily armed Botswana Defence Force (BDF) units.

Under the presidency of Ian Khama—a vehement opponent of hunting and a former commander of the BDF—an aggressive policy of the use of maximum force against suspected poachers, effectively of a shoot-to-kill policy, had been in force which had led to the killing of dozens of poaching suspects (mainly Zambians, Zimbabweans and Namibians)—in 2015 alone at least thirty Namibians and twenty-two Zimbabweans had been shot by anti-poaching units or the BDF on suspicion of poaching and dozens of Zambians had been shot over several years. This had led to angry protests from the Namibian and Zambian governments.

The claim that this was the largest incident of elephant poaching seen in Africa was preposterous, but it gained public attention. Botswana's poaching rate, even though it has risen since president Khama's ban on commercial and trophy hunting in 2014, pales into insignificance against the massive killing of elephants in Tanzania and Mozambique in recent years, and the toll taken by Sudanese and Central African poachers in northern Cameroon and the Central African Republic seven years ago (see pp. 234–236). I contacted the BBC reporter, Alastair Leithhead, who had spoken to Chase and broke the story. He told me that, "I honestly don't believe Mike Chase made up the 87 carcasses", but the Botswana government said they had not found the carcasses and denied the level of poaching reported by Chase.

The context of this row was highly political. In April 2018, when Mokgweetsi Masisi took over as President, he was immediately at odds with his predecessor, over issues such as the future political role of the former president's brother, Tshekedi Khama (the environment minister with responsibility for wildlife policy).

Soon after taking power, Masisi announced, to the relief of the governments of Namibia, Zambia and Zimbabwe, that he would halt the aggressive approach of shooting suspected poachers. He also responded to growing pressure from rural communities and from his own Botswana Democratic Party (BDP) MPs to re-examine the hunting ban (introduced without legislation by Khama in 2014) and overall elephant conservation policy. Rural communities, their traditional leaders and MPs had long argued that after the ban came into force there was a substantial increase in the losses they suffered through elephants eating their crops, breaking water pumps and lions attacking livestock. Popular pressure, exerted through village chiefs and parliamentarians, led to a large majority in the Botswana parliament for a motion calling on the government to lift the hunting ban, particularly the ban on elephant hunting.

The MPs' strongly supported motion was responded to by the Masisi government with the establishment of a ministerial committee to hold widespread consultations with all parties affected. This included traditional kgotla meetings (consultative sessions with the public), where Batswana have traditionally been able to question, challenge and even defeat government policy suggestions. The process of consultation was instituted in late 2018 and the report's recommendations made public by the government in February 2019. It contained a number of recommendations, including:

- *Hunting ban be lifted.*
- *Develop a legal framework that will create an enabling environment for growth of safari hunting industry.*
- *Manage Botswana elephant population within its historic range*
- *Department of Wildlife and National Parks (DWNP) should undertake an effective community outreach program within the elephant range for Human Elephant Conflict mitigation*
- *Strategically placed human wildlife conflict fences be constructed in key hotspot areas*
- *Game ranches be demarcated to serve as buffers between communal and wildlife areas.*

- *Compensation for damage caused by wildlife, ex gratia amounts and the list of species that attract compensation be reviewed. In addition, other models that alleviate compensation burden on Government be considered.*
- *All wildlife migratory routes that are not beneficial to the country's conservation efforts be closed.*
- *The Kgalagadi southwesterly antelope migratory route into South Africa should be closed by demarcating game ranches between the communal areas and Kgalagadi Wildlife Management Areas.*
- *Regular but limited elephant culling be introduced and establishment of elephant meat canning, including production of pet food and processing into other by-products.*

The Masisi government has made clear that it will consider and act upon the recommendations in some form, though it did not promise to enact them in full. It is clear that the hunting ban will be lifted, and a new regulatory and income distribution scheme is likely to be put in place, with the aim of restoring income to local communities, creating buffers between wildlife areas and farming ones and using this and other measures to cut human-wildlife conflict. A meeting was held with leaders from the KAZA (Kavango-Zambezi Transfrontier Conservation Area—uniting areas of Angola, Botswana, Namibia, Zambia and Zimbabwe to encourage safe movement of elephants other wildlife within the region) and they agreed to set out a scientifically-backed framework for elephant conservation policy. It is clear that while the jury is still out on whether Botswana would reintroduce culling (which could damage its lucrative tourist industry) it is bringing back regulated trophy hunting of elephants with a quota of 400 elephants a year, with part of the income directed towards local communities to give them an incentive to coexist with elephants and refrain from involvement in poaching. Hunting concessions are likely to also be used as buffers to prevent wildlife intrusion into and damage of farmland.

But while the government works on that, it has still to contend with the poaching row. Mike Chase gave his report on elephant numbers and poaching to the government for its consideration at the end of 2018, but also furnished further details to the BBC and took Alastair Leithhead on a helicopter trip to view some of the carcasses in January 2019. Leithhead told me he saw 87, namely those that Chase assured him were mainly victims of poaching. These 87 later increased in other reports to 88, then 128, and then to 157. Chase claimed that the carcasses he saw meant that there had been a 600% increase in poaching in northern Botswana. A Botswana government press release on 24 February 2019 questioned Chase's estimates of carcasses and of the level of poaching he claims, noting that there was no great change in overall elephant numbers that would suggest a serious rise in poaching.

Poaching has been rising (see pp. 269–272) and the hunting ban appears to have led to the greater involvement of Batswana assisting poachers from Zambia and Namibia. What is interesting is that Chase only publicised the poaching levels in 2018, after his friend and ally Ian Khama had left office and Masisi had announced a rethink in elephant policy—Chase has made it clear that he opposes a resumption of hunting. I wrote a series of articles from 2015 onwards for *African Arguments*, *Commonwealth Opinion*, *Talking Humanities* and *The Conversation* drawing attention to a rise in poaching following the hunting ban. On research trips to Botswana after the ban, Amos Ramakoti of the DWNP in Maun, Michael Flyman the organizer of the DWNP wildlife censuses, and Baboloki Autletswe, the head of the Kalahari Conservation Society, all told me that poaching had increased since the hunting ban and that Batswana were no longer cooperating with anti-poaching teams as they had in the past. Increasing numbers of local people were involved in helping ivory poachers from Zambia and Namibia and engaging in bushmeat poaching. Flyman said known poaching had risen from about thirty to thirty-five elephants a year before the ban to over fifty since 2014. I contacted Mike Chase in 2015, but he was too busy in Kenya to respond to my questions about poaching levels and the possibility that the rise was linked to the hunting ban. From 2016 onwards, despite requests on my behalf by the veteran southern African conservationist John Hanks, Chase declined to reply to my e-mails requesting his views on the rise in evidence of poaching. It was only after the change in government, the impending end of the Khama conservation regime and the strong likelihood of a return to legalised hunting that suddenly the possibility of an increase in poaching became an issue. Chase continues to openly oppose the restoration of legal hunting.

There has been a rise in poaching since 2014, though not a massive one. Even taking a conservative estimate of the Botswana elephant population of around 130,000, the Chase carcass figures do not show a serious threat to numbers—especially as the 130,000 figure is part of the 202,000-240,000 population of KAZA which is highly mobile and which moves in and out of Botswana's main elephant habitat in Ngamiland (particularly Chobe, Linyanti, Savuti and the Okavango) according to food and water availability and the greater safety in Botswana, given the high level of poaching in the southern Angolan and south-western Zambian parts of the KAZA range. But any rise in poaching should be taken seriously and cross-border KAZA action is needed to cut poaching but also to limit human-elephant conflict, which creates the grievances and impoverishes people, giving them incentives to poach rather than to protect.

The Botswana controversy is complex but important for future elephant policy in Africa. It involves an evolving mix of domestic politics and power struggles within Botswana's political elite, divisions over the best policy for conservation, competing views of the level of the poaching threat, and the tendency of the Western media to jump on animal advocacy bandwagons, in the process discarding in the process balance, verification and the views of African governments and, especially, the views and experiences of people who have to coexist and often come into conflict with wildlife.

Regionally, Botswana's change of policy has brought it back into line with Namibia, South Africa and Zimbabwe and they jointly and unsuccessfully applied to the CITES Conference of Parties in Geneva in August 2019 for permission to sell their ivory stocks. The vote against this at the conference led to angry responses from southern African states with President Mnangagwa of Zimbabwe suggesting the southern African range states might leave CITES or try to do their own deals with other countries to sell their ivory. How this will develop remains to be seen, but whatever happens will have a major effect on Africa's elephants as the southern African ranges are home to the majority of savanna elephants.

African elephant numbers

To return to the overall picture for African elephants, since Ivory was first published and despite the China and UK bans and some fall in poaching in crisis areas like Tanzania, elephant poaching remains a threat to populations in many areas and the most reliable figures from the *African Elephant Status Report 2016* (https://portals.iucn.org/library/sites/library/files/documents/SSC-OP-060_A.pdf) and the *African Elephant Database* (http://africanelephantdatabase.org/report/2013/Africa) show a continued decline in numbers across the whole Africa range—which suggests that poaching and probably also falling populations due to habitat loss are still outstripping reproduction rates.

In 2013, the *African Elephant Database* gave a basic estimate of 426,293 elephants in Africa with a margin of error of 25,527 either way but added that informed guesses suggested there could be another 134,135–180,901 elephants. *The African Elephant Database* and *Status Report* for 2016 gave a base figure of 415,428 with a margin of error $\pm$ 20,111, and informed guesses of another 117,127–135,384.

Estimates of East African elephant populations 1995–2013, from the Elephant Database, (http://www.elephantdatabase.org/)

1995		1998		2002		2007		2013	
Definite	Max	Definite	Max	Definite	Max	Definite	Max	Definite	Max
90,482	128,273	83,770	125,179	117,716	163,667	137,485	205,195	89,860	125,832

This table shows changes in East African elephant numbers, with poaching a major issue. The African Elephant Status Report for 2016, only recently available, shows a likely regional population of 86,373 with a possible absolute maximum of 108,922. The decline being almost totally a result of poaching in Tanzania. The table can be read in conjunction with the narrative in Chapter 7 starting page 224.

This book is dedicated to all those who have given their lives or who currently risk their lives in the name of conserving elephants and other wildlife. It is also dedicated to those who have the courage to question the ruling orthodoxy—that burnings and bans save elephants—an approach that has not ended poaching and is unlikely to do so in the future.

Keith Somerville
London, June 2016

CONTENTS

ACKNOWLEDGEMENTS

Although I started the intensive research for this book in 2014 and started writing in early 2015, the genesis of the work is in November 1981, in Kasungu National Park in Malawi. Liz and I visited Kasungu and drove round on the poorly maintained tracks, in the car belonging to the BBC Monitoring Service, for whom I was working in Malawi: a beat-up old Morris Marina with no second gear. We had a couple of close shaves with angry bull elephants. On our first game drive, as we came round a bend in the road with thick mopane bush on either side, there was a big bull by the road—a hand brake turn and screaming away in first gear was the only means of avoiding his angry charge. The bulls in Kasungu didn't seem to like us much. Maybe they took offence at the car. But they gathered in the area near the Lifupa dam because of the nearby game ranger and park HQ, where they felt safe. They would mock-charge every time they saw us. Trying to get out of the way fast in a car with no second gear was a bundle of laughs. It certainly amused Hugo Jachmann, who was researching the elephants in the park and shared a few beers with us during the nights we spent there; we'd occasionally bump into each other in Lilongwe. Hugo was even more amused when, on the first night at Lifupa, returning to our tent from the bar in the dark, we unknowingly walked through the middle of an elephant herd split across the path—it seemed they came into the camp at night for protection. Hugo has since been very helpful in filling in the detail of the poaching situation in Kasungu and telling me more about the Luangwa Integrated Resource Development Project (LIRDP) in Zambia. He also told me of the death of the researcher and conservationist Richard Bell, who worked in Kasungu and Luangwa, and whom I had the chance to interview in Gaborone in 1993.

My early interest in elephants—my appreciation of their magnificence and fear of what they could do to a Morris Marina—developed as I undertook more and more journalistic and academic research assignments across eastern and southern Africa. Some of these assignments were specifically on conservation, and on the issue of elephant conservation and the ivory trade, in particular. In Botswana I was lucky enough to see Foreign Minister Gaositwe Chiepe, Vice-President Festus Mogae, Seeyiso Diphuko of the National Conservation Strategy Board and researchers with the Kalahari Conservation Society, who gave me their views and described Botswana's elephant conservation and sustainable-use policy. In Maun, Tim Liversedge flew me to his camp in the Delta and introduced me to Karen Ross of Conservation International and Richard Bell, who gave me the benefit of their knowledge. On a number of trips to Serengeti, Ngorongoro and Lake Manyara, local rangers and game guides gave me invaluable information that revealed the extent of corruption among the wildlife authorities, the ruling party and enforcement agencies. In South Africa, Willie Mabasa, of the Kruger National Park, gave me his time to discuss the growing poaching problems there in 2012. Paul Ronan of The Resolve provided me with information and sources on the LRA's poaching.

As I started writing the book, I was able to contact a number of leading elephant and ivory trade researchers. I had a spikey but lively and incredibly useful exchange of e-mails with Ian Parker, and I am grateful that despite his clear doubts about what I was doing he gave of his time, answered questions and passed on his trenchant views in great detail. Iain Douglas-Hamilton provided very useful material and explained clearly his views on the nature and causes of the contemporary poaching wave. Lucy Vigne and Esmond Martin, whose work on the ivory trade is invaluable, gave me great insights into how the trade works; while another trade expert, Dan Stiles, was the source of a wealth of information and very kindly looked over sections of the book with a sympathetic but critical eye—helpfully spotting some of the many typos that litter my manuscripts and helping me fine-tune my conclusions. Ian Craig of the Northern Rangelands Trust in Kenya and Calvin Cottar both took time to give me the benefit of their knowledge

ACKNOWLEDGEMENTS

and experience of community-based projects and payment for environmental services (PES). Mary Rice put aside time to answer my questions about the Environmental Investigation Agency (EIA) and its approach to the ivory trade. Andrea Crosta, knowing I was highly critical of the Elephant Action League's work on Al Shabab and the ivory trade, was still willing to answer my questions at length. Andrew Dunn and Paul Elkan of WCS always answered my e-mails, helping me clear up areas of confusion about Boko Haram and get a clearer view of what was happening in South Sudan. Julian Blanc of MIKE was similarly very helpful and responsive to requests for information. Professor Anthony Turton was a mine of information on South African involvement in poaching with Renamo in Mozambique. Bugs van Heerden sent me on material from the Conservation Imperative group and was very helpful on approaches to conservation.

During a trip to Botswana in June 2013, Michael Flyman, who runs the wildlife department's aerial surveys, was very helpful, giving me his time and knowledge and passing on statistics from the surveys. Amos Ramokati, the deputy regional wildlife officer in Maun, was very helpful about poaching in the north. Steve Johnson of the Southern Africa Regional Environment Program (SAREP) was great company and a mine of very useful information; thanks to Zoe Parr for putting me in touch with Steve and for working hard, despite never having met me, to find people to whom I could talk in Maun and Gaborone. Baboloki Autletswe and Nthlotlang Konte of the Kalahari Conservation Society helped greatly to improve my understanding of the aims, but also the massive practical problems, of developing the Kavango-Zambezi Transfrontier Conservation Area (KAZA). Professor Rosaleen Duffy at SOAS, Jasper Humphreys of the Marjan Centre for the Study of War and the Non-Human Sphere, and Cathy Haenlein at RUSI have been very supportive, and kindly invited me to workshops and seminars that have been a very stimulating opportunity to exchange ideas. At one of those I got the chance to hear a fascinating report on anti-poaching work in the Central African Republic by Stéphane Crayne of the WWF, to whom I spoke after his paper.

John Walker, author of *Ivory's Ghosts*, was very supportive and looked constructively at the first draft of my first historical chapters. Grace O'Donnell of WWF in the UK very kindly went to the trouble of

ACKNOWLEDGEMENTS

photocopying and sending me documents and reports not available online. Tanya Knight at Care for the Wild helped me find copies of some of Dan Stiles's and Esmond Martin's ivory trade studies and sent them on to me. Daniel Reboussin of the University of Florida helped me trace vital documents in the Ian Parker East African Wildlife Collection at the University. At Flora and Fauna International, Sarah Rakowski provided me with the entire collection of *Oryx* and its predecessor publication on DVD, and she and Cella Carr kindly gave me permission to reproduce data and maps from the journal.

I'm particularly grateful to Michael Dwyer at Hurst for encouraging me to write the book in the first place, and to his team, especially Jon de Peyer and Lara Weisweiller-Wu, for seeing it through from the typo-filled manuscript to the final book.

As always, my wife Liz and son Tom were a source of constant support and periodic admonishment when research rage or Internet ire got the better of me. And, of course, I must thank the elephants, especially that first bull in Kasungu for only mock-charging. If it weren't for them this book would not exist.

ABBREVIATIONS

ADMADE	Zambian conservation and community development programme
AERSG/AESG	African Elephant (and Rhino) Specialist Group (IUCN)
ALC	African Lakes Company
ANC	African National Congress (South Africa)
AU	African Union, successor to the OAU (Organisation of African Unity)
AWF	African Wildlife Foundation (USA)
BDF	Botswana Defence Force
CAMPFIRE	Communal Areas Management Programme for Indigenous Resources
CAR	Central African Republic
CCM	Chama Cha Mapinduzi (Tanzanian ruling party)
CHA	Controlled Hunting Area
CI	Conservation International
CITES	Convention on International Trade in Endangered Species of Wild Fauna and Flora
DNPWLM	Department of National Parks and Wildlife Management (Zimbabwe)
DRC	Democratic Republic of the Congo (formerly Zaire)
DWNP	Department of Wildlife and National Parks (Botswana)
EAL	Elephant Action League
EC	European Community (now EU)

ABBREVIATIONS

EIA	Environmental Investigation Agency
ETIS	Elephant Trade Information System
EU	European Union
FFI	Flora and Fauna International
FNLA	National Liberation Front of Angola
FRELIMO	Front for the Liberation of Mozambique (governing party since 1975)
GMA	Game Management Area
GSU	General Service Unit (Kenya's paramilitary police)
IBEAC	Imperial British East Africa Company
IFAW	International Fund for Animal Welfare
INTERPOL	International Criminal Police Organization
ITRG	Ivory Trade Review Group
IUCN	International Union for Conservation of Nature (formerly IUPN, International Union for Protection of Nature)
KAS	British SAS-linked private security company
KAZA	Kavango-Zambezi Transfrontier Conservation Area
KWS	Kenya Wildlife Service
KY	Kabaka Yekka (Ugandan political party)
LIRDP	Luangwa Integrated Resource Development Project
LRA	Lord's Resistance Army (Uganda)
MIKE	Monitoring the Illegal Killing of Elephants
MNLA	Azawad National Liberation Movement (Tuareg separatists, Mali)
NFD	Northern Frontier District (Kenya)
NGO	Non-governmental organisation
NORAD	Norwegian Agency for Development Cooperation
NRA/NRM	National Resistance Army/Movement (Uganda)
NRT	Northern Rangelands Trust (Kenya) Renamo Mozambican National Resistance
REP	Ruvuma Elephant Project
SACIM	Southern African Centre for Ivory Marketing
SADF	South African Defence Force
SANP	South African National Parks
SAREP	Southern Africa Regional Environment Programme

xxiv

ABBREVIATIONS

SPLA/SPLM	Sudan People's Liberation Army/ Sudan People's Liberation Movement (South Sudan)
SWAPO	South West African People's Organization (Namibia)
TANU	Tanganyika African National Union
UAC	United African Company
UDI	Unilateral Declaration of Independence (Rhodesia)
UNEP	United Nations Environment Programme
UNESCO	United Nations Educational, Scientific and Cultural Organization
UNIP	United National Independence Party (Zambia)
UNITA	National Union for the Total Independence of Angola
USAID	United States Agency for International Development
UWA	Ugandan Wildlife Authority
WCS	Wildlife Conservation Society
WWF	World Wide Fund for Nature (formerly the World Wildlife Fund)
ZAWA	Zambia Wildlife Authority
ZANLA	Zimbabwe African National Liberation Army (ZANU guerrilla army)
ZANU-PF	Zimbabwe African National Union-Patriotic Front (Zimbabwe)
ZAPU	Zimbabwe African People's Union
ZNA	Zimbabwe National Army
ZRP	Zimbabwe Republic Police

LIST OF TABLES

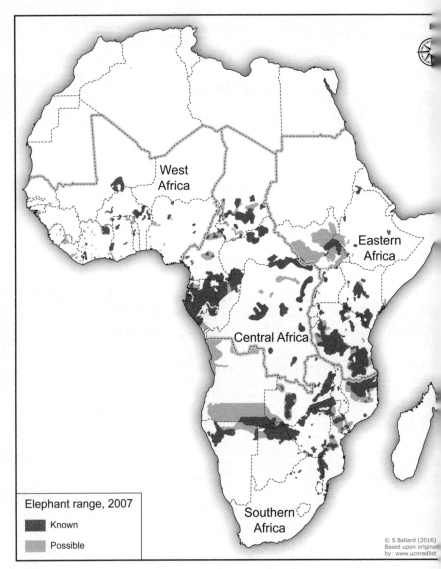

West Africa

Eastern Africa

Central Africa

Southern Africa

Elephant range, 2007

Known

Possible

© S Ballard (2016)
Based upon original
by: www.ucnredlist

Map 1. Past and present distribution.

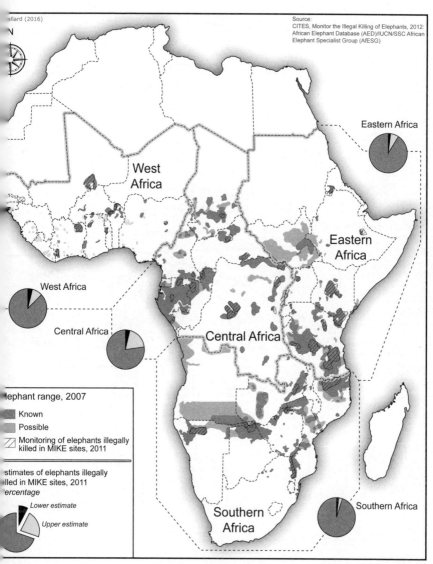

Source:
CITES, Monitor the Illegal Killing of Elephants, 2012:
African Elephant Database (AED)/IUCN/SSC African
Elephant Specialist Group (AfESG)

Eastern Africa

West
Africa

Eastern
Africa

West Africa

Central Africa

Central Africa

Elephant range, 2007

Known

Possible

Monitoring of elephants illegally
killed in MIKE sites, 2011

Estimates of elephants illegally
killed in MIKE sites, 2011
percentage

Lower estimate

Upper estimate

Southern Africa

Southern
Africa

Map 2. Elephant ranges and estimate of illegal killing.

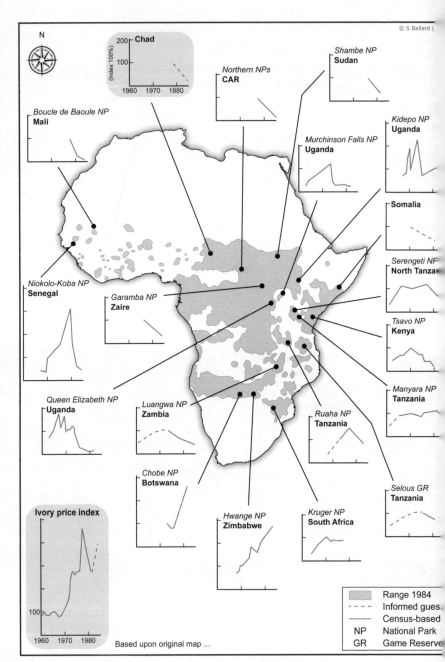

N

© S Ballard (

Chad (Index 100%)

Northern NPs
CAR

Shambe NP
Sudan

Boucle de Baoule NP
Mali

Murchinson Falls NP
Uganda

Kidepo NP
Uganda

Somalia

Niokolo-Koba NP
Senegal

Garamba NP
Zaire

Serengeti NP
North Tanza

Tsavo NP
Kenya

Queen Elizabeth NP
Uganda

Luangwa NP
Zambia

Manyara NP
Tanzania

Ruaha NP
Tanzania

Chobe NP
Botswana

Hwange NP
Zimbabwe

Kruger NP
South Africa

Selous GR
Tanzania

Ivory price index

100

1960   1970   1980

Based upon original map ...

	Range 1984
- - -	Informed gues
———	Census-based
NP	National Park
GR	Game Reserve

Map 3. National parks in current elephant ranges.

INTRODUCTION

As with the history and political economy of the ivory trade itself, the genesis of this book is complex and does not have an easily identifiable motive or start date. Over a period of nearly 40 years studying and reporting on African political and economic development, conflict and external relations, I have always had a keen and informed interest in wildlife, its utilisation and conservation. This manifested itself in making radio documentaries for the BBC World Service about African conservation dilemmas, especially the ivory question. A programme-making trip to Botswana in 1993 was key for me to develop a more detailed knowledge of the value of elephants and their ivory, and of the bitter debates over the ethics, viability and control of the ivory trade in order both to conserve elephants and to benefit populations in elephant range states. My area of work at the World Service and my freelance writing included coverage of the ivory trade ban, subsequent debates at CITES (Convention on International Trade in Endangered Species of Wild Fauna and Flora) and the fierce arguments between conservationists supporting a total ban and those who believed regulated trade and sustainable use were more viable long-term approaches to conservation and development. This interest and engagement was maintained over decades, deepened by first-hand observation on dozens of working and personal trips to Africa and by the chance to meet many of those most involved in conservation.

This abiding interest might have remained just that, with occasional research trips for journalistic purposes, had not a new narrative developed at the end of the 2000s, just as I moved into academia and had more opportunities for in-depth research. This narrative was concerned with ivory and insurgency. As this book will describe in detail, while there had long been a link between conflict and illicit hunting and trading in ivory, there now emerged a new discourse, arising out of a major escalation in poaching after 2008, the growing Western fear after the 9/11 attacks of "terrorists" based in Asia, the Middle East or Africa, the launching of George W. Bush's War on Terror and the evidence that some insurgent or militia groups in Africa (the Lord's Resistance Army of Uganda, the Sudanese Janjaweed and Somali's Al Shabab movement) might be engaged in poaching and illicit trading in ivory, among other wildlife products. This ivory–insurgency discourse became an important theme, along with the massive growth of Chinese demand for ivory, of media coverage and of Western and African government concern over the political and security implications of ivory poaching and other forms of the illegal wildlife trade.

This aspect of the worsening poaching problem became a dominant one, with the American, British and Kenyan governments all, for their own reasons, highlighting the insurgency–ivory link. Some NGOs and campaigning groups jumped on the bandwagon, and a mutual government/NGO interest developed in making the link a key one, both when fighting movements perceived as hostile or unacceptable and when getting funding and manpower to fight poaching. I wrote about these issues, and the early evidence seemed a convincing indication of the changing nature of the illegal trade. My early articles reflected this.[1] Based on the available evidence, there seemed to be a connection in parts of Central and East Africa between the increasing level of poaching and the role of insurgent or rebel movements. It seemed that ivory was being used to fund insurgencies.

But, as I dug deeper, discussed the issue more with conservationists and ivory trade experts and put the evidence, particularly on Al Shabab, under the microscope, the narrative became less, not more, compelling. I was increasingly struck by the complexity and constantly evolving inter-connections between ivory, conservation, corruption, crime and conflict, and by the links between the modern ivory trade and the history of the commerce, between ivory and the political economy of range states. As I had discovered writing my recently published book on Africa's contemporary history,[2] the ivory trade had not one but

INTRODUCTION

many histories. It is a highly complex and constantly shifting enterprise and the mix of corruption, crime and conflict varies across time and across range states. Readers will not find this a history of the elephant, or of ivory, or of conservation; nor is it a plea for the conservation of elephants, or a defence of any one particular approach to the ivory trade and conservation. It is a charting of the way that human coexistence and conflict with elephants, and our exploitation and enchantment with the animals and their tusks, has been inextricably linked with human history and political economy in those areas of Africa with substantial elephant populations.

Different regions have different histories; at times they merge, and at others they diverge. But they all feed into the modern ivory trade, the development of poaching and the corruption that enables the trade to continue—all driven by external demand. This history will be about the African supply end of the ivory trade, not an examination of demand or the structure of trade once the ivory leaves Africa—that has been written and is constantly being updated by experts whose knowledge of the trade far exceeds mine. The work of Esmond Bradley Martin, Lucy Vigne and Dan Stiles will be heavily referenced to guide readers to the expert studies on the demand side of the trade, which is the driving force for commerce creating the market that is then supplied by poaching. But the evolution of the African side of the trade in ivory—legal and illegal—is the sole focus of the book.

The book has an essentially chronological pattern, starting with a chapter on man's early relationship with and exploitation of elephants, charting the rise of the global trade in ivory and Africa's place within that trade. Chapter 2 traces the development of competition for ivory and of large-scale trade and hunting to meet growing demand in Europe and North America in the nineteenth century. A clear theme emerges of escalating killing rates to supply the growing market, of value both to wealth-seeking traders and hunters (especially the new breed of European hunters who moved to the continent in the latter half of the century) and to the newly established colonial administrations. Chapter 3 deals with the evolution of the trade under colonial rule, with the alienation of African peoples from control over wildlife and its utilisation and with the gradual replacement of commercial hunting and the big game business by conservation, which produced further alienation and disempowerment of local communities.

Chapter 4 examines the changes and continuities in the ivory trade and wildlife management after independence in East Africa. Chapter 5 does the same for Central and southern Africa. Chapter 6 examines and tries to unravel the bitter debates between rival conservation camps, the arguments over the viability of a legal trade in ivory, the events leading to the CITES trade ban and the subsequent debates over one-off sales and the best means of conserving elephants. These acrimonious debates will help illustrate the extreme difficulty of assessing the estimates of elephant numbers, effects of hunting and the level of poaching, and therefore of the best ways to conserve elephants in a manner that does not lead to greater conflict between wildlife and communities in the range states. Chapter 7 covers the post-ban period, giving particular emphasis to the rise in demand from China and the effects on the illicit trade and surviving elephant populations, as well as the increase in poaching in the new millennium and the ivory–insurgency narrative.

The concluding chapter will deal with the long-term trends and major factors involved in the political economy of the ivory trade, and will strongly affirm that the 1989 ban on exports of post-1989 ivory (apart from occasional one-off CITES-approved sales from certified stockpiles) has not stopped poaching and may even have encouraged it, once demand took off in China in the decade following the ban. The book's main conclusion is that, while demand reduction may help and rigorous anti-poaching measures may suppress poaching in some areas, ultimately, aligning survival of elephants with workable, locally-acceptable forms of sustainable use is likely to be the only answer that combines conservation with the needs and interests of the human populations of range states. This is not an easy or foolproof solution, but all others have failed elephants, the communities that live alongside them and the rangers who lay down their lives to protect elephants from the greed and corruption of others higher up the political, security and economic food chain.

Notes on methodology and sources

Derived from my wider study of African history and economy, one theme running through the book concerns the role of "gatekeepers", or the "gatekeeper state", as explanatory tools in analysing the nature and functioning of political and economic power in Africa. The idea of the gatekeeper state was developed by Frederick Cooper,[3] who argues that governments in newly independent African states "inherited both the narrow, export-oriented infrastructure which developmentalist colonialism had not yet transcended and the limited markets for producers of raw material… Colonial states had been gatekeeper states. They had weak instruments for entering into the social and cultural realm over which they presided, but they stood astride the intersection of the colonial territory and the outside world".[4] The new African governments took over this role, relying on the revenues from exports and import duties, and became the gatekeepers for the influx of aid and loans. Pre-colonial rulers had also played the role of gatekeepers in early trade with the outside world, during which the seeds of unequal relations and economic dependence were sown through the slave and ivory trades. Pre-colonial gatekeeping involved rulers of powerful polities and particularly coastal communities increasing their economic and military power through control of trade with Europe or the Arab world and Asia; this function was succeeded by the colonial occupation of Africa and then "by a domestic ruling elite… distant from the population it governed, exercising control over a narrow range of resources focused on the juncture of domestic and world economies, fearful of threats to its domination".[5] This model is one well suited to analysing the ivory trade and its economic, political and environmental consequences, as it was one of the forms of commerce that encouraged the development of export-oriented economic systems with political power and elite accumulation of wealth, derived from control of the gate.[6]

When it comes to sourcing, I have tried to tread a careful path. The field of elephant conservation, sustainable use, the future of the ivory trade and the ivory–insurgency narrative are fiercely contested by scientists, conservationists, trade experts and commentators. I have used a wide variety of sources: first-hand accounts by European traders/hunters/explorers of the development of the ivory trade; the hundred years and more of editions of the *Journal of the Society for the Preservation of the Wild Fauna of the Empire*, which then became *Oryx*; *Pachyderm*, the journal of the African Elephant and Rhino Specialist Group; *Traffic Bulletin* on the trade in wildlife; the Elephant Database, which contains the latest surveys of elephant numbers; the research and campaigning publications of conservation groups, NGOs and animal welfare organisations; government reports; think tank studies of security and environmental issues; scientific studies by zoologists, conservation biologists and elephant specialists; books and articles by leading conservationists and commentators; and correspondence or interviews with leading elephant conservationists, trade experts and campaigners.

The reader has to be clear from the start that even among elephant scientists, renowned conservationists and the international specialist groups and their publications, there are no neutral, totally impartial sources and voices—all have their particular approaches, their view of the future of the elephants, their methods of estimating numbers or the extent and effects of poaching and of the legal trade. These often contradictory starting points mean that the research produced may have built-in biases—passionate beliefs about the right course to take and the exclusion of the views of others. I have tried to mix and match accounts to give the range of estimates and contending views and to emphasise, as I do here, that even the most benign and trusted figures in the elephant world are pushing their own lines, in opposition to the views of others.

In presenting information and opinions, I have tried to identify as clearly as possible the source and, where relevant, the motivations of that source of information, and to provide corroboration or commentary on the more controversial data or views. It is a difficult field, beset by personal and professional animosity and the vested interests of governments and also NGOs. This has made sorting fact from fiction, researched data from campaigning material, and informed opinion from conjecture, difficult. One major question has been of how much credence to give research by NGOs with a major campaigning role that have strongly influenced African conservation policies and the framing of debates over elephants. A leading scientist involved in the study and conservation of elephants told me that many NGOs have extremely good research departments, especially the Environmental Investigation Agency (EIA), but that their published work involves a high degree of advocacy, emotional appeals and material designed to generate passion and raise money, rather than give a fully accurate and sourced account based on research.

INTRODUCTION

This dilemma was highlighted when I interviewed Mary Rice, the executive director of EIA. She said that it was a campaign-led organisation with the nature of the specific campaign as the starting point of any research. Closing down ivory trading was the basic goal, and investigative work and research derived its direction from that goal.[7] Linked to this was the problem of trying accurately to represent the views of the leading Kenyan-based scientists, conservationists and wildlife administrators, whom Bonner named the *prima bwanas*, who have bitterly fought each other and been dominant in framing debate and national policies on ivory and elephants. But the debates, heavily laced with vitriol, have not been conducted in the most constructive or strictly scientific manner.[8] The extensive referencing and use of extensive quotes is a direct consequence of the need for clarity and clear representation of research and opinions, which are heavily intertwined in many of the publications and studies cited. Vested interests and partiality abound in the research approaches, the estimates of numbers and effects of hunting and in published narratives of conservation and the ivory trade.

A final note about language—I share the reservations of many who write about the wildlife trade in using the term poaching.[9] It automatically gives a negative value to what is being described. Yet it is ubiquitous throughout the literature and used by many of those I have interviewed. I have retained the use, but would stress that I see it as a term with flexible meanings—from evil and brutal killing of animals for human gain to traditional practices rendered illegal by externally imposed law. At the heart of the word is the concept of hunting that has been criminalised by those in a position to try to control the utilisation of wildlife.

1

AFRICA AND IVORY

AN ANCIENT BUT BLOODY AND BRUTAL TRADE

People and pachyderms

The relationship between humans and elephants starts with people hunting animals for meat and hides. This developed wherever man lived in close proximity to them. Because of the quantity of meat and hides they provided, the value of dead elephants was evident to early man long before tusks became a commodity. It's not clear exactly when humans first used ivory for tools or decoration, but archaeological evidence from Germany and Russia suggests that people were beginning to fashion ivory ornaments and tools between 25,000 and 35,000 years ago.[1]

As economies expanded and became more sophisticated, they produced surpluses enabling wealth accumulation and the evolution of culture, valuing the production of beautiful objects and symbols of power such as thrones, sceptres or decorated weapons like swords and spears. In Europe, Central Asia and parts of China, mammoth tusks were the major source of ivory for these purposes. In China, India, West Asia and North Africa, resident herds of elephants began to be hunted for ivory, as tusks became more valuable than meat or hides. In Africa, it is hard to date the commencement of the artistic use of ivory.

The earliest known representations of elephant hunts in art come from rock paintings in the Hoggar (south-eastern Algeria), Fezzan (southern Libya, bordering Chad) and Tibesti (northern Chad) regions dating from 8000–4000 BCE.[2]

Hunting, climate and habitat changes led to the gradual extinction of many species of elephantidae across the world. Between 35,000 and 10,000 years ago they were reduced to the Asian elephant *Elephas maximus* (with three sub-species) and the African elephant *Loxodonta africana*, encompassing the savannah elephant (*Loxodonta africana Africana*), the smaller forest elephant (*Loxodonta Africana cyclotis*)[3] and the now extinct North African sub-species *Loxodonta africana pharaonensis*. In the last fifteen years, evidence has begun to emerge through DNA studies suggesting that there could be three distinct African species, with the elephants of West Africa possibly a separate species from the forest elephant and the savannah elephants of Central, East and southern Africa.[4] This is not fully accepted by the scientific community and the International Union for Conservation of Nature (IUCN) Red List of threatened species offers this taxonomic information: "Preliminary genetic evidence suggests that there may be at least two species of African elephants, namely the Savanna Elephant (*Loxodonta africana*) and the Forest Elephant (*Loxodonta cyclotis*). A third species, the West African Elephant, has also been postulated. The African Elephant Specialist Group believes that more extensive research is required to support the proposed re-classification."[5]

Living with elephants: the African experience

Elephants are a keystone species; "they modify their habitats by converting savannah and woodlands to grasslands and thereby provide new macro- and micro-habitats for other species... Elephants also provide water for other species by digging waterholes in dry riverbeds... Seeds (e.g. of acacia trees) are dispersed via their faecal material".[6] Elephants, in combination with other factors, like fire, can bring far-reaching changes. This can be heightened by artificially large elephant numbers, confined by human expansion or the creation of reserves; equally, if culling, poaching or drought reduce numbers significantly, woodland can turn to grassland and back to woodland.[7] Elephants are "powerful ecosystem engineers",[8] which can bring them into conflict with man.

AFRICA AND IVORY

If the initial relationship came about through man's hunting, the greater, lasting conflict developed from agricultural progress, which made elephants a threat to food security. A combination of the need or desire to reduce elephant threats to crops and the increasing demand for ivory as a valued possession was to have a massive effect on human-elephant relationships and the exploitation of elephants as a resource. When ivory began to represent a value beyond a pleasing by-product of hunting, man's acquisitiveness and lust for beautiful materials became a substantial threat to the elephant, a threat that would magnify as technology created weapons that could kill at a distance and in large numbers. Man's desire gave birth to a global trade in ivory, a system that could convert demand in Egypt, India, Japan, New York, London or Beijing into the killing of elephants in Cameroon, South Sudan, Kenya, Tanzania or Zimbabwe. The valuing of ivory as a substance from which beautiful artistic objects or valuable artefacts could be made has remained a major driving force of the trade—with demand shifting over time for economic and aesthetic reasons from early Egypt to Greece, Mesopotamia, Rome, India, China and then back to Europe, on to North America and thence to Japan and once again China. Ivory is desired as a beautiful object, as a symbol of wealth and power and, especially in the opening decade-and-a-half of the twenty-first century, as an investment commodity whose value is expected to keep rising. Changes in human attitudes towards ivory, generated by changing relationships with wildlife, discourses on conservation and the environment and ethical views of hunting for profit or sport, have all had their effect on the evolution of the trade and of opposition to it.

Ivory was not so revered or worshipped in Sub-Saharan Africa that it led to large-scale hunting, even if some communities became specialised elephant hunters, primarily for meat and hides. The increase in demand for tusks came about through the development of trade relations along the Mediterranean, across the Sahara, along the Nile and then on the Indian Ocean and Atlantic coasts. The growth in the ivory trade was externally driven through demand in the developing empires of Asia and Europe. This has been a constant factor throughout the thousands of years of the ivory trade.[9]

*The elephant economy: ivory exports and the growth pattern
of extraversion*

The globalisation of African economies over millennia has been significantly characterised by the development of dependence and subordination through extraverted, export-led income and wealth creation. Ivory
was one of the first commodities to encourage this concentration on the
export of raw materials. Such externalised trade encouraged wealth
accumulation, but not broad economic development, in African communities through control of the export gate and the receipt of income.
Ivory became a 'must-have' African commodity for rich overseas or
trans-Saharan buyers. This dynamic created growing demand and encouraged foreign merchants, middlemen on the coast and African traders and
hunters to increase exploitation of elephants for ivory.

Ivory became a source of wealth for traders on the coasts of both
East and West/Central Africa, but also for those communities or chiefs,
on the coast or inland, who controlled the trade locally and "kept the
gate" for the export of ivory and import of trade goods. As a result, in
some developing African polities or state systems, ivory became a factor in the development of political, military and economic power
within and between communities, and in the class or economic structures of those societies. The trade, wealth and political and military
strength that flowed from it played a role in the extraversion of political power—if a ruler or community could become established as the
primary supplier of ivory to external traders through hunting, raiding
or trade with other communities, then that external economic relationship could help to drive state-building, territorial expansion and
regional hegemony—a hegemony, however, dependent on continuing
control of the trade and enabling external political and economic penetration of Africa.[10]

That penetration was primarily concerned with expanding and controlling trade—whether in ivory, slaves or other valuable commodities.
In some areas of East and Central Africa, it led to the powerful
Zanzibar-based traders gaining political as well as commercial hegemony over the areas in which they operated, weakening local hierarchies of power, and taking advantage of regions where communities
had loose, flat and acephalous hierarchies (literally headless—lacking

kings, powerful chiefs or ruling lineages).[11] These societies, and even some of the more hierarchical polities with chiefs, monarchs or rule by dominant lineages, had another characteristic that aided penetration: "precisely delineated boundaries were rare. Power broadcast from the centre of a kingdom could dissipate the further a village was from the capital, and would ebb and flow according to the fortunes of a central administration".[12] Intrusion could start at the weak periphery and serve to undermine central power, or the arrival of well-armed, prosperous ivory and slave traders could decisively alter the balance of forces in or between societies.

The growth of the externalised trade and of gatekeeping was a forerunner of and building-block for the structure of export-oriented and dependent economic relations that persist today. It was not a mechanistic system, pre-ordained purely by the functioning of economic structures beyond communities' power to influence, but one that involved the exercise of agency by both external forces and hunting, trading and coastal communities across Africa. These communities, and the individuals or elite groups leading them, saw economic and political advantage in developing relationships, even though in many cases these were to become highly unequal, with control over the nature, size and ramifications of the trade progressively falling into foreign hands. It would be a gross exaggeration to say that ivory led to colonialism and occupation of Africa by European powers, but ivory was one of the commodities that attracted traders, those dubbed explorers and then hunters and financiers of hunting and slaving expeditions.

Some communities developed a role as elephant hunters and suppliers of ivory either directly to foreign traders at the coast or, like the Tonga of Zambia and Zimbabwe, the Wakamba in Kenya, the Nyamwezi in Tanzania or the Yao of Malawi and Mozambique, became middlemen in the trade between inland hunters and foreign traders at ports like Kilwa or Zanzibar.[13] They obtained ivory through hunting or barter and traded it for European or Indian cloth, manufactured goods and, later, firearms. Control over or local dominance in this trading system brought wealth and political and regional power, but not necessarily long-term development, as the wealth was related to the export of specific commodities and was not part of a broader pattern of development. The earnings from ivory, just as later with other extraverted commodities from cocoa to crude oil, became part of the accumulated wealth of chiefs, kings, political elites or powerful traders, used for patronage and to import foreign goods, rather than for investment in the local economy.

Trade in goods such as ivory, slaves and gold developed steadily between Sub-Saharan Africa and North Africa, the Mediterranean, the Middle East and Asia as early as the last millennium before the Common/Christian era (BCE) and through the first 1,500 years of the Common/Christian era (CE). Long-distance trade and growth in overseas demand for ivory began with Omani Arab, Chinese and Indian trading along the east coast, but expanded at the end of the fifteenth century, with the start of trading voyages by Portuguese, Dutch and later British and French merchants. The developing commercial relationship involved middlemen in coastal communities trading between Europe and Africa with the exchange of ivory, slaves, gold, spices and later copper for cloth, cowries, beads, firearms, and metal goods.[14]

The massive development that was to take place in the ivory trade had major consequences for those areas of Africa in which elephants were abundant or which became trading entrepôts and transit routes. This led to the reduction of elephant herds in some areas and the lengthening of trade routes into the interior of Central and East Africa, from both coasts as well as along the Nile. The expansion of commerce based at least partly on ivory had far-reaching consequences, as Edward Alpers, a leading historian of the development of the East African ivory and slave trades, has written: "I argue that the relentless hunting out of the elephant… can only be understood in the broader context of the exploitation of Africa's natural resources—including most especially its peoples—primarily by economic and social forces external to the continent."[15] From the perspective of African communities and societies, those best placed to benefit from the trade were not just peoples in areas with large elephant populations, but those with a long tradition of hunting and trading. In a few areas near the east coast or bordering the Sahel, this expanding commerce already involved the ivory trade with the Mediterranean, the Middle East or India.

A few communities specialised in hunting elephants as part of their culture and means of subsistence. The ivory trade specialist Ian Parker details the hunting practices of the Waliangulu of Kenya, writing of the importance of hunting and the rite of passage of the first elephant hunt. Because there was—at least until the nineteenth century—a relatively modest demand for ivory from the small coastal trade networks in that part of Africa, the Waliangulu killed primarily for meat and did not have a decisively destructive effect.[16] This was true of many other communities, like the Baka, Dorobo, Wakamba and Manyema, which engaged in elephant hunting as part of diversified subsistence strategies. But it would be wrong to assume that hunting was limited only to a few specialised or, from the viewpoint of the first Europeans, "primitive" hunter-gatherer communities. Their retained expertise in hunting, even as an economically peripheral activity, allowed communities to adapt to the opportunity when trading posts were established on the coasts of East, West, Central and south-eastern Africa by overseas merchants seeking ivory and other commodities.[17]

The early development of the ivory trade

Ivory's allure is such that potentates from as far apart in time and space as the Egyptian, Chinese, Greek, Roman, European baroque and Tsarist Russian empires and, currently, the emerging Chinese business elite, valued it as a symbol of wealth, beauty and status. Ivory was available from long-dead mammoths and was traded from Siberia to buyers in Europe, China and the Middle East. While elephants still inhabited areas of China, South-East Asia, the Indian sub-continent, Syria and the Mediterranean shores of North Africa, the demand from Mediterranean, Indian or Chinese empires was met locally. As elephants were killed off in those areas, their traders travelled further and further afield in search of ivory. The opening of trade routes by Chinese, Indian, Middle Eastern and Mediterranean merchants created demand for ivory in the parts of Africa they reached by sea, up the Nile or across the Sahara.

The most important impetus for extensive hunting in Africa came from external trade in the last millennium BCE and the early centuries CE. One good example is China, where there was both rapid population expansion and growth in the demand for ivory from the wealthy. Four thousand years ago, there were healthy elephant populations across China. Population growth, agricultural development and hunting for meat and ivory had, by the second century CE, confined the

elephant population to areas of the south and south-west.[18] Steady
demand for ivory for carving meant importing it—first from Asia and
then via the Middle East, which provided a commercial link to sources
in East Africa. Another major importer was Egypt. Its growing wealth
encouraged the development of art and rich ornamentation of palaces,
temples, and the living and death regalia of pharaohs. Tutankhamun was
buried with his neck on an ivory rest; other tombs contained ivory
perfume flasks, seals and figurines.[19] There were elephant populations
in North Africa, including in Cyrenaica (Libya), as well as on the upper
reaches of the Nile. These were hunted and eventually exterminated.
By 2750 BCE, elephants had been killed off in the eastern Sahara and,
by 2000 BCE, in the central Sahara.[20]

To obtain sufficient ivory, hunting and trading expeditions were sent
into Nubia during the period of the sixth dynasty, between 2420 and
2258 BCE. Ivory "became part of the natural wealth of Africa that successive Egyptian dynasties sought to control and acquire."[21] Ivory
imported into Egypt came from hunting in Sudan, Nubia, Syria and as
far south as Punt, which was located along the Red Sea coast of southern Sudan, Eritrea and Ethiopia, as far as Somalia. This stimulated hunting in those regions, which was given further impetus by contacts with
traders from Arabia.[22] The Assyrians, Babylonians, Egyptians and
Phoenicians all used ivory or traded it. Their consumption of ivory
required the killing of substantial numbers of elephants. By 500 BCE,
the Syrian herds had been wiped out and the ivory trade was redirected
to Africa's Red Sea and the Indian Ocean coast.[23]

India's tradition of ivory carving stretched back to the third century
BCE. Elephants were killed for their ivory but were also seen as valuable beasts that could be trained for agricultural uses as well as warfare.
This limited the destruction of herds and resulted in far greater domes-
tication. The demand for ivory for carving in India was increasingly met
by imports from abroad, rather than the hunting of indigenous animals.
Much of that demand was met from Africa, and Indian ivory purchasing
began to centre on the Red Sea and northern Indian Ocean. Arab traders supplying the Eastern Mediterranean, the Middle East and India
extended their voyages down the East African coast as elephant populations in the Horn of Africa, northern Sudan and North Africa were so
reduced they could not supply expanding demand.[24]

Meanwhile, on the North African coast, the Carthaginians had adopted the use of war elephants. Hannibal included elephants in his army when he attacked the Roman Empire in 218 BCE. The elephants were captured from the remaining herds that stretched along the coastal plains, across present-day Tunisia through Algeria to Morocco. Ivory was part of the plunder from Carthage when it was defeated by Rome. Scipio included 1,231 ivory tusks in his triumphal parade in Rome. The defeat of the Carthaginians established Rome's hegemony in the Mediterranean and North Africa and a substantial degree of control over the ivory trade. There is evidence that the Garamantes of the Fezzan region bordering the Sahara were obtaining ivory and slaves from West African region now divided between Niger, Nigeria and Cameroon, and selling them on the North African coast.[25] When the Roman Empire fragmented, the eastern remnant in Byzantium imported ivory from Asia overland, until war with Persia in 542 CE blocked the caravan route.

India and China then became the most important markets, relying on traders in Arabia to obtain tusks from the Indian Ocean coast of Africa. Traders went as far south as Sofala in Mozambique.[26] At this time, there was a growing globalisation of trade in the Indian Ocean, the Red Sea and Arabia, with ceramics from India and China traded in Africa for ivory, spices, timber and later slaves. As the traders moved south, their trading partners on the coast of southern Tanzania and Mozambique were sending caravans inland with porters carrying cloth and other manufactured goods, to trade for ivory. The ivory was sought-after in Asia because of the depletion of the continent's own elephants, and because African ivory is softer, whiter and easier to carve; savannah elephant ivory is superior in this respect to forest elephant ivory.[27] One of the key areas for the supply of ivory to ports on the eastern coast was between the Zambezi and Limpopo rivers, particularly the region where Botswana, Zimbabwe and South Africa now meet and the Limpopo is joined by the Shashi. This included the kingdom of Mapungubwe, where ivory hunting, trading and carving took place from the ninth to the early fifteenth centuries.[28] When the Mapungubwe civilisation went into decline in the late thirteenth century, the trade shifted to the Great Zimbabwe kingdom between the Limpopo and Zambezi.[29]

17

IVORY

The supply of African ivory to markets overseas was not limited to the east and south. The trade routes across the Sahara that supplied Egypt and Rome still operated, with European or North African goods being traded by Sahelian communities for ivory, slaves and gold from West Africa. Davidson believes that, as early as 750 CE, gold and ivory were the West African products most in demand among those Berber traders still able to cross the Sahara after its desertification, an obstacle to north-south trade.[30]

By the second millennium CE, China was importing ivory via Arabia from East Africa. Chinese writers recorded that tusks weighing up to 150 lbs were imported via Arab coastal trading communities, who called themselves Shirazi (taking their name from the Shiraz region of Persia).[31] In 1414, a fleet of 160 ships led by a Chinese admiral, Zheng He, reached the Indian Ocean. While in Bengal, Zheng saw a giraffe that had been sent as a gift from the Shirazi ruler of the trading settlement at Malindi (on the Kenyan coast). Zheng acquired it and sent it back to China. On his next voyages in 1417, the 1420s and the 1430s, he visited Somalia, as far south as the Juba river. Zheng brought back ivory, gold and spices. After the fifteenth century, Chinese importers of ivory continued utilising Arab or Indian traders. The growth of southern-central and East Africa's overseas trade had developed continuously between 1000 and 1500, dominated by the Swahili and Arabic/Shirazi communities on the Indian Ocean coast and by Sahelian communities across the Sahara. Swahili-speaking communities, produced by inter-marriage between Arab traders and coastal peoples, had established themselves as traders all along the East African coast, from southern Somalia to northern Mozambique, occupying more than 400 sites by the sixteenth century.[32]

Enter the Europeans

European state consolidation and expansion gave rise to the onset of the era of exploration along the coasts of Africa in search of trading opportunities. Ivory was keenly sought, but was only one among many commodities that Europe wanted. The Portuguese started the process when they tried to circumvent the hostile Islamic states monopolising trans-Saharan trade. A sea route had to be found to obtain gold and ivory from West Africa, and the Portuguese set their sights on offshore islands and the coast.[33] They sent trading fleets that eventually opened West and then Central, southern and East Africa to European trade. They later competed with the dominant Arab and Swahili merchants on the east coast of Africa.

In 1450, Portuguese traders reached the Senegal River and reported that the inhabitants hunted elephants for meat but made no use of their tusks. Expeditions went further round the coast to the kingdom of Benin (Nigeria) and brought the Portuguese into contact with a culture in which ivory played a role in economic and cultural life. The king, the Oba, claimed one tusk from every elephant killed. Ivory was part of the symbolism of kingship and there was a thriving carving industry. Benin was expanding its regional dominance northwards into Owo and Yoruba territory, gaining access to elephant herds there.[34] The Oba of Benin established a monopoly over ivory trade in the region. The Portuguese bought both tusks and carved ivory from Benin, but not always as much as they wanted, because of local demand. Portuguese traders established posts all along the West African coast and by the sixteenth century were buying ivory from the Temne people of Sierra Leone.

The Portuguese were able to take advantage of the opportunities presented by large elephant populations in coastal areas, and at the start of the century established regular trade on the upper Guinea Coast.[35] Hunting was carried out by communities in coastal forests and the hinterland using spears, pitfall traps and poisoned arrows; there was no transfer of firearms from the Portuguese to Guinean peoples until the end of the eighteenth century. The Portuguese were joined by the British and Dutch, who sent trading expeditions as far as Benin. A number of English merchants played a role in initiating the ivory trade between Britain and West Africa. They traded British cloth and metal goods for ivory, gold, tortoiseshell and slaves. The growing European interest in the region, and the subsequent opening of West and Central Africa to long-distance, overseas trade, became an unequal exchange. Unprocessed African commodities and slaves were traded in large quantities for smaller quantities of European manufactured goods.[36] Only in a few places did ivory remain the dominant commodity. The coastal trade led to the expansion of commerce within Africa, from the Atlantic Ocean ports into the interior.

19

As they moved down the coast, the Portuguese established strong links with the Bakongo Kingdom (covering northern Angola, the western DRC and southern areas of the Republic of Congo). They chose the kingdom as a major trading partner, buying ivory from the Bakongo, who had in turn obtained it from inland communities along the Congo River. The Portuguese also developed strong trading networks further south, with posts at Luanda and Benguela in Angola, and to the north of the Bakongo, establishing links with the Vili people of Loango.[37] The latter were energetic traders with the interior, bringing locally made cloth, ivory, slaves, redwood and copper to the coast. The Dutch likewise established trade in the Loango area, and between 1608 and 1612 exported 50,000 lbs of ivory annually.[38] The growing Dutch and Portuguese purchases of ivory required that the Vili travel ever further afield in search of elephants, as coastal herds were depleted. Most of the ivory was provided by hunters from the communities in the Congo Basin.[39] Evidence from Dutch and English shipping archives shows that the two countries imported 2,500 tons or 250,000 tusks from West and Central Africa between 1699 and 1725—during that period, at least 125,000 elephants were killed.[40]

When the Portuguese rounded the Cape and established trade along the Indian Ocean they had to compete for ivory with well-established Omani Arab traders, who had posts and forts along the coast from Mozambique to Somalia. Initial Portuguese trading was limited to the area from the Cape to Delagoa Bay (now Maputo), but gradually spread north. Once they had established trading posts, the Portuguese brought ivory from the interior of south-central Africa to the coast and exported it to India. From early on, the Portuguese traded guns and gunpowder for slaves and ivory.[41] The introduction of guns, expanding human settlement and agriculture and consequent human–elephant conflict all had the effect of reducing elephant populations.

Through the Portuguese export of ivory to the sub-continent, a class of Indian merchants, known as Banyans, grew up in the Indian Ocean trading ports and played an important role in the increasing demand for ivory and in the financing of caravans into the interior. The Gujarati town of Surat became the centre of the Indian ivory and carving industry.

The Portuguese for their part wanted to control trade along the coast, and were determined not to yield to the Arab and Swahili networks. Portuguese fleets were sent to subordinate the Arab and Swahili trading centres of Zanzibar, Mombasa, Kilwa, Mozambique Island and Sofala.[42] Although the Portuguese failed to establish hegemony, they did seize Sofala, where they established a coastal fortress and sent expeditions inland to obtain ivory and gold from Zimbabwe. Portuguese traders settled at Malindi on the Kenya coast, from where they traded with Kilwa. Most of the ivory taken to Kilwa went to the Arabian Peninsula or India. The posts at Sofala and Mozambique Island enabled the Portuguese to take part in the growing ivory trade dominated by the Yao people of Mozambique and Malawi, who hunted and also traded with peoples far inland for ivory and slaves. The Portuguese failed to gain a monopoly over Yao ivory and, in the end, forfeited much of the trade when they tried to finance their settlements through taxes on tusks.[43] The Zambezi trading posts became more important as a source when the Yao chose the Kilwa route for exports. The trade grew and it is estimated that during the sixteenth century 30,000 lbs of ivory passed annually through Sofala.[44] By the final years of the seventeenth century, the Yao had established control over much of the trade to Kilwa and Mozambican ports.

By the late sixteeenth century, however, even the experienced Yao traders were being reduced to players in a game increasingly controlled by coastal traders, whether Portuguese, Indian or Shirazi/Swahili. Moreover, the limits of the ivory trade's long-term economic benefits were becoming apparent. Income from ivory went to those within the Yao controlling the trade but, like later export-led commerce between Africa and the rest of the world, did not lead to domestic economic development. As Alpers concludes:

> "African traders suffered most through the fact that the market itself was not of their making and that this luxury trade was in no way contributing to the economic development of their own societies. Their rapid mastery of entrepreneurial skills could not free them from the disadvantageous relations by which this trade linked them to the world economy."[45]

The same pattern can be seen in Mombasa. Ivory routed through this important trading port came from regions under the control of the Galla of central Ethiopia and the Orma people. The accomplished hunters of the region between the coast and highlands were the Waliangulu and the Wakamba. The latter combined hunting with commercial networks linking the coastal trading communities and the interior. The Waliangulu traded ivory for cloth, cattle and goats from the Orma, who controlled trade with the coast.[46] The balance of power among the competing trading groups along the coast from northern Mozambique to Somalia changed at the end of the seventeenth century, when Kilwa, Mombasa and Zanzibar came under the control of the Omani Arab sultanate, the growing power in the Indian Ocean. The Portuguese competed with the Arab, Indian and Swahili traders and the rising Omani Sultanate, but were never able to triumph fully in any of these contests. The expansion of trade in the Indian Ocean region was not to benefit them as much as it did Indian merchants and the Omanis.[47] The former, the Banyans, gained an important middleman role in buying ivory on the coast to meet demand in India. Their power was such that the Portuguese granted some of them favourable terms to ensure the development of trade between India and the Portuguese settlements.

During the latter half of the eighteenth century, Omani power increased, with Zanzibar and Kilwa its chief trading centres. The Omanis ate away at Portuguese access to ivory by sending ships down the coast to what the Portuguese had considered their sphere of influence, on the northern Mozambican coast. They undercut the Portuguese by offering more trade goods for ivory and not applying tariffs. They also began to send trading expeditions inland to the north end of Lake Malawi and the interior of Tanzania. Caravans led by Arabs or traders of Arab-African descent had been venturing into these regions since the mid-century, and Kilwa's resurgence in importance led to a growth in trade. Arabs traded with the Ngonde and Tumbuka on the shores of the lake, buying ivory in exchange for cloth and glass beads. They reached as far as the area south of Karonga.[48] Finding substantial supplies of ivory, they established regular trade, and during the last half of the century pushed inland to Rumphi, south of the wildlife-rich Nyika Plateau, where "an abundant untapped supply of ivory" was reported to them.[49] The arrival of these Arab traders precipitated elephant hunting on a scale previously unknown in the region.[50]

Other developments in the evolution of ivory trading saw further decline in the Mozambican trade, amid attempts by Portuguese colonial officials to break the power of the Banyan traders. In 1781, the governor-general tried to ban Indian merchants from trading at

Mossuril, but ultimately was forced to compromise and establish a joint company of eighteen Portuguese settlers and thirteen Indian merchants. This period also saw the entry of the British, who began to gain a presence through Muslim Indian traders from Gujarat who traded with the Arabs and took ivory back to Surat. The town was now in territory controlled by the British East India Company, whose power had expanded greatly after the Seven Years' War of 1756–63.

During the eighteenth century, the greater availability of firearms made hunting easier and increased the rate of killing, just as demand from Europe was beginning to take off, with the growing prosperity of the developing capitalist consumer class. At the end of the century, the Scottish explorer Mungo Park travelled the Niger River and reported that Bamana hunters of Mali armed with muskets were shooting elephants to sell the ivory either through European traders or via the trans-Saharan trade routes. Park also noted the prevalence of the trade in Gambia, where, in 1795, he said that a Mandinke community known locally as Niumi were trading along the Gambia River. "The chief trade of the inhabitants is salt; which commodity they carry up the river in canoes as high as Barraconda, bringing down in return Indian corn, cotton cloths, elephants' teeth, and small quantities of gold dust". The hunters bartered the tusks locally with middlemen, who sold them on to coastal traders like the Mandinke.[51]

In South Africa, the ivory trade developed when the Dutch East India Company established Cape Town as a refreshment station for ships sailing to trading posts and colonies in Asia. Jan van Riebeeck arrived at Table Bay in 1652 to develop the settlement and set up farms to supply the merchant fleets. He found large herds of elephants at the Cape and more further inland. While Cape Town's major role was in supplying the ships, the Dutch wanted to make a profit from the settlement and ivory was a way of making it pay. Initially, the Dutch traded tobacco for ivory with local Khoikhoi hunters. As the farmed area and number of settlers increased, the settlers were encouraged to hunt elephants to supplement their income. As they spread eastwards, they cultivated more land and killed the elephants both for their tusks and to protect crops. Some, like Jacobus Botha, were such avid hunters of elephants that they made a fortune from ivory. Botha boasted how he would sometimes shoot as many as five elephants a day and sometimes more, on two occasions killing twenty-two in one day.[52] Khoikhoi hunters had hardly dented elephant numbers, but Europeans, with guns, settlement of land and the need to protect farms, drove them out. By 1760, there were no elephants south of the Oliphants River, and soon there were none within 500 miles of Cape Town.[53]

2

THE NINETEENTH CENTURY

ONE HUNDRED YEARS OF EXPLOITATION AND EXTERMINATION

If the centuries preceding the nineteenth had seen a steady but generally sustainable growth in killing elephants for ivory, the 1800s would see the large-scale introduction of firearms and the development of more organised and lucrative globalised ivory trading, to meet booming demand in Europe and later North America. The trade was supplied by African hunters initially, but by the latter half of the century increasing numbers of Europeans were hunting on a large scale or combining hunting with buying tusks cheaply from hunting communities. The power of the Omani and Shirazi traders on the Indian Ocean coast grew substantially as they accumulated wealth and power through meeting growing demand. But their power then peaked and declined as European involvement increased, culminating in colonial occupation. This was not a direct result of the ivory trade, even though it served as an economic incentive and a means of offsetting the cost of occupation. The earnings from ivory—but also from meat, hides and other wildlife trophies—became an important subsidy for the expansion of colonial control in East Africa. Hunting and the ability to profit from it also became an important lure for settlers, whom the colonising powers wanted to attract as another cost-effective way of reaping economic rewards from occupation.[1]

These factors led to the thinning out of elephant herds in coastal areas and their immediate hinterland and the large-scale destruction of elephants across broad swathes of East, Central, southern and West Africa, with an ever more frenetic search for new areas to exploit. The writer, environmentalist and daughter of Kenyan settlers, Elspeth Huxley, wrote that the arrival of high-velocity rifles in the hands of white hunters was a major influence on the accelerating slaughter of elephants. The hunters, she said, had the ability and appetite to kill scores of elephants or rhinos in a single day.[2] And some of the hunters were vastly destructive—the depredations of Selous, Gordon-Cumming and Harris, detailed below, and of others like Henry Hartley, who killed between 1,000 and 1,200 elephants in his career, or George Westbeech, who is believed to have killed 470–700 elephants a year between 1871 and 1888, display an even greedier pursuit of ivory. These same colonialists also encouraged the accelerated hunting of elephants by indigenous hunters.

The hunters and traders were reacting to, and exploiting for profit, the European and American demand for ivory. Its importance as a commodity and a lure for traders and explorers should not be underestimated. Ivory helped encourage the opening up of the Sub-Saharan interior to European commerce, and the exploration of navigable rivers like the Congo, Nile, Zambezi, Niger and Benue. Demand dominated the trade, and the decline of elephant populations in East and Southern Africa by the end of the nineteenth century is clearly related to the expansion of industrial capitalism and the rise in global ivory demand and prices. The *Gazette of Zanzibar and East Africa* in December 1894 estimated that by then 65,000 animals were being killed annually to meet global demand. This demand, and the ability of hunters, traders and adventurers to meet it, is at the heart of the narrative of the ivory trade and the decimation of elephants in the nineteenth century.

By the end of the century, ivory was booming, but elephants had been reduced hugely in numbers in many areas (especially south of the Zambezi); early calls for restrictions on hunting and embryonic attempts at conservation were emerging. A key aspect of the evolution of hunting towards the end of the century, after the start of colonisation, was the progressive exclusion of local communities from hunting at the expense of settlers, professional European hunters and visiting sport hunters, and the growing criminalisation of indigenous hunting. This set the pattern for the rise of what was labelled as poaching—hunting by communities, on the land they had occupied for countless centuries, became illegal, and indigenous peoples were alienated from wildlife, which was reserved first for European hunting and then for conservation, as dictated by the colonial authorities.

Expansion and increasing sophistication of the ivory trade

At the beginning of the nineteenth century, the ivory trade was expanding, building on existing routes and the role on the east coast of Arab, Indian and Swahili traders, as well as growing European commerce on the western, central and southern African littorals. Commerce was well established at trading posts from Senegal, south round the Cape and north to Ethiopia. Increasing numbers of European traders were involved, but the Omani Arab ports of East Africa were becoming the major focus. Long-distance trade networks, combined with the growing wealth of the capitalist class in Europe and North America, accelerated demand to the extent that elephants were killed and ivory harvested on an industrial scale. Towards the end of the century, the growing hegemony of Europeans in West, Central, East and Southern Africa, and the direct imperial competition for territory and resources, led to greater European penetration. This in turn quickened the pace of elephant hunting through the proliferation of firearms and the arrival of white settlers and hunters.

Demand for ivory in Europe had increased in the eighteenth century, overtaking the markets in India and China. In the last years of the century, advances in manufacturing techniques provided further impetus for the production of luxury goods made from ivory. This, and increased supply through established trade networks, led to major expansion of the ivory industries in Europe and North America. In the United States, Deacon Phineas Pratt received a patent in April 1799 for a machine to produce ivory combs, something Walker rightly says "initiated the transformation of world trade in ivory".[3] Mass production brought the price of individual items within the purchasing range of the middle classes. Market growth had a profound effect on the volume and nature of the trade. The price of ivory rose tenfold between 1780 and 1830. Initially, increasing demand was met by importing West African forest ivory—70 per cent of British imports in the first twenty years of the century came from there, averaging 125 tons annually, growing to 200 in the 1820s and then 275 in the 1830s. But West Africa could not meet the demand and manufacturers wanted softer savannah elephant ivory. By the 1840s, the West African trade had fallen to 35 per cent of imports. Zanzibar and Mombasa became the main suppliers, with British imports rocketing from 280 tons in 1840 to over 800 in 1875.[4]

British and American demand, and growing reliance on meeting this demand with ivory bought from Zanzibar and Mombasa, gave the powerful Omani Arab and Indian traders of East Africa a commanding role, but there was also growth in South African ivory exports, which reached over 50 tons a year after 1850, while supplies from Sudan through Egypt and Malta grew from more or less zero before 1850 to 165 tons a year in the third quarter of the century.[5] Nevertheless, Zanzibar was the ivory boom town. The British began to trade directly with merchants there rather than in India, and American firms established commercial offices.

The substantial expansion of ivory utilisation had a major effect in starting the century-long reduction in elephant numbers. Merchants based in Zanzibar, Mombasa, Kilwa, Khartoum, Mozambique and South Africa commissioned trading or hunting expeditions into the interior. They bought tusks from African middlemen, Arab hunters and later from itinerant traders and the growing breed of hunter—adventurers like Gordon-Cumming, Selous and Harris. The latter are prominent in accounts of the trade and, to quote Parker, "imbued with considerable blood-lust, may have shot anything they could lay sights on" but did not single-handedly reduce elephant numbers.[6] The search for ivory encouraged expeditions like those of Henry Stanley and played a role in further opening the interior to European trade and exploitation. Hunting, transportation and export of ivory became major sources of wealth and employment. The Omani Arab, Indian, Swahili, Sudanese and European ivory houses grew rich and were ruthless in pursuit of tusks. African communities hunting elephants and trading in ivory continued to bring in income without developing their economies, always feeding an externally generated demand.

THE NINETEENTH CENTURY

East and Central Africa: Slaves, Ivory and the Great Lakes Game

One leading American ivory trader in East Africa said that at the height of the trade in the latter half of the nineteenth century, 100,000 elephants were killed in the region annually.[7] The size of the trade meant that it was one of the dominant forms of commerce for much of the century, a source of great wealth, of political and even military power. Such an extensive undertaking was linked closely with slaving, and the effects of the combined trades were not just on the humans transported and the elephants killed, but also on the political, social and economic development of East Africa and the Great Lakes region. Ivory was a lure for the coastal Swahili people, Arab traders and Europeans to venture into the interior, open up trade routes and explore the rivers to the north.

The Arab trading ports of Zanzibar and Mombasa were the hubs of the east coast trade, drawing Yao traders from the south and west, peoples from the Nyika area of present-day Kenya and Tanzania, the Wakamba north of Mombasa, the Nyamwezi of central-southern Tanzania and the Manyema west of Lake Tanganyika. Arab and Swahili caravans, financed by traders, went inland as elephant herds near the coast were depleted. As commerce grew the Wakamba came to dominate the trade in Kenya, engaging in hunting and long-distance trade from Tanzania to northern Kenya. Relations between the Wakamba and the peoples into whose areas they moved were often ambivalent, with raiding developing alongside trade—raiding caravans of rivals became a quick way of obtaining tusks without significant cost. The Wakamba were in the right region to control trade routes and were able to adapt to changes in long-distance trade. As such, they were important in the nineteenth century ivory trade in Kenya, and later at the centre of the British criminalisation of African hunting, and so a focus, with the neighbouring Waliangulu, of the anti-poaching campaigns of the mid-twentieth century.

In common with the Waliangulu, Wakamba hunters used poison obtained from plants to coat arrows for elephant hunting. During the 1820s, they extended their hunting areas to Mount Kenya, towards Lake Baringo and as far north as Samburu country near Lake Turkana. Wakamba caravans of 200–500 men would bring ivory and slaves from the Nyika and other areas to the coast. In mid-century, they were supplying about 45 tons of ivory a year to Swahili and Arab dealers at Mombasa. But the wealth and influence this brought the Wakamba were transitory, and over the century, Arab and Swahili traders took control of the inland trade. Across East Africa, trading networks supplying the Arab, Swahili and Indian merchants at the coast were swallowed up or just pushed aside by the Arabs when they realised that they could control the whole chain, from buying from hunters to selling at the coast. Traders like Tippu Tip of Zanzibar became economically dominant, militarily powerful and able to exert control across swathes of East and Central Africa. Alongside the trade in tusks, they developed a lucrative one in people—ivory and slavery became mutually supporting.

Slavery was not new in Africa; the trans-Saharan and Indian Ocean trades and the European-driven slave commerce on the West and Central African coasts were barbaric commerces which had existed for centuries, each with their own ghastly dynamics of wealth accumulation through the misery of others. In the fourteenth and fifteenth centuries, the trans-Saharan trade saw between 4,000 and 7,000 people a year trafficked to North Africa, the Middle East and the Gulf annually from West and Central Africa. The Saharan and Indian Ocean slave routes operated from the start of the first millennium BCE to the late nineteenth century, while the Atlantic trade, sending captives to work on plantations in Brazil, the Caribbean and North America, started in the fifteenth century and survived until the middle of the nineteenth. European traders exploited existing systems of servitude and encouraged the massive growth in taking and selling slaves through middlemen among coastal communities and indigenous slave traders. Demand drove the trade but African chiefs, traders and powerful states were involved as suppliers of slaves through raiding, warfare and the sale of criminals, orphans and others deemed surplus to requirements within communities, valued only as a saleable commodity.[8]

Slavery existed within Africa prior to the development of widespread trade in people, with powerful empires, kingdoms and chieftaincies using slaves bought or captured in battle and raids in order to expand agriculture. These, then, could also become a commodity to be traded. There is no doubt that "the existence of Africans both capable and willing to capture other Africans was crucial to the emergence of the continent as a supplier of slaves".[9] But slavery became bound up with ivory through the need to transport trade goods inland from the coast to purchase ivory, which then had to be carried back to the coast. While paid porters were used, a more economical but brutal method was to capture slaves or buy them to carry the ivory, the slaves then also being sold for profit on the coast. This method was developed particularly by the Zanzibari-based traders, utilising willing middlemen among African communities.

By the early 1830s, Sa'id bin Sultan, the ruler of Oman, had established control over the Arab settlements along the coast and moved his capital to Zanzibar. He sought to establish dominance over the ivory and the slave trade, and established clove plantations on Zanzibar and nearby islands, which helped develop large-scale slaving to provide labour. Missionaries in the nineteenth century, such as A. J. Swann of the London Missionary Society, painted horrific pictures of slave caravans with people chained or yoked together carrying huge tusks.[10] While this did happen and the trade was barbaric, much of the ivory was carried to the coast by porters from the Nyamwezi or other indigenous inhabitants of the coast or hinterland, who were paid to carry trade goods into the interior and ivory out again. The local porters became known as *pagazi*. Experienced porters who had gained the trust of those running caravans became valuable labour, as was demonstrated by the competition to employ them when Europeans seeking out trade routes and access to the Nile began to use Zanzibar as the starting point for expeditions. Zanzibar's control of the ivory trade was boosted by American buyers' entry into the market from the 1820s, as the Salem- and Connecticut-based importers and factories started buying tusks. The merchants based in the Indian Ocean ports bought Indian, European or North American cloth and manufactured goods, including cheap firearms made in Birmingham, to trade for ivory and slaves, becoming important middlemen in the trade.

The Nyamwezi of Tanzania also became key middlemen in the ivory and slave trades. They inhabited the area between the coast and Lake Tanganyika, with an important settlement and trading centre at Unyanyembe (Tabora). Nyamwezi chiefs benefited by supplying ivory, being paid *hongo* for caravan transit through their territory, and fees for hiring porters, but the local economy was adversely affected over time as manpower was taken from the development of agriculture, and the wealth gained from the ivory and slave trades went only to a few. The power of chiefs began to rest partly on their access to external trade and their use of wealth to increase power. By 1856, the route to the lake through Nyamwezi territory was supplying substantial quantities of ivory; 218 tons were exported to Europe and 108 tons to North America and India. Between 1850 and 1890, the price of ivory at Zanzibar rose from £600 a ton to £2,100. This meant Zanzibari traders could make a profit of 200 per cent on caravans to the interior.

By the 1860s, merchants from Zanzibar and Nyamwezi traders had begun to go across and round the end of Lake Tanganyika to trade with the Manyema west of the lake. The search for ivory, especially from savannah elephants, took Zanzibari traders north to Buganda and Bunyoro (Uganda), where the local rulers exercised a monopoly over the trade. There, traders from Zanzibar and Mombasa competed with Sudanese Arab and European traders coming up the Nile from Khartoum. The growing economic power of the Arab traders and their Indian partners on the coast enabled them to assume ever greater control of the trade. Peoples like the Nyamwezi became bit-part players in the ivory and slave network, supplying porters and food for the caravans but losing control over the trade. The military strength of the Arabs meant they could project power inland and subdue recalcitrant peoples through whose territory they moved. They fought chiefs like Mirambo of the Nyamwezi, who tried to retain control of the trade in his territory.

One common factor among most of the peoples who became hunters and traders is that they were loose communities sharing a language and culture, rather than strongly organised or hierarchical states with clear territories. Local chiefs gained power and wealth through engaging in the trade, but this did not become the basis for the establishment of strong, clearly delineated states or the conquest of neighbouring territories. The Yao of Mozambique/Malawi would trade with neighbours, hunt in their lands and raid for ivory and slaves, but there was no major attempt by them, the Nyamwezi or the Chokwe to build what Europeans would have seen as territorial states with demarcated borders. Boundaries were fluid and related to people and resources rather than land. Unlike the Great Zimbabwe Empire based on gold or other polities based on mineral wealth, the trading communities of Central

Africa did not need to control large territories to harvest ivory, unlike the need to control ore-bearing areas to mine gold or iron. Strong defensive communities were unnecessary for the ivory hunters, but their loose societal structures made them vulnerable to the power of Arab traders, who exerted increasing hegemony over the trade and the communities involved in it.

The Portuguese lost influence in the ivory trade as Zanzibar grew, but in the late 1850s were still seeking supplies to meet their own domestic demand. Livingstone reported that during his expedition along the Zambezi in 1858 he encountered caravans of porters and slaves under locally recruited headmen, hunting elephants and buying ivory inland from Tete on behalf of the Portuguese. He also encountered Arab ivory and slaving parties as he travelled up the Shire River to Lake Malawi.[11] The British missionary believed the caravans only made a profit by combining trade in tusks and people. Sir Richard Burton also described in detail the ubiquitous nature of the ivory trade, emphasising the importance of the export of tusks for the economy of Zanzibar. He saw one caravan bound for Zanzibar carrying about 12 tons of ivory from the Congo Basin.[12] Burton said that at Ujiji (Tanzania), Omani Arabs had set up trading operations to obtain Congo Basin ivory, while Uvira on the north-western shore of the lake (now in the Democratic Republic of the Congo) was the northern depot for ivory and slaves. He relates the story of Musa Mzuri, an Indian from Surat in Gujarat, who went on a trading expedition from Zanzibar to Nyamwezi in 1825, taking twenty men's loads in cloth and beads and returning with 28,000 lbs of ivory.[13]

By the late 1850s, Arab traders were reaching as far as the Ruwenzori Mountains in Uganda. The ivory from these areas north and west of Lake Tanganyika was harder, darker forest ivory, known as *gandai*. It is the lowest-quality ivory for carving and colour. Traders were buying it because the savannah elephants of central Tanzania had been reduced to numbers that made expeditions unprofitable. Supply was failing to keep pace with growing demand and areas nearer to the coast were depleted, leading to ever longer expeditions by traders and the hunters they commissioned. The Zanzibari traders now had, like the Omanis, to send their ivory caravans beyond Lake Tanganyika to the Congo Basin.

IVORY

By the 1860s, an average of 24,000 tusks was passing through Zanzibar and mainland ports annually. There was huge demand for tusks from females, known as *scrivello*, which were smaller and vital to the billiard ball manufacturers. The need to send caravans further inland, with large numbers of porters and at huge cost, affected the nature of the ivory trade in East Africa, encouraging the rise of powerful traders who took over as middlemen from the Nyamwezi and controlled the chain, from buying tusks inland to selling in Zanzibar. Conflict with local people was fuelled by growing slave/ivory raiding by the heavily armed retainers of the Arab traders. This led to the militarisation of the caravans and the establishment of fortified trading posts between the coast and the lake. Many of the communities on the ivory and slave route west from the coast cooperated with the Arabs, deciding it was better to become slavers than be enslaved. Hamed bin Muhammad al Murjebi, known as Tippu Tip, was the most powerful of the traders. He owned seven plantations and an estimated 10,000 slaves, and organised caravans to buy or steal ivory and slaves across an area of 250,000 square miles of Tanganyika and Central Africa. He used his wealth, control of trade and military strength to dominate those with whom he traded and, when this domination was challenged by Nyamwezi leaders like Mirambo or Manyema chiefs east of the lake, to crush them. He was reviled but relied on by European and American missionaries and adventurers like Livingstone, Burton, Speke and Stanley. He supplied them with protection, caravan leaders and porters, and made a healthy profit from it.

By the 1870s the main elephant hunting area stretched from the Nile Valley and Bunyoro in the north through eastern Congo, down into Katanga and north-eastern Zambia. The trade routes went through Nyamwezi areas, with Unyanyembe and Ujiji remaining staging posts on the long-distance caravan route, and then to the north and south of Lake Tanganyika. In the account of his expedition to find Livingstone, starting at Zanzibar in March 1871, Stanley describes the ivory trade in Zanzibar and says that a merchant from there could finance an expedition to Ujiji on Lake Tanganyika for $5000 in payments to porters and trade goods and bring back 2.7 tons of ivory. This would give him a profit of $5,500 in 1871 prices.[14] On a later expedition west of the lake to the Lualaba River, Stanley saw that whole areas had been depopulated by the persistent slave raiding. Tippu Tip accompanied Stanley on this trip in 1876, seeing advantage both in assisting Stanley and using the expedition to extend his trading empire.

When Stanley reached the Ugandan shore of Lake Victoria, he wrote to the British *Daily Telegraph* and the *New York Herald* of the abundance of ivory, coffee and hides that could be the basis for lucrative trade with the Buganda kingdom to the west of the lake. The ruler of the king-dom, Kabaka Mtesa, told Stanley that Arab traders were already visit-ing him to trade guns, powder, wire, cloth and beads for ivory and slaves. Stanley's published accounts of the Congo and Central Africa's riches in ivory and other commodities prompted King Leopold of Belgium to ask him to lead an expedition exploring the course of the Congo and its tributaries to establish trading posts and tap the region's resources. Hochschild is surely right when he says that "Of the riches Leopold hoped to find in the Congo, the one that gleamed most brightly in his imagination was ivory. European and American mer-chants were already eagerly buying African ivory in the markets of Zanzibar"—and Leopold wanted his own source. After Stanley had agreed to undertake the expedition, financed by Leopold, the latter wrote to him that "I am desirous to see you purchase all the ivory which is to be found on the Congo".[15]

To the south in Mozambique, the Yao retained considerable control of the ivory and slave trades east and south of Lake Malawi. They had fire-arms obtained in exchange for both commodities, which made them more formidable hunters and slave raiders. As with other trading peoples travelling huge distances from their home areas, trade began to take over from hunting; the expeditions would be to buy or seize ivory and cap-tives through force of arms rather than hunt. For a long period in the latter half of the nineteenth century, the area between the south end of Lake Malawi and the confluence of the Shire and Zambezi was an impor-tant area for the gathering of ivory, with significant herds to be found at Liwonde Marsh near the lake and further south along the Shire at Elephant Marsh. Yao trade also spread west to the Luangwa Valley.

During the same period, the Chokwe of western Zambia/Angola were steadily expanding their trade in ivory to the west coast, where the Portuguese appetite, heightened by the decline of their east coast trade, was insatiable. Luanda became the main trading hub. Exports from Luanda increased from 52,690 lbs in 1844 to 1,698,248 lbs in 1857, most of it from the Chokwe. At first they were hunting elephants in their home territory, but the scale of killing led them to go further afield and, like other important ivory-supplying communities, to move much more into trading ivory. They travelled to Kasai in southern Congo and traded Portuguese goods for ivory and raw rubber with the Luba and Lunda. They were able to protect their long-distance caravans from raiding through their monopoly over the possession of firearms. This superior military power led to the Chokwe conquest of the Lunda towards the end of the century.

The ivory trade in northern Malawi and the region of southern Tanganyika and north-eastern Zambia between Lakes Malawi and Tanganyika was boosted by the growing demand centred on Zanzibar. The area had significant herds of elephants, as Livingstone had noted in accounts of his travels in the region, and the increasing availability of firearms and slaves to carry ivory and trade goods meant that the people of the region who hunted elephants could take advantage of both trades. The availability of slaves was particularly important because of the difficult terrain which had to be traversed to the coast. The value of the region as a source of ivory and slaves assisted the development of Arab trade hegemony. The descendants of the Arab traders from Kilwa who had established trading posts and intermarried with local peoples at the northern end of the lake were able to monop-olise trade with the Ngonde and Tumbuka along the western lakeshore as far as Karonga.

As the British increased their presence in the region in the 1870s, they moved round the western shore in search of trading opportuni-ties. Initially, they traded with the Arabs. The African Lakes Company (ALC) established a post at Karonga in 1879. British representatives, following the lead of Livingstone, characterised British commerce as legitimate and mutually beneficial, while portraying the Arab traders as violent, unscrupulous and therefore essentially illegitimate, pointing to the slave trade as the ultimate sign of dishonour. That they had been willing to trade with them when it suited company or wider British interests was conveniently forgotten. The ALC sent traders to buy and hunt for ivory in the elephant-rich area around the Songwe River, flow-ing from southern Tanzania into Lake Malawi. British criticism of the

Arab traders mounted as the legacy of Livingstone's public campaigns against slavery took effect, dovetailing with British commercial interest in taking control of regional trade. The spark that started a war between the British and the Arabs appears to have been an attempt by the Arabs to establish greater hegemony over the Ngonde, with whom the British were trading. The ALC's armed retainers became involved and it developed into a battle for control of trade. The Arabs were defeated by the ALC, supported by Ngonde warriors, bringing to an end a long period of Arab commercial dominance.

Towards the end of the 1880s, there remained significant elephant herds on both sides of Lake Malawi and in the region between the lake and the Portuguese at Quelimane. Alfred Sharpe, who was to become Governor of the Central African Protectorate, said that in 1887 he had hunted for ivory in what was to become Nyasaland (Malawi) and in Portuguese Mozambique, finding large herds.[16] The American ivory trader E.D. Moore said that, within a few years of the ALC's assumption of control and its encouragement of large-scale hunting with modern firearms, only a few small populations remained.[17]

In many areas once rich in elephants, herds became increasingly scarce, causing not a decline in the trade but a constant search for new and more lucrative hunting grounds. But voices were already being raised about the indiscriminate slaughter, the insatiable demand for ivory and the effects of modern firearms. Alvan Southworth of the American Geographical Society travelled up the Nile through Sudan and into Central Africa in 1874 and wrote that "ivory traders, wars and civilization" were destroying the elephant; he predicted the animal's demise if the pace of killing continued.[18] Joseph Thomson, who led the Royal Geographical Society's expedition to East and Central Africa in 1878–80, wrote of the disappearance of elephants. He said that at the southern end of Lake Tanganyika, where Livingstone had noted their great abundance, elephants were now absent. Thomson blamed those who imported ivory, writing that:

> "The fact that the trade in ivory... now almost entirely depends on the distant countries to which these routes lead, suggests a woeful tale of destruction. Twenty years ago countries between Tanganyika and the coast were rich in ivory... Now these countries are completely despoiled. Over that vast region hardly a tusk of ivory is to be got."[19]

This stress on demand driving the trade is one of the constant factors of the ivory trade up to the present. External demand created a market and drove first legal hunting in the nineteenth and early twentieth centuries, and then poaching in the last three decades of the twentieth century and the opening years of the current one. Thomson added that people in authority who talked of ivory as an inexhaustible commodity were wrong, and that in fourteen months' journeying in East Africa and the Great Lakes region he saw not a single elephant. The area between the coast and Lake Tanganyika had been largely cleared of elephants and the Zanzibari caravans were now concentrating on the Congo Basin, Uganda and what became known as the Lado Enclave, where northern Congo met Egyptian-controlled Sudan along the upper reaches of the Nile. Other accounts of the time and the later experience of hunters and travellers indicated that Kenya and Uganda still had huge herds of elephants, which were to become the new sources of ivory as demand soared in Europe and America.

Kenya's and Uganda's ivory-harvesting potential influenced the decision to build the Mombasa–Uganda Railway. The line was expected to transport 120 tons of ivory annually to Mombasa for export, with a charge levied of £45 per ton. The Imperial British East Africa Company (IBEAC) had been chartered to develop and economically exploit the area designated by the 1884–5 Berlin Conference and the 1886 Anglo-German Treaty as the British sphere in East Africa (with Tanganyika and Rwanda-Urundi constituting the German sphere). The company saw major advantage in using ivory to finance the development of commerce through income from ivory sales and taxes. There was already a modest but regular supply of ivory from the Waliangulu and Wakamba to the coast at Mombasa, but IBEAC and British hunter-traders wanted to open up the elephant-rich areas of central and northern Kenya, the Tana River area, Uganda, Somalia and southern Sudan. From 1899 there was also a British interest, through the Anglo-Egyptian condominium, in routing Sudanese ivory via Khartoum.

In Uganda, Lord Lugard, who had hunted elephants for the ALC in Malawi, was a key figure in developing British power, on behalf of first the IBEAC and then the British government. He was aware that ivory would be "an even more important subsidy to European imperial activities in East Africa than it had been in Central Africa".[20] Lugard combined military campaigns in Uganda with elephant hunting. The haul of ivory he amassed in Uganda, worth £5,300 annually, helped finance imperial occupation and suppression of communities that resisted. In the Equatoria region of southern Sudan to the north of Lugard's domain, Emin Pasha financed his sway there on behalf of the Egyptian rulers of Sudan through the ivory trade and accumulated huge stocks of tusks. Frederick Jackson, who became lieutenant-governor of Kenya and then governor of Uganda, was also involved in the 1880s in running ivory hunting and gathering expeditions for the IBEAC. As company and later Crown rule developed, administrators, employees of the railway and other officials had preferential access to hunting rights. The indigenous people, who had hunted elephants and sold the ivory to coastal traders, were progressively excluded from hunting by the new authorities, who had unilaterally assumed control over vast territories with no reference to their inhabitants' rights or traditional forms of subsistence.

The opening up of Kenya, Uganda and southern Sudan, and the stories of vast, untapped herds of elephants, led to an influx of hunters, which was welcomed by the IBEAC. The company saw them as a means of developing the ivory trade into a source of income and of encouraging white settlers, who would grow cash crops. The herds in Kenya, Uganda and Sudan were so vast and spread over such an area that it was presumed that there would not be the same serious depletion that had happened in southern Africa and east of Lake Tanganyika. The Waliangulu and the Wakamba were still pursuing a great deal of hunting in eastern Kenya, in the country the coastal side of Mount Kenya and around the Tana River. By the 1890s, the Arab traders who had wrested control of ivory trading from the Wakamba still had a major role in the commerce, but under the hegemony of the British. The Wakamba reverted to hunting as a subsidiary to farming, increasing the scale of hunting during periods of drought, as in 1897–8, when the access to game for meat and ivory became an important means of survival, as livestock died and crops failed.

Colonisation under the IBEAC, which lasted from 1888 to the formation of the Protectorate in 1895, fundamentally changed the relationship between indigenous communities and wildlife. An aim of the company was to use ivory for income generation and to reserve hunting for Europeans, as a commercial enterprise and for sport. Its policy was also guided by the British government's desire to make settlement pay. The latter gave the IBEAC the right to control hunting through licences, but it lacked the staff to implement this other than in the most superficial way. It couldn't control European hunting in the interior of Kenya, where there were few company representatives and those who were there were hunters themselves or sympathetic to white hunters. In 1894, the IBEAC introduced a £25 big game hunting licence and placed a 15 per cent duty on ivory. The company earned significant sums from ivory and wildlife product exports. In 1892, it had exported £23,153 worth of ivory to Zanzibar. Soon, exports started to go directly from Mombasa rather than through the Zanzibari merchants. Zanzibar's trade continued, but was almost entirely dependent on tusks from German East Africa (Tanganyika)—£116,169 worth of ivory in 1892 and £121,567 in 1894, after which it began to tail off, due to depletion of herds and diversion of Congolese, Ugandan and Kenyan ivory through other ports.

Uganda was keeping pace with Kenya as a source of ivory. In the 1860s, the explorer James Grant encountered Arab traders in Bunyoro and Buganda exchanging cloth and manufactured goods for ivory. At first this was an exchange of gifts, but it soon became regularised into a system of trade. Grant said that one Arab trader received 700 lbs of ivory, seven women slaves and fifty cattle in return for cloth, brass wire, and two muskets. Emin Pasha estimated that Arab traders from Zanzibar received five times the value of their trade goods in ivory from the rulers of the two Ugandan kingdoms.[21] The kingdoms both received regular visits from Arab traders from Zanzibar and from Khartoum, vying to corner the trade in ivory and slaves, tightly controlled by the rulers of the two dominant kingdoms and those of neighbouring Ankole.

The trade was tightly controlled by the rulers of the two dominant kingdoms and by those of neighbouring Ankole. They resisted attempts by the Arab traders, by Sir Samuel Baker (when he was governor of Equatoria before Emin) and by other trading expeditions to establish a free trade in ivory—which, of course, would have benefited the traders but not the Bunyoro, Ankole or Baganda. Baker had also tried unsuccessfully, on behalf of the Khedive of Egypt, to annex Bunyoro and

Buganda to Sudan. Baker and his successors did, though, open the way for Khartoum-based traders (Arab and European) to break the near monopoly of Zanzibar over Ugandan and Lado ivory. There was regional competition for hegemony between the Buganda and Bunyoro kingdoms. The Bunyoro used ivory sales to amass firearms and gunpowder to ward off any threat from Buganda.

Thus, under the IBEAC and then direct British colonial rule, ivory not only acted as a subsidy to the colonial treasuries but also enabled colonialism on the cheap, as colonial administrators and employees could augment poor salaries through legal hunting for elephants and the sale of ivory. Many, however, taking advantage of poor hunting regulation enforcement and also exploiting their positions within the colonial hierarchy, would hunt illegally, amassing wealth from what amounted to poaching while decrying the allegedly destructive effects of indigenous hunting.[22] The ability to use office or networks of allies and friends within the colonial system to accumulate wealth through illegal hunting was a forerunner of the corrupt systems of clients and patronage networks that are at the heart of contemporary poaching and smuggling networks in east and central Africa.

Stanley, Leopold and the plundering of the Congo

The other great reservoir of elephants that was only partially exploited by the 1870s was the Congo basin. Tippu Tip and other traders had benefited from it to an extent through trade with and then domination of the Manyema, through economic means and by force of arms. But huge areas of the Congo River and its tributaries were untouched by external commerce. Henry Stanley was instrumental in opening up vast areas to trade, and was as willing as the Arab traders to use force. Stanley saw huge benefits to European trading interests and to himself of opening up the river systems of the Congo and their hinterland to commerce. Ivory would initially be at the forefront. He knew there were large herds of forest elephants to be found and stocks of tusks held by communities across the region which had not been accessed for the global market. When he failed to enlist British interest in exploiting the region, he was approached by King Leopold II of Belgium, who was desperate to enrich himself and build an overseas empire. Stanley took up Leopold's request to establish trading posts along the Congo River. Financed by him, Stanley undertook an expedition from August 1879 to June 1884, setting up armed trading posts along the river and using local labour to build a road from the lower Congo up to Stanley Pool (the site of Kinshasa and Brazzaville). Steamers were built from components hauled round unnavigable cataracts, to be launched on the upper reaches of the river to transport ivory, and later rubber, from as far up-river as Stanley Falls (1,000 miles inland from Stanley Pool).

Leopold's rule and trading interests spread along the river, competing with French expansion in central Africa. It took the Berlin Conference of 1884–5 to sort out the new frontiers. Leopold emerged with recognition of the Congo Free State—which was a huge and unmanageable personal empire stretching from the Atlantic to the Great Lakes. The new borders theoretically cut the Zanzibar traders off from their sources of ivory, their Manyema clients and their trading posts east of Lake Tanganyika. This divorce was not simple and required the use of force and negotiation by Leopold and Stanley, ending with the co-option of the slaver and ivory trader Tippu Tip as an ally.

Stanley's initial expedition along the Congo was followed by his Egyptian-funded expedition in 1887 to rescue Emin Pasha, Governor of Equatoria. Emin had been pushed south by a revolt in southern Sudan and was based at Wadelai, in present-day Uganda, on the border of Sudan, Uganda and the Congo Free State. He was trapped but had an immense stockpile of ivory. Stanley's expedition progressed into the Ituri region, where he came upon first the Arab-controlled ivory and slave settlement of Ugarrowa on the upper Aruwimi River, and then the ivory camp at Ipoto run by a trader known as Kilonga-Longa. These sites were engaged in slave raiding and the seizure of ivory by force.[23] In his account of his journey to Wadelai, Stanley claims that vast stores of ivory had been collected by Ugarrowa, Kilonga-Longa and Tippu-Tip.[24] Stanley described Tippu Tip as the "uncrowned king of the region between Stanley Falls and Tanganika Lake."[25] The rescue expedition found Emin Pasha, but he was forced to leave Wadelai in 1889 after Stanley's arrival. The ivory was abandoned, presumably all taken by Tippu or other local traders. Prior to his forced move south, Emin Pasha had made a profit for his Egyptian masters of £8,000 a year (about £616,000 in current values) from ivory, coffee and cotton from Equatoria.

Leopold sent further expeditions along the Congo to entrench control over the interior. One, led by Belgian officers, journeyed to Wadelai in search of Emin's ivory hoard, to take control of the region and expand Congo Free State territory into the Lado Enclave bordering Congo, Sudan and Uganda, at the expense of the British and Egyptians. The region was teeming with elephants. The British blocked this move, but bought off Leopold by allowing him exploitation of the enclave in southern Sudan for the remainder of his life—on his death, it would revert to the Anglo-Egyptian condominium of Sudan.

Sudan: ivory and slaving

In the nineteenth century, despite the Ottoman Empire's gradual decline in political and economic power, its rulers in Egypt, the khedives, still sought to enrich it and themselves through ivory and slaves obtained from southern Sudan. Trade was primarily in the hands of Arab traders known as *jallaba*. They sent south caravans protected by armed retainers to buy ivory and slaves—they had to compete for these with traders from Borno in present-day Nigeria, who were moving east. The ivory they obtained was transported back to Borno, where it was sold to merchants in Maiduguri or at the regional trading centre of Kano. In 1839, the ruler of Egypt, Muhammed Ali, sent a trading expedition of ten boats up the Nile in the hope of finding gold and ivory in southern Sudan, Uganda and northern Congo. They reached the settlement of Gondokoro (just north of Juba, the capital of South Sudan), nearly 1,000 miles south of Khartoum. There was no gold, but a huge area stretching along the White Nile densely populated by elephants. The potential for trade was huge and opened the way for Arab traders from northern Sudan and an increasing number of Europeans to mount expeditions to the south. The Arab traders established armed and fortified trading posts, known as *zaribas*, from which to gather ivory and mount slaving operations. The traders effectively divided up the area between them, to avoid damaging conflict or competition.

By the early 1840s, regular voyages were taking place between Khartoum and the area around Gondokoro, bringing out cargoes of around 40,000 lbs of ivory at a time. The traders did not hunt but exchanged glass beads and copper wire for tusks with the Dinka,

Shilluk and Nuer. They also used force to steal ivory from weaker communities. Khartoum became a key market for ivory trading. The Egyptian authorities encouraged European, Turkish, Arab and Abyssinian traders to buy ivory and sell it there. Traders were urged by Cairo's representatives in Khartoum to penetrate further into the Upper Nile and Bahr el-Ghazal regions, and into the elephant-rich area of South Sudan, northern Uganda and Lado. One agent sent by the rulers of Egypt, Zubair Rahma Mansur, pushed into Bahr el-Ghazal and southern Darfur and became a ruler in his own right, trying to build his own power base and source of wealth utilising both ivory and slaves. He established considerable freedom of action as more of a tributary potentate than an officer of the khedive. He made an annual payment of £15,000 worth of ivory to Egypt. In the first thirty years of the new ivory trade along the Nile, conflict was regular between the traders, warlords like Zubair and the Egyptian authorities in Khartoum. The latter gained a reputation for seizing shipments of ivory sent by the traders and treating them as Egyptian property, refusing to pay the traders or requiring them to have an army escort and taking a third of their ivory in return.

Pressure from Britain and France forced the Ottoman Empire to give up its attempts to enforce a trade monopoly in Sudan and along the Upper Nile. The need for technical expertise and skilled people to help them build their empire in Sudan meant that the Turkish-appointed overlords in Egypt had to cooperate with Europeans. This brought people like the Welsh mining engineer, John Petherick, to Khartoum to help develop the town and its trade. He became part of the ivory rush in Sudan. By 1856, he was British vice-consul in Khartoum and was reporting back to London that the ivory trade had grown from 40,000 lbs in 1851 to 140,000 lbs in 1856. The initial source of ivory was the store of tusks many peoples of the region had from animals hunted purely for meat, or collected from carcasses. Little value was attached to ivory locally. But as demand increased peoples like the Shilluk, Nuer, Dinka and Bari were encouraged to hunt. They were also encouraged to sell their own people, or captives they had taken in cattle raids, as slaves to the Arab traders.

The well-armed Arab traders used their *zaribas* as slaving bases and holding camps for slaves. As with the connection between the East

African ivory and slave trades, in Sudan the growing cost and need for armed escorts made ivory-gathering expeditions expensive, but also gave the traders the opportunity to use military power to develop the profitable slave trade. Baggara and Rizeigat Arabs from Darfur and Kordofan were increasingly involved in the ivory and slaving raids led by Arab merchants from Khartoum. These created a vicious cycle of growing local hostility towards traders, the depredations of slavers leading to armed clashes and retaliatory raids. When he started his expedition down the Nile in 1860, Speke relied on Petherick and Khartoum merchants to help provision the Sudan end of his journey and transport him to Khartoum. During his trip through Bunyoro territory towards Gondokoro, where Petherick had arranged to pick him up on one of his ivory-gathering operations, Speke traded cowries for ivory. When he reached southern Sudan, Speke reported meeting an Egyptian raiding party south of Gondokoro. The force was a mixture of Egyptians, Arabs and slaves. They were raiding for cattle, which were traded with other communities for ivory and slaves or labour. Speke describes how the Egyptian force joined a local chief to fight one of his enemies and, in the process, steal cattle and a stock of ivory. The stolen cattle were then used to pay local villagers to carry the ivory to Gondokoro.[26]

Violence became a means of obtaining ivory, and the pursuit of elephants and their ivory developed into a system of raiding and theft, with the brutal slave trade expanding alongside. Under the khedive's administration, Khartoum thrived on ivory, tax on the trade and the blood money of slavery—400,000 slaves were estimated to have been sold in Egypt and Turkey between 1846 and 1860, according to Romolo Gessi, an official serving the khedive. The Dangala and Ja'alyin Arab communities in central and northern Sudan played a major role in the river trade, while the Baggara, Rizeigat and Shaiga Arab communities were raiders, armed tax collectors and hunters, who preyed on elephants and people alike. "Each province maintained its own force of these irregulars, who were widely loathed and described in one official report as 'swaggering bullies, robbing, plundering, and ill-treating the people with impunity".[27] The Arab traders spread beyond the Bahr el-Ghazal and Equatoria regions and began to open up trade routes to the Azande kingdom (straddling northern DRC, the eastern CAR and South Sudan). Many of the routes developed were maintained over time despite changes in ruler, the drawing of colonial boundaries and then independence—with the smuggling of ivory, rhino horn, drugs, tobacco and weapons thriving across the porous borders of the Sahel belt—from Mali across to the Red Sea along routes which are over 160 years old. The Baggara and Rizeigat evolved over time into the Janjaweed militias, which gained notoriety for their brutality and massacres during the Darfur conflict in the first decade of the twenty-first century—they also continued to poach or smuggle ivory across a broad swathe of central Africa, across the CAR and Chad into Cameroon.

The growing power of the Arab traders and their plundering of the region's resources generated a strong response from some southern Sudanese peoples. Violence escalated and, to bolster their Baggara forces, traders paid the Azande people of southern Sudan and the eastern Congo to fight for them. Partly as a result of the violence, European traders began to disappear from the region in the 1860s, to be replaced by more Arabs, who relied increasingly on the slave trade. Only when the European powers put pressure on the Egyptian khedive and Samuel Baker was appointed governor of Equatoria did Egypt agree to suppress the slave trade, in exchange for the European powers' acquiescence in the Egyptian annexation of southern Sudan.

By the time of Samuel Baker's appointment in 1869, the ivory trade through Khartoum was worth £40,000 a year (approximately £2.3m in 2015 values). Baker was able to suppress the open slave trade, and spread Egyptian control to the borders of Congo and Uganda, though a covert slave trade persisted. Baker himself was not above using captives from his raids to transport ivory and other goods, as slaves had been forced to do by Arab traders. He also engaged in cattle raiding, trading the spoils for ivory. The exchange of stolen cattle for ivory continued to develop between the Arabs, Baker and some southern cattle communities, and with the Acholi of Uganda. Baker contributed income to the Egyptian coffers through ivory confiscated from Arab traders whom he accused of slavetrading or of failing to pay duties owed to Khartoum. The ivory he obtained has been estimated at 150,000 lbs, worth £50,000 (nearly £3m in 2015). Baker calculated that in a good ivory season, a trader sending an 150-man expedition from Khartoum could bring back 20,000 lbs of ivory worth £4,000, as well as hundreds of slaves that could be sold for £5 each. As the trade and its penetration south continued, the Arab traders tried but failed to dominate the Azande, who had experience of the Arab style of raiding and the foresight to trade their large stocks of ivory for guns.

With British influence in Egypt increasing as Ottoman power declined, there was growing reliance in Cairo on British finance and personnel in governing Sudan. Egypt was to come under effective British hegemony from 1882, though remaining legally part of the Ottoman Empire until 1914. When Baker finished his term as governor of Equatoria in 1873, he was succeeded by General Charles Gordon. Gordon established a government monopoly over ivory. By the end of his governorship in 1880—by which time he was governor-general of the whole of Sudan—Gordon had amassed a stockpile of £60,000 (today about £4m) worth of ivory, but had lost the trade in ivory with the Bunyoro kingdom, which instead started sending all its ivory out via Zanzibar. During this period, there was continuing unrest among Arab groups opposed to overall Egyptian control. Gordon employed Romolo Gessi to defeat traders linked with Zubair in Bahr el-Ghazal, and Gessi was able to seize ivory worth £90,000 from the defeated Arabs. In 1878, the Egyptians appointed Emin Pasha as governor of Equatoria, with the principal aim of maintaining control in order to maximise income from ivory. His success was such that while he was cut off from Khartoum by a Sudanese Arab "Mahdist" revolt, he built up the massive stock of ivory that Stanley saw as part of the prize for himself, Tippu Tip and the Egyptian khedive when he mounted the rescue mission described above.

Emin had not only bought ivory from the Equatoria region of what is now South Sudan, but opened trading links for tusks with the Acholi of Uganda and the Turkana of Kenya. His advances, however, were not without opposition. Emin was as unsuccessful as Baker in trying to annex areas of Uganda, and there was frequent conflict between Emin's forces and the Acholi as he persisted in raiding them for cattle with which to obtain ivory from other communities. The revolt, led by Muhammad Ahmad (known as the Mahdi), temporarily ended Egyptian control of Sudan and the Nile route south; the ivory trade was disrupted. The Mahdi gained the support of the Baggara, whose experienced horse-mounted fighters were a huge asset in overrunning outlying Egyptian garrisons and advancing on Khartoum—where his army defeated and killed General Gordon.

Following the overthrow of the Mahdist forces in April 1898 by an Anglo-Egyptian army, the condominium over Sudan was formalised and the British became the effective rulers, spreading the area under their control to the Azande kingdom to block French and Congo Free State attempts to reach the Nile. The British wanted control of the Nile from Uganda up to the Mediterranean, and to monopolise the ivory trade in the region. The new condominium was energetic in exploiting wildlife resources such as ivory, rhino horn and ostrich feathers, for which there was a ready market in Europe. In 1901, 15 tons of ivory were exported from the south, rising to 125 tons in 1913. The condominium's monopoly of rail and river transport brought significant income for the government through the ivory trade.

South and southern Africa: the effects of European settlement

The British extension of settlement in the Cape when they seized the region in 1806, and the migration of Dutch Trekboers inland away from British control, very rapidly took its toll on Cape elephants. This was so serious that in 1830 the Cape government introduced a ban on elephant hunting to protect the few remaining herds in the Knysna Forest and Addo, near Port Elizabeth. In less than 200 years, white settlement and the introduction of firearms had destroyed an elephant population in the Cape estimated at 25,000 animals. The ban in the Cape did not end the ivory trade in South Africa and tusks were still exported via the Cape, and later through Natal. To escape British control, and with the Cape no longer a viable hunting area, the Trekboers and hunter-adventurers moved up through Natal, Zululand and into what became the Orange Free State and Transvaal, and then onwards into Bamangwato country (Botswana) in search of ivory.

Some of the indigenous communities, like the Zulu under Shaka, hunted elephants. Shaka organised huge hunts in which game would be driven towards concealed hunters. The method of killing elephants was brutal and dangerous. The hunters, including Shaka, would rush out behind the elephants and cut their hamstrings before killing the animals with multiple spear thrusts. Ivory trade with Europeans predated the arrival of the Trekboers and the British; the Portuguese had first established trade with Zulu and other Ngoni peoples, exchanging cloth and manufactured goods for ivory. Some hunters and traders, like Henry Francis Fynn and Nathaniel Isaacs, settled in Natal and traded with the Zulu with the permission of Shaka and then Dingaan. They hunted elephants in Natal and Zululand and bought ivory from Zulu hunters, selling it at a huge profit at Port Natal. Various Xhosa communities began to hunt elephants in the nineteenth century in response to demand from European ivory traders. The Mpondo king, Fako, keen to get British support in the 1840s as a defence against Boer encroachment, instructed his son, "Diko, my son, go and hunt elephants so that I may send government a present of ivory".[28]

The opening up of South Africa to European settlement and trade through the subjugation of Xhosa, Zulu and other indigenous peoples also enabled hunters and traders to gather ivory, through either barter with local hunters or long-distance hunting expeditions. The progressive destruction of herds meant that journeys needed to last months to find sufficient ivory to be commercially viable. A typical example is that of William Harris, who travelled from the Cape to the Magaliesberg in Transvaal in 1851 without seeing an elephant until the very end of the journey. The famed traveller, Frederick C. Selous, was a single-minded elephant hunter, who killed hundreds of animals for profit in a number of long expeditions through southern Africa. When he first landed in South Africa, at Algoa Bay (Port Elizabeth) in 1871, he had to trek 1,400 miles into Matabeleland before he saw an elephant, such had been the slaughter since white settlement.

On their migration north away from the British, the Trekboers took oxen and other livestock but also shot huge amounts of game for meat. This meant they could maintain their flocks and cattle as the basis for a livestock-centric economy when they settled. Elephant hunting produced large amounts of meat and a tradable commodity. British settlers and hunters also became involved in large-scale hunting, especially of elephants. Some, like R.G. Gordon-Cumming, who wrote of his experiences, hunted for ivory and traded firearms for tusks with Tswana communities, who themselves bought ivory from San hunters. He made no pretence about the level of profit he derived—trading a musket worth £1 for ivory worth £30.[29] He could earn as much as £1,000 from a single trip (£90,000 in 2015) and wrote that he killed at least 105 elephants. The effect of this hunting for meat and ivory meant that, by the 1860s, elephants had been wiped out in the eastern Cape; by the 1870s, few survived south of the Limpopo.

Selous noted with regret the steady extermination of game across southern Africa, in which he had played an active part. He wrote in 1909 that in the early nineteenth century elephant and buffalo had abounded in the forests of the Cape Colony, but the spread of farming and hunting for hides and ivory wiped them out by the century's latter half. He admitted that between 1860 and 1870 there had been enormous destruction of game inhabiting the open plains of South Africa. Hunting by settlers and indigenous hunters, many of whom had worked as mine labourers and been able to buy guns, led to the eventual disappearance of many species throughout much of the Cape, Free State and western Transvaal. Selous said that exports of ivory from South African ports were practically zero in the closing years of the nineteenth century, and that the remaining elephants in remote areas of southern Africa had become "so wild and cunning, and ranged over such vast areas of country" that it no longer paid either white or black hunters to go after them; this allowed the remote herds gradually to increase their numbers.[30] Nevertheless, the exports of ivory rose in the Cape and then fell as the herds were wiped out, and hunters and traders had to move north and west to gather tusks. Thus export records from the last half of the nineteenth century show that ivory steadily rose in price per pound from 4.4 shillings in 1862 to 9.6 in 1883, but the quantities exported fluctuated. From 1861 to 1875, there was an increase from 58,330 lbs worth £14,731 (£1,500,000 today) in 1861 to 161,234 lbs worth £60,402 (£5,800,000 today) By 1883, the price was higher, reflecting demand, but the quantity exported was down to 11,915, worth £5,764.

The destruction of game and elephant herds in South Africa pushed hunters north into Zimbabwe, Botswana and Zambia. Chief Khama of the Bamangwato Tswana levied a tax of half the value of tusks shot in his territory. By the 1880s he had started to control hunting, as herds in Chobe and surrounding areas were wiped out. He was concerned about the rapid extermination of animals that had a long-term value for his people as sources of ivory and hides. The restrictions imposed by rulers like Khama were often aimed at the Trekboer hunters, who gained a reputation for killing anything that crossed their path.[31] Khama allowed

British hunters access to his territory as long as they obtained his permission. After Bechuanaland became a Protectorate (1885) he wrote to the British government and stressed that he wanted to maintain the traditional pastoral, cultivation and hunting traditions of his people, warning that if hunting wasn't controlled, "the game will come to an end in the future, but at the present it is in my country, and while it is still there I hold that it ought to be hunted by my people".[32] The hunter-turned-conservationist H. A. Bryden published an article in the London *Fortnightly Review* in 1894 bemoaning the slaughter caused by the availability of breech-loading rifles in southern Africa. He said that one group of hunters in the Okavango, adjacent to Khama's territory, had killed 104 elephants on one hunting expedition. Boer farmers from the Marico district of north-west Transvaal made regular hunting trips to Chobe and along the Zambezi to supplement farm incomes with ivory.

European hunters had been shooting elephants in Ndebele country in Zimbabwe since the 1830s. By the 1870s, the kingdom was producing 50,000 lbs of ivory a year, exported through South Africa. In 1872–4, 100,000 lbs was exported, 40 per cent from elephants killed by white hunters, Selous estimated. This would have involved the killing of about 2,000 elephants.[33] In 1883, to the consternation of hunters like Selous, the Ndebele king, Lobengula, sought to introduce restrictions on hunting to stop the shooting of elephant cows. Ndebele hunters were finding game extremely scarce and the king wanted to protect his people's resources. This is not surprising given that, by his own admission, Selous alone killed 548 head of game on one long hunting expedition there. Another hunter, William Baldwin, collected 350 lbs of tusks on one trip, and once killed eight elephants in half an hour. In his books and articles, Selous gives exhaustive details of his hunting trips and the numbers of elephants and other game he shot. In 1872, for example, he shot elephants carrying 450 lbs of ivory and bought another 1,200 lbs from Ndebele hunters. He always blamed Africans for the decline in elephant numbers, ignoring the fact that their hunting of elephants was at the instigation of white traders. In the late 1870s, he ventured into the Chobe region of Botswana, where on a single trip he shot twenty-four elephants and nine rhino. By 1877, he said that elephants were becoming scarce in Chobe, but still shot twenty of them between January 1877 and December 1880. Prior to the onset of demand from outside these societies, elephant hunting had been a sporadic activity among local people and not one that seriously reduced numbers.

By the time his book, *A Hunter's Wanderings in Africa*, was published in 1881, Selous was lamenting that there were too few elephants in Matabeleland for him to make a decent profit and that they were becoming scarce all along the Zambezi. The scarcity of animals in these areas meant that Selous and other hunters moved into Mashonaland and began to wipe out herds south of the Zambezi. He also hunted in Mozambique, where he said that a Portuguese merchant on the Zambezi near the river's junction with the Luangwa had just sent 10,000 lbs of ivory back to Quelimane for export to Europe. In 1885, well after he had noted the general decline in elephant numbers in southern Africa, Selous was involved in the killing of large numbers in the Lomagunda district of Zimbabwe, where the British South Africa Company's administrator for Southern Rhodesia had issued free licences for the killing of elephants that were raiding farms. Selous says that, although elephants were declining in numbers, in this locality they were plentiful. He said there "was a hearty response to this invitation, and in a short time about 100 elephants appear to have been killed and some 2,000 lbs of ivory obtained. Judging by the average weight of the tusks, the majority of these elephants must have been young females."[34]

By the end of the nineteenth century, hunting had led to a massive fall in elephant numbers between the Zambezi and Limpopo Rivers. The process was being repeated to the north in the Barotseland area of Zambia. The Barotse king permitted hunting by Europeans and this increased as the British took over and settlement grew around the copper mines. Selous reported that one hunter, George Westbeech, sent between 20,000 and 30,000 lbs of ivory out of the region between 1871 and 1876, having received permission to hunt from the Barotse ruler, Sipopa. Another hunter, William Finaughty, killed ninety-five elephants in one year there. Westbeech earned £12,000 (just under £800,000 at today's values) from his ivory hunting. It has been estimated that by 1900 there were fewer than 6,000 elephants south of the Zambezi, and total extermination there was not beyond the bounds of possibility. In South Africa there were a few elephants in the Tsitsikama Forest along the south coast, about 150 in Addo, a few in remote areas of Zululand in the Tembe and none in the Sabi and Shingwezi areas that were later to form the bulk of the Kruger National Park. In Botswana, the once huge herds of the Chobe and Savuti rivers now numbered a few hundred and very few survived in the southern half of Mozambique and Namibia. In Zimbabwe, there were fewer than 4,000 elephants.

West Africa: ivory and the decline of herds in Nigeria and Cameroon

Having been a major site of the European-African ivory trade, by the nineteenth century West Africa's ivory exports were in gradual decline, though still a lure for British, French and other European trading companies. Cameroon was a major centre for French purchases of ivory, while the British—though also buying Cameroonian ivory—came to concentrate on Nigeria. The Cameroonian trade had developed during the late seventeenth and eighteenth centuries, but by the early 1800s the herds in coastal swamps and forests around Douala had been depleted and the hunting of elephants moved northwards. The region's Duala people controlled the trade, buying ivory from Kunda hunters in the inland forests once the coastal herds disappeared. This replicated the pattern in many areas where coastal hunters became traders as scarcity cut income from hunting. The Duala community used ivory for personal adornment, usually in the form of bracelets, but did not accord it great value. The increased level of elephant hunting and engagement in extensive commerce in ivory was rather a reaction to demand from European traders.

One of the first clear references in Europe to large quantities of ivory available at the Cameroonian coast came in 1820 from a British naval officer, Lieutenant Bold, who reported after a voyage to the region that Cameroonian tusks were large and of good quality for carving. He estimated that European traders had obtained 60 tons of ivory in one season and that much of the ivory had been collected from dead elephants over a long period of time rather than hunted.[35] Guns, powder and salt were exchanged by British, Portuguese and French traders for the ivory, some of which may have come from as far as northern Nigeria and Mali. The availability of good-quality ivory made for competition between the coastal and the trans-Saharan trades during the nineteenth century. By the closing decades, Batanga on the south coast of Cameroon had been established as a major ivory trading port and very little Cameroonian ivory was reaching Europe by way of North Africa—about 10 tons a year of an average of 70 reached Britain via the Sahara route. Much of the ivory going via the northern desert route was sold through Hausa and Borno traders in Kano, which remained an important ivory commerce centre for the region. Kano was a focus for traders from Adamawa (straddling the Nigeria-Cameroon border), Ouaddai in Chad and the Benue River.

Samuel Crowther, an African missionary and later the first Nigerian to become an Anglican bishop, reported in 1854 that on his travels from the Niger Delta up along the Benue River he came across extensive ivory trading, much of it from Adamawa, mostly controlled by Hausa and Borno merchants owing loyalty to the Sultan of Sokoto.[36] The British traders on whose vessel Crowther was travelling were keen purchasers of ivory. They had to compete with the existing commerce between the region and Kano and Katsina merchants, who also bought slaves in exchange for cloth, carpets and iron weapons. The Kano traders, in turn, were selling ivory to Sudanese Arabs who had come westwards in the early to mid-nineteenth century seeking ivory and slaves. The Kano dealers were also seeking their own supplies beyond Nigeria and West Africa, with reports of traders reaching Gaza in present-day Central African Republic and southern Sudan. By the late the 1870s, with ever greater British interest in the region, the Royal Niger Company was buying large quantities of tusks—65 tons at £800 a ton in 1878, with duty paid by the company to British government representatives. Interestingly, ten years later, the price of West African forest ivory had fallen to £500–600 a ton, perhaps in competition with the better-quality savannah tusks from East and southern Africa.

Over the final decades of the nineteenth century, the demand at the coast and the growing power of the Royal Niger Company, as well as French and German companies—all of which competed with each other—had put many of the Kano traders out of business. Some trade remained, however, and ivory dealing has survived in northern Nigeria up to present times, with Kano as a regional centre for illegal ivory trading in the late twentieth and early twenty-first centuries. The German traders, based in their new colony of Cameroon, fought to divert tusks from within the territory and from neighbouring areas of

Nigeria and Chad to Douala, away from Kano and the trading ports at Calabar or on the Benue River. By 1902, the German traders had succeeded in concentrating the market within Cameroon and in that year 66 tons were exported, compared with 7 tons going to Borno and 12 to the Benue ports. Gradually, as in other areas of Africa, European hunters were arriving in Cameroon and replacing local ones. This, as elsewhere, led to a more rapid decline in elephant numbers there. By 1910, the British trade through Nigeria and the German supplies from Cameroon were drying up, never to recover as a legal trade.

3

THE IVORY TRADE AND CRIMINALISATION OF AFRICAN HUNTERS UNDER COLONIAL RULE

At the end of the nineteenth century, European powers were entrenching themselves in their African colonies and seeking to pay for colonial occupation through exploitation of local resources and trading opportunities. Among the consequences were evolution of the ivory trade and changes in the relationship between Africans, land and wildlife. Key centres of the trade—Zanzibar, Mombasa and Khartoum— became part of the British Empire. The eastern networks of Arab, Swahili or Indian traders who exported tusks remained, but control and taxation was in the hands of the British. Taxation of commerce in ivory helped colonial powers fund government and extract profit.

The influx of European officials, traders, hunters and settlers also changed the nature of hunting. Oblivious to or antagonistic towards indigenous hunting, colonial administrations banned or severely restricted it. In many colonies, especially those with settlers or opportunities for commercial hunting, indigenous hunting was criminalised. Where there was minimal settlement, control over hunting might be left to chiefs or other traditional leaders to administer, unless it became expedient to ban it. Any trading in ivory falling outside colonial control became illegal, where before it had been legal and of long standing. This did not stop Africans hunting or trading outside the official system. They didn't simply give up, and traders using centuries-old networks did not cease to trade but often mixed legal and illegal trade. According to David Anderson, African agency was not eradicated, but this "should not obscure the fact that the disempowerment of African communities in the face of colonial policy-making was real enough. Nowhere in Africa were Africans participants in the colonial decision-making processes that defined development goals… with little or no sensitivity to indigenous African husbandry practices."[1]

The institution of alien and arbitrary wildlife regulations was accompanied by the development of a justificatory discourse. Regulation was imposed on the grounds that it was necessary to protect a resource or prevent the destruction of a species. Banning Africans from hunting was said to be a necessity, because they were held to blame for the destruction of game. Hunters-turned-conservationists, like Selous, blamed them for the scarcity of game, ignoring the scale of their own hunting. The narrative of elephant survival being threatened by African hunting became and remains dominant.[2] Settlers could hunt and professional European hunters could make a living from ivory, but indigenous farmers whose crops were destroyed or lives threatened by elephants had to appeal to the authorities for help, or buy hunting licences to protect their own land. Those who hunted as part of their subsistence strategy were simply criminalised. When protected areas or areas of exclusive European hunting were established under colonial rule, resident communities were pushed from their land, thereby losing both their homes and farmland and the ability to hunt as they had prior to colonial rule. The process of expulsion from wildlife areas continued throughout the period of European rule and did not end with independence, but became part of the continued practice of dispossession or exclusion of local communities to make way for national parks and/or tourist areas as part of a "fortress conservation" approach backed by Western NGOs and corporate sponsors in a highly capitalist approach to conservation—one which denied local communities the right or ability to exploit natural resources.[3]

For Europeans, colonisation enabled the development of commercial and sport hunting on a grand scale. This became part of the settler way of life and the stuff of romanticised legends of white hunters and big-game hunting as a sport for the rich and privileged. Officials, employees of European companies and settlers could supplement incomes by shooting elephants and selling the tusks. Thus the colonial governments, their employees and the settlers became the new gatekeepers of the ivory trade—though Arab, Swahili and Indian merchants still prospered by exporting ivory. European hunting alone did not rapidly deplete populations, but was part of the increased killing, enabled by the spread of modern firearms and driven by European and American demand for ivory, as well as the enthusiasm of colonial administrations for ivory as a source of income. As we have seen, European hunters had already been shooting for ivory prior to colonialism, but they now had a near monopoly and could buy ivory held by indigenous peoples cheaply and at great profit. Men like W. D. M. Bell were famous for their exploits as hunters—though, as the elephant specialist Ian Parker cautioned me, we have to take Bell's published works and those of other hunters with hefty pinches of salt, as they exaggerated their exploits.[4] Bell killed over 1,000 elephants during his career, hunting across a broad swathe of East Africa and the Lado Enclave; Ian Parker puts the total at 1,011 based on Barclay's game records.[5]

At the beginning of the twentieth century, some hunters and colonial officials also developed a belief in the need for regulation and protection of rare species, leading to the emergence of the conservation movement. At first this concentrated on ensuring that indigenous hunting was banned to protect game animals for sport hunting and the ivory trade. Some conservationists did argue that protecting species and habitats because of their inherent value or environmental significance was important, too, but their voices were not dominant at first—and when that strand became more influential it became another justification for banning African hunting, with exclusion of Africans from the conservation discourse and practice. For many decades, the new regulations had little effect on professional hunters. The era of the "white hunter, black poacher" was upon Africa, in many territories up to independence and even beyond.[6]

The ivory trade was booming at the turn of the century and, despite a downturn during WWI, this continued up to the Depression in 1929. While the middlemen in African ports accumulated wealth from ivory, European and American trading companies also prospered from a trade with few ethical standards. The veteran ivory trader-turned-critic E. D. Moore says that, from the turn of the century to the outbreak of

WWI, the European and American traders knew that a considerable portion of the ivory they purchased was stolen or obtained illegally. Moore was responsible for buying ivory to meet demand in the USA, which was overtaking Britain as the largest market. By 1922, the Illinois Billiard Association estimated that 4,000 elephants were killed annually to meet the demand for billiard balls.[7] As the global trade expanded, there was concern among dealers that the public might become sickened by the scale of slaughter. A brochure produced by the London dealers Lewis and Peat misleadingly told potential customers that "ivory for the most part is found dead in the jungle and collected by natives from the 'Cemeteries' so called because the herds of elephant … are supposed to have chosen spots in which to die… Only a very small percentage of ivory is shot by hunters".[8] Moore estimated that between 1905 and 1912 30,000 elephants were killed annually to meet demand, and during the first two decades of the twentieth century, 600,000 elephants were shot for the American market alone.[9] Researcher and chronicler of the trade Esmond Martin puts the rate of killing higher, at 44,000 elephants a year from 1850 to 1914.[10]

The movement towards conservation co-existed with this trade, explaining why the thrust was to sustain numbers and colonial wildlife department income, rather than end killing. The proponents of conservation initially showed few ethical concerns about the trade itself. A former hunter who became governor of Uganda, Harry Johnston, publicly condemned the ravages of European and American sportsmen and commercial hunters. He said killing on an unrestricted scale was a blot on civilisation,[11] but didn't call for an end to ivory trading. In 1899 he wrote to British Prime Minister Lord Salisbury attacking uncontrolled hunting by settlers. He singled out for criticism the leading settler in Kenya, Lord Delamere, portrayed as a lovable rogue in books by settlers and the film *Out of Africa*. Johnston criticised him for shooting elephants with no regard for the game laws.[12] A year later, Johnston wrote to the Foreign Office that: "The fact is Lord Delamere, who secured 14,000 [pounds] on ivory in the Baringo District by shooting elephant with a maxim gun, was exceedingly annoyed on returning to his old hunting ground to find that I had created Baringo Game Reserve which was intended to preserve elephants".[13] Delamere's hunting companion, Dr Atkinson, ended up in court on far more serious charges when he blew up and killed a Rendille chief and several retainers after they refused to sell him a stock of ivory at the price he set. A jury of settlers acquitted him, despite evidence of deliberate murder—he kept the late stock of ivory he took after killing the men.[14]

Conservation measures in East Africa were not the first attempts to limit hunting or create reserves. Chiefs like Khama and Lobengula had initiated controls over European hunting in their domains to prevent over-hunting. As early as 1858, the Transvaal and Orange Free State Republics introduced laws to limit hunting. The British Cape Colony followed in 1886, with specific protection for elephants. The introduction of reserves and game laws then progressed across colonised Africa. Reserves were established in Kenya and Uganda. In British Central Africa, High Commissioner Sir Alfred Sharpe introduced regulations limiting the shooting of elephants according to tusk size. A former elephant hunter himself, Sharpe went down the well-trodden path of blaming not sports hunters or global demand for the demise of elephants, but "indiscriminate hunting" by local peoples.[15] The German authorities in Tanganyika introduced hunting restrictions in the Moshi, Kilimanjaro and Rufiji areas in the last decade of the nineteenth century, when they observed a serious decline in elephant numbers.

This trend was exemplified by the May 1900 conference of colonial powers in London to discuss coordinated conservation. It produced the Convention for the Preservation of Wild Animals, Birds and Fish in Africa. The British, French, Germans, Portuguese, Spanish and Italians all signed. Few ratified or translated it into enforceable laws, but it formed the basis of much British policy, with Africans excluded from hunting or owning modern firearms in most colonies. Reporting the conference, *The Times* said, "It is necessary to go far into the interior to find the nobler forms of antelope, and still further if the hunter wants to pursue the elephant, the rhinoceros, or the giraffe… very soon those animals, unless something is done to prevent their extermination, will be stamped out as completely as the dodo". But the preamble to the convention makes no great claim to ethical motivations, and says the signatories are "desirous of saving from indiscriminate slaughter, and of insuring the preservation throughout their possessions in Africa of the various forms of animal life existing in a wild state which are either useful to man or are harmless".[16]

Following the conference, a number of hunters, naturalists and colonial officials came together in London in 1903 to form the Society for the Preservation of the Wild Fauna of the Empire (henceforth referred to as the Fauna Preservation Society). It lobbied the British government to enact the decisions of the 1900 conference and published the *Journal of the Society for the Preservation of the Wild Fauna of the Empire*, which printed articles calling for legislation to conserve wildlife, along with annual reports by colonial game departments. For many years, most members of the Society propagated the view that they had to protect the fauna from the Africans. In 1905, Colonel Delme-Radcliffe, a colonial official in Uganda, wrote that Africans were to blame for the widespread killing of elephants there, while European hunting was controlled and had little effect on numbers. African hunters were presented as primitive, cruel and indiscriminate.[17]

Preservation of fauna was seen by conservationists and colonial officials as the domain of Europeans. The encouragement of European sport hunting was in fact seen as a viable route to conservation, as Africans could not be trusted. One Society member, writing about conservation in Nigeria in 1937, said that "the evincing of intelligent interest in fauna on the part of Europeans is essential to successful preservation... Thus the use of the rifle should be encouraged as the only means of making Europeans take genuine interest in the fauna of so difficult a country."[18] Some recognised that indigenous peoples had hunted as part of their livelihood, but failed to appreciate the way this often supplemented more important economic activity. This outlook meant that "colonial governments not only alienated large swathes of territory, but also assumed responsibility for and asserted rights over the natural environment... the rise of bureaucratic conservationism often led to the criminalization of local resource extractors,"[19] creating conflict between conservation and local communities. As Beinart and Hughes concluded, "barriers led to deepening alienation, and growing hostility to conservation. This set governments, conservationists, and indigenous peoples on a collision course that became increasingly acrimonious in parts of Africa".[20]

Although the commercial ivory trade was generated by demand external to Africa, involved Arab, Swahili or Indian middlemen, and saw white hunters killing large numbers of elephants, Charles Hobley, a former colonial administrator and proponent of hunting-friendly conservation, wrote that the attempts at regulation should be aimed not at European hunters and the colonially encouraged ivory trade, but at Africans and small-scale traders outside government control. He posited that the "aim is to persuade those in authority overseas that the slaughter of wildlife for profit can no longer be tolerated. As long as avenues exist for the sale of illicitly obtained ivory... natives will slaughter without compunction and petty traders will arrange for export either openly or surreptitiously."[21] Hobley contended that the "natives" were adept at bending the rules and that where game departments bought natural-mortality ivory, "90 per cent of the alleged old stocks had been killed recently, but had probably been buried for a few months until the odour of decomposition had passed off and had then been smoked over a wood fire" to disguise their poaching.[22] Hobley simultaneously—and hypocritically—praised the way that the game departments in colonies funded their work through revenue from ivory hunted by Europeans on licence, acquired from control operations, or confiscated from poachers. He reported in 1938 that in British East Africa "the Elephant has for many years provided the money for the upkeep of the Game Departments and the proceeds from ivory, plus licence fees have year by year... resulted in a substantial balance to the local treasuries". In 1926–35 inclusive, the revenue collected by the game departments of Kenya, Uganda, and Tanganyika totalled £665,400 (£39,479,845 in current values). Game department spending in the same period was £292,290, leaving a surplus to government of £373,000 (about £22m today).[23]

European or settler conservationists—at one stage dubbed the "penitent butchers"[24]—established protected reserves. In 1884, Paul Kruger, the last president of Transvaal and a keen elephant hunter in his youth, proposed the establishment of the reserve that would later bear his name in the Sabi area—it was expanded in 1926 by joining the Sabi and Shingwedzi reserves. Etosha reserve was established in South African-controlled South West Africa (Namibia) in 1928; Addo Elephant Reserve in the Cape in 1931; Albert National Park in Belgian Congo in 1925; Sumba and Lukusuzi reserves in Northern Rhodesia (Zambia) in 1942, building on earlier measures to create protected areas at Mweru Marsh and in the Luangwa Valley. What is now the

Serengeti National Park was established as a reserve in 1940. Each foundation of a reserve involved the expulsion or exclusion of local communities and a ban on hunting by Africans.

Some colonial governments implemented regulations to stop the indiscriminate shooting of elephants for ivory, banning the killing of cows and immature bulls. The measures were put to a meeting of colonial powers in 1921 to try to get international agreement on a tusk weight below which it would be illegal to shoot an elephant, unless for crop protection. It was recognized that without creating protected areas, the combined effect of expanding human cultivation and settlement would squeeze out elephants and other wildlife and this would be exacerbated by shooting elephants indiscriminately—this was conservation with shooting and continued sales of ivory in mind. This was strongly argued by a leading zoologist, Dr Peter Chalmers Mitchell, who wrote that "the most direct menace to elephants in Africa is the increase of settlements, the multiplication of farms and shambas. Africa is becoming a white man's country at a pace that would have seemed incredible ten years ago."[25]

Some sections of the conservation movement, though, did begin to develop a more critical attitude towards European hunters, and to recognise the damage they were inflicting, particularly on elephants. The future warden of Kruger National Park, James Stevenson-Hamilton, wrote in the *Journal* in 1921, under the pseudonym *Sabi*, that it was European penetration and the introduction of the breech-loading rifle that had led to the rapid decrease in elephants. He said Africans had hunted elephants for thousands of years to sell ivory to traders, and "no great inroads were made upon the elephants, nor were they driven from many… of their natural haunts until the arrival of the European with his firearms…" Since 1900, by contrast, elephants had been driven from entire areas of British East Africa, "retiring before the settlers, and European hunters in the south, and west, finding small rest among the Abyssinian and Swahili traders, whom they encountered to the north and east".[26]

Stevenson-Hamilton lamented that regulations were not enforced in many territories:

"For instance, if the hunter is untroubled by a conscience it is possible that a person, who by his licence is allowed to dispose of two warrantable bull elephants, should not shoot a dozen or more, keep the ivory of the two largest, and place the remainder at the disposal of some local fund [game department or colonial administration coffers], wherein the ivory is shown as 'found in the bush'.[27]

But ivory income was of increasing importance. By the 1920s, "the sale of ivory by the East African administrations had become a not inconsiderable part of the exiguous income", and helped administrations in Kenya, Tanganyika and Uganda through the Depression.[28] This income ivory, including poached or otherwise illicit tusks, explains in part why the game departments' awareness of poaching by Europeans who had taken out licences did not lead to action. Stevenson-Hamilton took a realistic approach to the case for better regulation, and said:

> "Ivory, with due care, might remain a permanent though small asset to a country, if the killing of the beast that provides the ivory were duly restrained within limits. To kill the goose that lays the golden eggs, or, more correctly speaking, to kill all the geese that perform that useful function, should not appeal to the educated financier".[29]

Stevenson-Hamilton and a growing number of game officials joined forces with naturalists like Drake-Brockman to urge international action to conserve elephants and stop smuggling. Drake-Brockman warned that, without this, hunters could evade regulation by hunting

> "in the lesser known regions of the Uganda Protectorate and the Belgian Congo, in the hope of amassing wealth rapidly by elephant-hunting... there are still regions in the neighbourhood of the White and Blue Nile [Lado and southern Sudan], where a daring elephant-hunter can elude capture and carry on his illicit trade."[30]

Hunters from British colonies, for instance, were regularly hunting in Portuguese, French and Belgian territories, with scant regard for regulations.

The recorded exports from African colonies had reached 921,210 lbs in 1919, equivalent to about 40,000 elephants. This halved by 1934, with lower demand resulting from the Depression. In the six years from 1929 to 1934, the average annual total of ivory exported from Africa (excluding Ethiopia, Italian and British Somaliland and British West Africa) was 556,472 lbs. This represented well over 20,000 elephants killed annually in addition to those poached, or killed in regions which did not keep records.[31] The threat posed by this was recognised at another conference on the conservation of wildlife in Africa, held in London on 8 November 1933 and attended by South Africa, Belgium, Britain, Egypt, Spain, France, Italy, Portugal and Anglo-Egyptian Sudan. It discussed the importance of establishing reserves and attempts to regulate the trade in ivory to ensure coordination, minimum legal tusk sizes for exports and identification of the origin of ivory. The participants drew up and signed a convention calling for "the regulation of the traffic in trophies... Every trophy consisting of ivory and rhinoceros horn exported in accordance with the provisions of the present article shall be identified by marks which, together with the weight of the trophy, shall be recorded in the certificate of lawful export".[32] Again, this agreement had little effect on the ground.

Kenya: white hunters, black poachers and celebrity slaughter safaris

Ivory was an important factor in Kenya's colonial economic development and the implementation of wildlife management policies. It paid for the game department, established to regulate hunting, protect crops and prevent poaching by indigenous communities. In 1897, indigenous peoples were banned from hunting without the express permission of the authorities. Game ordinances banned the existing, unregulated ivory trade, requiring that ivory be sold through official auctions and that natural-mortality ivory be surrendered to the game department for a small payment. Hunting using traditional methods like poisoned arrows, spears and traps was criminalised. Peoples like the Waliangulu and Wakamba, who had hunted elephants for centuries, were turned into poachers overnight. The Waliangulu would be the most seriously affected, as tusk-gathering and hunting were important in community life, providing income, hides and meat. For the Wakamba, hunting was supplementary to pastoralism and cultivation; they also retained a minor role in buying ivory from others and selling it to merchants in Mombasa.

Neither community was prepared to stop hunting and lose part of their livelihood because of what they saw as an arbitrary whim of the British. The Wakamba hid their ivory, hoping the British would leave and they could resume trading. When the British showed no signs of departing, the sale of what was now illegal ivory resumed.[33] Wakamba bought ivory from Dorobo, Waliangulu, Giriama or Boran hunters and sold it on, paying two shillings per pound and selling it for double that to the Mombasa merchants, who in turn sold it to foreign buyers for 35 shillings per pound.[34]

A Game Department was formally established in the colony in 1899, run by a keen hunter, A. Blayney Percival. He was on close terms with many of the European hunters and showed little enthusiasm for monitoring their adherence to regulations.[35] But Africans were a different matter. They were labelled poachers. The ivory from white hunting and trading passed through the official system, accounting for half of the government's tax revenue in 1902 and 75 per cent of protectorate trade income. One of the new game department's first tasks was the buying of ivory stocks held by indigenous peoples. Had a fair price been paid, then it is possible that there would have been less of an incentive for illegal networks to thrive, but government prices paid to Africans for old or found ivory was half the market rate, and any ivory deemed to have been hunted by Africans since the new regulations was confiscated. Percival admitted at the time that the ivory-smuggling business had been created by the regulations.[36]

The authorities also established reserves. The Northern Reserve stretched from the Ugandan border to Marsabit, south of the Guaso Nyiro River, and to Lake Baringo; the Southern Reserve touched the Uganda railway in the north, reached German East Africa in the south, the Ugandan protectorate in the west and the Tsavo River in the east. The Game Department had insufficient manpower to police the reserves and many European hunters ignored regulations with impunity. The commissioner of the protectorate, Sir Charles Eliot, was aware that the settlers were ignoring hunting restrictions in the reserves, and that they felt the laws had "no moral force, and may be violated without loss of moral character when they can be violated with impunity".[37] Eliot foresaw the spread of European settlement as a major threat to game and said in 1903 that there was still game in Kenya in areas not settled by whites. Opposition to the regulations among the settlers was led by Lord Delamere. He blamed everyone but settlers for killing too much game—Africans, Boer immigrants, Germans from Tanganyika and officials of the government and the Uganda Railway.[38]

Many of the hunters involved had moved to Kenya from elsewhere in Africa as elephants and other game dwindled through over-shooting. Bell and J. A. Hunter were among those who based themselves in Kenya and felt they had a right to hunt what they chose, where they chose, with scant regard for regulations. One prolific hunter, Arthur Neumann, was quoted as saying, "shoot anything in case it is valuable".[39] Some officials, hunters themselves, were critical of commercial hunting but supportive of what they saw as gentlemanly "sporting" hunting. Robert Foran, a senior colonial official in Kenya and a keen hunter, who accompanied former US president Theodore Roosevelt on his expedition of incompetent butchery in 1909, was highly critical of commercial hunters engaged in "heartless profit seeking", but encouraged sportsmen to sell ivory to finance what he saw as their noble sporting forays.[40] Foran was later to write that he killed 400 elephants over a period of six years—more than most Waliangulu and Wakamba hunters killed in a lifetime, yet the latter were blamed by settlers and officials for the depletion of herds and excluded from Tsvao, when it became a reserve.

Mombasa became the major port for ivory exports from East and Central Africa. There Bell and Neumann would sell the ivory they hunted in Uganda, Sudan and Lado. A single trip to Lado and Uganda brought Bell 14,000 lbs worth £23,000 (£2.4m today)—he returned to Kenya with 180 tusks carried by 100 porters.[41] Bell didn't shoot all the elephants that provided that number of tusks. In his published works he doesn't say how many tusks were bought from local hunters, but he purchased tusks from them for two or three shillings, then sold them for £50–60. In his 1909 Lado foray, he shot 210 elephants in nine months.[42] Neumann hunted in northern Kenya, between Mount Kenya and Lake Turkana, and in 1906 earned £4,500 (over £477,000 today) from one expedition, thought to involve the killing of 200–250 elephants.[43] The publishers of African big game records, Rowland Ward of London, said that in 1914 sales of ivory in London, Liverpool and Antwerp (the latter chiefly of ivory from the Belgian Congo) totalled 2.5m lbs and that between 50,000 and 62,500 elephants were being killed annually to feed these markets.[44]

In 1908, R. B. Woosnam took charge of the Game Department and warned that the ivory trade, "whether disguised or under a system of government purchase or allowing a limited number of licensed traders, must inevitably encourage the slaughter of Elephants and lead to their eventual extermination in the not very distant future". He was in favour of an end to all trade in ivory, but this was not likely given its contribution to Kenyan finances. Woosnam still upheld the total ban on hunting by indigenous Kenyans and the development and implementation of game laws and practices that, according to Parker, made "no concessions for Africans to use wildlife... nor was the possibility entertained that they might want to hunt for the same recreational reasons that white men hunted".[45] This policy was an extension of the British elite attitude to land and hunting—the gentry hunted for sport, poor rural dwellers were grubby poachers and the overtly commercial trade was to be looked down on.[46]

Early reports by the department show that licences to hunt elephants were being issued regularly to settlers, colonial officials and visiting hunters, and numerous elephants were being killed in crop protection operations. The reports also indicated concern that poaching by Somalis and Baluchi traders from Mombasa was being carried out to the north-east near the Somali border, in the Jubaland part of the Northern Reserve. The first chief warden, Percival, had warned that the department did not have the resources to police this area and that commercial poachers were entering the Baringo reserve and killing elephants.[47] The Game Department had started a permit system to limit access to the reserve and established a local minimum weight of 30 lbs for legally traded ivory. Interestingly, the report on elephant poaching in the *Journal* noted that Percival was in favour of allowing groups like the Dorobo and Waliangulu to hunt within their own districts—though again nothing came of this, because of the wider settler and official opposition to hunting by local communities. At the same time, he was adamant that the Wakamba had to be stopped from hunting in reserves, on the grounds that this threatened the income of £20,000 a year (£2.1m) from visiting European and American hunters.[48]

In 1909, the lieutenant-governor of Kenya, Frederick Jackson, wrote to the Colonial Office to report that elephant numbers were falling from the tens of thousands believed to have inhabited Kenya in the late nineteenth century. He gave the following estimates of those remaining: in the Southern Reserve, none resident and some migrants from Kilimanjaro, southern Sotik and Mau, and possibly Aberdares; in Laikipia, 100 cows, a few calves and a very small population of small bulls; in the Rift Valley, none resident but visitors from Laikipia and Mau; in the Nyando Valley, sixty; in the Northern Reserve, numerous at times on Marsabit and Lamasis; in Uasin Gishu, 1,000–1,500 from Ketosh, Elgon, Karamojo and Elgeyu; on the coast, 60–100. Jackson added that there was little killing of elephants by the local people for ivory and only a few were killed for meat.[49] The main hunters were now European sporting or commercial hunters on the one hand, and, on the other, a few organised Somali, Abyssinian and Baluchi poaching gangs supplying the illicit export trade through either Mombasa or Ethiopia. Jackson also said that since hunters had accessed areas north of Mount Elgon and the Karamoja area of Uganda after 1900, these had become overrun by Europeans, Indians, Baluchis and other hunter-traders, with the killing of elephants having increased by 50 per cent in recent years.[50]

If commercial hunting was threatening wildlife, the growing popu-larity of sporting safaris also contributed to its decline. In 1909, former US president Theodore Roosevelt undertook a long safari in Kenya. His own account of this expedition celebrates it as being in the cause of conservation—specimens were sent back to the Smithsonian Institute.[51] By his own count, Roosevelt and his son killed 512 animals, and the entourage as a whole shot a total of 5,013 mammals, 4,453 birds and 2,322 reptiles or amphibians, prompting Frederick Jackson to accuse Roosevelt of exceeding all reasonable limits of hunting.[52] This sort of celebrity safari became popular with rich Americans and British or other European royalty, nobility and wealthy businessmen. They and others with the money and time to spend flocked to hunt in Kenya on safaris run by people like Denys Finch Hatton and Baron Bror von Blixen, profiting from this new source of income. A Kenyan govern-ment report printed by the *Journal* in 1913 recorded a rise in game licences issued, from 829 in 1910–11 to 973 in 1911–12, with a par-ticular increase in travellers' licences. The report added that in the Northern Reserve there were large numbers of elephants but "bulls with heavy tusks are now scarce, as is only to be expected seeing that ivory hunting has been carried on for so many years". Big bulls were much sought-after as trophies for sporting hunters.

CRIMINALISATION UNDER COLONIAL RULE

The First World War, in which Kenyan settlers and Game Department personnel joined up to fight the Germans in Tanganyika, saw an increase in poaching in the area between the Tana River and Jubaland and the smuggling of ivory and rhino horn into Italian Somaliland, which continued after the war. The Commissioner of Coast Province, J. McLellan, estimated that in 1921, 1,314 tusks had been cached or smuggled out of the province into Somaliland. He also believed that another 250 elephants had been killed in eastern Kenya that year and the ivory sent to Somaliland. Keith Caldwell, chief game warden in the early 1920s, was convinced that the existence of the smuggling route and encouragement from traders in Somaliland had led to an increase in elephant poaching by Somali, Boran, Wakamba and Waliangulu hunters.[53] Despite demands from the British Colonial Office, the Italian authorities were unwilling to stem the trade and even accepted tax payment in ivory.

After the war, more settlers arrived, attracted by cheap land but with little capital and needing to hunt for meat and ivory as they waited for cash crops to grow. While lamenting killing by Africans, the Game Department freely issued elephant licences to settlers and European visitors. Under the 1921 ordinance, two elephants could be shot on a £45 licence. Settlers were permitted to kill elephants to protect crops, but the tusks had to be surrendered to the local game warden or district commissioner.[54] The regulations established payments for found ivory. In Wakamba areas, this meant that some of their hunting was disguised through the sale of tusks as found ivory. In 1924, the district commissioner in Kilifi on the coast said the demand from what he described as "non-Native" traders at Mombasa was driving an increase in Wakamba hunting of elephants.[55] The Game Department believed that in the mid-1920s the illegal ivory trade through Somalia was worth between £30,000 and £80,000 a year (£1.5m to £4m today). This route was well established, predating European colonialism. The Somalis operated between the Tana River area, Jubaland and ports like Kismayu and Mogadishu in Somalia, and Lamu in northern Kenya, where ivory was bought by Arab and Indian traders.[56] The ceding of Jubaland to Italy in 1925, far from disrupting the trade and making control easier, merely shifted the Italian border closer to where elephants were hunted.

In the mid-1920s, the Game Department, headed by A. T. Ritchie, worked with white hunters, who became honorary wardens, to stop all African hunting, even to protect crops. The "ability to act in immediate defence of property, always recognized as a right of landowners, was denied to Kenya's African farmers. In the case of elephants... Africans were forbidden to do more than chase them from their *shambas* using the 'weapons of the weak', sticks, stones and fire."[57] Professional white hunters were often sent to carry out crop protection, with the proceeds from the ivory split between the hunters and government. In 1923 the department earned £16,000 (£793,000) from ivory and £8,000 from hunting licences. In a speech to the Kenya and Uganda Natural History Society in March 1924, the chief warden encouraged this partnership, emphasising that white hunters buying a £15 elephant licence could earn £75 (£3,718) from the ivory.

As game wardens continued to prosecute African hunters, the double standards employed became ever more apparent. An elephant killed by an African was an elephant lost to the treasury and hunting industry. Most settlers, hunters and officials had rigid views on this, and game wardens like George Adamson, of *Born Free* fame, were single-minded in their persecution of African hunters. In his book, *Bwana Game*, Adamson makes clear his obsession with hounding hunters like the Wakamba. He makes little effort to hide his view of Africans as inferior, even talking at one point of being "sorely tempted to acquire a native girl" when the urge came upon him.[58] When he carried out crop protection work, killing hundreds of oryx and zebra at the start of WWII, he admitted developing "a ruthless blood lust",[59] while decrying the supposedly brutal killing of game by Africans.

By the late 1930s, the age of the big hunting safaris was in decline and opinion was shifting towards the establishment of hunting-free areas for wildlife protection. Ritchie was keen to establish national parks, but progress was slow; the department's efforts, devoted to crop protection and game control, contributed to killing rather than conserving elephants.[60] In 1931, Ritchie reported that the department had generated income from legal and confiscated ivory of £14,643 (£834,000) and £11,754 from game licences. Following the Depression in 1929, the price of ivory dropped from 20 shillings a pound to four to five shillings in 1934. Kenya's income from ivory dropped to

£7–9,000 a year in the mid-1930s, without any significant drop in ivory available from controlled or licensed hunting. In the long term, according to Ian Parker, Ritchie was keen to end the Game Department's funding through the commercial exploitation of ivory.[61] Many of his wardens had a different view. While they prosecuted African hunters, many relied on shooting elephants on licence and selling the ivory to supplement their income. Adamson bought licences for £25 and sold the tusks for £100. He said he sympathised with indigenous communities who had lost the right to hunt, but pursued them ruthlessly when they did so, while spending much of his time shooting elephants in the Tana River area to protect crops[62]—the very area where game wardens were stamping out Wakamba, Dorobo, Giriama and Somali hunting.

Tanzania and Uganda: elephant control dominates

In the last years of the nineteenth century, Germany adopted a policy of colonisation. The Society for German Colonization was used to establish a presence in Africa. It concluded treaties with several chiefs on the Tanganyika coast in the early 1880s. On 3 March 1885, the German government granted it an imperial charter with the objective of establishing a protectorate in the region. German ambitions conflicted with rule of coastal areas by the sultan of Zanzibar, who was forced to concede when the Germans dispatched five warships to that end in August 1885. The British and Germans agreed to divide the mainland between them and confirmed the borders in a treaty of 1890. German rule was established over Bagamoyo, Dar es Salaam and Kilwa. Progressive occupation and military conquest of mainland communities followed. The sultan of Zanzibar was forced to accept subordination to the British and with it loss of his control over the ivory trade.

Even under the hegemony of the powerful ivory traders like Tippu Tip, the mainland communities had retained some freedom to hunt as they chose, and the lack of territorial borders had given the trade fluidity; mainland communities retained some agency in the trade.[63] There was no central authority or government interested in or capable of regulating or limiting hunting. The imposition of German administration changed everything. The Germans didn't ban locals from hunting, but, like the British elsewhere, introduced licences and sought to control commerce. Licensed hunters had to give one tusk from every elephant to the authorities. Most licences were issued to European hunters, including those coming across the border from Kenya. But when the authorities decided that control was necessary for crop protection and income generation, indigenous hunters were also allowed licences. The Germans sought to limit hunting in certain areas. The 1896 Wildlife Decree controlled where hunting was permitted. In 1907, the Serengeti, Ngorongoro and territory along the Rufiji River became ordained protected areas.[64]

The Germans exported ivory in large quantities, much of it through Zanzibar, where Arab, Swahili and Indian traders were still active, though under British rule. The Hamburg dealers, Meyer and Company, became one of the biggest ivory trading companies in the world through access to Tanganyika ivory.[65] At first, exports were buoyant, but reduced with depletion of herds and then the combat in Tanganyika during WW1. In the 1880s, German exports via Zanzibar were around 400,000 lbs a year, rising in 1894 to 412,920 lbs and remaining at this level until the late 1890s, when the effects of over-exploitation and regulation began to bite. By 1899, exports were down to just over 100,000 lbs. They rose slightly after the turn of the century and were then maintained near 150,000 lbs annually until war broke out.[66] One of the causes of the decline in exports was the drawing of borders and Belgian exploitation of ivory, which ended the trade across and round Lake Tanganyika from the Congo Basin. Towns like Ujiji and Unyanyembe lost their central role in continental trade.[67] By the turn of the century, Mombasa had overtaken Zanzibar as the main export port, and the dhow traffic that carried ivory from Malindi, Lamu and Kismayu to Zanzibar diverted to sell through Mombasa.

Before the turn of the century, the imperial authorities banned the killing of elephant cows and trade in tusks under 14 lbs—the latter limit meant that hunters in British territories would smuggle ivory between 14 and 30 lbs (the British limit) to German territory for sale. By 1919, when the British were given control of the territory under a League of Nations mandate, there were twenty protected reserves in Tanganyika. The combination of limits on hunting and the effects of the war meant that elephant numbers recovered,[68] despite reports that during the campaign against German forces in Tanganyika British troops had shot elephants for their ivory. The ivory trader Moore says that British aircraft bombed elephant herds, with ground forces retrieving the ivory.[69] When the British assumed authority over Tanganyika, they exerted closer control of its ivory under a Game Ordinance of 1921, which regulated local hunting to encourage the generation of income from rich, visiting hunters. This provided revenue for the new administration, as did substantial sales of ivory from crop protection and licensed hunting.[70] It also, however, furthered the progressive exclusion of local communities from hunting, and, as elsewhere, the creation of reserves frequently involved their expulsion from farming or grazing land.

Professional hunters were responsible for much of the ivory income, but poaching by hunters without licences (indigenous and European) was common, as was poaching in the Belgian Congo and Portuguese Mozambique and smuggling of the ivory through Tanganyika. One successful hunter-poacher operating in the territory was George Rushby. He moved to Tanganyika to mine for gold, but made most of his money from ivory. He turned to poaching as he could only shoot three elephants on each licence. He poached in the Belgian Congo and smuggled the ivory out through Tanganyika. In 1923, the Tanganyika authorities became concerned about increasing crop damage by elephants and issued new licences, under which twenty-five elephants could be shot as part of a control programme. Rushby took out a licence to hunt in the Kilombero Valley, east of the present-day Selous reserve, and shot fifty-three elephants, but was not prosecuted. When the control scheme ended, he continued to hunt illegally along the border between Tanganyika, Northern Rhodesia and Congo, and is believed to have killed seventy-five elephants there, earning £5,000 (£263,700 today). Rushby continued hunting in the Congo and then French Equatorial Africa, where he is believed to have poached ivory worth £15,000 (£791,000).[71]

The British set up a Game Department in Tanganyika and Charles Swynnerton became its first director. In 1926, he was successful in getting the administration to fund salaried game officers to control elephant numbers. He rightly assumed that under the twenty-five-elephant licences only large tuskers were being shot, rather than animals actually responsible for crop damage.[72] Swynnerton was also aware that Indian traders at coastal and inland trading centres encouraged farmers to fake reports of crop damage to maintain ivory supplies. They were also buying illicit ivory and smuggling it out in sacks of produce that attracted no export duty and weren't inspected.[73] Extensive shooting of elephants continued on licence into the 1920s. One visitor reported to the Fauna Preservation Society in 1929 that over the previous eight years the number of large, ivory-bearing bulls had dropped dramatically, though large numbers of elephants remained. The visitor said he had seen twenty-three herds of elephants, but none with large bulls or ivory he believed to be over 30 lbs. He lamented that "the impetus that leads the majority of men to shoot in this country is the chance of making money out of the animal he kills and the real sportsman who pursues game for the thrill of the chase and beauty of the trophies is almost non-existent".[74]

In 1935, Major Hingston of the Fauna Preservation Society carried out a survey of game regulations in East Africa and recommended that Serengeti (including the Ngorongoro and Natron reserves), Selous and Kilimanjaro be declared national parks with no hunting. Hingston emphasised that "the elephant is the most harassed of all African mammals, and its numbers, since the introduction of European firearms, have decreased more rapidly than those of any other species. Its reduction in numbers is still progressing, and special measures may become necessary in order to save it from extinction."[75] Despite concerns about numbers, the Game Department reported that it had killed 2,716 elephants in control operations in 1934 and earned £20,653 ($1.2m today) from ivory sales.[76]

In Uganda, tension between elephant conservation and crop protection was the key influence on the ivory trade. Despite prolonged hunting in the Bunyoro, Buganda and Karamoja regions in the nineteenth century, there were substantial herds across the protectorate. A sustained rate of killing to protect crops and reduce numbers in certain areas meant a steady supply of ivory for export via Mombasa. During its brief period of rule, the Imperial British East Africa Company (IBEAC) sought to control commerce in tusks, and aided the establishment of a fort between Bunyoro and the IBEAC headquarters in Kampala. The company employed professional European hunters to ensure a steady supply of ivory. Game regulations licensing elephant hunting were introduced in 1897, partly to protect the population in the Murchison Falls region, where colonial administrators saw large herds, some 700-strong. They moved regularly between the Falls and feeding grounds to the north-west by the White Nile. Migratory routes ran east, too, through Lira and Acholi country. There was sustained killing of elephants in these areas to harvest ivory and protect farms, but not with the intention of reducing numbers, as the IBEAC and then the colonial government wanted a steady supply and would not risk depleting the herds.

Regulation and the establishment of reserves in Uganda led to an increase in elephant numbers and the development of a long-term control programme, which generated steady income from ivory. In the Bunyoro and Buganda kingdoms and other indigenous communities, hunting by local people was regulated, but not banned. The need to balance the needs of agriculture, local demands for crop protection, conservation and ivory income meant policy was erratic. Plans were put forward for costly hunting licences to limit the shooting of ele- phants and institute fines for over-shooting or poaching, only for rising elephant numbers and crop damage to force the authorities to lift restrictions on hunters so they could control numbers in areas where crop damage was serious. Sir Harry Johnston, commissioner for Uganda, established game reserves in the north-east, Bunyoro and Toro, specifically to protect elephants. Like many other administrators, he was particularly concerned about the effects of African hunting on wildlife. His successor, Sir James Sadler, under pressure over elephant damage to African *shambas*, instituted a licence system allowing hunters to shoot two elephants.[77] These licences were available to chiefs in areas with elephant problems and not limited to Europeans. Sadler believed regulation had been so effective that numbers were increasing rapidly and measures would have to be taken to control numbers more rigor- ously in farming areas.[78]

Colonel Delme-Radcliffe noted in 1905 that large migratory herds of elephants moved between Gondokoro in the Lado/South Sudan area to the Acholi and Karamojong areas and the region around Lake Albert. Despite the large numbers, he joined the colonial chorus bewailing African "slaughter" and calling for elephants to be protected from the "natives" and reserved for responsible hunting by Europeans.[79] He admitted that elephants were doing huge damage to local peoples' crops but wanted officially employed hunters, and not the local people, to kill for control purposes. By contrast, Sadler and his deputy, George Wilson, were meanwhile lobbying the Colonial Office for greater protection for African farmers, including their right to kill marauding elephants. In 1906, Wilson, probably not coincidentally, told a meeting of the African Society in London that the value and volume of ivory exports from Uganda had fallen recently, reducing colonial income.[80]

Sadler's successor as governor, Sir Hesketh Bell, called on the British government to put the hardships of the local population before European sport or conservation. He told the Colonial Office that in Toro in 1905, 105 people had been killed by elephants and countless *shambas* destroyed. He wanted professional hunters to be given licences to kill twenty elephants each to reduce numbers, though he was less keen on giving indigenous people freedom to kill crop-raiding elephants. This led in some areas to a reduction in numbers, but not in crop raiding—as Swynnerton noted in Tanganyika, the hunters concentrated on large tuskers rather than the herds which were to blame for the damage. Bell reported in 1909 that only two cows had been killed on the control licences, compared with 130 bulls.[81] He added that hunters were killing elephants illegally and taking the ivory out through the Baringo region of Kenya, to evade Ugandan Protectorate regulations. During the war, the loss of hunters to active service in German East Africa induced the government to relax regulations, allowing local communities to kill elephants to protect crops. Between 1917 and 1921, 4,000 elephants were killed by African and European hunters under these measures.[82]

After the war, the new governor, Robert Coryndon, reported that elephant numbers in Uganda were still high, with the heavily forested areas and expanses of elephant grass in Buganda, Bunyoro and Western Province providing ideal habitats, making control difficult. While he thought that numbers were increasing, he pointed to the absence of large tuskers, noting that the tusks handed in to the authorities from elephants shot for crop protection were small. Coryndon put the volume of ivory handed in at 12,500 lbs,[83] from between 2,000 and 4,000 elephants. The government instituted a strict programme of control, with substantial shooting of elephants starting in 1925, when the Game Department was established. Parker estimates that between 1929 and 1969, control measures in areas of cultivation and later culling—in which he took an active part in Murchison Falls in the 1960s—reduced the range of elephants from 70 to 11 per cent of the country; he suggests that the extent of control shooting and the resulting ivory sales prevented large-scale poaching right up to independence, because there was a steady and substantial legal supply.[84]

The first annual report from the Game Department, containing details of ivory sales in the preceding years, showed quite how much the Ugandan administration was earning. In 1920, sales totalled £27,391; for some reason, there were no sales in 1921, but in 1922 income rose to £44, 065 (£1.8m today). The report affirmed that, despite the level of cropping, elephants remained plentiful and that "it will be possible annually for many decades to carry out a thinning process amongst the extensive herds of the Protectorate without causing any serious diminution in the numbers… [a] large number of elephants must be destroyed each year to prevent them overrunning the country".[85] The department continued to pay for found ivory at a reasonable rate per pound, but it was believed this was being used to launder illicit ivory, by poachers or those hunting more than licences allowed. When the payment was reduced, the quantity of found ivory being handed in fell dramatically and the report suggests that the level of poaching was reduced. In 1935, the chief game warden, Charles Pitman, said 14,000 elephants had been killed in the last decade under the control programme. This did not seem to have seriously depleted numbers and in 1936 culling rose to 2,300. Just before the start of WWII, estimates of elephant numbers in Uganda varied between 20,000 and 50,000.[86]

Sudan and the Lado killing fields

Southern Sudan was a lucrative source of ivory for traders based in Khartoum and Ethiopia. Under Anglo-Egyptian rule, Sudan was subject to similar regulations to the British colonies. One of the problems facing the British was the existence of traditional routes for selling local ivory that took it out of their control—through western Ethiopia. Ethiopian buyers looked to Sudanese hunters as their own elephant herds were depleted through hunting or human expansion. Sudanese hunters, and also some from northern Kenya, could find more lucrative markets for tusks in areas like Maji in south-west Ethiopia than in Khartoum.[87] The British consul in Maji estimated that, in the 1920s, £10,000 (£426,000 today) worth of ivory was being traded there annually.[88] Small tusks below the British weight limit were purchased in Ethiopia, enabling hunters in Kenya to evade these limits. Swahili, Arab and Baluchi traders bought poached or underweight ivory from British territories and sold it there. This has been a common feature of the ivory trade over time: the ability of poachers and traders to move illicit or even legal tusks across borders to find more lucrative markets, unregulated markets beyond government control or corruptible markets operating with the connivance of officials benefiting from the trade.

Game regulations were gazetted in southern Sudan in 1904, introducing licences: £5 per elephant. A 20 per cent duty was charged on income from elephant products.[89] Game reserves were established between the White and Blue Niles and the Baro River, in the south, but licence holders and local people were allowed to hunt in reserves. In 1902, thirty elephants were shot on licence in the south; no estimates are given for elephants poached or shot for crop protection. According to game records submitted to the *Journal* in 1907, twenty-nine elephants were shot by licence holders, most of them in the Upper Nile region. This level of licensed shooting was maintained until just after WWI. The game department earned £4–5,000 a year from ivory, but total exports from Sudan, including illegally obtained ivory and tusks from Lado, were ten times that amount. No figures are available for numbers killed by the cruel method local hunters used in Bahr el-Ghazal—elephants herds would be trapped within a huge ring of burning grass and burned to death or asphyxiated by the smoke.[90] James Stevenson-Hamilton, later chief warden of Kruger National Park, served as a district commissioner in Upper Nile Province and wrote that on one occasion in 1921, "more than two hundred elephants were killed in one place by a 'ring fire'... The procedure is to surround a herd in long, dry grass, and having fired the latter all round, to drive the wretched creatures back into the flames by yelling and drumming, until they succumb."[91] In some areas of south-western Sudan, Arab horsemen killed elephants with firearms—descendants of the ivory and slave raiding communities such as the Baggara and Rizeigat (fore-runners of the Janjaweed militias who were involved in the Darfur conflict and in poaching ivory across the CAR and Chad into Cameroon in the twenty-first century).

The ivory trade in southern Sudan became part of the competition between different ethnic groups. It provided money to buy guns with which to protect cattle or raid others' herds. Ivory earnings could alter delicate regional balances of power. This was particularly the case with the Murle and Nuer communities of Jonglei. Johnson has detailed how some Nuer leaders gained considerable local influence and prestige through their role in trading ivory with the Oromo across the Ethiopian border, getting guns in return. One such leader, Gai Jang, gained con-siderable power among the Jikany and Lou Nuer by trading ivory for firearms. He also acted as a link between the Dinka to the west and Oromo traders—another case of hunters increasing their wealth and influence by doubling as middlemen. Oromo traders conducted expe-ditions into southern Sudan to buy ivory and trade guns and cattle using Nuer intermediaries.[92] This trade lasted into the 1930s, when the British suppressed much of the commerce into Ethiopia and diverted ivory to established Arab traders, who exported it via Khartoum.[93]

The British aim in suppressing the smuggling was not conservation, but ensuring that revenue accrued to the colonial administration. In the first decade-and-a-half of the British presence in the south, from 1901 to 1913, ivory exports grew from 15 tons with a value of £7,295 to 125 tons of ivory worth £113,236 (£11.5m today), or 10 per cent of Sudan's total exports. Between 1902 and 1919 the average annual exports of ivory totalled 67 tons.[94] It wasn't only southern Sudanese who were smuggling ivory into Ethiopia—European commercial hunt-ers were, too. One British hunter, Henry Darley, was involved in the ivory trade with merchants in Maji.[95] He had hunted in northern Uganda in 1924, where he blamed Egyptian, Swahili, Arab and Baluchi hunters for finishing off the herds. In his own account of his expedi-tions, Darley says he then moved to hunt on the Boma Plateau on the Sudan-Abyssinia frontier, where he "shot elephants till I was tired of shooting them".[96]

One of the most rapacious episodes in the colonial ivory trade took place in the Lado Enclave, the area of southern Sudan 220 miles long and 100 miles wide extending along the west bank of the Nile and inland to the borders of the Belgian Congo. It was ceded temporarily to King Leopold in 1894. Between then and the resumption of British control six months after Leopold's death in December 1909, hunters almost stripped the area of elephants.[97] Prior to extensive hunting by Europeans, the Azande had gathered ivory there, using the "ring of fire" technique to kill large numbers of elephants. They hunted primarily for meat, but increased their hunting as traders from Zanzibar and Khartoum reached the area to buy tusks.[98] Hunters like Bell were drawn there as the Belgians charged just £20 for a licence for unlimited elephant hunting; he was told by the Belgian officials that few bothered to pay and the administration did nothing about it.[99]

Bell wrote of the mad rush by hunters to take advantage of the inter-regnum between Leopold's death and the reassertion of Anglo-Egyptian rule. Hundreds of elephants were killed in a few months, and many more wounded by inexperienced but greedy hunters out to make quick money.[100] The colonial official Foran was later to admit to poaching regularly in the enclave between 1904 and 1910.[101] He reported seeing herds of elephants numbering over 2,000, with large numbers of bulls carrying tusks estimated at over 100 lbs each. Foran said that between the end of Congo Free State rule and the entrenching of a British presence, hunters made a fortune from the slaughter, amassing profits of £3,000 to £4,000 (£311,000 to £415,000 today) from a six-month safari for ivory.[102]

Central and southern Africa: from the Congo to Kruger

Even after the loss of Lado, the Congo remained a valuable source of ivory for the Belgians and visiting hunters. There hadn't been any con-vincing scientific surveys of numbers anywhere in Africa at this time, but visitors like the British naturalist T. Alexander Barns believed: "There are a great many elephants in the Belgian Congo, so many, in fact, that their numbers very probably exceed the native population". He said that the forests around Ituri (near the border with Uganda and Lado) were full of elephants.[103] The entrenching of colonialism and accelerated economic exploitation led to the brutal expropriation of ivory. King Leopold's officials and their troops would sweep through areas seizing whatever tusks they could find and killing elephants indiscriminately. Local peoples who had hunted elephants for centuries were required to deliver all their ivory to the authorities. The official monopoly and seizures from indigenous people went alongside a laissez-faire attitude towards foreign hunters, who entered the territory to hunt elephants and export the ivory without let or hindrance by regulations, which could be evaded by bribing venal officials.[104]

In Northern Rhodesia and Nyasaland, over a century of hunting had taken a heavy toll. The colonial administrator and former hunter, Sir Alfred Sharpe, carried out a survey in Nyasaland in 1903 and found only 605 elephants—it is not clear if this was supposed to be a figure for the whole protectorate, as just four years later he wrote in the same journal that there were 1,000 elephants in the central Angoniland region. In 1908, a reserve was established in this area, running from Dedza along the Dedza-Lilongwe road and west to the Dzalanyama Range and the border with Mozambique. Hunting of elephants was allowed on licence and thirty-seven were killed by licensed hunters in 1906–7, mostly in Nkhotakhota and Angoniland. The colonial administrations in what were to become Zambia and Malawi followed the patterns of other British colonies, introducing hunting restrictions, licences and protected reserves.[105] Administrators like Sharpe shared the view that the decline that had occurred in elephant herds and other wildlife was the fault of indigenous peoples, and the European hunters or global demand for ivory had little share in the blame—despite the clear evidence that the market for ivory within Africa was tiny. In a letter to the Fauna Preservation Society *Journal* in 1905, Sharpe said that colonial hunting regulations were keeping European hunters within the law but left "the native free to slaughter all he wishes without let or hindrance". Contributions to the *Journal* over the next few years, however, noted the growing regulation of hunting in the region and pointed out that, prior to the arrival of Europeans and the introduction of firearms, the local peoples had not hunted elephants in large numbers, and that the introduction of guns had created the biggest threat to elephants.[106]

In Southern Rhodesia and South Africa, European settlement and the crushing of opposition from nations like the Zulu and Ndebele led to efforts to prevent local people owning guns. The presence of large numbers of settlers and the expansion of farming had continued the work of earlier hunting by Europeans in vastly reducing elephant herds. Despite the slaughter of wildlife, the extinction of species like the blaaubok and quagga and the severe reduction in elephant numbers, it was South Africa that led the way in establishing protected areas in which numbers could recover.[107] After the Second Boer War, the Sabi Reserve was created along the border with Portuguese Mozambique, with Stevenson-Hamilton as the game warden. On his first tour of the reserve, he was disappointed to see very little large game and saw it as his task to turn the area "from a hunter's paradise into an inviolable game sanctuary".[108] The Transvaal government agreed to his call for the expansion of Sabi and the creation of the Shingwedzi reserve to the north.

Stevenson-Hamilton had to contend with poaching in the reserves, particularly by Portuguese and indigenous hunters crossing from Mozambique, but also with South African hunters using the reserve to cross into Portuguese territory to poach elephants, which were rare in Sabi. At first it was thought that there no elephants in the reserve or the surrounding area, but Sir Alfred Pease, a resident magistrate in Transvaal, reported in the *Journal* in 1908 that there was a small herd of elephants in the by then combined Sabi-Shingwedzi reserve, which might have crossed from Portuguese territory. In the following year, Stevenson-Hamilton reported in the *Journal* that a herd of thirty elephants was now resident and more herds were to be found just over the border in Mozambique.

Sabi and Shingwedzi were later joined to form Kruger Park. In 1926, Kruger became a national park with full protection, covering an area of 200 miles north to south and 40 miles east to west. It had two herds of elephants, near the Letaba and Tendi Rivers, with migrants entering from Portuguese territory to avoid hunters. In 1932, Stevenson-Hamilton's annual report in the *Journal* indicated an increase in numbers, with several breeding herds and small groups of males encountered regularly. Although some poaching of antelope occurred on the edges of the park, killing for ivory was not reported as an issue. A year later, the Chief Warden reported 150 elephants split between herds in the north of the park and small parties of males or single bulls around Letaba and the Olifants River. A small herd of elephants also survived in the Addo region of the eastern Cape. They were protected and the herd numbered 126 in 1919. But persistent crop raiding led to a cull at the insistence of local citrus farmers. All but sixteen were shot and the remainder confined within a very small reserve.[109] After several more were shot for crop raiding, the group was further reduced to eleven, but these provided the basis for the herds which now inhabit what became Addo National Park—where there are now 600 in the park, many of which I saw on a trip there in 2010.

West Africa: steady decline in numbers and ivory sales

In the early twentieth century, naturalists and colonial officials noted the decline in elephant numbers throughout the region. The Fauna Preservation Society wrote to the secretary of state for the Colonies to draw attention to this, noting falling ivory exports from the region. The letter, published in the *Journal* in 1907, reported that sales in Gold Coast (Ghana) had fallen from 33,003 lbs worth £5,417 in 1892 to 2,749 worth £725 in 1904. Gambian exports were down from 2,046 lbs in 1898 to 1,071 in 1905; elephants were on the point of extinction there. 1906–7 game returns for licensed hunting in Gambia show no elephants killed. In a later letter, the Society said a total ban on elephant hunting in Gambia was unlikely to work, as poachers would just kill the elephants and smuggle the ivory into the surrounding French Senegal territory. By the 1930s, it was evident from the lack of sightings over decades that elephants had been exterminated in Gambia,[110] and it was believed that there were no more than 300 left in Gold Coast; Sierra Leone had a population of 500–600.[111]

While small numbers of elephants survived in Nigeria, hunting, the expansion of agriculture and clearing of forests had taken their toll. Reserves were set up by the British in several areas to protect elephants, apes and other forest species, but had only a limited effect in halting their decline. A report on game preservation, published in the *Journal* in 1931, noted the popularity of hunting among many peoples and the trade in wildlife products through centres like Kano. It also lamented that it had proved impossible to further preservation or economic and controlled exploitation of wildlife through big game hunting, which was rare in Nigeria and rendered difficult by forests and thick bush in areas with game. This emphasised the belief that European, supposedly regulated hunting went hand in hand with successful conservation of habitats and species. The only area reported to have significant numbers of elephants was the north of Borno region on the shores of Lake Chad, where crop damage was reportedly serious and human-elephant conflict an issue.

The report noted that European hunters would be needed to reduce their numbers as, contrary to accepted colonial wisdom, "The native professional hunter, of whom there is one or more in every village, does not take a very large toll of life, for he is armed in northern Nigeria with bow and poisoned arrow or spear only, and is not allowed to carry firearms; while in the Southern Provinces only smooth bores and 'Dane' guns may be carried."[112] In 1932, the number of elephants in Nigeria was estimated at 2,000, with the largest groups in the areas bordering Cameroon, in Borno and in Gwoza; forty-five were killed in 1932 for crop protection, mainly in Cameroon region.[113] In 1933, the arch-critic of African hunting, Charles Hobley, wrote in the *Journal* that poaching by "natives" was widespread and reducing elephant numbers in Nigeria—a direct contradiction of the earlier reports by people on the ground. In 1934, the *Journal* reported that there was no evidence of elephant hunting by local people in the north of the country.

From 1945 to independence: national parks and the war against poachers

This period saw the spread of national parks, tougher regulation of hunting, and the first militarised campaign against poaching in Kenya. There was growing concern about falling elephant numbers, which was still blamed on African poaching rather than on the actual effects of global demand, the rapid killing of elephants by professional hunters, expanding human settlement and clearance of land for agriculture. The creation of national parks went alongside attempts to develop tourism to generate income. Local peoples were relocated or just ordered out of reserves and parks. This exacerbated the conflict between conservation through national parks and local rights. Communities on the margins of national parks lost livelihoods, elephants damaged crops and indigenous hunters became public enemy number one. The African as a destructive force remained the dominant discourse.

As the national park movement progressed, it was a given that the main threat to their foundation and the establishment of a tourist industry would be local communities, who were not consulted about the parks or the future of wildlife, even as independence approached.[114] The parks were modelled on Yellowstone in the United States, where the indigenous population had been exterminated or moved to reservations. Where communities inhabited areas gazetted as national parks, they were forced out and parks established free of human populations—the development of tourism as part of conservation was stressed and the rights and livelihoods of communities ignored. That approach continues to a great extent today, and is often reflected in the "fortress conservation" approach of both many Western NGOs and corporate interests profiting from tourism, which pay too little heed to the interests and rights of indigenous communities, thus facilitating poaching by alienating the people who live with wildlife.[115]

The creation of fully protected areas did not end the licensed hunting of game outside the parks. Between the end of the war and the start of the independence period, national parks were set up by colonial regimes and settler states across Africa. In December 1946, Kenya gazetted Nairobi National Park; in April 1948, Tsavo; December 1949, Mount Kenya; and in May 1950, the Aberdares National Park. Between 1942 and Ian Smith's Unilateral Declaration of Independence in 1965, Southern Rhodesia established parks at Hwange, Victoria Falls, Matopos, Gonarezhou, Lakes Kyle and McIlwaine, Mana Pools and Matusadona. In Tanganyika, the Serengeti National Park was gazetted in 1950. The Uganda National Parks Act was passed in 1952, establishing the Queen Elizabeth, Ruwenzori and Murchison Falls parks. Northern Rhodesia turned reserves at Sumba, Lukusuzi and Kafue into parks between 1942 and 1950, with Luangwa to follow. In all the national parks, hunting was banned and resident communities were excluded, further marginalising indigenous peoples and distancing them from control over wildlife, even though it was they who suffered from relocation and the damage to crops or livestock when animals moved out of protected areas into grazing or cultivated land.

As the emphasis on totally protected areas took hold, the conservation movement developed internationally. The International Union for the Protection of Nature (IUPN) was expanded at a conference attended by twenty-three governments and 126 national institutions, organised by the United Nations Educational, Scientific and Cultural

Organization (UNESCO) at Fontainebleau, France on 30 September 1948. The IUPN had existed for decades, but had played only a minor role in international conservation. It was now re-launched and expanded with support from the UN and the United States. The new body was to "encourage and facilitate co-operation between governments and national and international organizations concerned with and persons interested in the protection of nature", and to protect wildlife through international action to legislate for the formation of national parks, reserves and wildlife refuges, and to protect threatened species from extinction.[116] In 1956, it was renamed the International Union for the Conservation of Nature and Natural Resources (IUCN); in 1973, the IUCN in turn established CITES (the Convention on International Trade in Endangered Species of Wild Fauna and Flora), to regulate trade in wildlife products, including ivory.

The Fauna Preservation Society was closely involved in these developments and in the 1961 establishment of the World Wildlife Fund (WWF) as a charity to raise funds in support of IUCN projects.[117] This was part of a continued process of disempowering local people and integrating conservation into the global capitalist economy. The late colonial and post-colonial approach—based on alliances between international organisations (including the World Bank and IMF), NGOs like the WWF and governments (Western and African)—mirrored the earlier colonial approach of banning indigenous exploitation of wildlife and criminalising indigenous hunting. Local communities were still viewed as backward, potential or actual "despoilers of nature".[118] However, it was also part of a growing narrative of conservation for environmental or ethical reasons, replacing the pre-war emphasis on conservation to sustain hunting and income from ivory.

The new narrative did not have an immediate or strong influence over the ivory trade, which began to pick up after the war. The Fauna Preservation Society *Journal*, renamed *Oryx*, reported in 1950 that the ivory trade was flourishing in Africa, bringing in significant sums for colonial administrations. Sudan earned £15–20,000 annually from ivory (£462,638–616,852 today); Southern Rhodesia took £25,000 (£771,065 today) from hunting licences, ivory and rhino horn.[119] Kenya exported 684,300 lbs of tusks in 1946, and export figures remained around 500,000 lbs annually up to independence.[120]

Kenya: the battle for Tsavo

Post-1945, Kenya and its neighbours continued to operate a legal trade in ivory obtained through licensed shooting, tusks confiscated by the Game Department, found ivory and ivory imported from neighbouring territories (much of it of dubious provenance). Ivory auctions were held in Mombasa, and the experienced Swahili, Arab and Indian traders were still in business, often mixing legal and illegal tusks. The illegal trade in ivory poached in Kenya and smuggled out through Somaliland also continued, though the scale is hard to estimate. Somali pastoralists moving their herds in search of grazing across northern Kenya and Jubaland gathered ivory they found, occasionally killing elephants but also trading with local hunters among the Dorobo, Waliangulu and Wakamba. The livestock traders operating in the north and the network of coastal traders in both territories were key to the operation.[121]

The Game and National Parks Departments continued to take a tough line on indigenous hunting. The head of the Game Department, Willie Hale, wrote in the 1953 annual game report: "Every African is a poacher... [the department] recognises no customary hunting rights, though certain sub-tribes, such as... the Wasanye [Waliangulu] in the Coast Province, not to mention the ubiquitous forest-dwelling Dorobo, are nearly all full-time hunters... Poaching must be stopped and, therefore, poachers must be prosecuted". Some department officials, like Ian Parker, felt that this was unworkable and would not help conservation. For practical reasons, Parker believed that some accommodation had to be reached allowing indigenous groups to hunt in a regulated fashion.[122] The newly-established national parks had only a few hundred visitors a year at first, but by 1955 this had grown to 120,000, providing employment and bringing in hard currency.[123] Only a small proportion of local people were employed and local communities saw little benefit in return for the loss of grazing, of access to water for their herds and of crops or livestock.

Tsavo National Park was formally established in April 1948 in what National Parks head Mervyn Cowie called "an area of almost discarded heterogeneous bush lying in the semi-desert belt between the Kenya Coast and the Highlands."[124] Tsavo was remote, with no settled agriculture. It was huge, with scattered populations of elephants, black rhino and other game. But it bordered areas where the Waliangulu and the Wakamba lived in close proximity and were known to hunt, despite the regulations. They had continued to hunt in territory encompassed by Tsavo's boundaries, though this wasn't fully appreciated at the time. Once it was known, the only solution considered was aggressive and took no account of local needs. Tsavo wardens like David Sheldrick and Bill Woodley became intent on stopping all indigenous hunting. North of Tsavo, Adamson continued his personal crusade against poachers.

The level of hypocrisy towards indigenous hunting was staggering—in terms of the denial of rights but also of the discourse of African destruction of game. Adamson was single-minded in his pursuit of poachers, especially those hunting for subsistence rather than the organised commercial poachers. Yet he himself had hunted elephants for profit and, as Ian Parker of the Game Department has written, used what most would consider inhumane methods in the control of game that were specifically banned when it came to local people: "As a poisoner George Adamson had no rival in the Game Department", using strychnine to kill hyenas, which he considered pests, oblivious to the other animals that would die in large numbers as a result.[125] He and other game wardens had an "almost conspiratorial attitude" towards white hunters, overlooking their hunting misdemeanours but never giving the same consideration to Africans.[126] Only a few of those involved in conservation, such as Parker, realised that "In the long run the future of conservation depended more on African acceptance than anyone else's and this would be withheld while they were not allowed to hunt and were thrown in jail for doing so."[127] But this acceptance was not to be sought for many decades as the new global conservation discourse took hold and grew in influence.

When Tsavo was given national park status, few resources were put into development, patrolling, surveying animal numbers or assessing the level and effect of hunting by communities bordering the park. It was soon realised that the area was unmanageable as one huge unit and was split into east and west parks. The east had the main elephant herds, but was an arid region of dry woodland and bush. David Sheldrick was appointed warden of Tsavo East, assisted by Bill Woodley. On taking up the post, Sheldrick became aware of hunting (or poaching as the authorities saw it) by the Wakamba on the northern edge of the park and the continuing hunting of elephants by the Waliangulu.[128] He believed this to be a threat to elephant numbers and persuaded the National Parks and Game Departments of the need for concerted anti-poaching operations. Sheldrick was given the resources to recruit an anti-poaching unit. No scientific surveys had been carried out of the elephant population but there were few signs of decline. It is hard to argue with Steinhart's assessment that even though the Waliangulu and Wakamba were hunting regularly, it was not convincing "that a centuries-long symbiotic relationship between hunter and prey had been so thoroughly upset by commercial motives as to represent a credible threat to the survival of elephants in eastern Kenya".[129] Even the former head of the Game Department and experienced conservationist Keith Caldwell said, after a visit to Tsavo in 1951, that he was aware that the Wakamba and Waliangulu hunted in the reserve, but that "I doubt if they do serious damage".[130]

The 2,000 or so Waliangulu living on the margins of the park had hunted there for generations, using the meat and hides as well as selling ivory. They had a small but experienced group of hunters, who became the chief targets of the anti-poaching operations mounted by Sheldrick and Woodley. These hunters were hard to catch, as they travelled in small groups on foot, using poisoned arrows rather than guns. With relatively few hunters involved and limited numbers of Wakamba hunters in northern areas of the park, there was a regular but not substantial off-take; there are no accurate estimates of numbers. Ofcansky puts the figure in the early years of the park at 3,000 over two years,[131] but there is no firm evidence for this figure or scientific estimate of what proportion of the population it represented. Ian Parker believes that the leading Waliangulu hunters, like Galogalo Kafonde, Boru Debassa, Abakuna Tise and Abakuna Gumundi, rarely killed more than forty to fifty elephants each a year, and that in the 1950s there were only ten such hunters among the community.[132]

The initial anti-poaching efforts bore little fruit. Small ranger teams were based at outposts around the park and would patrol those areas to catch poachers and find carcasses of animals killed by them. When they caught poachers the latter would be prosecuted, though little success was achieved and little effort made to prosecute the traders exporting the ivory. The traders were not only adept at hiding their tracks and mixing legal and illegal ivory, but could hire lawyers and bribe officials to ensure they continued in business.[133] Sheldrick's efforts to develop more efficient methods were interrupted by the Land and Freedom Army rebellion in Kikuyu areas, in what became known as the Mau Mau Emergency. Woodley was called up to join the security forces and Sheldrick used periods of leave to serve with the units combing the forests of the Central Province for insurgents. He then adopted military-style tactics against the poachers, with a strong emphasis on mobility and intelligence gathering. The killing of a Kenyan game ranger by a Waliangulu hunter on 15 January 1955 was the turning point in operations against poachers, and not just in Kenya. The militarised nature of Sheldrick's new measures was to be copied in many countries, with a stress on fast, tough responses by well-armed units of rangers acting like counter-insurgency forces. There was often an implicit shoot-to-kill policy. The rangers were recruited from among the Turkana, Samburu and Somali communities in Kenya and given intensive military-style training. Locally recruited staff were not permitted to take part in the operations.[134]

Although Sheldrick and Woodley, who led the new-style anti-poaching force, developed sympathy for the Waliangulu, the philosophy behind the militarised operations combined a simple desire to stop the killing of elephants within the conservation area with the belief that all Africans were potential poachers. In Daphne Sheldrick's account of the fight to protect elephants, while clearly committed to conservation, she damned the Waliangulu as professional elephant poachers, but lambasted neither her ex-husband Woodley nor her second husband, Sheldrick, who both hunted elephants for profit—though she admitted it was difficult to reconcile "the obvious pleasure [Woodley] derived from it with his role as the custodian of the elephants' safety". While recognising that the growth in the price of ivory and external demand was driving the trade, she lamented that the African hunters had allowed money from ivory to erode "their hitherto strict code of ethics and commercialism has taken hold", and said that elephants were "being ruthlessly killed for gain" by Africans. She concluded that the Waliangulu and Wakamba were a "more sinister threat" to elephants than white hunters, declaring that "almost the entire population of the Waliangulu tribe had either served, or were serving prison sentences" relating to ivory poaching.[135] This outlook was shared by other game wardens and those involved in the lucrative safari hunting business. Sydney Downey, who founded the Ker and Downey safari company, wrote that among the Wakamba, some "elders, or the 'evolved' young-sters, are impressive and trustworthy... Other members of the tribe could hardly be described in polite phraseology", having no aesthetic or ecological values when it came to wildlife; the Waliangulu were "savage destroyers... [engaged in] a vast and fiendish trade".[136] Downey insisted that control shooting and hunting on game licences did not damage elephant numbers, but indigenous hunting did.[137]

It was against the background of these conflicting viewpoints that the Voi Field Force started operations in April 1955. During its first patrol, one poacher was shot dead after shooting an arrow at the rang-ers. The Force had thirty men, with army-style NCOs leading sections linked by radio. It began to have an effect, capturing poachers and establishing a reputation for toughness and a willingness to fire on them. Sheldrick established an intelligence system, with files on known hunters and their associates. He obtained permission to raid locations outside the park in search of tusks, horns and poachers. The Force even caught—and then lost—the most famed Waliangulu hunter, Galogalo Kafonde. In one series of operations between the Galana and Tana Rivers, in the area of the park known as Dadimabule, Sheldrick deployed all three of Tsavo East's anti-poaching units, recovering 352 tusks totalling 6,604 lbs of ivory and 1,589 lbs of sawn tusk pieces. They found 1,280 elephant carcasses, including 200 corpses of orphaned calves that had died after their mothers were killed.[138]

The operations proceeded at full pace until the end of 1957, by which time poaching in the park had largely been stamped out. Lower-level anti-poaching operations and surveillance of known poachers continued. By the end of this episode, 429 Waliangulu and Wakamba had been caught and prosecuted, and 25,179 lbs of ivory recovered and sold through the government auctions. It is estimated that there had been 200 Waliangulu, 250 Wakamba and fifty people from other com-munities involved in the poaching.[139] Despite his initial decision not to use local people in the anti-poaching units, by the end of the campaign, Sheldrick had started employing former poachers and other Waliangulu to provide them with alternative means of earning a living. Sheldrick's crowning glory came when Galogalo gave himself up on 13 June 1959 and said, "The elephants are finished. Rich people wanting more and more are responsible. Like you, I fear the demise of the elephants, for they are at the core of our culture and our daily lives. Always the Waliangulu have lived among elephants and have hunted them honourably as true men, only targeting large bulls and never killing cow elephants or their babies. Now 'others' who do not care about them kill them clumsily for mere gain. I want no part of that and I swear I will never hunt an elephant again."[140]

Some felt that the Field Force operations' aggressive suppression of hunting was not the answer. Ian Parker, who worked with Sheldrick's anti-poaching unit, lamented the half-hearted efforts made to trace and prosecute those involved in trading in illegal ivory, in comparison with the substantial resources put into catching hunters. He also highlighted corruption within the Game Department, with the ivory handed in by professional hunters unrecorded and sold for private profit by officials and police officers. When a Game Department official was found to have illegally sold £30,000 worth of government ivory, he received a light suspended sentence, in contrast with the imprisonment of those caught poaching.[141] Parker also recorded that three detectives with the Criminal Investigation Department in Mombasa were involved in ivory smuggling, but nothing was ever done about them.[142]

Parker believed there was a need to find more inclusive approaches to illegal hunting, ones which might, in the long term, gain the support of local communities. Sheldrick and Parker set up a scheme to enable the Waliangulu to hunt in a regulated way, with limited off-take. They were backed by an influential Kenyan settler and conservationist, Noel Simon, and drew up plans to set up a zone along the Galana River, just outside Tsavo. This would enable locals to hunt without breaking the law and so meet their needs, while dissuading them from poaching in the park. Parker strongly believed that if these communities had no other livelihood they would have to hunt. He wrote that he regretted his role in having them jailed for following their traditional way of life.[143] He said that he had become acutely conscious "that the game laws had been formulated with total disregard for the Waliangulu's existence and need".[144] The scheme was developed with the idea that hunters, receiving income from the ivory, would be convinced that the project was for their benefit and not a European operation. The plans were met with scepticism from the colonial authorities and outright hostility from the East African Professional Hunters' Association, which did not want to see Africans licensed to hunt. But, with lobbying by Simon, who had been appointed head of the East African Wildlife Society, they obtained a grant of £10,000 from the Nuffield Foundation in Britain, and were supported by the IUCN.

This backing persuaded the Kenyan colonial administration to endorse the plan, but it insisted upon certain changes—these proved the undoing of the whole project. Rather than the ivory providing direct income for the Waliangulu hunters, it was to become government property with the proceeds accruing to the treasury. Parker told the author that some of the value was returned to the Waliangulu through an annual grant based on the previous year's ivory production,[145] but the hunters lacked a sense of ownership or control. Only the meat and hides would stay with the project. Daphne Sheldrick believed that this "deprived the scheme of its most valuable source of income from the start and had a ham-stringing effect on its viability".[146] Another drawback likely to discourage experienced hunters was that they would have to use guns and not poisoned arrows, preventing them from following their traditional hunting methods.

The scheme went ahead, managed by Parker; 3,000 square miles along the Galana River on Tsavo's eastern border were set aside as the controlled hunting zone. Only Waliangulu hunters and their families would be permitted to reside in the area. They were allowed to kill 200 elephants annually. The scheme ran for several years, but was doomed by the hunters' lack of autonomy and loss of direct control of ivory income, exacerbated by the colonial government's requirement that private hunting safaris also be allowed to operate on the scheme's land. This further alienated the Waliangulu, who saw white hunters shooting on what they thought was their land, with no income accruing to them.[147] Also problematic was the migration of elephant herds, both in search of food and water and to avoid danger. Once the culling started, many herds moved back into the safety of Tsavo. Gradually, the Waliangulu began to drift away and some, it is believed, may have resumed hunting inside the park's boundaries.[148] Those who remained became employees rather than autonomous hunters, and the scheme became a private enterprise involved in a combination of conservation and game ranching.[149]

The failure of the Galana scheme may have led to a small-scale resumption of poaching in Tsavo, but the elephants there were soon facing a greater threat, which ironically resulted from the increase in numbers under the park's protection. In 1959, it became evident that increasing elephant numbers were leading to the destruction of vegetation on a massive scale, changing woodland to dry savannah. Daphne Sheldrick said areas of Tsavo began to resemble "a battlefield or lunar landscape".[150] The loss of woodland vegetation reduced numbers of browsers like black rhino, gerenuk and other antelope. The increase in elephant numbers, without any poaching or licensed hunting within the park, was because birth rates exceeded natural mortality. When drought hit, the growing herds depleted food sources and destroyed trees. Cruelly, the elephants' successful protection from local hunters led to a situation where a cull well into the thousands might be needed to protect the park from damage. David Sheldrick initially accepted that a cull might be necessary, but insisted that it be carried out by the park rangers and not commercial hunters.[151] In the event, the resumption of rains and the recovery of some vegetation then put off a decision on a cull.

Ivory trade in eastern and southern Africa before independence

Between the end of the war and independence in 1962, the elephant issue in Uganda revolved around conservation in some areas, crop protection in others and preventing poaching. Rising meat prices in local markets and the high prices for ivory meant that killing elephants—legally or illegally—could be a lucrative source of income for local people or professional hunters. The establishment in 1948 of the Murchison Falls and Queen Elizabeth National Parks saw the banning of all hunting in these areas, which contained large numbers of elephants. But throughout the 1940s and 1950s, elephant control work continued in other parts of the territory, with over 1,000 animals shot annually. The former Kenyan chief warden, Keith Caldwell, estimated that the number of elephants in Uganda had been reduced from 18,700 in 1925 to 8,000 in 1950; 25,892 elephants had been shot by the Game

Department during this period and 7,650 on licence by professional or indigenous hunters.[152]

In 1950, with ivory prices rising as the global economy picked up, 699 licences were issued for elephant hunting and 1,500 elephants were killed in control or licensed hunting. The Game Department reported in 1952 that poaching was becoming a problem in the Toro reserve. The department's report also noted that there were fewer and fewer big tuskers and "that of the elephants shot nearly 70 per cent had tusks of under 40 pounds apiece, and 40 per cent were under 30 pounds". It lamented that most of those now taking out the licences were not true "sportsmen" but were in it for the money.[153] While hunting outside the parks and reserves was reducing numbers, they were increasing appreciably inside the parks and threatening the sort of damage witnessed in Tsavo. A scientific survey using aerial counting in Murchison Falls revealed 4,000 elephants in the mid-1950s; by October 1957, this had increased to 5,000.[154] This was problematic because, with poaching deterred, the elephants were increasingly confined and concentrated. As numbers increased in the parks a new problem of over-stocking and environmental degradation developed, leading to huge culls in the 1960s.

In Tanganyika, control shooting and hunting continued outside the national parks. Between 1947 and 1956, the government earned £506,437 (over £15.6m today) from ivory. There was a growing tension in and around reserves, where local people were prohibited from hunting and earning income from ivory and other products, while the Game Department and professional hunters reaped the rewards of government-sanctioned hunting. In the late 1950s, 300–450 convictions were recorded each year for poaching by local people, while the numbers of licences issued to white hunters increased.[155] The Game Department estimated the elephant population of the territory at around 30,000 in 1950. A Fauna Conference held in Tanganyika accepted the need for continued control shooting, concluding that the hunting of game by local communities should be allowed on a limited basis for meat, but that they should not be permitted to hunt for trophies—still allowing for professional or visiting hunters with licences.[156] As Tanganyika approached independence, it was clear that with the expansion of the Serengeti National Park's boundaries, strenuous efforts by the warden, Myles Turner, to combat poaching[157] and expressions of support for a national park-based conservation strategy from independence leader Julius Nyerere and his Tanganyika African National Union (TANU), the existing policies on hunting and conservation would be maintained and even strengthened after independence; Nyerere effectively accepted the exclusionary conservation practices that were becoming the norm.

In southern Africa, similar policies were implemented. In Bechuanaland (Botswana), the British, with support from Tswana traditional leaders, established reserves at Moremi in the Okavango Delta, the Central Kalahari and Chobe. Chobe had been a focus of heavy elephant hunting in the late nineteenth century, but protection led to a massive increase in elephant numbers. Harvesting was controlled through private safari areas and hunting concessions around the reserves—meaning those running the concessions strenuously combated poaching—and because local chiefs and community leaders were broadly in favour of creating protected areas, to keep out South African crocodile hunters and visiting safari hunters. They also realised that these areas were unsuitable for cattle due to the presence of tsetse flies and the aridity of the Central Kalahari.[158] In South Africa, it was estimated that the population of elephants in Kruger had risen appreciably to 1,750. The growth was due to a good birth rate, protection from poaching and migration into the reserve from Portuguese Mozambique, to escape hunting there.[159] The sustained population growth became a problem in later years and led to substantial culling.

4

CONSERVATION, CORRUPTION, CRIME AND
CONFLICT IN EAST AFRICA

Changing the guard at the ivory gate

Sub-Saharan African countries achieved independence with an inherited system of wildlife management and a developing system of conservation through national parks and reserves. In other words, the
systems established to benefit colonial powers, along with the measures
instituted to conserve habitats and species, were part of the legacy. For
the nationalist parties, political leaders and educated elites who had led
the demands for independence, ending rule from abroad and, to para-
phrase the Ghanaian leader Kwame Nkrumah, seeking the political
kingdom, were the number-one priorities. Few nationalists paid much
attention to wildlife management and utilisation, largely because the
speed of transition catapulted them into power with little opportunity
to gain knowledge, let alone experience, of the gamut of government
responsibilities in areas such as conservation.

In the first years of independence, there was little change to the style
or personnel involved in running parks and reserves. Africanisation of the
public service varied in its speed across Sub-Saharan states, but everywhere the priority was control first of key state institutions and security,
and then over the economy. National parks and wildlife were barely on
the radar. Many of those who ran the parks and had implemented colo-

Table 1: Estimates for East Africa's elephant populations, 1979 and 1989

	1979	1989
Ethiopia	900	6,650
Kenya	65,000	19,000
Rwanda	150	70
Somalia	24,300	6,000
Sudan	134,000	40,000
Tanzania	316,300	80,000
Uganda	6,000	3,000
Total	546,650	154,720

Source: David Western, 'The Ecological Role of Elephants in Africa', *Pachyderm*, 12, 1989.

nial conservation policies—Sheldrick, Turner, Woodley and so on—stayed in place, albeit with huge misgivings about what was to come—misgivings based on the "black poacher" mentality developed so assiduously under colonialism. Ian Parker, who empathised with African hunting communities, wrote that conservationists, rangers in national parks or wardens in game departments were scared that at independence the game laws so resented by local peoples would be abolished and hunting thrown open to all Africans with disastrous effects.[1]

None of the newly independent states made drastic or immediate changes to conservation or hunting laws. Independence meant a change of guard at the gate, but not empowerment at a local level. Ownership of the parks and reserves was vested in the state; land policies reinforced state control and continued to legalise the exclusion of communities from reserves, sanctioning relocations when parks were established or expanded. Where wildlife utilisation was permitted it was at the discretion or under the control of new political leaderships and their client networks. When large-scale poaching or other forms of illegal wildlife use occurred it was frequently under the patronage of a powerful local, regional or national politician, or as a result of conflict or rebellion against the systems of government and economic exploitation that grew out of the colonial system.[2] Trade in ivory continued under the auspices of the new governments, driven by external demand and largely dominated by non-African traders and buyers—the Asian, Swahili and Arab traders adapted to independence as their forebears had adapted to colonial rule. In the growing sphere of international wildlife conservation, the creation of international conservation organisations and conservation or animal welfare NGOs gave great scope for extensive interference in and influence over the wildlife policies of the new states.

Western influence was derived not just from the colonial inheritance, but also from the growing and potentially valuable tourist trade, African states' need for Western loans for conservation and tourism development, and the continued external demand for ivory. The dominance of Western scientific and conservation experts and Western elephant researchers continued, and, if anything, expanded despite independence with substantial influence developing over African conservation policies and the elephant debate, with them often pursuing agendas that served their outlooks on conservation. Most passionately believed in the efficacy of their own approaches, leading to divergent and often contradictory population estimates and narratives on conservation; in the following chapters I have tried to reflect this, to identify both sources of population estimates and the positions from which contending camps approached conservation and the future of the ivory trade.

There also developed a romanticised, highly emotional and widespread European and American attachment to African wildlife and to key species like elephants, rhinos and lions through the rise of safari tourism, and TV and film documentaries; these also influenced policy and practice in African range states. Gibson summed it up well: "Wildlife has become an increasingly important part of the relationship among many African countries and industrialized countries, international nongovernmental organizations (NGOs), and international businesses. Revenue from wildlife tourism is an important source of foreign exchange… Residents of industrialized countries ascribe growing importance to the fate of animals in Africa".[3] On a continent where the new rulers understandably had little time for wildlife, the willingness of Western governments, institutions, NGOs and public opinion to place a value on conservation and to put pressure on the new governments was to have a lasting effect on conservation policies, and largely stopped local communities from taking back the ownership they'd lost under colonialism. This often gave those conservationists close to the NGOs strong influence over international and national policies, control of discourses over future policy and favourable coverage in the media.

IVORY

The fears of white hunters and game wardens about independence were based on an idealised view that colonial wildlife policy had been effective, organised rationally and, above all, fair. There was an implicit belief in the integrity of the system, with the expectation that this integrity would be lost under independent governments. As we have seen, this was a straw man. The colonial system of hunting and conservation was riddled with corruption, abuse of power and the self-serving actions of those in charge of the system. This is not to denigrate those who implemented policy on the ground, but to point out the problems inherent in the whole system—that game wardens protecting elephants in a reserve could profit by killing elephants on licence, while local people were banned. Illicit ivory had been laundered by the system for the benefit of those who were part of the colonial elite and its patronage network of settlers, hunters and safari operators.

Under independent governments, the gate for exports and rent-seeking from the ivory trade was in the hands of the new authorities, politicians and their networks of clients. In essence, they continued the system of profiting from ivory and enabling those controlling the gate to profit. The legal trade continued side by side with the illegal. Illicit trade routes through ports like Mombasa and Dar es Salaam that operated under colonialism continued to function and even expand after independence. Kismayo in Somalia remained a centre for exporting ivory poached in Kenya, usually by dhow to the Gulf, while Khartoum was a focus for the Central African ivory trade, with tusks from southern Sudan sold there along with ivory smuggled from Congo, the CAR, Chad, northern Uganda and Kenya. It wasn't a matter of new trade routes springing up with independence, but of old ones evolving. Conflict and disorder in many of the independent states (notably in Congo and Sudan, but later also conflicts in Mozambique and Angola in which South African forces played a role) created opportunities for the killing of elephants on a massive scale through the breakdown of conservation and anti-poaching controls. It also helped to enrich political and military elites and, to a lesser extent, to fund insurgencies or sustain conflict. Disorder was an opportunity for poaching and smuggling, but not a cause of it.

The 1960s was a decade of relative peace for most of Africa's elephant populations, but the 1970s and 1980s witnessed an explosion in poaching, influenced by significant increases in global ivory prices, driven as ever by external demand, not by African factors. The consequent rise in prices and ready markets, generated to a great extent by increasing prosperity in Hong Kong and Japan as well as continuing ivory commerce in North America and western Europe, provided an incentive to poach, especially at a time when African economies were in decline and living standards falling. The price of ivory had remained largely unchanged during the 1960s at around $5 per kilo; it now soared to $7.50 in 1970, $74 in 1978, $120 in 1987 and $300 in 1987. The profits for middlemen and those who controlled the trade were huge. Hunters could earn a year's income from one expedition. The situation was summed up by David Western, the chairman of the AESG in 1983, when he said that, as a result of demand from overseas buyers expanding the market and increasing prices, "There has been a crescent of heavy poaching extending from Somalia, through northern Kenya, South Sudan, the CAR, Chad, northern Zaire, and probably the Congo Republic…"[4] Corruption, conflict and poverty provided the opportunities for poaching to thrive, but only because of the demand and high prices paid outside the continent for African ivory.

Conservation, corruption and catastrophe in Kenya

Kenya's elephants, its conservation policies and poaching problems were always likely to be at the forefront, because of the settler population, the growth of safari tourism and the greater global media attention given to the country due to Western investment and familiarity. The poaching war in Tsavo had been widely reported; books and films like *Born Free* and *Living Free*, and the basing there of conservation groups and researchers studying elephants, all contributed to the focus on Kenyan wildlife. Kenya experienced growth in almost every sector of government activity and, along with it, in the economy of patronage, corruption and criminal activity, masked by the country's image as a successful developing economy with pro-Western policies.[5] Corruption and the failure to ensure that revenues from tourism and related activities flowed down to local communities continued to reinforce their alienation from wildlife and conservation policies, dominated by the conservation-capitalism-NGO nexus already described.

By independence in December 1963, control over wildlife resources had been well and truly wrested from the hands of local Kenyan communities. Legal hunting, carried out by professional hunters and visiting Americans and Europeans, was a source of foreign exchange income, though not a huge one. The national parks were established facts on the ground, from which local people had been forcibly excluded but which were to form the basis of a lucrative tourist industry.[6] By the 1970s, tourism ranked in the top three hard currency-earners, along with tea and coffee. Some communities still hunted, despite the bans, but the nature of the Kenyan economy and of people's means of subsistence had changed so completely that there was no realistic prospect of a return to pre-colonial systems of farming mixed with hunting. Parker, in his analysis of the ivory trade for the US Fish and Wildlife Service in 1979, asserted that the breakdown of social structures in African communities during the colonial period had played a role in changing traditional attitudes to hunting. The relatively low-profile hunting that Sheldrick had stamped out in Tsavo was largely replaced by a more rapacious form, driven by the rising price of ivory. Some Waliangulu still hunted in traditional ways and on a limited scale, but the devastating rise in poaching was not down to them. To the frustration of communities deprived of the right to hunt, the Kenyatta government did not reverse bans on hunting, but it did demonstrate awareness of the role that ivory could play in the development of political patronage, and members of the Kenyatta family were quick to profit from ivory.

This took the form of a new source of ivory coming on to the market. Kenyatta decided that he needed to reward allies and buy off those who had fought in the Land and Freedom Army (Mau Mau) but then been politically marginalised. In a very obvious move to use ivory income as a form of patronage, he ordered Chief Game Warden Ian Grimwood to issue permits for ivory said to be held by former fighters and supposedly gathered during the revolt in the 1950s. This led to large amounts of ivory being sold by people purporting to be ex-fighters, using what became known as Collectors' Permits. There was no check on whether this was old or newly poached ivory, and poached tusks were laundered using permits. One very active collector, known as Field Marshal Muthoni Kirima, was not one of the better known fighters if she had been a fighter at all, but she received a permit and then acted as an agent gathering and selling illegally held or poached ivory. There was no pretence of only collecting ivory from forests where the insurgency had taken place; Kirima travelled all over Kenya gathering tusks.[7] The Collectors' Permits were an early indication that the illegal trade would flourish under a government for which political patronage, wealth accumulation and the gatekeeper mentality would trump integrity and regulation.

During the 1960s, poaching remained a relatively insignificant problem in Tsavo and the other parks. The elephant problem that faced Tsavo was that of the massive destruction of woodland and other vegetation. Sheldrick reluctantly suggested a reduction in elephant numbers through culling. But a period of good rains, the deaths of elephants during the drought and the resurgence of woodland in some areas had enabled the park authorities to put off a decision. By the mid-1960s, elephant numbers in the Tsavo-Galana-Mkomazi ecosystem were rising, with destruction of woodland and creation of semi-arid grassland. Sheldrick, with backing from botanists looking at vegetation cycles, believed culling would not be necessary to stop the damage, as vegetation would recover and the grasslands created had increased bio-diversity, with rising numbers of grazers like buffalo and zebra. What was needed, Sheldrick believed, was a long-term view of these cycles, rather than precipitate culling. The parks board initiated a study to establish elephant numbers and provide a solution to woodland damage. Dr Richard Laws, who had worked on reducing elephant numbers in Murchison Falls National Park in Uganda, was appointed to study the Tsavo elephants, assisted by Parker, who had overseen a substantial cull in Uganda.

Laws decided he needed to shoot 300 elephants in each zone he identified in Tsavo and through detailed examination of their carcasses assess the effects of the increasing numbers on the elephants and the environment. Parker's Wildlife Services company carried out this cull and a similar one in Mkomazi, across the border in Tanganyika. Parker says that numbers were up to 40,000 in the Tsavo ecosystem, having recovered from losses in the earlier drought, and that they were under increasing stress from competition for food. Laws and Parker believed there were about twelve different population groups in the ecosystem and that each would have to be reduced to prevent further damage.[8] Having shot 600 in the scientific study, Laws recommended that 2,700 more be culled. The cull would bring in substantial income for the government and for Parker, who would conduct it and share in the income from meat, hides and ivory. Sheldrick vehemently opposed the cull, arguing that long-term cycles of vegetation change had to be studied first and that it was fundamentally wrong to cull large numbers of animals in a conservation area. There was an outcry in the press in both Kenya and Britain when news of the cull leaked out. The park trustees supported Sheldrick and Laws resigned. The polarity of the two positions on this cull was a forerunner of the fierce scientific and personal conflicts that were to develop in the late 1970s and 1980s over elephant numbers and the effects of the ivory trade on their survivability.

If Sheldrick had won that battle for Tsavo's elephants, an even tougher campaign was to come against the dual enemies of drought and resumed poaching. Drought hit again in 1970–2, causing even greater destruction than before. Elephants and black rhino, deprived of browse by the loss of woodlands, were the main victims. Elephants died in their thousands. Far more perished in the drought than would have been killed in the cull. At the request of the East African Wildlife Society, Tim Corfield, carried out a survey to assess mortality during the drought and came up with a figure of 6,000 in Tsavo East.[9] More died in the wider ecosystem. Hard on the heels of the drought came a massive wave of poaching. A number of factors appeared to prompt it: 1) the opportunity to gather ivory from the thousands of elephants that had died in the drought attracted local people, made destitute by the loss of livestock and crops, into the park; 2) the rise in ivory prices prompted traders in Mombasa and Somalia to encourage both gathering of natural-mortality ivory and poaching; 3) anti-poaching forces had been wound down; 4) the growing availability of modern automatic weapons in the region and the presence of Somalis who had fought in what was called the Shifta War (1963–8) between Somali insurgents and Kenyan security forces north of Tsavo; 5) Kenyan poachers could legalise poached ivory through the Collectors' Permits, and the politics of patronage gave protection to poachers and smugglers—at a price.

The poaching started outside Tsavo, in regions not designated as protected. Many elephants had died in Tsavo and surrounding areas like the Galana Game Ranch and people started outselling natural-mortality ivory to traders. Despite the extensive die-off there were still substantial herds in and around Tsavo. Demand and rising prices meant that gathering turned into poaching. David Sheldrick alerted the authorities to the new onslaught developing outside the park and persuaded them to allow him to establish a combined force of park staff, police and the paramilitary General Service Unit (GSU) to fight the poachers if they entered the park,[10] which they soon did to pursue the remaining large herds. Over a period of four years, Somali gangs and local poachers took a heavy toll on the 30,000 elephants that had survived the drought. Sheldrick believed that between 1974 and 1976, 15,000 elephants were killed in Tsavo and surrounding areas.[11]

These Somali gangs were associated with the remnants of Somali insurgents who had fought a long but low-intensity war in north-eastern Kenya during the 1960s. They started poaching in the wider Tsavo region and near the Tana River in 1971, perhaps prompted by drought, which decimated the livestock herds of the region's nomadic Somali pastoralists, many of whom had been sympathetic to the insurgents. The poachers could use the herders as cover, and the networks of Somali traders in the region as the means of smuggling tusks across the border and out through ports like Kismayo. The Somalis weren't the sole poachers; organised Kenyan gangs as well as Walinagulu and Wakamba hunters took advantage of the vulnerability of the park after the drought. It was always convenient for the wildlife ministry and the Kenyan government to highlight the Somali role in poaching, as it took attention away from the far more extensive poaching by gangs linked with corrupt officials, the Kenyan business and political elite and rogue rangers from the wildlife ministry or Game Department.

Sheldrick's rangers were outnumbered and out-gunned in the new poaching war. The fight against the poachers and smugglers was complicated by the involvement of high-profile politicians and businessmen organising or providing protection for the smuggling of poached ivory through Mombasa, where there was still a legal ivory trade through which illicit tusks could be laundered. Poaching was a major temptation for poor rural dwellers who were struggling to survive after the drought, but this was also a chance for the new political and business elites to entrench their role as gatekeepers for the illegal as well as the legal ivory trade, and they chose to benefit through corruption and poaching rather than try a more regulated and sustainable system that would conserve elephants and generate income. The new gatekeepers saw ivory as "a natural (and renewable) resource that could be exploited, this time by Africans for Africans", or at least those Africans placed to benefit.[12] The godfathers of the new poaching networks were rarely in danger of arrest, either belonging to or enjoying the protection of the political class that ruled Kenya. Those traders who were caught generally had the political clout or wealth to avoid imprisonment; they rarely appeared in court on smuggling or illicit trafficking charges.

The border between Kenya and Somalia had long been a problematic one for those concerned with protecting wildlife. There were centuries-old trade networks used by herders and merchants moving between Somalia and Kenya—routes intersected by the colonial borders. Despite the transfer of Jubaland to Italian Somaliland in 1925 and its inclusion in independent Somalia in 1960, Somali nationalists and Kenyan Somalis agitated in the early 1960s for the secession of Somali-populated areas of northern Kenya before their incorporation into Somalia at Kenyan independence in 1963. Within the colonial Northern Frontier District (NFD), there had been considerable support for unity with Somalia, favoured by a majority of respondents to a British-appointed commission—62 per cent of the district's population, including the entire Somali population. However, non-Somali communities including the Boran and the Oromo of Marsabit favoured remaining part of Kenya, creating conflict with the Somali population. Similarly, at the centre, Kenyatta's Kenya African National Union (KANU) and other parties opposed the loss of the region. The British chose to ignore the commission's findings and the NFD remained part of Kenya.

Just prior to Kenyan independence, agitation by Kenya's Somali nationalists developed into attacks by militants on police stations and raids on non-Somali settlements, in which people were killed and livestock stolen. This continued after independence in 1963 and developed into a low-level insurgency. At first there was no evident involvement in poaching on the part of the Somali insurgents, known as *shifta* (from an Amharic word for bandits), during the conflict, which lasted until 1968. During that time, the *shiftas* killed three district commissioners and a

Boran chief and fought 385 engagements. The Kenyan army and police carried out counter-insurgency offensives, adopting tactics of indiscriminate violence against the Somali population, using extra-judicial killings, torture, rape and the killing or theft of livestock to intimidate Somali civilians into ending support for the insurgents. Of the 437 Somalis killed during the conflict, most were civilians. The *shifta* were armed and supplied by the Somali government but received support from and were able to hide among the Somali pastoralist communities.

The low-level war ended in January 1968 with the signing of a peace deal by the Somali and Kenyan governments. Many of the insurgents stayed in Kenya and cached their weapons. The Somali population was cowed but angry at its treatment and impoverished by the loss of livestock. Estimates based on compensation claims to the Kenyan government suggest that 15,847 cattle, 3,352 goats or sheep and 214 donkeys were stolen or killed by Kenyan forces. Hogg believed that between 1963 and 1970 the Isiolo camel population declined by 9 per cent, small stock by 90 per cent and cattle by 7 per cent.[13] In the eyes of many Kenyans, including the political elite, the revolt had resulted in the "criminalisation of a community based upon social, economic, and cultural values that were deemed un-Kenyan".[14] While Somalis undoubtedly were involved in stock theft (as were other communities) and took part in poaching and ivory trafficking, they became convenient whipping boys for the government—a community that could be blamed for anything and everything in order to mask official unwillingness to get to grips with the role of political corruption, police graft and criminal networks with official protection in poaching and smuggling.

The combination of massive livestock losses and the drought impoverished Somali communities and fed grievances with the authorities and non-Somali communities. This was fertile breeding ground for the poaching gangs that began to operate in the region, also engaging in livestock raiding against the Boran, Orma and Turkana. As early as 1968, there were reports of Somali involvement in poaching elephants in the Samburu area. Game Warden Rodney Elliott in Maralal said that Samburu was threatened by *shifta* straight after the end of the war, and the government feared that tourists would be attacked there. Elliott was given an expanded force of rangers to deter the Somalis and adopted militarised methods in fighting Somali poachers. His rangers killed fourteen *shifta* in 1966, fifty in 1968 and thirteen in 1969. The raids declined in 1970–1. An unfortunate by-product of the fight against the poachers was that the Kenyan army, police and paramilitary GSU entered reserves or national parks and themselves engaged in poaching—and, unlike the Somali poachers, were more or less beyond the law, often part of patronage networks involving high-ranking politicians, the police and civil servants, including in the Game Department. There was even evidence that senior army and police officers were involved in poaching, and wardens found it impossible to press charges against them because of obstruction from the head of the Game Department.

The Somali incursions and cattle raiding led to resumed poaching by other communities around Tsavo. The Orma, Wakamba and Waliangulu had also been hit by drought. They were aware of the massive elephant death toll during the drought, which gave them an incentive to enter the park to gather tusks from animals that had succumbed. The Orma and Wakamba had also been affected when Somali pastoralists crossed the Tana River in 1970 looking for pasture for their livestock. Including former *shifta* and armed with modern weapons like AK-47s, they had pushed Wakamba and Orma from their grazing and raided their livestock. Some members of the two communities reverted to ivory gathering and hunting to survive. The growth of non-Somali poaching in Tsavo and other reserves was also linked to the growing involvement of powerful members of the ruling elite in the legal and illegal ivory trades—helped by the issuing of Collectors' Permits which could be copied and used to legalise poached ivory. But no cases involving corrupt officials, politicians or their relatives were brought to court as investigations by game wardens were nipped in the bud—impunity for ivory dealing among the powerful became the order of the day.

In 1976, the National Parks were amalgamated with the notoriously inefficient and venal Game Department, under the overall control of the Ministry of Tourism and Wildlife. This led to chaos in the parks, with no funding and no fuel for patrol vehicles. The corruption evident in the use of Collectors' Permits and other means by which Game Department ivory ended up in the hands of clients of the governing patronage network now infected the amalgamated department and reduced the ability of wardens to deal with poaching. Sheldrick was moved from Tsavo and replaced by a less energetic warden. He feared he was "leaving the elephant and rhino population at the mercy of poachers and their corrupt masters".[15] The Fauna Preservation Society reported in July 1977 that 100 elephants were being killed every month in Tsavo, some with poisoned arrows, but most with modern weapons.[16] Some ivory went north to Kismayo, but Somali and other traders in Nairobi also channelled tusks through established networks using Mombasa. Tsavo became a killing field, with poachers operating with impunity and growing evidence of wildlife department personnel directly involved in poaching and transporting ivory.

By 1977, there was growing concern among conservation groups, wardens and researchers at the rapid decline in elephant numbers in Kenya. The research by Ian Parker and his EBUR report on the ivory trade and corruption in Kenya (see below) also provided growing evidence of the role of political patronage and high-level corruption in illicit trading. The accusations were getting ever closer to President Kenyatta's family, with one of his wives, Mama Ngina, said to be involved in poaching and smuggling of ivory; there was also evidence that his daughter Margaret—Mayor of Nairobi, then Kenyan Ambassador to the UN, and head of the United Africa Corporation (UAC)—was being issued permits to sell ivory obtained without legal certification. Amidst these embarrassing stories, President Kenyatta announced a ban on all hunting in 1977 and on ivory exports the following year. This helped obtain a World Bank grant of $17m to improve management and security in Kenya's national parks. The government was hailed by conservation and animal welfare groups in the West for the ban, but the situation was getting worse. The Kenya Rangeland Monitoring Unit reported in 1978 that there were only about 60,000 elephants left in Kenya, down from an estimated 167,000 in 1973.[17] The Tsavo region's population had fallen to 11,000, a quarter of its level in 1970.

Kenyatta gave every appearance of reacting positively to appeals from conservationists and Western governments to stop poaching, while the real situation worsened with widespread poaching and endemic corruption within government, the security forces and the wildlife department. Kenyan ministers issued constant denials that Kenyatta's family was involved, but the evidence mounted and details that the government had tried to suppress were increasingly widely known—notably Parker's

EBUR report.[18] The *Daily Nation* newspaper, which dared not directly accuse the president's family, was increasingly critical of the minister for wildlife and tourism, Matthew Ogutu, for failing to deal with corruption within his department or the estimated 1,300 poachers killing elephants.[19] Parker wrote in EBUR that "Illegal ivory transactions concern all strata of Kenyan society. The supposed guardians of the Trade—the Game Department—appears to have become a pivotal institution in the business it is supposed to suppress. Subordinate staff and wardens in the field actually indulge in poaching elephant."[20]

In one of the few areas where they both agree, Iain Douglas-Hamilton and Parker recount an attempt in 1973 by a research officer in the Game Department, Peter Jarman, to reveal the extent of the corruption. At a seminar in Nairobi, Jarman said the Collectors' Permits were an abuse of power encouraging the laundering of illegal ivory. He believed only 44 per cent of the ivory harvested in Kenya was sold through official channels and that the situation was getting progressively worse. Jarman estimated that 42,000 elephants had been lost in Kenya between 1969 and 1973 (of which 15,000 died in the drought). He accused members of the political elite and their clients, including assistant ministers, of getting ivory illegally and from government stocks (at a vastly reduced price) to sell at a profit.[21] The seminar was told of elephant poaching in Maasai Mara using government vehicles, of illicit exports of ivory through Mombasa and Nairobi Airport. In his report on the seminar, Douglas-Hamilton praised Parker for exposing the level of corruption in the government when it came to ivory. He quoted Parker as saying that $160m worth of ivory would leave Africa in 1973, the equivalent of about 200,000 dead elephants.[22] Little was done in reaction to the evidence presented, but Jarman's contract with the department was not renewed and he had to leave Kenya.

In late 1973, Ian Parker had been commissioned by Jack Block, a Nairobi businessman and founder of the Kenyan section of the WWF, to compile the report on poaching and corruption in the ivory trade, which became known as EBUR (Latin for ivory). It detailed evidence of poaching, corruption, laundering of illegal ivory and the use of permits to legalise illicit tusks. The corruption went to the core of the Kenyan political establishment. Parker sent copies to Block, the British high commissioner and the American ambassador—who returned them, indicating it was a danger to the stability of the Kenyan government and too hot to handle. But a leading domestic critic of Kenyatta, former assistant minister of tourism and wildlife J. M. Kariuki, is believed to have seen the report and intended to use it in parliament to embarrass the government.[23] The report was deemed so sensitive by the government that the copies were seized by Kenyan Special Branch on the orders of the president, and may have contributed to Kariuki being kidnapped and murdered shortly after he threatened to reveal "a report which documents corruption by the highest in the land" to parliament.[24]

In the report, Parker identified that Kenya's principal dealers in ivory were of Indian or Pakistani origin. They bought ivory for local currency from auctions and traders or illicitly, exported it and received payment abroad in hard currency, only a small portion of which returned to Kenya. Parker calculated that in the first six months of 1973 Kenya lost $2.3m in revenue in this way. About 214 tons of ivory were legally exported in that period, 76 per cent of it accounted for by Collectors' Permits, which were being used to launder poached ivory.[25] The EBUR report is packed with detail and worth reading for those who want to go deeper into the mechanics and fine detail of the trade. One of the channels for corrupt trading was the sale of ivory to private dealers directly from government stocks rather than through the official auctions. Dealers obtained this ivory at very low prices in return for payments to officials.

The report also detailed the poaching and smuggling of ivory by wardens and rangers, with the Game Department having a pivotal role in illicit dealing. It said that two assistant ministers of tourism and wildlife, and Kenyatta's daughter Margaret, were obtaining ivory from the Game Department and selling it privately for massive profit. Kenyatta had permits issued to her retroactively to legalise ivory she had obtained, and Parker discovered that in March 1974, the UAC sent eight shipments totalling 6,052 kg (or 521 tusks) of ivory by Pakistan International Airlines to buyers in China; he estimated that, if that month was representative, then the UAC could have been exporting 73 tons—equivalent to 3,000 elephants—a year.[26] EBUR also accused the chief game warden, Mr Jonathan, of substantial involvement in illegal trading, along with senior police officers, and asserted that the Attorney-General, Charles Njonjo, had on a number of occasions intervened to prevent charges being brought against those involved in illegal deals. At the very top, President Kenyatta is described as personally authorising permits to export ivory, in direct contravention of Kenyan laws; State House stationery was used for letters instructing officials not to seize the ivory of two men who had been issued with Collectors' Permits but had been found in possession of illicit ivory.

The report put flesh on the bones of the stories that had been circulating about the extent of corruption at all levels of wildlife administration of wildlife, right to the top of the government, though Parker told me that he never found direct evidence of Mama Ngina's involvement. He says that when he later discussed the EBUR report with the British high commissioner, Tony Duff, he was told that conservation was "tertiary" in human affairs, and Duff wrote that the "primary problem of corruption could not be solved by going after the Kenya Government for mismanaging ivory and elephants; but if corruption in general was brought under control then the ivory problem would be resolved".[27] Yet corruption wasn't resolved and still hasn't been; poaching has continued with the protection of politicians, with scandals over the decades such as the Anglo-Leasing affair, right up to the suspension of five ministers and numerous heads of public bodies by President Uhuru Kenyatta in April 2015 following evidence of serious corruption.

Kenyatta's banning of all hunting and sales of ivory was a very public attempt to gloss over the corruption, but nothing was done to stem graft or stop poaching. A year after the ban, a Wildlife Awareness Week was organised in Nairobi to publicise the government's claim to be protecting wildlife and combating poaching. Douglas-Hamilton said that Margaret Kenyatta turned up at one of the events wearing ivory bangles. When he suggested that she remove them, she shouted in a rage that, "you conservationists are the ones who say bad things about my father". He says that to smooth things over he had to write her a letter of apology.[28]

The decline in integrity and efficiency in the running of the national parks continued into the 1980s. The first African head of parks, Perez Olindo, had resigned soon after the merger with the Game Department, in protest over corruption. The income from tourists was not used to build up an efficient administration or strengthen the anti-poaching teams, but disappeared into government coffers or the pockets of senior officials. This led to increasing demoralisation but also maintained networks of graft and the involvement of wardens and poorly paid staff in poaching, often at the behest of their bosses. Rangers had little motivation to fight poaching and, even if they did, National Park vehicles were in poor condition and perpetually short of fuel. Rangers lacked modern weapons to combat poachers who were frequently armed with AK-47s. Tsavo continued to suffer particularly heavily and, by 1989, when Richard Leakey was made head of the Kenya Wildlife Service, he estimated that it had just 5,000 elephants, compared with 40,000 two decades before;[29] Kenya lost half its elephants between 1970 and 1977.

Leakey believed that the combination of rising ivory prices in the 1970s and '80s and a corrupt and poorly run wildlife administration enabled poaching by a variety of groups (Somali gangs, corrupt wardens and rangers, and to a lesser extent, the Waliangulu and Wakamba) and illicit trade in tusks.[30] A poached elephant could be a meal ticket for a poor Kenyan and the route to riches for his patrons. Throughout this period, Tsavo's elephants were hit hard. There had been a brief period of respite in the early 1980s when the Tsavo East warden, Joe Kioko, and Bill Woodley in Tsavo West worked in tandem to tackle local and Somali poachers, and to root out rangers poaching or transporting ivory, but that didn't last. Given to big gestures rather than root-and-branch reforms, President Moi (as much part of the gate-keeping, rent-seeking patronage system as his predecessor) sacked the wildlife department director and invited back Perez Olindo. Olindo tried to get to grips with the rampant corruption, but had few resources and found his hands tied by the political connections of officials he tried to sack or move. Moi trumpeted his determination to combat armed poachers but didn't put the resources or political will into restoring anti-poaching capabilities or combating graft, because the latter was a key component of the Kenyan elite's hold on power.

Olindo tried to establish how many elephants remained in Kenya and commissioned Douglas-Hamilton to carry out a new survey of the Tsavo/Galana/Mkomazi elephant population. Douglas-Hamilton had a passionate commitment to elephants, after many years studying them at Lake Manyara. His estimates tend to be on the pessimistic side, and have consistently been used to support moves to ban any trading in ivory (see Chapter 6 for a detailed account of the competing estimates of elephants numbers and interpretations of them). His survey in the wider Tsavo region estimated that the population was down to 5,363; he counted 2,421 dead elephants, estimating that between 5,000 and 7,000 had been killed in eight years. He accompanied his survey findings with a report calling for a purge of the wildlife department, which was sent to Moi and to the European Economic Community (which was funding conservation programmes), the United Nations Environment Programme (UNEP), the WWF and the International Union for Conservation of Nature (IUCN).[31] Pressure on the government to act more decisively grew when armed groups of Somali poachers carried out attacks on foreign tourists in Tsavo, giving the Kenyan government the pretext once more to blame the majority of poaching on Somalis. The GSU was sent in, but to no great effect. By 1988, tourism was bringing in $435m a year, with earnings increasing by 24 per cent in one year. Attacks on tourists in national parks could destroy this bonanza quickly. But corruption could damage it more seriously in the long term. The elephant and wildlife researcher David Western, chairman of the AESG, claimed in 1988 that less than one per cent of tourism earnings were ploughed back into conservation, park facilities and anti-poaching.

The growing evidence of an increase in Somali poaching, the use of military weaponry and attacks on tourists caused a hardening of attitudes, particularly after the discovery that a poaching gang led by a Somali army colonel, Abdi Ibrahim Faha, had entered Kenya in February 1989, killed six elephants and wounded three members of the Kenyan security forces. Though the poaching-smuggling networks were far more complex than mere groups of Somali bandits, and politically sensitive because they involved senior politicians and government officials, the Kenyan administration simply stressed further that Somalis were to blame—that they were poaching, had smuggled substantial amounts of ivory back to Somalia and had attacked tourists. Kenya formally protested to the Somali Foreign Ministry and vowed to fight incursions with force.

The level of Somali poaching and smuggling in Kenya became evident when the US Fish and Wildlife Service announced that it was banning any ivory imports from Somalia. The Director, Frank Dunkle, said his department had discovered that Somalia had exported 21,000 tusks in 1988, when it only had an elephant population of 4,500. The majority of the tusks came from elephants poached in Kenya. In August, three Kenyan game rangers were killed in Kora National Park, north of Tsavo, when their unit confronted a gang of Somali poachers. There was evidence that among the poachers were Somali veterans with experience of fighting in the Ogaden or in Somalia's civil war, which had started in the late 1980s. The London-based magazine *New African* reported in November 1988 that President Siad Barre had authorised the smuggling of poached ivory to Somalia from Kenya—this was denied by the Somali Embassy in Nairobi, but the magazine had a copy of a letter signed by Barre, instructing two Somalis to bring Kenyan ivory to Somalia to sell. [32]

The rate of elephant killing continued to accelerate. In 1988–9, it was estimated that three elephants were being killed daily by poachers in Kenya, [33] putting increasing pressure on Moi to act. This came to a head at a wildlife conference at the National Museum of Kenya on 29 August 1988, two days after the Somali poachers had shot the rangers in Kora. The tourism and wildlife minister, George Muhoho, addressed the conference and made ritual promises about catching the poachers. Leakey, as head of the East African Wildlife Society, had knowledge of corruption in the wildlife service, evidence of which had been gathered by Olindo. Disappointed with what the minister said, Leakey called his own press conference, where he "likened the slaughter of our elephants to economic sabotage: elephants were the flagship species of our wildlife and the basis for Kenya's biggest industry, tourism. The decimation of elephants and other wildlife therefore posed a direct economic threat to our country."[34] He spoke of a secret report uncovering the high-level corruption that enabled poaching and smuggling to continue, implying he knew who was involved. Muhoho accused Leakey of "a cheeky white attitude" and said the report was nothing new. [35] Soon after, Leakey met Moi and told him of the extent of the poaching problem. Moi reacted by declaring a shoot-to-kill policy—misinterpreted in the press as a shoot-on-sight policy for all poachers, rather than a preparedness to kill poachers who used firearms to resist arrest.

In April 1989, Moi removed Olindo as head of the wildlife department and appointed Leakey to lead the renamed Kenya Wildlife Service

(KWS), with a mandate to fight poaching and corruption. Leakey found the service bankrupt and riddled with corruption. A senior member of staff told him that corruption was everywhere, from theft of property to misuse of funds and turning a blind eye to poaching or even profiting from it. Wardens and rangers were dispirited or corrupt, and didn't have enough fuel for the spotter planes or Land Rovers. When Leakey visited Tsavo, both Kioko and Woodley—wardens of the East and West—told him that their rangers needed modern rifles, ammunition and fuel for their vehicles to stand any chance of fighting the poachers. They also needed decent pay and conditions for the rangers, who "earned barely enough to feed and clothe their families, certainly not enough to pay their children's school fees, too".[36] Leakey wanted the rangers paid, supplied with vehicles and petrol, and armed to take on the poachers.

After a battle with the police commissioner, who wanted the notoriously corrupt police to take on anti-poaching duties, Leakey was able to get modern G-3 rifles, new aircraft (funded by US donors) and fuel to carry out patrols. The government was hustled into this when, in June 1989, a tourist was killed by poachers. In the month that followed, armed game rangers killed twenty-two poachers in Tsavo. Leakey's energetic approach and high international profile enabled the Kenyans to raise funds for conservation and anti-poaching enhancement from Western governments and institutions (see Chapter 6). The effective quid quo pro was that Kenya now supported international moves for a ban on the ivory trade, rather than listening to those who favoured some form of sustainable-use programme for ivory without a complete ban. Kenya has maintained this position with support from Western governments and NGOs, whose financial backing for the Kenyan approach was slow to reduce poaching, but who were able to tie campaigning to Kenya's anti-trade position and its high-profile approach, declaring war on poaching and organising major media events like ivory burnings.

Tanzania: conservation undermined by corruption and poverty

The Arusha Manifesto announced by Julius Nyerere in 1961 was the declared policy of the government of independent Tanganyika, and represented a public commitment to national parks and protecting wildlife as a national inheritance. Nyerere and his party, the Tanganyika African National Union (TANU), wanted to maintain the national parks and garner foreign assistance in running them. The expertise of existing wardens, like Myles Turner, was retained for several years. Tanzania (formed in 1964 through the merger of Tanganyika and Zanzibar) didn't have the problems of elephant poaching experienced by Kenya before independence. The main wildlife issues were controlling poaching of buffalo and antelope for meat and hides, and elephant control in areas outside the parks and reserves. In 1962, 14,000 game animals were shot under licence in Tanganyika, but poaching amounted to over 150,000. Turner reported from Serengeti that elephant poaching really wasn't a concern there—rather, his problem was the use of snares or muzzle-loading rifles to hunt for meat. Where there was poaching of elephants, however—and this also applied to Selous, Manyara and other areas with large elephant populations—corrupt government, army and police officials were involved, often using government vehicles to transport poached ivory and meat. Poaching linked to corrupt officials developed during the 1970s, and worsened from the mid-1980s onwards.

Licensed hunting, including for elephants, remained legal in much of the country. It was banned for five years after 1973 amid concern that poaching for meat and over-hunting had reduced game numbers and could damage the increasingly valuable tourist industry centred on Serengeti, Ngorongoro and Manyara. Selous was a source of revenue from visiting trophy hunters. Yet licensed hunting resumed after 1978. Although major evidence was to emerge later of large-scale elephant poaching in Selous, in the first decade of independence there was more concern over elephants causing damage in the national parks. It was reported in December 1968 that an increase in Serengeti's elephant numbers had caused damage to the relatively small areas of woodland there. A survey was undertaken to see if culling would be necessary. It was found that growing numbers of elephants were moving into the Serengeti-Mara ecosystem as human activity around the parks forced them to seek sanctuary in protected areas. But numbers declined rapidly in the 1970s and early 1980s, when the border with Kenya was closed during a dispute between the two countries over the break-up of the East

African Community. This affected the number of tourists visiting Serengeti, as they had previously crossed into Tanzania from the Mara, and the falling park income meant reductions in anti-poaching patrols and a subsequent rise in poaching—elephants and rhino were the targets, because of the substantial rise in the value of ivory and horn.

The Serengeti elephant population declined from 2,460 in 1970 to 467 in 1986; of these, 1,500 were killed by poachers, while the remainder migrated to the Mara.[37] The poaching was carried out by local people, government employees, the police and army personnel, with tusks often transported in government vehicles for sale in Burundi or Dar es Salaam. This information was given to the author by National Parks staff in Serengeti and Manyara in 1988 under condition of anonymity. They said that senior members of government departments and officials of TANU (later the Chama Cha Mapinduzi, or CCM) were heavily involved in the sale and smuggling of wildlife products. They named a very senior party and government leader, but were unable to provide documentary evidence to back this up. These accounts were supported by information from a former game warden, Eric Balson. Among those he named as providing protection for Game Department and government officials involved in poaching were members of the Arusha Game Division, four game scouts, a game permit officer and Saidi Kawawa, brother of Rashidi, Nyerere's vice-president (1964–84) and general secretary of the CCM. Rashidi Kawawa denied playing a role in any form of corruption when I interviewed him in Dar es Salaam in February 1991. In the same month, the Tanzanian minister of the interior, Augustine Mrema, told me that government revenue problems and IMF and World Bank structural adjustment programmes had deprived the government of funds to pay officials, so the police and some government officials resorted to poaching, black marketeering and smuggling. As in Kenya, Tanzania's ivory trade (legal and illegal) was in the hands of the Indian business community.[38]

In 1970, the government declared a state monopoly over the legal ivory trade, but illicit ivory was still smuggled out by Asian businessmen. In 1991, the author was offered ivory by an Asian shopkeeper who was involved in the black market in foreign currency—this was during investigative reporting by the author on the currency black market in Dar es Salaam, during which he was also held up at gunpoint by corrupt policemen.

CONSERVATION, CORRUPTION, CRIME AND CONFLICT

The growth in poaching during the 1970s also parallelled that in Kenya, affecting the northern parks and the large population in Selous. A study by Douglas-Hamilton noted rapid decline and evidence of carcasses in elephant ranges in Tabora and Arusha in 1979 and 1980. Selous registered a 20–30 per cent fall in elephant numbers between 1976 and 1981, far in excess of natural mortality or licensed hunting and only explicable as a result of poaching.[39] Similar trends were evident in Ruaha and Serengeti. The director of Tanzania's National Parks, Derek Bryceson, and his wife, the primatologist Jane Goodall, wrote that organised poaching for ivory was so pervasive, with the involvement of corrupt officials, that banning it was untenable, because Tanzania was a poor country immensely rich in wildlife—creating the incentive to poach, with corruption providing the networks to sell.

Bryceson and Goodall said that, while Tanzanians were proud of their wildlife and their national parks, to get people surrounding the reserves to support conservation and oppose poaching, wildlife had to contribute to their standard of living. Tourism brought in some money, but was concentrated on Serengeti, Ngorongoro and Manyara, and did not make a big difference to local incomes. Though not keen on hunting, Bryceson and Goodall believed that controlled cropping schemes could contribute to conservation. They envisaged communities appointing hunters who would carry out the cropping. The communities would sell ivory, horn and skins to generate income. They also said that ivory from crop-raiding elephants that were shot should be sold for the benefit of the local community.[40] The scheme never got off the ground and poaching continued on an increasing scale alongside the legal trade, with evidence of high-level corruption within the government, ruling party and police that sustained the trade and deterred a serious search for alternative conservation strategies.

Although studies in the early 1970s had shown a large elephant population in Selous and gave no indication that poaching was seriously reducing numbers, by 1981, an aerial survey counted about 85,000 elephants but a significant number of skeletons, with the number of deaths increasing by 50 per cent over a five-year period, something unlikely to be due to natural mortality. The skeletons were concentrated in areas near to settlement and along access routes that had been cut during oil exploration. The African Elephant and Rhino Specialist

Group (AERSG) publication, *Pachyderm*, concluded that this was due to poaching and that elephant numbers had not shown a natural level of increase over previous surveys, suggesting a marked increase in hunting. Nothing was done about this and a survey reported by the same publication in December 1984 indicated a further 20–30 per cent decline in elephant numbers in Selous since 1981—though, as with most estimates, it had a wide margin of error. Moreover those conservationists and researchers most deeply committed to ending the ivory trade, and the international media which reported their interpretations of figures uncritically, highlighted the most pessimistic estimates and extrapolations of the threat to African elephants that could be derived from them.

That said, there was a clear and substantial drop in elephant numbers during this period. Despite this evidence of a decline, Selous continued to be used for licensed sports hunting of elephants. This brought in $2m in foreign exchange in 1985 ($4.36m today), but little went towards reserve management or anti-poaching; ninety-five elephants were shot there legally in 1985, but it was estimated that at least 500 were poached and regulation was so poor that licensed hunters could exceed quotas with little chance of prosecution.[41] It was clear that the decline was the result of poaching and human encroachment rather than legal hunting, but those conservationists and NGOs opposed to any trade in ivory came out against the legal hunting industry, too.

Rather than the discourse on elephant conservation being about realistic, community-friendly measures to protect habitats and species while gaining the support or at least the acquiescence of local communities, the narrative of NGOs and many researchers became one of bans and exclusions, rather than diverse and inclusive solutions.[42] Although at one stage prepared to accept that in southern Africa regulated trade and hunting could play a role in conservation, leading researchers like Douglas-Hamilton gradually moved to a total ban position, as did NGOs that had previously been less dogmatic, like the WWF and the American AWF, or African Wildlife Foundation (see Chapter 6 for greater detail on the hardening of the ivory–elephant conservation debate arteries). Douglas-Hamilton, who had been studying the elephants of Lake Manyara, reported a rise in poaching there, with increasing numbers of carcasses found. Some had been shot with large-calibre rifles and others speared. In one aerial count he saw 181 live elephants and ninety-two carcasses.[43] This contributed to convincing him that a complete ban was necessary—he had been studying the herds at Manyara very closely and was horrified by evidence of the large-scale killings there. For him and many other researchers, the issue of the ban became a highly charged emotional issue, in which estimates of numbers and the extent of decline became weapons to be wielded in arguments over policy.

Evidence of smuggling and corruption involving Tanzania was increasing. Belgian customs officers found 1,889 tusks weighing nearly 10 tons in a freight consignment labelled beeswax which had come from Dar es Salaam and was in transit to Dubai. Inspections carried out by Convention on International Trade in Endangered Species of Wild Fauna and Flora (CITES) officials indicated that these were tusks from elephants killed in Tanzania in 1985. It was the biggest seizure of ivory made outside Africa.[44] The growing evidence of poaching, corruption and smuggling led the Tanzanian government to ban imports and exports of ivory in December 1986, though little was done to investigate the systemic corruption which enabled illicit trading to survive the bans—trading that continues now through similar networks in the police, revenue services and ports authority (usually with protection at ministerial or senior party level). Registered dealers were instructed to return their licences and any unworked ivory to the government. At the same time, trying to project an image of toughness towards the illicit ivory trade, the government announced that 245 poachers had been arrested in 1986 (161 in Serengeti; no figures for the worst affected area, Selous), and 3,283 tusks confiscated.[45]

Nevertheless, by 1987, Tanzania's elephant population had declined to about 85,000 from around 300,000 in 1979;[46] in Selous, the numbers had dropped from 110,000 in 1976 to 55,000 in 1986 and 50,000 by 1988, and have continued to decline, despite the global ivory trade ban by CITES in 1989. The measures to stop poaching and combat smuggling had a propaganda effect but were cosmetic in nature; as in Kenya, there was no root-and-branch attempt to fight corruption, which got steadily worse in the late 1980s and 1990s as Tanzania's economy remained in crisis, partly as a result of ill-designed structural adjustment polices imposed by donors and international financial institutions. The import and export ban and declaratory policy of fighting corruption, while in effect doing little of substance, paved the way for a tougher policy towards the legal ivory trade, which would see Tanzania apply at the 1989 CITES conference to have African elephants relisted to Appendix 1—effectively banning trading in ivory.

Uganda: culling, conflict and catastrophe

In Uganda, elephant over-population and crop damage dominated in the years after independence, continuing the pattern of previous decades. Between 1929 and 1959, extensive control shooting, licensed hunting and poaching reduced the range of Uganda's elephant from 70 per cent of the territory to 17 per cent; during the same period, Uganda's human population grew from 3.5m to 5.5m. Elephants were increasingly confined to parks like Murchison Falls, Queen Elizabeth, Rwenzori and Kidepo Valley, where protection caused their numbers to increase dramatically. The expanding populations were crammed into limited areas, with consequent damage to vegetation. Extensive control shooting had kept up a regular supply of ivory to the legal trade, but in the years after independence poaching and smuggling of tusks poached in Congo increased, with strong evidence of government complicity.

Soon after independence, it became evident that, while elephant numbers in reserves were threatening vegetation and bio-diversity, a longer-term threat was developing to the survival of substantial numbers of elephants inside and outside reserves. This was posed by corruption and illicit ivory dealing among senior government officials, army officers and politicians, right up to the prime minister, Milton Obote. He and deputy army commander Idi Amin were discovered to be benefiting from the proceeds of poached ivory—much of it from Congo. In 1965, General Nicholas Olenga, a Congolese rebel supporter of the late Patrice Lumumba, said that Obote and Amin were involved in the smuggling of ivory and gold from eastern Congo, where Uganda stationed army units to protect its borders from the effects of the civil war there. The Ugandan army was involved in the trade, as were Congolese rebels, who poached or bought the ivory from local hunters. The proceeds went to the rebels and to senior Ugandan army officers and the prime minister.

At the time, Obote did not have an absolute majority in parliament and relied on some support from the Buganda royalist Kabaka Yekka (KY) party. There were increasing tensions between the parties and Obote was signalling his intention to curb the power of the Buganda king, Mutesa. In 1966, a KY MP, Daudi Ochieng, put forward a motion in parliament to suspend Amin from duty over the smuggling allegations, and accused Felix Onama, Minister of State for Defence, Adoko Nekyon, Minister of Planning, and Obote of involvement.[47] Rather than suspend Amin or investigate the allegations, Obote promoted Amin to army commander, and Amin spearheaded the forced exiling of Mutesa, though this was not a direct result of the smuggling accusations. It is believed that, had Obote made an attempt to prosecute or demote Amin, the latter would have revealed how Obote and government ministers were benefiting from illicit trading. Uganda had a legal ivory trade and the ivory brought in from Congo was laundered through government ivory sales.

Corruption and the involvement of the army in poaching and smuggling were to become even greater problems throughout the 1970s and the early 1980s, as Amin's overthrow of Obote in 1971 bred violence, total impunity for the army and then civil war, invasion and insurgency. But in the late 1960s, fear of overpopulation in the parks and the consequent need to cull to prevent environmental damage led to a major culling operation, with a consequent increase in legal ivory sales and therefore the ability to launder poached ivory. The main focus of the culling was Murchison Falls, where Laws judged that the growth rate of 6 per cent a year, combined with the concentration of elephants within the park, was causing the sort of vegetation destruction seen in Tsavo. Laws believed the population could suffer a catastrophic decline if culling was not carried out to prevent woodland destruction. The game department agreed with Laws's conclusions and Ian Parker's company, Wildlife Services, was contracted to kill 2,000 elephants and 4,000 hippos and to get maximum income from ivory.[48] Parker said that as soon as he was asked to carry out the cull he was approached by Indian businessmen in Kampala who demanded to know why he had not sold the ivory through them—his reply was that he hadn't started the culling and had no ivory to sell. The businessmen revealed that large quantities of ivory had already come onto the market, before the cull had started in earnest. These turned out to be some of the tusks that the Ugandan army was smuggling out of Congo, which Parker describes as "the first large ivory heist in post-colonial Africa and a sign of things to come".[49] Although Uganda had been a source of ivory for much of the twentieth century, with 34,792 elephants legally culled or hunted on licence between 1925 and 1959, the country had never developed its own ivory auctions. Ugandan dealers, mainly Asian businessmen, sold ivory via the auctions and traders in Mombasa. So when Parker's culling and export operation started in 1965 it was all run effectively from Kenya, where Parker was based.

In 1968, in a move interpreted as a way of laundering illicit tusks and using ivory as part of the system of political patronage, the government declared an amnesty for anyone possessing illegal ivory, offering a reward for any handed in. Within six months, over 81 tons had been surrendered. This was a huge amount by Ugandan standards. Exports had averaged 20–30 tons a year for most of the century and reached a peak of 60 tons in the late 1960s during the culling in Murchison Falls. The move followed Obote's decision to set up ivory auctions in Kampala rather than sell Ugandan ivory through Mombasa's auction and export system.[50] The amnesty brought large quantities of ivory onto the market to be sold in Kampala and so boost earnings without the Kenyans taking a large cut. Parker wrote that the chief game warden, Lawrence Tennant, refused to say much about the amnesty or who had ordered it, leaving the impression that it had been ordered directly by Obote.[51] There was circumstantial evidence to suggest that much of the 81 tons that flooded the new Kampala auctions was not old illegal stock but included a large amount of newly poached ivory. Surveys of elephant numbers in Murchison Falls and the Gulu Elephant Sanctuary in 1970 showed evidence of large-scale hunting of elephants there, above and beyond the scope of licensed culls. Enormous numbers of carcasses were spotted in aerial surveys, along with camps for butchering and drying the meat.

Far worse was to come. From the early 1970s through into the 1980s violence perpetrated by the army and the insurgency created a situation in which protection of wildlife became almost impossible. The Ugandan army, under the military dictatorship of Idi Amin, fought for power with invading Ugandan rebels and Tanzanian forces, and later

Obote's army and the National Resistance Army (NRA) of Yoweri Museveni, all fought for power. In an environment of mounting brutality, lawlessness and the impunity of the army and armed groups, ivory poaching became rampant, whether by Amin's army, by its remnants fleeing from defeat at the hands of the invading Tanzanians and their Ugandan allies, or later by the army fighting the NRA. The breakdown of national park administration and the inability of rangers to stop the army or insurgents from poaching led to the mass slaughter of elephants across the parks. It wasn't a case of ivory being used to fund armies or rebel groups, but of conflict creating a state of disorder in which corrupt soldiers and officials could poach and defeated forces would retreat taking whatever resources they could carry. Uganda's elephant population plummeted.

There were also indications that the growing instability in Uganda was rendering its parks and reserves vulnerable to incursions from Sudan, with armed Sudanese rebels who had taken refuge in northern Uganda using poaching to provide them with meat, as well as taking ivory and rhino horn to sell or exchange for arms. Uganda's parks director said in 1974 that Sudanese refugees in Uganda had poached in Kidepo Valley National Park, through which they moved to return to Sudan after the conclusion of a peace agreement between the rebels and the Sudanese government.[52] The Ugandan army had supported some of the rebels groups and, as with Congolese rebels, poached ivory was part of the relationship between them. Poaching was also increasing hugely in the Murchison Falls (now also known as Kabalega Falls), Queen Elizabeth and Rwenzori Parks, mainly a result of incursions by the Ugandan army.

The director of the Ugandan Institute of Ecology, Eric Edroma, wrote in 1975 that poaching of elephants had more than trebled in Rwenzori since 1971 and numbers in Murchison Falls had been reduced dramatically. He blamed large-scale commercial poaching for the wave of killing.[53] The following year, a conference on wildlife conservation was held in Rwenzori National Park and, as scientists flew over the park to reach the conference venue, they counted far more carcasses than live elephants.[54] The elephant researchers Eltringham and Malpas told the meeting that their study of elephants in Uganda indicated that the population of once over-crowded Murchison Falls had plummeted from 14,300 in 1974 to 2,250 in 1975, and that the national population was down from 60,000 to 6,000. They predicted a grim future for the country's elephants if poaching was not stopped.

The authors said that up to their annual survey in late 1973 they had seen large numbers of elephants in Murchison, Rwenzori, Queen Elizabeth and Kidepo Valley. When they conducted aerial surveys in September 1974, "a startling and radical change was detected when our counts revealed that, in twelve months, numbers had fallen to less than half in the Kabalega [Murchison] Falls Park and showed a considerable drop in the Rwenzori Park... our next counts in September 1975 dismally confirmed the decline without a shadow of doubt...the number of elephants in the Rwenzori Park was only a third to a quarter of what it should have been, while at Kabalega [Murchison] the drop was of the order of 85 per cent".[55] They concluded that gangs of poachers had shot family groups using automatic weapons. There had been no attempts to butcher the carcasses for meat or hides—only the tusks had been taken. It was "clear that the recent spectacular rise in the price of ivory has been the incentive".[56] At the conference, Parker said that in 1973 Uganda had exported ivory from between 11,000 and 20,000 dead elephants, with one ton of ivory equivalent to 100 elephants. During 1973, Douglas-Hamilton and Parker had carried out aerial surveys of Murchison and Queen Elizabeth; in the latter, there were 1,230 living elephants and 953 carcasses; in Murchison they found only 2,000 alive.[57]

By 1975, Murchison's elephant population was put at 1,061 (a tenth of its level in 1973), while Rwenzori was down from 2,864 to 931. The major cause was the combination of significant ivory price rises and virtually unlimited opportunity for soldiers and government officials, who could act with total impunity. The poaching severely reduced numbers, caused a breakdown of family structures and forced elephants in large, amorphous herds to take refuge in the remotest areas of the parks. Other studies indicated that the population in Queen Elizabeth of about 4,000 in the early 1970s had fallen to just a few hundred in the middle of the decade.[58]

Poaching slowed towards the end of the 1970s, simply because there were so few elephants left. But in 1979, another onslaught started when the Tanzanian army and Ugandan rebel forces invaded the country following Amin's incursions into northern Tanzania. Not only did retreating Amin loyalists kill game for meat and take ivory with them into southern Sudan—their flight also enabled Ugandan poachers to enter the parks without the danger of clashing with heavily armed military gangs, and the Tanzanian army also became involved in game poaching. The Tanzanians reportedly hunted for both meat and ivory, selling the meat to Ugandans and across the border in Zaire. In a report for the Uganda Institute of Ecology, Van Orsdol, who had been working in Rwenzori since 1977, estimated that 14,000 of the 46,500 large mammals in the park had been killed, including kob, hippo, elephant, buffalo and topi. Apart from the ecological effect, the "loss in economic terms is enormous, for tourism cannot be restored without the wildlife, and Uganda's three parks are estimated to earn some $15m per year".[59]

When researchers returned to Murchison Falls in late 1979, they saw only 400 elephants remaining, all gathered in one large herd and terrified of humans.[60] In the southern portion of the park, only 160 remained of a population that seven years before had numbered 9,000, while the north of the park had 1,200 remaining, of 5,000. In Rwenzori, numbers had collapsed from 3,000 to 150. A team from the IUCN examining carcasses from both parks found that most had been killed using automatic weapons, indicating that the end of the war had not meant the end of poaching by well-armed gangs.[61]

In late 1980, it was estimated that Uganda had a population of no more than 2,000 elephants. Edroma summed up the causes as: "The breakdown in law and order, the declining economy, the get-rich-quick drive, the spread of human settlements, the ease of access to elephant ranges, and the inability of the park and game staff to control the situation".[62] He noted with a certain irony that Amin's regime had banned licensed hunting in 1975 and the new government had banned all hunting of game in September 1979, but that in Uganda such laws "remain on paper only". In the early 1980s, poaching continued as the parks were under-funded and could not mount anti-poaching patrols. The political and economic chaos had taken their toll on the integrity of the staff and in Murchison a senior warden, Mishak Adupa, was found to be the ringleader of a group of rangers poaching the few remaining elephants in the park. One ranger told Douglas-Hamilton that during

Amin's time the park staff had no option but to cooperate with the army in poaching and smuggling ivory.[63]

As the parks were rehabilitated, the rangers adopted a shoot-to-kill policy and made little attempt to capture poachers or even retrieve their bodies. In the northern Kidepo Valley Park, Douglas-Hamilton said that Sudanese troops camped across the border were regularly raiding the park to hunt ivory. They were deterred when the rangers were given modern weapons and permission to fire on the Sudanese if they crossed the border.[64] Over the next couple of years there were reports that poaching had been reduced in Murchison, particularly the northern section, and that the park saw a slow recovery of elephant numbers to about 1,250. In Rwenzori, it seemed that numbers had risen slightly to 200, with reports of elephants moving back into the park from across the Zairean border. On the other hand, in the late 1980s, it was reported that there was an increase in poaching in Kidepo Valley as personnel from the Sudan People's Liberation Army (SPLA), which had started a rebellion against the government in Khartoum in 1984, were using Ugandan territory as a safe haven and harvesting game in the park.[65]

Sudan: poaching and war maintain the centuries old ivory trade

Following Sudan's independence in 1956, the long-established ivory trade run by traders from Sudan, but also involving the smuggling of ivory from southern Sudan into Ethiopia in return for guns, evolved but retained many basic structural characteristics, such as the role of Arab traders, and of Baggara or Rizeigat (or Janjaweed) militias raiding the south and neighbouring countries for ivory and cattle. The British departed leaving a country already experiencing conflict between communities in the south and the ruling Arab elite in Khartoum. This started in August 1955 as a mutiny by southern Sudanese troops based in Torit, Equatoria Province. Southerners rose up against northern officers and 366 northerners were killed in two weeks of fighting. Northern army units were flown in by the British and the mutiny was crushed. Mutineers who escaped became an insurgent movement that was to develop in the early 1960s into the Anyanya revolt, one of the many rebellions of the periphery against the northern, Arab-dominated centre that have plagued Sudan since independence.[66]

CONSERVATION, CORRUPTION, CRIME AND CONFLICT

The southern rebellion continued until the signing of peace accords between the rebels and the Khartoum government in 1972. It had three main effects on the ivory trade in the country: disruption of the established trade network in which hunters from among the Dinka, Nuer and other southern communities supplied ivory to Arab traders; growing disorder which, as in Uganda, prevented serious attempts to curb poaching and saw the government creating militias (notably the future Janjaweed) to fight the rebels (notably among the Baggara and Rizeigat, later known as Janjaweed) who had free rein to raid for cattle and hunt elephants; and evolution of the role of Sudanese armed groups, including the Janjaweed and South Sudanese armed groups as part of the secessionist movement of splintered from it, in hunting elephants beyond Sudan, in Uganda, Congo/Zaire, Chad and the CAR.

According to Parker, who gained inside knowledge of the Sudanese ivory networks while involved in gathering ivory for the southern autonomous government after the end of the Anyanya rebellion, rebels poached elephants in Sudan, Uganda and Congo and sold it via illicit networks in Ethiopia, Kenya, Uganda and Congo/Zaire.[67] The rebels, supported by successive Ugandan governments, traded ivory for arms with Amin's forces and later through networks of corrupt army officers and officials in the governments that succeeded him. In 1973, after the peace accords to end the first southern rebellion, Parker was asked to help the new regional government in the south to sell ivory, to raise funds needed to rehabilitate the economy. As he travelled around the southern provinces, he found that ivory had become a form of currency traded by the rebels, the Sudanese army and merchants. His role was to gather ivory held by a range of communities, former rebels, traders and government officials; he estimated that 200 tons of ivory worth more than $4m ($21.5m in 2015 values) had been taken out of Sudan before 1973, and much of the revenue squirrelled away by Sudanese politicians and officials in accounts abroad.[68] It was all illicit, but was rendered legal by a government amnesty intended to assist the sale of ivory to gain hard currency.

Parker drew up regulations for Juba's control over the issuing of hunting permits and for the certification and export of southern ivory, recommending that a Juba ivory auction be created. During this period

131

he bought ivory from Dinka, Nuer and other southern Sudanese hunt-ers, from Indian, British, Greek and Arab traders, from former Anyanya fighters and from Sudanese civil servants, including a judge and a num-ber of game wardens. The rising global price of ivory encouraged people to sell their stocks. He has said that Sudanese records for ivory sales were hugely inaccurate, under-estimating the amount sold abroad and the number of elephants killed. Sudan exported raw ivory but also had an old and thriving carving sector, with about 200 carvers working ivory and selling figurines, ornaments and other articles, mainly to foreign customers.

Saudi Arabia was an important staging post for illegal exports from Sudan. In his 1979 ivory trade report, Parker said that Sudan exported 52 tons of ivory in 1977 that were not recorded on customs records, although Saudi customs figures indicated that Saudi Arabia had actually exported 315 tons that year—all of which he believed came from Sudan.[69] Records of imports from Sudan for Hong Kong, the UK, West Germany, Spain, India and Saudi Arabia show that Sudan exported a huge 348 tons that year. The 315 tons which went to Saudi Arabia was all traded by one organisation, rather than multiple traders—Parker and Martin also reported that Sudan sold ivory to Japan, 43 tons in 1980 and 60 tons in 1981.[70] Given the Japanese preference for hard ivory (over the soft ivory of Sudan's), the presumption is that much of this quantity was ivory poached in Zaire or the CAR from forest ele-phants and smuggled to Sudan for export. Sudan's ivory exports had fallen in the final two years of the 1970s, only to rise again to levels above 180 tons a year in the early 1980s.

The period of relative peace in the south began to fracture in the early 1980s as the military ruler, President Numeiry, dismantled the autonomous structures created by the 1972 peace deal. One of his motives was to regain control of southern resources because of the discovery of oil there. This led to increasing conflict and to the full-scale resumption of civil war in 1984. But even before the rebellion by John Garang's SPLA in 1984, armed groups of Arabs from Darfur had been raiding southern regions for ivory and cattle. The horse- and camel-mounted groups (soon to be used as armed militias to fight the SPLA) were reported to have slaughtered large numbers of elephants in Bahr el-Ghazal.[71] Douglas-Hamilton supported this account, reporting that Arabs from the north, in gangs as large as sixty and armed with Kalashnikov or G3 automatic rifles, raided protected areas in the dry season, when elephants gathered near water, killing large numbers of animals.[72]

Western gave further evidence of this trend when he wrote that concern over the killing of elephants in Sudan seemed justified by the steep rise in Sudanese ivory exports, which had been low, but by 1983 amounted to a quarter of Africa's entire recorded trade. Western said that heavily armed groups from northern Sudan were regularly killing elephants in the south[73] and crossing into the CAR, Uganda and Zaire to poach. In 1984, Douglas-Hamilton estimated that Sudan had lost at least half its elephants since 1975.[74] Illegal hunting was taking place in Bahr el-Ghazal, Equatoria and the Upper Nile region, and the poorly armed game wardens had little chance of stopping poaching by insurgents, Janjaweed and the army. According to Günter Merz, a lecturer in wildlife management at the University of Juba, the SPLA rebels—like Anyanya rebels before them—were killing elephants and trading the ivory across the southern and eastern borders to Uganda and Ethiopia for weapons and ammunition. Merz said that the range of elephants in the south had been 650,000 square km in 1976, but poaching and uncontrolled hunting had steadily reduced it to 500,000 square km by 1984.[75]

The Sudanese role in poaching across eastern and central Africa was highlighted in an October 1983 article by the wildlife writer Brian Jackman in the British *Sunday Times*. He reported that Khartoum had become the transit point for tusks from about 100,000 elephants killed across the region. Large quantities of illicit tusks were being laundered through Sudan to facilitate their sale overseas. Sudan had become the largest source of raw ivory in the whole of Africa. Between 1979 and 1983, Douglas-Hamilton estimates that 900 tons of ivory had been exported by Sudan, the equivalent of 100,000 elephants. He says that one trader, Mohamed Awadalla el Awad in Khartoum, had become the single biggest ivory exporter in Africa. According to Martin, in 1982, he sold 220 tons of ivory worth $7m, and 164 tons in the opening nine months of 1983.[76] Martin added that much of the ivory must have come from outside Sudan, as he believed it was impossible for the ivory of 100,000 elephants to have been harvested in southern Sudan in the space of four years, given that the population of the country had been put at just 134,000 in 1975.

In 1984, the Sudanese government banned the export of raw ivory, but this did not stop the illicit trade and extensive poaching. It was from that same year that the government began using the Baggara and Rizeigat militias, often heavily involved in poaching, to fight the SPLA in Bahr el-Ghazal. There was also considerable evidence that the army, the police, ethnically recruited militias in the south and the SPLA rebels were all involved in killing elephants in protected areas, as well as across the border in Uganda, the CAR and Zaire.

5

THE KILLING FIELDS OF CENTRAL
AND SOUTHERN AFRICA

Although East Africa grabbed global attention in the early years of independence, central and southern Africa remained important areas for elephants and the ivory trade. The dense forests and savannahs of the Central African region housed a large proportion of Africa's elephants, while southern Africa's herds, depleted in the nineteenth century, staged a remarkable recovery before facing a new onslaught in Angola, Mozambique and Zambia and culling programmes in Zimbabwe and South Africa. Amid the seeming successes of conservation in some countries, there were serious problems posed by the continuing alienation of indigenous peoples from ownership or involvement in decision-making on wildlife, and by the nexus of crime and corruption. In southern Africa and Congo/Zaire, conflict played a role in creating incentives and opportunities for poaching on a substantial scale. The unresolved conflicts across central Africa undermined the work of game rangers in parks in Zaire/DRC/CAR and Chad, while politically motivated poaching operations in Angola, organised by South African Military Intelligence and the Angolan UNITA movement demonstrated how conflict could lead to the exploitation of ivory both to fund insurgency and to enrich those involved in the prosecution of war—as ever, the Angolan episode was far more complex than a simple case of elephants being killed to fund war.

IVORY

Table 2: Estimates for Central Africa's elephant populations, 1979–89

	1979(a)	1987(b)	1989(c)
Cameroon	16,200	21,200	21,200
Central African Republic	63,000	19,000	19,000
Chad	15,000	3,100	3,100
Congo	10,800	61,000	70,000
Equatorial Guinea	1,300	500	500
Gabon	13,400	76,000	76,000
Zaire	377,700	195,000	85,000
Total	497,400	375,800	274,800

Sources: (a) and (c): David Western, 'The Ecological Role of Elephants in Africa', *Pachyderm*, 12, 1989; (b): D. H. M. Cumming, R. F. du Toit and S. N. Stuart, *African Elephants and Rhinos: Status Survey and Conservation Action Plan*, Gland, Switzerland: IUCN, 1990.

Central Africa: conflict, corruption and confusion over numbers

These figures demonstrate one of the major problems in counting central Africa's elephant populations. For some countries there were no viable surveys and for others estimates varied considerably—both because of the extreme difficulty of counting elephants in heavily forested areas and because the growing use of low or high estimates to support the arguments of the competing camps in the bitter conservation arguments, which meant serious discussion of how to reconcile different census figures was overtaken by points scoring by all sides involved. The calculation of numbers in the CAR, Congo-Leopoldville (Zaire), Congo-Brazzaville and Gabon have varied wildly but are of particular importance, as these countries held the majority of Africa's forest elephants—the hardest species to count because of the thick forest canopy. Their populations make a huge difference to estimates of Africa's elephant population but, as Douglas-Hamilton explained to me, what we "barely know now is what goes on in Central Africa, under the forest canopy", and what density of elephants per square kilometre can be used to estimate overall populations from surveys.[1] This can lead to major difficulties in assessing the extent of poaching. The estimates of Cumming et al. suggested a consistent pace of decline in Central African populations, but admitted the problems of monitoring numbers in the lowland rainforests of Cameroon, Gabon, the Congo, Zaire and the CAR.

It wasn't just the region's forest elephants that were at risk. The savannah areas of central Africa (northern Zaire, the CAR and southern Chad), where elephants were more accessible and law enforcement weak, saw as fast a decline as any other African range states, with the ivory trade the primary cause. Even with varying and sometimes suspect estimates, it was clear that numbers were declining fast. The existence of a plethora of armed groups across the region had an effect on the level of illicit trade, though the role of conflict in providing opportunities and weapons for poaching and smuggling routes should not be interpreted in simplistic terms as a causal relationship between ivory and funding of war or insurgencies. Rather, conflicts limit anti-poaching measures and law enforcement and expand the number of groups equipped to kill elephants on a large scale, while opening up opportunities for corruption and cross-border illicit trade. The extent of legal and illegal hunting in the region meant that by the 1980s the average tusk size fell sharply, with hunters killing more and younger elephants (or more cows) to produce the same weight of ivory. As Martin, one of the leading analysts of the ivory trade, remarked, "the small size of tusks being exported and used in domestic carving industries supports the contention that the populations in these countries have been greatly reduced... Illegal hunting is extremely high in most of the Francophone countries which I visited."[2]

Gabon was a refuge for forest elephants as populations in the CAR and Zaire were depleted, but it, too, was exporting large quantities of ivory—about 6 tons a year according to official figures, but considerably more according to Parker's 1979 study of the African ivory trade. Large amounts were smuggled across the border into the Congo. The key traders were Senegalese who had established themselves in the smuggling networks of Central Africa.[3] Parker noted that the Congo Republic admitted to legal shooting of 150 elephants a year and domestic production of 11–16 tons of ivory, but that officials told him that exports in 1977 totalled 83 tons, suggesting that the vast majority sold through Brazzaville was brought in from Gabon and Zaire; this was confirmed by Douglas-Hamilton during his surveys of elephants in the region.[4]

Chad's elephant population was lower than that of Sudan, Cameroon or the CAR, and consisted mainly of savannah elephants in the south and east. A state of almost constant insurgency from the mid-1960s made law enforcement and surveys difficult, and served to flood the country with weapons that could be used for poaching. While much of the fighting was concentrated in the arid north, the presence of myriad militias and shifting alliances enabled opportunistic poaching and the development of smuggling routes to Sudan, Nigeria, Cameroon and the CAR. Research suggested that there was considerable commerce in ivory among government and military officials and incursions by Chadian poachers into the northern CAR. The conflict's intensification into a war in 1979, with Libyan and French intervention, led to increased poaching and "a catastrophic reduction in elephants"; Martin et al. wrote that eye-witnesses saw entire herds killed by military personnel using helicopters and vehicle-mounted anti-aircraft guns.[5] There is no suggestion that the ivory proceeds were used to fund continued warfare; rather, they were the source of wealth for faction or militia leaders, who used the conflict and resulting dislocation of government control to engage in criminal activity with impunity.

Chad's elephant population numbered around 15,000 before 1979, but estimates in the mid-1980s put it at 2,000–3,000 spread over a large range in the south. In 1985 there was still considerable commerce in ivory, much of it from the neighbouring CAR, where Chadian hunters on horseback, armed with spears and automatic weapons, hunted with little impediment in border areas. The period of continuous civil war (1979–1990) saw shifting alliances in Chad and the use of Darfur in Sudan as a safe rear base for various of the armed political factions and militias. Many of the Chadian troops were related to the Zaghawa or Rizeigat communities that straddled the border and provided a route to Khartoum for illicit ivory. The porous border allowed armed groups from Sudan, notably the Janjaweed militias from the Baggara-Rizeigat, to poach and smuggle contraband across the border—continuing a trading role that, as we have seen, they had engaged in across this area of the Sahel for centuries.

Zaire: corruption and conflict, a catastrophe for forest and savannah elephants

The forest basin of the Congo was home to huge numbers of elephants, the majority in the dense eastern forests. Consistent exploitation had reduced numbers in the nineteenth century, but there were no reliable estimates of the population either then or when Congo achieved independence in 1960. It was believed that the vast forest areas could hold more than a million forest elephants, with a sizeable savannah population in the northern Garamba National Park, but no scientific surveys were available to confirm this, and even when censuses were attempted they were far from authoritative because of the difficulties posed by counting in thick forest. The civil war and insurgency that followed independence made the protection of national parks impossible in areas of the east, where rebels, local militias and the army plundered local resources. Although external demand for ivory—providing a constant and expanding market—was a major factor in encouraging exploitation of wildlife resources, there was also a need for food and income to replace that swept away by conflict and the displacement of populations.

Garamba National Park was occupied by Congolese rebels from 1963 to 1965. They brought weapons in from Sudan and smuggled out ivory, which was sold to buy arms and enrich their leaders. A 1966 study by Kai Curry-Lindahl for the International Union for Conservation of Nature (IUCN) found that the north of the park had been almost denuded of wildlife as animals were killed for meat, ivory or horn. The park staff had been forced out of most of the park, their vehicles stolen or destroyed. The report lamented that in the north of Garamba elephants had suffered severely. Aerial and ground counts produced a total of 519 elephants. The killing of rhinos and elephants was largely for horn and ivory.[6] In 1969, Garamba was hit again when Sudanese Anyanya rebels moved into the park to avoid counter-insurgency sweeps in southern Sudan. Needing money to buy more arms, they virtually exterminated the white rhino population and killed many elephants. Dr Jacques Verschuren, the director of national parks in the Congo, said that elephants had been depleted across the park, from about 10,000 at independence to around 5,000 in November 1969.[7] Curry-Lindahl was even more pessimistic, calculating that conflict had reduced elephants in Garamba from 9,983 in 1960 to 1,202 in 1963 and 700 in 1966. He believed that the decline was a result of both Congolese rebel activities while occupying the park and regular incursions by poachers from Sudan. Park rangers were helpless against these groups and many have been killed in Garamba over the last five decades trying to protect the wildlife.

IVORY

In the 1970s, with the rise in global ivory prices and increased demand from outside Africa, Zaire's forests and northern savannahs became the single biggest source of ivory, according to Parker's authoritative 1979 report on the trade. Harvesting of elephants was enabled through the corruption of government officials and shifting insurgencies in the north and east, which meant that many remote areas were not under government control; those that were suffered from plundering of wildlife and other natural resources by the army. Military commanders, local militias and rebels competed for resources, including ivory, both to finance their forces and to accumulate personal wealth.[8] The remnants of Laurent Kabila's rebel forces—on the Lumumbist side in the civil war—retreated to the forests of South Kivu, remaining an irritant to the Mobutu government. They survived by smuggling ivory, diamonds and gold into Tanzania. But the bulk of ivory poached in Zaire was smuggled out through Burundi, Zambia and Sudan, or laundered through trade networks in Antwerp. Parker estimated that at independence the country's recorded exports were around 50 tons a year. Legal sales fell during the civil war as smuggling increased, but rose under Mobutu's rule to 100 tons in 1969.

Verschuren wrote in 1975 that Zaire remained an important refuge, though elephant ranges were shrinking because of human settlement, exploitation and war. Elephants were no longer present in lower Zaire, Kwango, Kasai or Ubangui, but were abundant in the large intact forest blocks, particularly in the Salonga National Park in central Zaire. In the savannah areas of the north, notably Garamba, they were vulnerable but numbers had recovered enough for gatherings of 600 animals to have been seen by researchers.[9] Outside the reserves, elephants had become more or less nocturnal, sheltering in the marshes or dense vegetation, and their presence could only be confirmed through dung pile counts. In Virunga, between 1960 and 1970, over 80 per cent of the park's elephants were killed. The main threat there came from hunters and soldiers coming across the border from Rwanda.

The account so far of the fate of Zaire's elephants has focused on conflict and the actions of rebel groups or foreign poachers. But corruption was the most serious problem, as it encouraged and facilitated poaching and smuggling, ensuring there was little effective law enforcement. Douglas-Hamilton was told by US embassy officials in Kinshasa that diplomats had seen Zairean soldiers loading ivory onto military planes in the north of the country and that Political Bureau members of Mobutu's ruling Mouvement Populaire de la Révolution were using the army to smuggle ivory to South Africa.[10] As prices rose in the 1970s and corruption increased, poaching and smuggling became a way of life for many. The rising price of ivory meant that gold and diamond smugglers branched out into ivory, supplied by those hunting to survive or by army officers, militia leaders and rebel forces. There was legal hunting alongside poaching, but the scale is impossible to assess, as legal permits were often copied multiple times to enable laundering of poached ivory. In August 1978, the Mobutu government banned the hunting of elephants and the trade in ivory, but with no workable enforcement apparatus and corruption rife, it remained a paper commitment, especially as the officials charged with enforcing it were often as venal as the poachers.

Corruption, patron-client networks and the pure need for government employees and poor rural dwellers to engage in a variety of illicit economic activities were the hallmarks of Zaire under Mobutu and, to a great extent, his successors—Laurent and Joseph Kabila. During Mobutu's rule, civil servants, junior officers and even government ministers were so badly paid that embezzling public funds or smuggling—of coffee, gems, precious metals or ivory—was a necessity to pay rent, buy food or clothes and pay for children's schooling.[11] Ivory shipments as large as three tons were being facilitated by senior government officials. Smuggling was masterminded by senior politicians, who used corrupt officials and members of the armed forces to gather and transport the tusks. Much of the illicit exporting of ivory was in the hands of Asian businessmen, who had networks of contacts in Kenya, Uganda and Tanzania. The ivory was frequently exchanged through such merchants for goods in short supply in Zaire, creating a lucrative two-way trade (a modern version of the trade between Zanzibar and eastern Congo in the nineteenth century). The traders and their political patrons banked a substantial part of the earnings from illicit ivory outside Zaire. This was just part of the extreme gatekeeper or rent-seeking activities of the elite under Mobutu.

A 1983 census estimated that elephant numbers had declined by 60 per cent between 1976 and 1983 and that large areas of north-eastern

Zaire outside the parks were completely devoid of elephants, as a result of regular incursions by Sudanese Arab raiders armed with automatic weapons.[12] In an assessment of Africa's elephant population in 1987, Douglas-Hamilton emphasised that the elephants of northern Zaire were under constant threat from Arab poachers entering the country from the CAR and Sudan. He concluded that Zaire still had a larger elephant range than any other country, but the reduction through hunting meant that estimates of 500,000 in the mid-1980s were highly optimistic—though Douglas-Hamilton's estimates were criticised by Parker for being too pessimistic.[13] It is by no means certain which of them was nearer the mark, but all estimates showed a steady decline in elephants in the Congo Basin.

In the Salonga National Park and surrounding areas of central Zaire, corruption remained the main threat. Rangers frequently confiscated automatic weapons from poachers and returned the guns to the army or police, only for them immediately to turn up again in the hands of other poachers. Large areas of Salonga and Maiko National Parks were reported to be in the hands of poachers, and one group of researchers who carried out repeated surveys in Zaire's parks in 1989 concluded that it was impossible to distinguish between poachers, soldiers and bandits: "often they are one and the same". They reported that on one verified occasion in 1989, poachers were able to kidnap forty local villagers to make them carry the tusks to Kisangani, with no attempt at interference by the police or army.[14]

The estimate of numbers from the surveys at the end of the 1980s was 8,330 in Salonga, 4,000 in Maiko and the surrounding areas, 7,290–7,630 in Ituri, 8,040 in Lomani and 8–10,000 in the Kahuzi-Biega region. Zaire had domestic ivory stocks of 1,500 tons and official figures indicated that, despite the ban on hunting and domestic ivory trading, the country exported 705 tons between 1979 and 1988. This is believed only to be the tip of the ivory iceberg, with considerably more exported illegally to Burundi, Zambia, the CAR and Sudan. Alers et al. believe that as many as 400,000 elephants were killed in Zaire in the decade leading up to the October 1989 ivory trade ban by CITES (the Convention on International Trade in Endangered Species of Wild Fauna and Flora).[15] By 1989, estimates suggested that Zaire had between 85–112,000 elephants; about 25,000 of these were in savannah areas in the north-east, the rest forest elephant populations spread across the rainforests of central and eastern Zaire. Two thirds of Zaire's forest elephants had disappeared over a thirty-year period from the mid-1960s.

Emperor Bokassa oversees the destruction of CAR herds

For over a century, the CAR has been a great reservoir of resources, from ivory to meat, diamonds, slaves and gold. In the nineteenth century, over three million elephants were thought to have been killed there to supply demand from Europe. After colonial rule, successive governments plundered elephant herds for ivory, with the meat sold in local markets. Hunting in the CAR became so intense that, of an estimated population of 80,000–100,000 elephants in 1976, numbers crashed to 10–15,000 by the mid-1980s.[16]

The progressive depletion was a result of the substantial legal hunting overseen by President Jean-Bedel Bokassa, as well as poaching by CAR hunters and raiders from Chad and Sudan.[17] During Bokassa's reign (1966–79), the ivory trade in the CAR was run by a private company, La Couronne, of which he was a major shareholder and chief executive by proxy. It had a monopoly over the legal trade but was also involved in illegal trading, including of ivory poached in Zaire. Parker said the company encouraged poaching and smuggling, and that in 1978 around 4,000 elephants were killed in the CAR to feed the export market.[18] Exports by the company in that year totalled 165 tons, approximately 16,000 elephants—indicating that the legal trade was outweighed by domestic poaching and the smuggling in of ivory from neighbouring countries. The *Traffic Bulletin* said in March 1981 that only 1 per cent of the company's ivory came from the CAR, with 79 per cent from Zaire and 20 per cent from Sudan. La Couronne organised the harvesting of ivory domestically and acquired its ivory from a network of middlemen, who gave guns to villagers to bring in the ivory, ruthlessly suppressing all competitors. Poachers in the CAR and those who entered the country from Chad and Sudan used automatic weapons but also hunted from horseback, using spears to cripple the animals. It was estimated that 6,000 elephants were poached annually in the CAR during the last years of Bokassa's rule,[19] some of the ivory crossing the borders into Chad and Sudan. Income from ivory up to the mid-1980s averaged $10–25m ($21.8–54.5m in today's values), enriching Bokassa and La Couronne and accruing after his downfall to the corrupt traders and officials involved in illicit trade.

Bokassa was deposed in 1979 by the French army's Operation Barracuda, which returned to power former president David Dacko (whose own overthrow, also with French backing, had brought Bokassa to power in 1966). The new government banned elephant hunting and ivory trading and, in August 1980, joined CITES. However, *Traffic* reported that, despite this, 120 tons of ivory, the equivalent of about 12,000 elephants, was exported from Bangui in the first six months of Dacko's rule.[20] Smuggling increased hugely because the legal trade had been suppressed, but also because La Couronne and Bokassa had previously enjoyed control of all aspects of it. Their removal gave poachers greater freedom to operate. Despite having imposed a ban, Dacko allowed trusted allies to export ivory without permits and persuaded the French government to release ivory from the CAR that had been seized by French customs—there were indications that, for some time, France had been allowing imports of ivory from the CAR without adequate checks on documentation, on the orders of senior members of the government.[21] In December 1981, Dacko reversed his ban on elephant hunting and the trade in ivory grew, with the CAR exporting 350 tons between 1979 and 1983; a large proportion of the total was believed by trade monitoring groups to have come from Zaire.[22]

The CAR's own elephants suffered at the hands of indigenous poachers and those from Chad and Sudan. In 1983, a joint WWF-IUCN survey of the population in the northern national park, Gounda St Floris, showed that 532 of the park's 3,000 elephants had been killed that year, many of them speared, with horse tracks found near the carcasses by survey teams. When Douglas-Hamilton carried out a survey of both Gounda St Floris and Bamingui-Bangoran, on the border with Chad, he found Chadian pastoralists in the parks with large numbers of cattle. Poaching was continuing, with the involvement of senior CAR ministers. One politician was said to have seized guns paid for as part of a UN anti-poaching project and handed them over to hunters working for him. Douglas-Hamilton counted 4,300 elephants but 7,900 carcasses.[23] It was estimated that poachers killed 80 per cent of the elephants in savannah areas in the late 1970s and 1980s. Most of the hunters were part of large, horse-borne gangs of Sudanese and Chadians. They would poach scores of elephants in expeditions that could last as long as a year, with several gangs operating in CAR parks.

Under the rule of General Kolingba, who overthrew Dacko in September 1981, there was a brief period when the army suppressed poaching, after Kolingba visited one of the parks, saw the carcasses of poached elephants and was fired on by poachers as he flew over in a helicopter. One raid by the army captured twenty-four poachers carrying 220 tusks loaded on horses and camels. This crackdown was short-lived, however, and a 1984 survey estimated that the CAR had only 10–15,000 elephants, compared with 80–100,000 in 1976.[24] Poaching was most serious in the vast areas of savannah along the Sudanese and Chadian borders. By 1982, the CAR was again one of Africa's largest exporters of its own and others' poached ivory, with 150 tons (about 15,000 elephants) exported under legal permits; most was believed to have been poached, with a massive forging operation under way to provide false certificates.

Burundi: the focus of the illegal trade in the Great Lakes region

The most blatant example of a country profiting from illicit tusks was Burundi. It had no wild elephants, but it exported 1,300 tons of ivory between 1965 and 1986—the equivalent of 12–13,000 elephants. Ivory was smuggled in from Tanzania, Zambia, Zaire, Gabon and Mozambique. Successive Burundian governments allowed imports of poached ivory, certifying it as legal before exporting it. A country with few resources, torn by civil war, Burundi was in desperate need of income and freely allowed the smuggling of ivory, coffee, gold, and other commodities from neighbouring states. Soon after independence, Burundi became a regional entrepôt for ivory and its annual sales rose steadily. Belgium joined CITES in October 1983 and thereafter adhered to its import and export regulations, limiting its role as a channel for illicit tusks exported from Burundi. However, Burundi continued to act as a major trading hub for ivory from East and Central Africa, using different routes to export it to Asia.

Much of the Burundian trade was organised by one Asian businessman, Zulfikar Rahemtullah, who had connections across East Africa and

Asia. He bought tusks from Senegalese, Malian and Guinean traders, who trucked ivory from Zaire and Francophone states. When Burundi wanted to join CITES, the latter asked Parker to examine Burundi's ivory stocks and trading networks; he found that Zairean ivory made up about 33 per cent of Burundi's exports, Zambian ivory about 30 per cent and Tanzanian ivory 23 per cent, with small quantities from Sudan, the CAR, Zimbabwe and Botswana.[25] The Environmental Investigation Agency (EIA) was told by Costa Mlay, of the Tanzanian Wildlife Department, that ivory poached in the Selous game reserve was transported to Burundi by Somali truckers through Dodoma, Singida and Kigoma, in the north. He said that the smugglers had no problem getting it through customs, because Burundi allowed anything of value to be imported tax-free, adding, "They only tax the ivory when they export it". The other route, according to Mlay, used containers of second-hand clothes exported from Dubai to Burundi via Tanzania. Halfway across Tanzania, ivory was hidden in the containers. A Burundi customs official would arrive and seal the containers, and they would go back to Dubai without ever entering Burundi. The Tanzanians discovered this when a container lorry crashed—they confiscated 475 tusks.[26]

In the early to mid-1980s, the adherence of increasing numbers of states to CITES and the development of a quota system reduced Burundi's income from ivory. Ivory with CITES certificates fetched a higher price, undercutting Burundi's uncertified tusks. Burundi decided to apply to CITES, which wanted Burundi to join in order to close an illegal route. But it would be a problem if the country had large stocks of illegally acquired ivory, which could lead to CITES being accused of laundering poached tusks. When Parker was surveying the stockpile in Bujumbura, he was approached by Rahemtullah, who said he had 40 tons of ivory and would pay Parker to help him sell it on a CITES permit, which would double its price. He was working on the belief, according to Parker, that "If Burundi joined CITES all the ivory legally in the country at the time would be 'pre-convention stock' and become CITES-acceptable". Parker says he marked the tusks with an indelible pen to indicate that they had been inspected. But Rahemtullah had a more cunning scheme in mind and bought up 20 tons more from rival dealers at low prices, with the intention of legalising it with CITES codes. Parker found that when the list of registered tusks was drawn up it included 300 tusks he had not seen, the tusks bought by Rahemtullah. He says he had little choice but to leave them on the list rather than start the certification process again.[27]

Parker explained the discrepancy to CITES, who remained keen to get Burundi onside and were prepared to see the stocks exported so that Burundi would have no more illicit ivory. Rahemtullah's ivory was exported to Antwerp but another 30 tons of unregistered ivory was said to have been sent to Singapore. After this episode, Burundi promised CITES that it would bring no more illicit ivory into the country, a condition of fully certified membership, yet it somehow exported another 110 tons between November 1986 and October 1987—giving an indication of the CITES's inability to deal with the continuing illegal trade.

Negotiations for Burundi to join CITES resumed in 1988 under the new president, Pierre Buyoya, and once more Parker was involved. He was again contacted by Rahemtullah, who said that an ivory trader called White was in Burundi with another man trying to buy stocks of unregistered ivory. Parker identified the man as Ant White (a former Selous Scout special forces soldier from Rhodesia, who was involved in trading poached ivory from Zimbabwe and Mozambique, and enjoyed close connections with South African Military Intelligence);[28] the other man was said to be the notorious South African spy Craig Williamson, later involved in the Operation Lock affair. White was a dealer who had previously bought 10 tons of ivory from Burundi and exported it via Dar es Salaam. Burundi now had a total of 109 tons of ivory worth $13m, which CITES refused to register. Jacques Berney of CITES told Burundi that if it sold the ivory before full membership and devoted the money to conservation or donated it to CITES, then it could still become a member. The Burundians insisted the ivory was legal under Burundi law. Parker says he advised the government to sell the ivory straight away, before joining CITES.[29]

There was to be another twist in the story. Parker came to believe that ivory from Burundi was being shipped out via Mozambique and that there was a connection with both the rebel movement Renamo (Mozambican National Resistance) and corrupt Mozambican government officials in Beira[30]—this fits in with information given to the author by South African intelligence sources about the Renamo link and White's involvement. The missing piece of this complex jigsaw was that, just as

IVORY

Table 3: Estimates for southern Africa's elephant populations, 1979–89

	1979 (a)	1987 (b)	1989 (a)
Angola	12,400	12,400	12,400
Botswana	20,000	51,000	51,000
Malawi	4,500	2,400	2,400
Mozambique	54,800	18,600	18,600
Namibia	2,700	5,000	5,000
South Africa	7,800	8,200	8,200
Zambia	150,000	41,000	41,000
Zimbabwe	30,000	43,000	43,000
Total	282,200	181,600	181,000

Sources: (a) David Western, 'The Ecological Role of Elephants in Africa', *Pachyderm*, 12, 1989; (b) D. H. M. Cumming, R. F. du Toit and S. N. Stuart, *African Elephants and Rhinos: Status Survey and Conservation Action Plan*, Gland, Switzerland: IUCN, 1990.

Burundi was trying to shift its ivory before joining CITES, the Mozambican government informed CITES that its quota for ivory exports would increase from 1,000 tusks in 1987 to 19,000 in 1988. The Mozambicans said this was a result of huge stocks of ivory captured from Renamo when their Gorongosa base was taken. Parker thinks that there was a plan for White to buy the Burundi ivory at a low price, as it was not CITES-certified, and then sell it at full CITES price through Mozambique. The Burundian ivory would be sold on Mozambique's quota at $200 per kilo, bringing in at least $16m, double the price obtainable in Burundi. From accounts of the Renamo-South African connection (see below), however, it is likely that the stock of ivory really was from elephants poached in Mozambique by the rebels or the South African Defence Force (SADF) and transported to Burundi. In the end, Mozambique didn't export the 19,000 tons on the quota, and no one knows what happened to the massive stock in Burundi.

South and southern Africa: conflict, corruption and ivory as an apartheid war asset

Between 1981 and 1989, southern African elephant populations showed a 42 per cent decline, with Zambia and Mozambique experi-

148

encing catastrophic falls, while Botswana, Namibia and South Africa showed growth. Zimbabwe's drop in numbers was largely a result of culling to keep the population around the 45,000 mark,[31] but also reflected a growth in localised poaching.

Botswana: conservation, community support and the culling dilemma

If one country seems to have gone in a different direction to most range states, and avoided major problems of poaching and illicit trade in ivory, it is Botswana. Since independence, its elephant population has risen steadily. In 1993, government ministers and wildlife officials told the author that the country had 60,000 elephants with a carrying capacity of 50,000, but the number is now between 130,000 and 207,545, according to dry-season aerial surveys by the Botswana department of wildlife in 2012 and 2013.[32] The large variation results from the two surveys varying in timing and the areas covered, according to Michael Flyman of the Department of Wildlife and National Parks, and also because of elephant migration across northern Botswana, Zimbabwe, Zambia, Namibia and Angola.[33]

Under British colonial rule, control over Botswana's wildlife had shifted gradually from chiefs to the administration, though without entirely stripping them of influence. Communities owned the wildlife through the office of the chiefs, and Tswana-speaking groups like the Bamangwato had been effective overlords for Khoisan and others whom they permitted to hunt in their territories. When white hunters moved in to hunt ivory commercially, they did so only with permission from the chiefs, but British and Boer hunting severely depleted the elephants of Chobe. Those that survived moved into inaccessible areas of the Okavango Delta. However, protection measures instituted by chiefs like Khama and then the regulation of hunting under the British enabled elephant numbers to recover. The government veterinary officer reported in 1935 that elephants and buffalo were becoming common along the Chobe River, after years of few sightings. The Chobe Forest Reserve became a major breeding area for elephants and the region a gathering place for herds moving from Namibia's Caprivi Strip and Zimbabwe.

In 1960, the Chobe Game Reserve was established and had a growing elephant population, with many animals migrating from Hwange in Zimbabwe to avoid overcrowding. The reserve was established with the support of local chiefs and with limited opposition from the sparse population in the area, though there was a problem of elephants from the reserve raiding gardens that lay outside, leading to the shooting of a number of crop-raiders in the early 1960s. The role of traditional leaders created a popular perception of game as common property, with chiefs playing a key role in deciding its utilisation.[34] This shifted somewhat after independence in 1966, with the government taking ownership of wildlife, leading to conflict, as rural people lost control over wildlife resources they considered to be theirs. Another cause of antagonism was "dissatisfaction with compensation for wildlife-caused losses... the disappearance of benefits from wildlife-based tourism that now go into central government coffers or to private enterprise; and constraints on resource harvesting in historically utilised areas... there is little sense of responsibility to protect wildlife... when it is perceived that these no longer belong to nor benefit them".[35]

Prior to independence, some European residents had called for protected areas, taking the view that "The African, when he has not been made aware of the value of the game to himself, is likely to slaughter indiscriminately if control is removed". To give them their due, the writers of that comment, Robert and June Kay, did also bewail the damage caused and paltry benefit brought by European hunting parties killing large amounts of game.[36] These concerned white residents called for the formation of a Bechuanaland Fauna Preservation Society, but also for measures to ensure that local communities benefited through taking a percentage of profits from hunting safaris. Another conservationist wrote that African subsistence hunting was having a negligible effect on game numbers, but a threat could develop as commercial hunting companies moved into Botswana because of "scarcity of game concentrations elsewhere and by political strife in countries where safari firms have hitherto flourished."[37] The white conservationists sought support for protection of these areas among Batswana communities near Moremi, Chobe and the Central Kalahari. The Tswana community in the Moremi region of the Okavango voted to create the Moremi Wildlife Reserve in 1963, following the earlier establishment of reserves in Chobe and the Central Kalahari. This community lived in an area where tsetse flies discouraged cattle raising and the soil was unsuitable for cultivation. At a *kgotla* meeting (a traditional forum allowing for community discussion and a role in decision-making) presided over by Batawana regent Elizabeth Moremi, the majority of the community present voted to establish a reserve and limit hunting to areas outside its boundaries.[38] What was important, despite the initial pressure having come from Europeans, was that the Batawana leaders and *kgotla* had made the decision, rather than having a decision imposed on them. As Beinart and Hughes emphasised, the process was under African control through the Batawana community, in cooperation with the Fauna Preservation Society, and was "a community management model, forty years before its time".[39] The reserve and other parts of the Okavango that had been protected became national parks or reserves in 1977, with the transfer of local control to the government.

After independence, attempts by the Botswana government and cattle-owners to increase cattle herds (the main national asset until the discovery of diamonds) began to falter in the north. Outbreak of disease, notably tsetse-borne trypanosomiasis, led plans to expand cattle farming there to be abandoned, leaving large areas open to game and the expanding elephant population. In unprotected areas of the north there was an increase in hunting, with concession areas created around reserves/parks developing a lucrative industry attracting foreign hunters. But the off-take did not slow the increase in elephant numbers. In the 1970s, about 500 elephant licences were issued annually. Between 1979 and 1982, a total of 1,515 were provided, prior to a temporary suspension as a result of concerns over falling tusk weights. Botswana Game Industries was established by a commercial hunter called Peter Becker, who had moved to Botswana from Kenya. The company dealt in ivory, skins and meat products and became one of the largest dealers in ivory and other wildlife products in Africa.

Although the extension of state control reduced local control over wildlife, the retention of some involvement of chiefs and communities in wildlife decision-making perhaps explains how a lingering sense of ownership helped prevent widespread poaching. The sense of local involvement has been developed through an accountable political system combining parliamentary government with *kgotla* meetings. The relative sparseness of populations in rural areas, the limited role of cultivation and the progressive fencing of cattle-rearing areas to prevent the spread of disease has also helped. The wetter areas around the Okavango, Chobe, Savuti and Linyanti and the very arid areas of the central Kalahari and Tuli have remained havens for wildlife, with less conflict with local people than might have been expected, though this varies from area to area; for instance, the Okavango Panhandle experienced greater problems, because of settlements in areas through which elephants moved regularly between wet and dry seasons. The ability to manage human-wildlife conflict went hand in hand with efforts to educate people about wildlife and ways in which it could be turned into an economic asset.

The increase in the size of protected areas did not put an end to legal hunting and ivory trading. Botswana Games Industries played a major role in the trade and Botswana started keeping records of sales in the mid-1970s. Between 1975–8, Botswana exported 14,192 kg of ivory a year.[40] Botswana was one of the early African signatories to CITES and kept tighter control over its hunting industry than did most other African states. Poaching of elephants was not widespread, compared with buffalo or antelope poaching for meat, which was more prevalent on the margins of protected areas or safari concessions. In his ivory trade survey in 1979, Parker suggested that some of the ivory sold on Botswana permits may have been brought into the country from poaching in Angola or Zambia. In 1982, concerned at an increase in poaching, Botswana suspended the issuing of elephant hunting licences. In a 1984 report on the Botswana ivory trade, Martin estimated that, with a steadily growing elephant population, around 1,000 elephants could be removed each year without seriously affecting numbers, providing enough ivory both to supply the small domestic demand and to generate export income because of high external demand. He also noted that wildlife officials were becoming concerned at a significant increase in poaching in the far north bordering the Caprivi Strip, and that "poachers from Namibia have crossed the eastern Caprivi Strip and shot elephants along the Chobe River".[41] The increase in poaching, along with migration patterns, may explain the rise and fall in elephant numbers in northern Botswana: 39,511 in 1980 to 42,792 in 1984 and 50,000 in 1985, but dipping to 44,670 in 1987 and then rising again to 69,500 in 1989.

THE KILLING FIELDS OF CENTRAL AND SOUTHERN AFRICA

Poaching was a threat both to income from hunting and to the growing and lucrative high-cost, low-volume tourist safari industry in Okavango and Chobe. This was why the Botswana Defence Force (BDF) became heavily involved in anti-poaching and wildlife protection. It helped that the BDF deputy commander (son of the president, and later president himself), Ian Khama, had developed a strong personal commitment to conservation and a financial stake in the tourism industry. The BDF was formed in 1977 as a response to the growing conflict on Botswana's borders and the dangers of spill-over or incursions resulting from the war in Rhodesia, as well as the South African SADF's occupation of parts of southern Angola and fight against SWAPO (South West African People's Organization) in Namibia. The areas most vulnerable were along the northern and north-eastern borders with Namibia's Caprivi Strip and with Zimbabwe. These were areas of elephant concentration and migration routes, tourist attractions and hunting concessions. While poaching had always taken place around there, it had chiefly been small-scale subsistence hunting for meat. The growth in poaching of elephants and rhino near the borders was a new phenomenon, and the anti-poaching units in the park were often facing poaching gangs armed with automatic weapons.

The BDF was deployed in border areas and used to hunt down poachers—a deployment and mode of operation that continues today. Although there was some surprise when it was first announced, there was a logic to the move, as "the BDF was the only institution with the firepower to combat well-armed poachers—that most of the poachers were foreign did mean that there was some public support for efforts to stop them. The government portrayed this as defence of economic security against an external threat."[42] The poachers entering northern Botswana, particularly organised Zambian gangs, were after rhino horn and ivory. Botswana had only a small rhino population and it was soon more or less wiped out, though the poachers made less of a dent in elephant numbers.

The BDF used small, mobile commando squadrons with specialist trackers to hunt down the poachers. When poaching increased in the mid- to late 1980s, with thirty-five elephants killed in 1987, the patrols were stepped up, and the level of poaching quickly reduced. Dan Henk, who carried out a study of BDF anti-poaching operations, was told that by 1989 regular BDF units were supporting the commandos, with four 100-strong companies deployed. Poachers were regularly being intercepted and many were killed in clashes with BDF units. Increasing numbers of the poachers were found to have come from Namibia. The anti-poaching measures kept the killing of elephants to a minimum. Elephant numbers increased to well over 60,000 in 1989, reaching a point where the government and wildlife officials were concerned that they were exceeding the carrying capacity.[43]

With poaching under control, Botswana's main connection with the ivory trade centred on its use as a transit route for poached ivory linked to the SADF in Angola and for illicit tusks from Zaire and Zambia. These were moved through Botswana by road, to South Africa. As Botswana was a member of the Southern African Customs Union (SACU) there was little checking of South Africa-bound freight at border posts, especially if it came from Namibia, also part of the SACU area. This trade through Botswana had no effect on the country's own population—numbers rose steadily and in the early 1990s topped 60,000, increasing to 78,304 in 1994. Conservation officials, NGOs and the Botswana foreign minister all told the author in interviews in Gaborone in November 1993 that the major expansion in elephant numbers meant that culling might prove necessary. It was for this reason that the government wanted Botswana's elephants removed from CITES Appendix 1 listing and sought permission to sell ivory stocks and tusks harvested in culls or in hunting concessions, which would generate income to support conservation.

Zimbabwe: increasing numbers despite culling and poaching

Protection measures introduced by the British and maintained by the settler administration in Rhodesia excluded the African population from hunting, but provided extensive opportunities for settler and big-game hunting, while enabling steady growth in elephant numbers. Estimated at just 4,000 in 1900, they had grown to 60,000 in the 1960s, resulting in regular culling in areas where large populations were believed to be damaging the environment and destroying woodland. The major populations were in Sengwa and Matusadona in the north-west around Lake Kariba, Mana Pools, Hwange in the south-west and Gonarezhou in the south-east. In Hwange alone, 3,000 elephants were culled between 1971 and 1974, with the aim of maintaining numbers at 13,000. At least 2,500 elephants were culled in Gonarezhou in the 1970s. One of the game wardens in charge of the cull, Ron Thomson, believed that the need to cull should be adapted to provide substantial income to poor rural dwellers in areas of high elephant density, to prevent poaching and ensure regulated off-take and utilisation of meat, hides and ivory.[44] This was later to be taken up through the Communal Areas Management Programme for Indigenous Resources (CAMPFIRE).

The rationale behind the cull was that elephant numbers were increasing beyond the ability of habitats to support them without destruction of woodland and the consequent effect on browsers, like rhino, sable and roan. But the policy was also part of the overall approach to wildlife involving substantial commercialisation through safari hunting, tourism and the sale of ivory, horn, hides and meat. The wildlife authorities advocated these policies as they garnered funds for development and anti-poaching operations in national parks and they represented, in their view, a sustainable-use approach to wildlife.[45] African communities also approached wildlife on a utilisation basis, but had been excluded from legal hunting and even required the wildlife department's assistance when animals threatened crops, livestock or people. The only role for Zimbabwean Africans in the settler wildlife set-up was as trackers, skinners, drivers or domestic staff at hunting or tourist camps.

The isolation of the country after Rhodesia's Unilateral Declaration of Independence (UDI) in 1965 limited the influence of international conservation NGOs on wildlife policy. Sanctions also had the effect of creating a trade relationship with South Africa in ivory and wildlife products, the best way to evade sanctions. White-ruled Rhodesia sold considerable quantities of ivory from culling operations but also, according to Parker—who had the chance to inspect tusks exported via South Africa—forest elephant ivory from central Africa. Parker says that through his ivory trade connections he knew that, despite sanctions, Rhodesia was exporting beef to Gabon in exchange for ivory, which was sold via South Africa with Rhodesian certification.[46]

Following UDI, a bush war was waged by black nationalist groups (including future ruling party ZANU, the Zimbabwe African National

Union) against the white settler regime. One side-effect of this conflict, fought from the mid-1960s to 1980, was a decline in poaching, due to the dangers of hunting in remote wilderness areas where guerrillas and the Rhodesian army were operating. This is the opposite of what happened in many elephant range states in Africa when conflict occurred—in most, it reduced anti-poaching capabilities, introduced automatic weapons into the countries and forced people to find new means of subsistence when war disrupted local economies. In Rhodesia, subsistence hunters stayed out of the bush, fearing being shot during counter-insurgency operations. The spread of the war into wildlife areas also interrupted culling operations, leading to an increase in elephant numbers. The one place in Rhodesia where the liberation war—and later the civil war in Mozambique—provided the right environment for poaching was Gonarezhou, along the Mozambican border. Rhodesian special forces conducted operations into Mozambique to assist the rebel Renamo movement and fight Zimbabwean guerrillas. Members of Rhodesian special forces were believed to have become involved in both selling natural-mortality ivory and poaching elephants (see section below on Mozambique). Right at the end of the liberation war, when the end of white-minority rule was in sight, there was a massive slaughter of elephants by Rhodesian special forces and other soldiers in the Chizarira Game Reserve. Hundreds if not thousands of elephants were killed using machine-guns and automatic weapons, the tusks flown out to air bases in South Africa under close cooperation between the Rhodesians and South African Military Intelligence and special forces.[47]

By 1980, the country had reached its highest recorded number of elephants. David Cumming, director of research in the Department of National Parks and Wildlife Management, put the population at 43,000, confirmed by aerial surveys in 1979 and 1980.[48] Appropriate habitat, a decline in hunting during the bush war and migration of herds from Zambia and Mozambique, where poaching was rife, contributed to the increase in numbers. The largest single concentration of elephants was in the Hwange National Park area, where a census in 1980 estimated 15,000–20,000. This prompted planning for a cull of nearly 1,000 elephants. The next largest population—of 11,000—inhabited the Sebungwe region of north-central Zimbabwe, which included Chizarira National Park, Chirisa Safari Area, and the Sengwa Wildlife Research Area. Here, research led to a decision to cull 392, mainly in Sengwa, to alleviate damage to woodland.

After the end of the war, the establishment of the Republic of Zimbabwe and the election of Robert Mugabe's ZANU-led government in 1980, the wildlife department began to look at ways of bringing conservation and wildlife utilisation in line with development programmes to stress community involvement and provide benefits for local people. New policies were designed to enable local communities, through district councils, to engage in regulated hunting for meat, hides and ivory, and to tap into the lucrative but controversial safari hunting market. With elephant licences costing visiting hunters $3,000, there was clearly a way of dovetailing the perceived need to reduce elephant numbers with generating income for local communities and conservation. This was seen as a desirable part of the new government's economic and social development goals, but also a way to stop a rise in poaching, which began at the end of the liberation war, particularly in Hwange.[49] This rise, though, was not on a scale to seriously reduce elephant populations, and culling continued under the new government. The elephant researcher Katy Payne says that 25,000 elephants were culled between 1981 and 1988, earning $13m from ivory, meat and hides;[50] 44,000 were killed between 1970 and 1990.

A large population was concentrated around the Gonarezhou-Savé Valley area on the border with Mozambique. Here efforts were made by conservationists in the late 1970s and early 1980s to gain the support of local people to stop poaching of elephants and rhino. Clive Stockil, founding chairman of the Savé Valley Conservancy and an honorary warden in Gonarezhou, says there was extensive poaching by the Shangaan community in the early 1980s but that, by working with elders and with the development of community-based sustainable-use strategies, poaching was reduced.[51]

In the mid- to late 1980s there was a major increase in poaching in Gonarezhou resulting from the conflict in Mozambique. Renamo, the Mozambican army, SADF/Military Intelligence and the Zimbabwean Army were all involved in poaching and smuggling ivory during the war against Renamo and the destabilisation of Mozambique by South Africa. Zimbabwean army units were based in Gonarezhou, where clashes took place between them and Renamo. Zimbabwean troops poached in the park under cover of the counter-insurgency operations. In 1981–2, one Mozambican gang operating in the park killed eighty elephants and sold the ivory for $9 per kg inside Zimbabwe, in order to buy food and other goods in short supply because of the war in Mozambique.[52]

In the Zambezi valley in the north, rhino were the main target for poachers from across the border in Zambia, helped by Zimbabweans, who saw the chance to make money fast. Relatively few elephants were targeted, because horn was increasingly valuable and easier to smuggle. A shoot-to-kill policy was instituted and joint operations conducted by the wildlife service and army. The overall death toll among illegal hunters between 1984 and 1991 was 145. This sort of militarised operation wouldn't work in the south-west, where poaching was being carried out by organised gangs enjoying the protection of senior government officials, by members of the Zimbabwean National Army (ZNA) in collusion with wildlife officials, or by South Africa-backed insurgent groups. As Duffy put it, "The case of ivory poaching indicates that illegal users of wildlife drawn from outside the state apparatus can be dealt with by coercive arms of the state, whereas illegitimate wildlife users from within the state's own apparatus constitute a greater challenge to state wildlife agencies."[53]

The fight against the rhino poachers was highly publicised to garner international support and funding from conservation NGOs. By contrast, the ivory poaching in the south-west was hidden, and it took investigative work by the EIA and Stephen Ellis, editor of the newsletter *Africa Confidential*,[54] to uncover what was going on, including the connection with the other state-linked poaching operations involving the SADF and South African Military Intelligence. The details, which only emerged after the CITES relisting in 1989, were used by the EIA and others as a counterweight to the arguments of Zimbabwean wildlife officials like Rowan Martin that a regulated ivory trade would work in Zimbabwe.

The picture that emerged from Gonarezhou was a complex one, involving poaching not only by local people from the Sengwe communal lands in cooperation with the army, but also by ZNA troops ordered to poach by their officers, by Renamo guerrillas and Mozambican nationals who crossed the border, and by illegal Zimbabwean migrant workers in South Africa who were armed and sent by the SADF to poach and smuggle ivory back to South Africa. It was a tangled web that also involved former Rhodesian special forces personnel, who had become involved in the illicit trade while fighting Zimbabwean guerrillas in Mozambique. The closure of the park, due to poaching and because of the deployment of ZNA units there to fight Renamo incursions, helped hide ZNA poaching. Ivory poached in the park or across the border in Mozambique was frequently transported to Harare on the Mozambique-Zimbabwe railway, which ran through the park, or trucked out in army vehicles. EIA investigations suggested that ivory was being carried out of the park on the trains, along with rhino horn and commodities smuggled in from Mozambique to avoid customs duties. The trade was run by the army with the help of railway officials.[55]

The ZNA's role in poaching was suspected by national parks staff, and some of its own officers tried to blow the whistle. Captain Edwin Nleya, serving with the ZNA along the Mozambican border, discovered that his unit had been ordered to poach ivory and that army personnel were poaching, smuggling and also stealing cattle in Mozambique to sell in Zimbabwe. After he reported this to his commanding officer, he had a gun pulled on him and was told to keep quiet. On 31 December 1988, he reported to the police that he was being threatened. Soon after, he was taken away by intelligence officers. His body was found three months later.[56] An inquest decided that he had been murdered, though the army claimed he had killed himself. Over a period of nearly three years, between September 1987 and June 1990, at least nine National Parks investigators, intelligence officers, army and police officers died suspicious deaths while investigating reports of poaching by the army and senior officials.[57]

When reports emerged in the press of a growth in poaching in Gonarezhou and the killing of 260 elephants and thirty-two rhino there, the Zimbabwean government blamed Renamo, the SADF and poachers crossing from Mozambique, even though much of the killing was taking place in areas occupied by the ZNA. Conscientious parks staff tried to alert the government to the extent of poaching. Several conservation officers told the EIA that three reports had been compiled warning government ministers about the poaching and implicating senior parks staff,

army personnel, the SADF and organised smugglers. Unpublished wildlife department reports said that aerial surveys had discovered the car-
cases of 823 elephants in the park, and the EIA said that 1,000 elephants
were killed there at the end of the 1980s.[58] The central players in the
smuggling operation were Gonarezhou warden Enoch Mkwebu, game
scout Zephania Makatiwa and Bill Taylor. Taylor was an American-born
dentist who had links with the Rhodesian Selous Scouts and the SADF,
but also cooperated with poachers working for the ZNA. Mkwebu was
moved from Gonarezhou after accusations that he was involved in poaching and transferred to be acting provincial game warden at Gokwe,
where there was a sudden and major rise in killing of elephants, allegedly
for crop protection reasons.

Another smuggler involved was former Selous Scout Ant White
(whom Parker had come across in Burundi). According to the EIA,
White collected tusks in Mozambique and trucked them through
Zimbabwe into South Africa. Some ivory was flown out by private
planes to northern Mozambique and Tanzania, from where it was sent
to Seychelles or Comoros before ending up in the Middle East and
Singapore.[59] By 1991, the Zimbabwean authorities were reporting that
the population had risen from 42,960 in 1987 to 70,000 in 1991,
despite heavy poaching and culling to reduce numbers in Hwange,
which cut the estimated population there from 20,000 to 13,000. The
culling had been necessitated by a two-year population rise of 8,600,
from 13,000 in 1987 to 21,600 in 1989.

The start of the constitutional negotiations in South Africa, the scal-
ing back of South African involvement in Mozambique and then the
signing of the peace deal to end Mozambique's civil war in 1992
brought a decline in poaching. The large ZNA presence in Gonarezhou
was removed and Renamo demobilised, and better enforcement by the
National Parks authorities deterred local poachers. Clive Stockil said
that this produced a major improvement and a reduction in illegal killing. Nevertheless, he warned that "the main organisers of the poaching
ring that operated in the 1980s have not disappeared and consistently
try to find new ways to reopen poaching rings in the area", which they
were to do in the late 1990s and the first decade-and-a-half of the
2000s.[60] The Gonarezhou pattern was to be repeated in Zimbabwe and
elsewhere in Africa; it was a primary demonstration that illegal hunting

by those from within the state itself presents a greater challenge to agencies responsible for wildlife protection than poaching by poor communities or criminal groups outside the networks of power and patronage. In these situations, the wildlife authorities struggled to combat illegal resource use, because the "illegitimate users" of that resource were from powerful state agencies or highly placed military and government officials.[61]

The end of the war in Mozambique and the decline in poaching in Gonarezhou did not mean the end of poaching in Zimbabwe, but the situation improved, and attention began to centre on the development of the CAMPFIRE initiative, which sought to benefit local communities through sustainable use of wildlife resources. The leading Zimbabwean elephant researcher and pro-trade advocate, Rowan Martin, who was closely involved in CAMPFIRE's development, said it aimed at achieving the long-term conservation of natural resources in communal areas (black farming areas, designated as such when the settler government handed the best land to white farmers), "by placing custody and responsibility with the resident community".[62] There would be a national programme, but with local control exercised by adult members of communities as the effective shareholders and with coordination carried out by regional and national boards. The core of the idea was that communities would benefit directly from the sustained utilisation of local resources through income generated from hunting for meat—to be sold and consumed locally—from the sale of hunting concessions or licences to hunt elephants and other big-game, and from a share of the income from trophies and ivory sales.

This would return ownership and provide sustainable resources for economic development in the communal areas, a priority for the Mugabe government, given the marginalisation, disempowerment and impoverishment of these areas under white rule. Communities would be given a direct role in managing wildlife. Local communities could opt into CAMPFIRE schemes and negotiate versions of the sustainable-use strategy that would suit them, mixing hunting for meat and wildlife products for sale, trophy sales and concessions for safari hunting. While the plans for CAMPFIRE included the sale of ivory, by the time the schemes came into being the CITES ivory ban was in place, and ivory did not figure as a source of income (other than as legally hunted trophies which could be exported by the foreign hunters who paid to shoot in CAMPFIRE areas with elephant quotas).

Implementation of the policy enabled CAMPFIRE to become, for a period, a globally renowned sustainable-use scheme in the communal areas, with a major and very overt utilisation of elephant hunting. Local CAMPFIRE projects had the right to sell quota-based elephant hunting concessions to safari operators and then take a share of income from elephant products, though not ivory after 1989. Martin and the Department of National Parks and Wildlife Management (DNPWLM) were clear when the schemes were launched that the utilisation of wildlife relied on an off-take that didn't reduce the size of a species population, and that income derived from exploitation should be ploughed back into the scheme to ensure both the continuation of that species in sustainable and realistic numbers and the preservation of habitats, while still benefiting and ensuring the buy-in of local communities.[63] The importance of ivory income to these plans, as the single most valuable commodity that would be produced by regulated hunting, was such that it became a major influence on the Zimbabwean government's opposition to the relisting of African elephants by CITES in 1989, and its subsequent attempts to get CITES approval for ivory sales—though this was also influenced by Zimbabwe's possession of large ivory stocks.

Zambia: culling, corruption and the fight for Luangwa's elephants

At independence in 1964, Zambia had a number of national parks and reserves with significant herds of elephants. Hunting was permitted under licence and for crop protection, but poaching for meat and hides was also taking place around the reserves, and in some areas reports of crop raiding by elephants were exaggerated to provide a pretext for shooting them, harvesting the ivory and distributing the meat among local people.[64] During the campaign for independence, nationalist politicians had attacked colonial wildlife regulations. Kenneth Kaunda, who became the first president of independent Zambia, was highly critical of restrictions that stopped Africans hunting. But by the time he led the first independent government, he had modified his approach and upheld the inherited wildlife laws, taking a pro-conservation line, and not opposing the wildlife department's policy of culling and control shooting where necessary.

The Luangwa Valley, which had some of the greatest concentrations of elephants and other game, was a focus of culling operations. Culling—of elephants, buffalo and hippo—was conducted on ecological grounds but was intended to produce economic benefit. A butchery and freezer unit was established to provide meat for sale, which could be transported frozen to population centres. The meat did not sell well and the operation failed to make a profit. Hides were processed and the ivory and hippo tooth exported, though a high level of theft of ivory occurred. During the culling operation (1965–9), 1,453 out of 15,000 elephants in the southern part of the reserve were shot. The northern section of the Luangwa Valley had an estimated elephant population of 17,700 animals; the whole region was estimated by the early 1970s to have a population of 86–100,000.[65] This high population led to plans to cull even more elephants from 1970 onwards. This was successfully opposed by international and local conservationists led by Peter Scott, one of the founders of the WWF, and John Hanks of the Zambia Wildlife Society (who later joined the WWF).

In 1968, the Kaunda government passed the National Parks and Wildlife Bill, which put the ruling United National Independence Party (UNIP) stamp on updated colonial wildlife legislation. Introducing the bill in parliament, the natural resources minister, Sikota Wina, said the government believed Zambia's wildlife to be a national heritage, but that the government had to find ways for wildlife to pay its own way. While licensed hunting was allowed to continue, most ordinary Zambians in rural areas were still excluded from ownership, control or utilisation of the wildlife. Four years later, UNIP gazetted seventeen more national parks and warned that anyone poaching in the parks risked being shot. But the system of licensed hunting, including of elephants, was continued. The UNIP government retained charge over the issuing of licences, ensuring political control over permits for the export of ivory, appreciating that permission to hunt and utilise wildlife was a "distributable benefit" that could be used for patronage, to reward allies.[66]

Despite the licensing system, illicit hunting became widespread and little serious effort was made by the wildlife authorities or police catch poachers or to examine why poaching was so prevalent. Few Zambians, according to reports of the Game Department, saw poaching as a serious offence, given that many of those poaching had been excluded from traditional hunting areas by the establishment of protected areas, and there was no great public or political pressure to stop it.[67] The country had a large elephant population that grew to 150,000 in 1979, but Zambia kept a low profile in the global ivory trade. During the 1960s and 1970s, exports averaged 26 tons, with a high point in exports between 1967 and 1971 as a result of the culling programme: an average of 49 tons a year and 113 tons in one year. Ivory was exported through Portuguese-controlled Mozambique. In 1975, Zambia's economic crisis—resulting from drastically falling copper prices—led to restrictions on trade, which curiously included ivory exports. However, this period saw a growth in smuggling, as global ivory prices rose just as copper price fell. Ivory was smuggled out by road to Tanzania or Mozambique and most went to Hong Kong—Parker believes large quantities of ivory were smuggled out in this way, including tusks from animals poached in Zaire and Malawi.[68]

South Luangwa, with its large elephant population, was the focus of an explosive increase in poaching. The park had been expanded; local communities had lost land and what little control they had had over its wildlife resources. Local people assisted gangs of commercial poachers, who targeted the rhino and elephants in the national park and adjacent wildlife management area. The anti-poaching units were poorly armed, underfunded and no match for highly organised poaching by gangs armed with automatic rifles. Richard Bell, who became head of the Luangwa Integrated Resource Development Project, believed poaching was organised in Mpika (situated between North and South Luangwa and the Bangweulu National Reserve) by Senegalese and Malian traders, who were encouraging local people to hunt for meat, ivory and rhino horn.[69] The latter didn't need much persuading, as the copper price crisis and the hardship it caused left many people impoverished. Local truckers who carried dried fish from Lake Tanganyika to Mpika were paid to carry tusks on their return journey to the Lake. Zambian, Senegalese and Malian middlemen provided arms and ammunition for the poachers.

Despite the evidence of a rise in poaching, in 1977 plans were advanced for another massive cull. Richard Laws argued, with support from some NGOs and sections of the Zambian wildlife department, that the Luangwa elephant population of around 100,000 was ecologically destructive and a huge cull was needed to reduce it to 25,000. On this occasion, Peter Scott of the WWF and other conservationists were won round and the Fund gave its support to the intended cull of 75,000 elephants—with Scott commenting on "this unhappy paradox of world depletion and local over-abundance".[70] Iain Douglas-Hamilton was strongly opposed to the cull and became involved in the debate, arguing that there had been no proper survey of elephant numbers since 1973 and that there was evidence of poaching. He was funded to carry out a survey of Luangwa's elephants before the cull started and found that the huge population of the early 1970s had been reduced by poaching to about 50–60,000. With ongoing extensive poaching, the population was continuing to fall.[71] During his aerial surveys, Douglas-Hamilton saw not only large herds but also incredible numbers of carcasses of poached animals. The cull was abandoned, but there was no halt to the poaching, and later surveys suggested that by 1979 the population was down to 33,500. By the late 1980s, the Luangwa population had been reduced to 9,000, with an estimated nine elephants killed daily.

Local people either helped the poachers or failed to report their activities. The incentive to help them—in return for cash—was substantial, and, having been excluded from protected areas and barred from traditional hunting to provide meat, local communities felt no ownership of the wildlife. Ownership was instead vested in central government, with fees from tourism and hunting accruing to government or to prosperous businessmen who controlled tourism and sold hunting concessions in the Lupande Game Management Area adjacent to the park. Local communities gained nothing from tourism or wildlife. In the context of Zambia's continual economic problems, local people has little choice but to turn to harvesting wildlife resources in a totally unregulated way through poaching, aided by poor law enforcement and the increased availability of modern weapons.

These were obtainable with comparative ease from the large numbers of guerrillas in bases in Zambia in the 1970s and 1980s—from ZAPU (the Zimbabwe African People's Union), the ANC (South Africa's African National Congress) and Namibia's SWAPO (South

West African People's Organization). It is thought that rebels groups from Angola and Mozambique also engaged in ivory poaching in Zambia. Again, this was a case of regional conflicts providing weapons and opportunities for poaching, and economic necessity providing the incentive for local people to engage in or assist poaching. One estimate was that in the late 1970s and early 1980s the value of ivory poached in Luangwa was $16–33m a year.[72] Zambia recorded legal ivory exports of $10m between 1979 and 1988, but illicit exports for the same period are estimated at $172.8m.[73] In the 1980s, Burundi and South Africa via Botswana became the preferred routes for smuggling the ivory out.

Although the government, with support from the WWF and other international conservation groups, made attempts to strengthen anti-poaching capabilities, the practice continued unabated and there was considerable evidence of corrupt army personnel and government offi-cials taking part in and profiting from it—including people at army-command and cabinet level, or in senior leadership positions within UNIP.[74] In 1980, the Zambian government and the WWF launched a $3-million anti-poaching programme in the Luangwa Valley but it proved ineffective—far more resources were needed, along with a purge of government corruption, which wasn't going to happen. The 1982 ban on elephant and rhino hunting and all exports of ivory was similarly ineffec-tive. It was only in 1986, after the launching of the Luangwa Integrated Resource Development Project (LIRDP), that local people began to withdraw support from the poachers and to back anti-poaching mea-sures. This change did not come in time to stop an upsurge in poaching in 1987–8 in which 12,500 elephants disappeared—too large a number to be accounted for by natural mortality.

The LIRDP was a community-based management scheme funded by the Norwegian Agency for Development Cooperation (NORAD), with the support of President Kaunda—it was based in Kaunda's political heartland of Eastern Province. The scheme, launched in May 1986, covered 15,000 square km of the South Luangwa National Park (SLNP) and the Lupande Game Management Area (GMA). "At its core, LIRDP was concerned with the survival of the SLNP and the wildlife in the buffer Lupande GMA, and especially the harnessing of this wildlife to improve the livelihoods of the Kunda people who inhabit Lupande

GMA".[75] The scheme was similar to CAMPFIRE in Zimbabwe, aiming to combat the rural deprivation that encouraged poaching by tying conservation goals to poverty alleviation through the generation of wildlife revenues from tourism and hunting directly benefiting local communities. A key aim was to create a local programme to restore powers and responsibilities that had been taken by central government. The project was opposed by the National Parks Department, which lost power over the Luangwa region. Local chiefs bought into the scheme as a way of trying to garner local resources for their patronage networks, taking on the role of local or regional gatekeepers. There was a constant battle between those running LIRDP and the chiefs over the allocation of income, with the chiefs trying to get their hands on the revenue to the detriment of local people.[76]

The biggest conservation battle was controlling the poaching epidemic that had reduced elephant numbers in the project area from 35,000 in the mid-1970s to 5,000 in the mid-1980s. Fighting poaching on this scale took money, manpower and the buy-in of local communities that had benefited from poaching. Those implementing and garnering local support for the scheme had to consider that local people relied on game for about 30 per cent of their protein intake, as the land quality was poor and tsetse infestation precluded livestock rearing. This was accommodated through the retention of revenues raised by LIRDP in a revolving fund, with 60 per cent reserved for project operations and 40 per cent allocated for local development initiatives, as determined by committees made up of local community leaders. The revenue for the scheme was derived from national park entry fees, hunting licences, culling operations (buffalo, hippo and impala) and commercial ventures established by the project—there was no direct culling of elephants for ivory, only crop protection shooting, and ivory was not a source of income for the project.[77]

Anti-poaching teams were funded and 200 local people were employed as rangers, who worked to get elephant poaching under control by the time of the CITES ivory trade ban in October 1989. Poaching was reduced by 90 per cent, to a level of ten elephants a year between 1988 and 1995. In areas of Zambia outside the LIRDP, poaching continued at the same rate as before. As a result of these two factors, elephants began to migrate back into the park, with numbers rising from 2,400 to 5,400 and reaching 9,000 by 1996. The success in controlling elephant poaching was a major plus for community-based schemes, but LIRDP was not all plain sailing, and there were serious arguments over jurisdiction with the national parks department, including the attempts by local chiefs to take more of the income.

Zambia's poaching was connected with the illicit trade in Malawi, where there was persistent but low-level poaching around national parks and reserves. I lived in Malawi from September 1981 to April 1982 and was a frequent visitor to the main park, Kasungu. Zambian poachers came across the border into the park to poach elephants for ivory, while local people killed mainly for meat but occasionally for ivory when need drove them to it. In the mid-1970s, the country had about 4,500 elephants. Malawi exported 1.2 tons of ivory annually, and it was on sale legally in curiosity and souvenir shops in Lilongwe and the commercial capital, Blantyre.[78] On an almost daily basis in the shopping and embassy district of New Lilongwe, I would be approached by street traders selling ivory carvings—though much of this "ivory" was actually hippo tooth. Most of the illegal ivory and hippo tooth was smuggled across the border from Zambia, as the Malawian currency was worth more than the Zambia kwacha. Malawi's strong currency and the availability of consumer goods made Malawi "an attractive market for ivory smugglers who can sell their tusks there at reasonable prices and pick and choose from imported and locally produced consumer items available in the shops".[79]

Through repeated trips to Kasungu, I got to know Hugo Jachmann, who was studying the elephants there. Having seen very large herds in Kasungu on several occasions—some numbering over 100—I'd presumed that they were not under threat. Hugo told me that at night the elephants congregated in and around the main tourist lodge in the park, as it was a place of relative safety. This was where I unknowingly went through the middle of a herd that had gathered on each side of the track back to my tent, as Hugo gleefully informed me the next morning. Hugo worked with Richard Bell, a senior wildlife officer with the Malawian National Parks Department, studying Kasungu's elephants but also trying to catch poachers and ivory traders. He believes that the level of poaching by Malawians was low and the major threat came from Zambians crossing the border, which ran along the park boundary in the west. During the late 1980s, President Banda's power was waning and crime, including poaching, increased. This, and continuing Zambian incursions, reduced Malawi's elephant population to 2,400. Kasungu's population fell from 900 in the early 1980s to 672 in 1992, 391 in 1995 and fifty-eight in 2005. It didn't help that park organisation suffered when Richard Bell moved to run the LIRDP in Zambia.[80]

During his work in Malawi, Bell wrote that the local poaching at Kasungu was principally by small-scale tobacco farmers on the margins of the park, who would turn to poaching when crops failed or tobacco prices were low. Farmers would sell the small amount of ivory they harvested to buy fertiliser and so bolster their commercial farming.[81] In Kasungu, poaching pushed the elephants into the south-east of the park, near its headquarters. Bell believed that improvement in farm incomes in areas around national parks would cut Malawian poaching, and that wildlife departments needed to learn the lessons of the Galana scheme in Kenya—that "poaching should be recognized and made use of as a legitimate form of land use… we would like to encourage commercial poaching for high cash value products (particularly ivory) at the expense of subsistence poaching… The objective would be to allow the commercial poaching to provide the cash injection into the priority rural areas", to assist the transition to the point where poaching was no longer a requirement to fund cash cropping.[82]

South Africa: Kruger, culling and population control

The recovery in South Africa's elephant numbers, which were concentrated in Kruger with just a few in Addo and other parks, was such that from the mid-1960s the national parks agency implemented a policy of culling. By the mid-1960s, the population had grown to 9,000; culling aimed to produce the target population of about 8,000, to limit damage to woodland. Between 1967 and 1994, 16,027 elephants were culled. The culling operation was highly organised to avoid distressing scenes for the large number of tourists visiting Kruger. A processing factory was set up at the Skukuza headquarters in Kruger to butcher the carcasses, make biltong, can some of the meat, grind down bones for use in fertiliser, make boots and belts, and store ivory—which was exported under legal permits until the ban in 1989. Culling was suspended in 1994 after protests by animal welfare groups and questioning of the cull's scientific basis. The result was that elephant numbers in the park rose to 13,750, according to a survey in 2010,[83] and may reach 20,000 in the foreseeable future. Some estimates put the figure even higher—15,500 in 2006.

Poaching was a relatively minor problem when it came to elephants in South Africa, but over the last decade rhino poaching has been a major and worsening problem. When poaching of elephants did occur, it was generally thought (conveniently so, perhaps) that the main culprits were poor, rural Mozambicans coming across Kruger's long border with Mozambique at the behest of middlemen who organized the trade. In April 1983, *Oryx* reported that 137 elephants had been killed in Kruger National Park by poachers entering from Mozambique. The estimated value of the ivory taken was $550,000. With its security forces engaged in fighting South African-backed Renamo rebels, there was little the Mozambican government could do to stop cross-border poaching and smuggling. In the late 1970s, South Africa exported 1.9–6.2 tons of ivory annually, mainly from the culls. Kruger ivory was of good quality and its legal provenance meant that it sold for a high price globally.

Under South African rule until 1990, Namibia had well-run parks, but poaching was common near the Angolan border and along the Caprivi Strip. From the 1970s onwards, as the fight against the SWAPO liberation movement escalated, the influx of army, security and Koevoet (a special operations unit with a reputation for assassinations and brutality) personnel worsened poaching and obstructed anti-poaching operations. Game wardens discovered poaching by army or other security personnel but were ordered not to detain them or confiscate the ivory. The Namibian conservationist Garth Owen-Smith was transferred away from the area at one stage in the 1970s because he was too outspoken about poaching by the security forces. When working on conservation projects in the Kaokoveld in 1982, he found that government officials and security/military personnel were frequently poaching elephant and rhino, using government vehicles to transport the ivory or horns to South Africa for sale. The local Himba and Herero men hunted, but this was limited and they killed no more than they needed for food, selling found ivory or tusks from elephants killed as part of subsistence rather than commercial hunting. Poaching by the security forces prompted greater hunting by local communities concerned that their sources of food, skins and money would dry up.

In 1962, an official estimate had put the elephant population for the Kaokoveld/Damaraland region at 3,000.[84] From a population of 1,200 in 1968, Kaokoveld's elephants fell to fewer than 300 by 1982. No serious attempt was made by security and government officials to stop the killing. As Douglas-Hamilton put it, poaching was "a widely known perk of senior government officials, and the illegal slaughter of animals by known individuals went unpunished".[85] Hunting by local communities in the north was facilitated when the South Africans distributed guns to trusted community leaders for protection against SWAPO. Poaching also affected the desert elephant population in Damaraland, where aerial surveys in 1982 showed evidence of only thirty to sixty elephants, compared with a population of 200–300 in 1970. The much larger elephant population in Etosha National Park was more secure as the park was well-known, visited by large numbers of South African and German tourists, and had a bigger force of rangers.

The end of the independence war in 1989 and official independence from South Africa in March 1990 ended the opportunities for poaching by South African security forces and their Namibian units. The elephant populations in Kaokoveld and Damaraland began to recover and the total Namibian elephant population at independence had risen slightly to 5,000.[86] Part of the recovery in this region may have been the return in larger numbers of elephants that had migrated between northern Namibia, Caprivi and Botswana, as the threat of poaching declined. Ironically, on the disbandment of Koevoet, many of its members were recruited to work for the Namibian wildlife department in armed anti-poaching units, while others went into business as hunting safari operators.

Overall, the public face of South African conservation was one of well-regulated parks and scientific methods of control. Despite the opprobrium of apartheid, Kruger and other parks were popular tourist destinations bringing in hard currency, and the country's reputation as a custodian of wildlife was strong. This reputation was, though, to be marred significantly by the discovery of the role that ivory and rhino horn had played in apartheid South Africa's wars of destabilisation against Angola and Mozambique, waged to deter these countries from supporting the ANC and SWAPO, to punish them economically and to damage their attempted pursuit of socialist development policies.

Apartheid, ivory and destabilisation in southern Africa

In January 1996, a report was released by an official commission of inquiry in South Africa into the clandestine poaching and ivory/horn smuggling network established by South African Military Intelligence and SADF personnel during South Africa's destabilisation of Angola and Mozambique. The commission, headed by Justice Kumleben, con-firmed what many knew or suspected about the massive poaching operation that had wreaked havoc with Angola's and Mozambique's elephant populations.[87] Suspicions had surfaced long before the end of South Africa's involvement in the two countries and the demise of apartheid. Investigative journalists and those monitoring the illegal trade in tusks had begun to see signs of a South African role in poaching and selling illicit ivory as early as the end of the 1970s.

The ubiquitous Parker, in his 1979 report on the ivory trade, had found proof that Angolan FNLA and UNITA rebels were selling ivory to buy weapons, and that guerrillas in remote parts of south-eastern Angola killed elephants for meat as well as ivory.[88] The investigative journalist Stephen Ellis wrote that ivory trade sources had been approached as early as 1974 by senior officials of the South African Finance Ministry inquiring about the selling of illegally-obtained ivory, who had implied that this interest came from the highest levels of gov-ernment.[89] The picture that emerged from the work of Ellis and the Kumleben Commission was of a highly organised poaching and smug-gling ring involving UNITA, the SADF and criminals in South Africa and Namibia, which took ivory poached in Angola and some from northern Botswana and transported it to South Africa, where it was certificated and smuggled out or sold to buyers from Asia.

The most authoritative source on the Angolan operation was Colonel Jan Breytenbach, commander of 32 "Buffalo" Battalion (which operated in southern Angola in support of UNITA). He was a keen conservationist who was appointed but never allowed to serve as con-servator in the Caprivi Strip. He told the author in November 1990 that UNITA had used ivory to fund arms purchases and that elements of the SADF had been involved in smuggling tusks, but more detail came out in his own books and in his published interview with Ellis. Breytenbach first visited southern Angola and the Caprivi Strip when he was sent to survey waterholes in 1970, as South Africa became concerned about SWAPO infiltration through Angola. He says that during this mission he discovered that a large area of Angola's south-eastern Cuando Cubango province was a concession run by Simoës Hunting Safaris, with rich Portuguese, Americans and Germans hunting there, but never in such large numbers that they reduced the game. Poaching of elephants and rhino was being carried out by Portuguese tsetse control teams working in the area, but again not on a huge scale.

In Namibia, Breytenbach found that South African and South-West African (colonial Namibian) government officials and security personnel were regularly hunting elephants and other game in the Caprivi Strip.[90] As South Africa militarised the Strip and set up military bases to combat SWAPO infiltration, construction companies working there engaged in poaching, taking tusks back to South Africa. Breytenbach also became aware that the increased military presence in northern Namibia had created opportunities for senior SADF officers to poach in Kaokoveld and Caprivi. He identified a particularly active brigadier based in Rundu in northern Namibia, but despite repeated complaints, the SADF tolerated his illegal hunting, the selling of tusks and horn, and even the use of military helicopters to collect ivory.[91] The town of Katima Mulilo, in the eastern Caprivi Strip, became a major trading centre for ivory. The dealers were white businessmen who ran the illicit trades under the cover of legitimate businesses. They organised poaching, supplying transport and weapons, and it began to develop into "one of the biggest ivory and rhino horn smuggling rackets that the African continent has ever seen".[92] However, as SWAPO incursions from Angola increased and Angola achieved independence amidst a civil war between the rival liberation movements—involving the USA, Zaire, China, South Africa, Cuba and the Soviet Union—Rundu in northern Namibia became a major South African military base and the centre for the ivory and rhino horn trade with UNITA.

The Kumleben Commission discovered that the UNITA leader, Jonas Savimbi, had asked South Africa to help him sell hundreds of tusks in the late 1970s. He needed funds to fight the war against the Angolan government and its Cuban allies. South African Military Intelligence officers working with UNITA, senior SADF officers and Savimbi planned an operation to kill elephants for their tusks in UNITA-controlled areas, smuggle them out in military vehicles to Rundu or Katima Mulilo, truck them to South Africa and then sell them to dealers for export to Asia. Starting in 1978–80 with the use of army vehicles to carry the tusks, the operation became increasingly organised. Lieutenant General du Preez of South African Military Intelligence, with backing from the SADF high command, funded the formation of a company called Frama Inter-Trading in 1980. It was run by two Portuguese businessmen known for their links with smuggling, Jose Lopes Francisco Lopes and Arlindo Manuel Maia.

Frama was to be used to truck food, equipment and weapons to UNITA-controlled areas, and bring back illegally obtained timber, ivory and rhino horn for export via South Africa. The Kumleben Commission was told that the head of wildlife conservation in Namibia, Polla Swart, was told that Frama Trucks were not to be searched, and that if by chance ivory was discovered it should not be confiscated. General du Preez had told the South African-appointed administrator-general of South West Africa, Danie Hough, that Frama trucks and employees should not be stopped by the police or wildlife wardens.[93] Proceeds from the ivory would go to UNITA, but some was retained by Military Intelligence; it is believed that senior intelligence officers also siphoned off funds for themselves from this highly covert and illegal operation.[94]

The Kumleben Commission found that initial press reports of the operation had led to an internal SADF inquiry, which had discovered but not disclosed the extent of the smuggling, only admitting that the SADF had smuggled 500 tusks out for UNITA. The cost to the Angolan elephant population, however, was far higher than the 250–300 elephants needed to produce 500 tusks. As early as 1979, Parker had visited Rundu and seen 3,911 tusks and 700 rhino horns, which had been issued with veterinary permits in Namibia and were "owned" by SADF personnel. Thanks to the permits, these could be legally exported through South Africa, even though this was poached ivory and horn. Parker said that he was convinced the ivory at Rundu had all come from Angola. Parker also interviewed South Africa's biggest ivory dealer, Cheong Pong, who admitted handling Rhodesian ivory, tusks imported from Mozambique via Swaziland, Zambian ivory smuggled through Botswana in boxes labelled as machine parts and ivory from Namibia.[95]

The vast majority of the ivory sold by South Africa went to Taiwan and Japan. Breytenbach said that the scale of the poaching operation in Angola was huge, and that while there were tens of thousands of elephants in southern Angola in 1970, in 1986 he only found the spoor of five in the region, because they had been wiped out by the UNITA/SADF poaching operation. A census attempted in the late 1980s found only 180 in south-eastern Angola. Savimbi was astute enough to protect game in the immediate region around his base at Jamba, so that journalists and politicians would see plenty of game when they visited him and so dispel rumours that he was using illegal ivory to fund his guerrilla force. But he admitted to his biographer, Fred Bridgland, that he paid for South African supplies with ivory and diamonds.[96] Savimbi sent US Defence Secretary Frank Carlucci a model of an AK-47 carved in ivory and wood as thanks for US support and also sent a life-size AK-47 carved from ivory to South African State President P. W. Botha. South African Defence Minister Magnus Malan confirmed that he and Botha had both been on hunting trips in Angola at Savimbi's invitation, but denied taking ivory from elephants.[97]

UNITA's former London representative and current president, Isaías Samakuva, told the author in June 2015 that, while a UNITA liaison officer on the Namibian border, he discovered the SADF's and the Central Intelligence Service's involvement in hunting elephants in southern Angola and northern Namibia, often using helicopters during the hunts and to get the ivory out. He denied a major UNITA role in poaching, which is not really believable in the face of all the evidence that the ivory and rhino horn harvesting was a joint enterprise. There is no definitive estimate of the amount of ivory produced by the Angolan poaching operation, but the Kumleben Commission found that of South Africa's 328 tons of ivory exports in 1980–8, only 192 tons were covered by domestic production—leaving 136 tons (equivalent to well over 100,000 elephants) unaccounted for. Breytenbach believes that 100,000 elephants were killed over the decade that the

SADF assisted UNITA in poaching and smuggling ivory.[98] It is also suspected that Cuban forces fighting alongside the Angolan army shot elephants for ivory. A Cuban general who led the forces there in the 1980s, General Arnaldo Ochoa Sanchez, was tried and executed by the Cubans for drug and ivory smuggling in 1989.

Mozambique was a major but declining source of ivory before and during Portuguese colonial occupation. The long independence war fought by Frelimo (the Front for the Liberation of Mozambique) disrupted what remained of the colonial ivory trade, but created new opportunities for the exploitation of elephants. There is no clear evidence that Frelimo was actively engaged in poaching, but there is some to suggest that in 1977 the Frelimo government allowed guerrillas of Mugabe's Zimbabwean African National Liberation Army (ZANLA) to kill elephants for meat in areas near the Mozambique-Zimbabwe border. Solomon Mujuru (alias Rex Nhongo), the ZANLA second-in-command and later a key mover and shaker in Zimbabwean politics, asked Mozambican President Machel if his guerrillas could kill elephants in protected areas near the border to feed themselves. Permission was given, but Nhongo killed more elephants than needed for food. He is said to have sold the ivory in the Gulf States and deposited the funds in London banks.[99]

ZANLA's Rhodesian opponents, notably the Selous Scouts, also became involved in Mozambique's ivory trade during the Zimbabwean war. According to their own accounts of the war, they were not involved in smuggling, and vehemently denied this when the unit's commander, Ron Reid-Daly, was accused of smuggling ivory at a Rhodesian army court-martial (he was acquitted).[100] Rather, one former soldier suggested to Ellis that troops operating along the border or inside Mozambique simply found natural-mortality ivory or ivory from elephants killed in minefields. The ivory was then flown, presumably by military transport, to South Africa, where contacts in South African Military Intelligence arranged its sale. It was also said that as part of their insurgency operations these units may have established relationships with communities on both sides of the border who poached elephants. Ellis believed that the Selous Scouts were partly financed by South African Military Intelligence, and may have repaid them with ivory.[101] When rumours of this trade emerged, the head of the Rhodesian army, General Hickman, had Reid-Daly's phone monitored. Reid-Daly emphatically denied being involved in ivory poaching or smuggling and claimed that the bugging of his phone may have endangered members of the unit engaged in clandestine work in Zambia—including Ant White, whose name comes up repeatedly in connection with ivory smuggling.[102]

Ellis's investigations convinced him that the Selous Scouts were in fact involved in ivory smuggling in Mozambique and that former members of the unit continued to engage in the trade after Zimbabwe's independence, many of them joining South African Military Intelligence or special forces units heavily implicated in ivory and others forms of smuggling linked with Angola, Mozambique and Burundi.[103] After the war, White moved to Beira and developed links with the Frelimo governor as well as the SADF; he featured regularly in reports of poaching by Renamo and corrupt officials within the Mozambican government. Renamo had been established by the Rhodesian Central Intelligence Organisation to weaken the Frelimo government and make border areas of Mozambique unsafe for Zimbabwean guerrillas and ZANLA bases. When the war ended, the South Africans took over support of the group, to weaken the Mozambican government and stop it from allowing the ANC to establish guerrilla bases along South Africa's north-eastern border.

Through this backing of Renamo, the SADF became involved in poaching in Mozambique and south-eastern Zimbabwe, smuggling tusks poached by Renamo and also encouraging illegal Zimbabwean migrants in South Africa to poach in Zimbabwe and bring back the tusks. When Mozambican troops captured Renamo's Gorongosa headquarters in August 1985, they discovered large quantities of ivory, and another 19,700 tusks were said to have been found when they recaptured Gorongosa in 1989. According to the EIA, former Renamo officers told the agency that their commanders and the SADF had ordered them to kill elephants and they might kill 150 in a day. One former platoon commander said that the South Africans were getting 200 tusks a month from Gorongosa alone.[104] Evidence of the Renamo and SADF roles accompanied increasingly pessimistic reports about elephant numbers. *Traffic* said they had fallen from 54,800 in 1981 to 27,400 in 1985 and 18,600 in 1987, chiefly as a result of poaching for meat and ivory by Zimbabwean and Mozambican combatants and the SADF.

In 1990, South Africa declared that it had ended its military support for Renamo, but there is evidence suggesting that elements in Military Intelligence and related covert groups continued to help Renamo, were involved in the ivory trade and were also using weapons previously supplied to Renamo to arm members of Mangosuthu Buthelezi's Inkatha Freedom Party (IFP), which was fighting a vicious war against the ANC in KwaZulu-Natal and in townships around Johannesburg. The South African journalist Eddie Koch reported that, as late as 1991, the SADF was assisting Renamo and smuggling ivory from Mozambique and Zimbabwe into South Africa for sale to Asia through illegal trade networks.[105] The Kumleben Commission found evidence that the Renamo leader, Afonso Dhlakama, had ordered the continued killings of elephants and smuggling of tusks via South Africa.[106] The continuation of the SADF/Military Intelligence link with Renamo after 1990 led to the South African National Intelligence Service infiltrating Mozambique to investigate whether the relationship was connected to ivory and covert SADF backing for the IFP campaign of violence, which was disrupting the process of constitutional negotiations. The South African National Intelligence officer Anthony Turton, who went undercover for eighteen months, told the author that in areas of Mozambique near the South African border there was no wildlife remaining—it had all been killed. He also said that two white Rhodesian missionaries, the former Selous Scout Ant White and other Rhodesian special forces personnel were involved in smuggling ivory with help from South Africa Military Intelligence.

White has also been linked with the South African intelligence officer Craig Williamson, who was involved in the bizarre Operation Lock. An almost surreal covert operation aimed at identifying and killing leading figures in the southern African ivory and rhino horn trades, Lock involved former British SAS soldiers working for a security company called KAS. This was funded through WWF officials by Prince Bernhard of the Netherlands, who had decided he wanted to smash the smuggling rings. In 1987, John Hanks, director of Africa Programmes for WWF-International and later head of the SA Nature Foundation, flew to London to meet Sir David Stirling, founder of the British SAS and of KAS, whose personnel would pose as smugglers, infiltrate smuggling rings in southern Africa and assassinate key members.[107] The head of Operation Lock, Colonel Ian Crooke, also identified a series of con-servationists—including Ian Parker, Richard Bell and Rowan Martin—as possible targets because they had in some way annoyed him.[108] Hanks agreed to the deal in a letter to KAS, in which he said that the operation should not be regarded as WWF-funded. Hanks told the Kumleben Commission that funds from Prince Bernhard had been passed to KAS, though he continued to deny that this was an official WWF operation.

KAS obtained rhino horn to use as bait to catch smugglers and started trying to work up entrapment operations.[109] However, the whole project was infiltrated by South African agents working for Craig Williamson, who tried to use Lock personnel to spy in Zambia and Zimbabwe. The whole operation began to fall apart, and questions were asked about missing rhino horn, the alleged spying activities in neighbouring countries and the links with South African intelligence bodies. A number of journalists were digging into the story and, despite KAS threats to sue and *Africa Confidential*'s retraction of a story about Lock under pressure from the newsletter's owners, Ellis published an exposé of the whole botched operation in the London *Independent* on 8 January 1991, revealing the WWF's involvement and effectively bringing the sorry episode to an end. There were accusations that Lock had been infiltrated by South African agents led by Craig Williamson and had become involved in the killing of ANC activists. Hanks, in his own account of the affair (which is an extended damage-limitation exercise), denies any connection with killings or attempts to destabilise neighbouring states in the guise of undercover anti-poaching operations, and says that the infiltration of Lock by Williamson did not lead to Crooke or any other Lock personnel carrying out work for the Civil Cooperation Bureau or other apartheid security agencies.[110] Hanks also defends the use of both undercover and military-style tactics against poachers, and supports the operation's basic aim of tracking them down, only admitting that "mistakes were made in how parts of the operation were conducted".[111]

6

THE CITES SAGA

The conflicts within the conservation, wildlife management and NGO communities over the ivory trade were hugely influential in the development of international and African policies. They governed approaches to conservation and sustainable use of elephant populations. The fierce debates and bitter personal battles between conservationists had a profound effect on how much sovereignty African states could exercise over their resources. The roles of Western-dominated international bodies like the Convention on the International Trade in Endangered Species (CITES), Western conservation and animal NGOs, and the "prima *bwanas*"[1] of elephant conservation—experts living and working in Africa—have been crucial in determining the content and consequences of debates about elephants. Western NGO and "expert" influence maintained Western hegemony over conservation in Africa. Influence over the global conservation debate was exercised through NGOs like the African Wildlife Foundation (AWF), the World Wide Fund for Nature (WWF), Born Free and the Environmental Investigation Agency (EIA). They had strong voices in the debates over the ivory trade and elephant conservation, pushing for bans and shutting down the potential for community-based, sustainable-use approaches favoured by many African states and local groups. African governments and peoples have been deprived of much agency over the formal, internationalised system of wildlife management and the utilisation of wildlife as a national resource.

The WWF-backed International Union for Conservation of Nature (IUCN) was instrumental in the formation of CITES. It came into force as a convention governing wildlife trade between signatory states in July 1975.[2] It aimed to ensure that trade in wild animals and plants did not threaten their survival in the wild. CITES is legally binding on signatory states, but does not replace national law. Elephants were to become a species whose population status, future and ivory would be argued over at conferences of the parties to CITES and at meetings of species-specialist groups. Acrimonious feuds and deep distrust coloured the elephant experts' debates, which dominated CITES meetings. Population estimates and interpretations of the ivory trade's effects presented by experts with competing conservation policy objectives must be viewed as part of the debate, rather than as objective projections untainted by campaigning aims. The antagonisms and polarisations of the debates may well have prevented them from agreeing to positions that would have been of greater benefit. Entrenched positions were adopted, insults hurled and compromise prevented, notably at the CITES meeting in Lausanne in October 1989 and the preceding meetings of the IUCN's African Elephant Specialist Group (AESG). African states were often reduced to mere appendages in these debates, pushed into conflict among themselves through the pressure, media propaganda and actions of the rival camps, especially increasingly powerful NGOs with funds to distribute to those who toed the "appropriate" line.[3]

The debate over elephant numbers and the effects of the ivory trade

A major disagreement developed over the extent and causes of the huge drop in elephant numbers in the 1960s and 1970s, which set the scene for verbal warfare between different conservation camps. Douglas-Hamilton was asked to produce a report for the US Fish and Wildlife Service on Africa's elephant population and the ivory trade. He estimated elephant numbers based on extensive surveys conducted over years across elephant range states, and asked Ian Parker to examine the ivory trade. What emerged from the latter's study was a meticulous report on the workings of the trade, which Parker knew from extensive research and from having traded ivory himself. It differed from Douglas-Hamilton's assessment of populations and downplayed the role of the ivory trade in reducing populations. Douglas-Hamilton says that he doesn't "doubt the integrity of the figures he produced. What I do worry about is how he came to be a leading protagonist of the ivory trade",[4] objecting to what he saw as a move from a critical stance in Parker's EBUR report and statements to the media in the mid-1970s that the ivory trade could be killing 100,000 elephants a year,[5] to a position of greater sympathy for ivory traders and their interests than for conservation.[6] This contrasted with Douglas-Hamilton's much more pessimistic report on numbers and his growing opposition to the ivory trade in all its aspects.

Parker believed that legal ivory exports between 1976 and 1978 represented less than 5 per cent of the continent's elephant population and were sustainable,[7] and that much of the ivory traded was natural-mortality ivory.[8] But there was no clear estimate of the amount of illegal ivory being traded, nor how much of it was laundered through the legal trade. The disagreement escalated in 1979 when Douglas-Hamilton released his minimum estimate of the African elephant population, putting it at 1,343,000—a fraction of the earlier 1970s estimates of 3–5 million.[9] Douglas-Hamilton's figure, as he confirmed to me, was a minimum—a good point to work from, as there were still huge unknowns, particularly populations in canopy forest.[10] Parker thought the estimate unscientific, if not outrightly dishonest. He later said the error was demonstrated by the amount of ivory exported from Africa during the 1980s, which he believed amounted to the equivalent of 1 million elephants. Parker suggested that there could be as many as 2–2.5m elephants in Africa, basing this on a conviction that the number in the Congo Basin forests was far higher than estimated.[11] Parker denied that there was an elephant crisis, but not that poaching was increasing. He contended, however, that this was not endangering the future of African elephants; rather, that the threat came from human population growth, the increase in cultivated land and habitat loss.[12]

Battle lines were drawn over elephant numbers. Conservationists like Douglas-Hamilton believed that the decline in numbers was a result of the legal trade and the catastrophic rise in poaching, and that this threatened elephants. He was so concerned about Parker's conclusions in his report that he wrote to the IUCN advising them to ignore

Parker's criticisms and consider trade bans "in selected countries".[13] On the other hand, the ivory trade experts like Parker argued that Douglas-Hamilton's minimum figure was wrong and, to quote Meredith, believed conservationists and allied NGOs were "using false statistics to conjure up an elephant crisis to raise funds for their own purposes".[14] At first, Parker's argument had the upper hand at meetings of the AESG, but this was not the end of the argument. Ultimately, the more conservative figures were to become widely accepted and serve as the basis for far-reaching decisions.

The row over population size was crucial, as it was used to assess the threat to the elephant's survival. Of equal importance was the estimate of how many elephants were killed for the legal and illegal trades, and whether this exceeded the rate of reproduction (thus leading to a decline in numbers). There was broad acceptance of a figure of around 1,000 tons of ivory exported from Africa over a five-year period in the mid-1970s but, as Barbier et al. have written, the figures, including Parker's on the extent of the ivory trade, were best guesses, likely to have underestimated the legal trade without providing any clear estimate of poached exports.[15]

The problem of assessing the level of legal and illegal exports was compounded by the media's seizing on the worst-case scenarios and writing sensationalist, inaccurate stories that increased Western public distaste for any trade in ivory. When Douglas-Hamilton made a rough estimate that in 1976 between 100,000 and 400,000 elephants had been killed to supply the ivory exported from Africa, basing his calculations on an average tusk weight of 4.8 kg, the media stressed the upper figure, giving an impression of a greater rate of killing than could be proved and declaring the imminent extinction of the African elephant.[16] This led to some suspicion of Douglas-Hamilton's estimates, but he stressed in an interview with me that he did not intend the 400,000 figure to be adopted as "the" estimate. One effect of the growing media attention in America was that the California congressman Anthony Beilenson put forward a bill to ban US ivory imports and helped to start an anti-ivory campaign; the bill only became law in a much-amended form in 1988, after the anti-trade rollercoaster had gained momentum and support from AWF and other influential NGOs.

As the fight to control the elephant conservation discourse developed, there was a measure of consensus that the threat to elephants from poaching was far from uniform across Africa. Evidence suggested that poaching was a major cause of the decline in East Africa, along with human population growth and the consequent increase in the area of land used for agriculture or pastoralism, reducing available elephant habitat. Illicit killing increased dramatically from 1970, when the price of ivory went up tenfold to around $30–50 per kilo. Before that, Kenya's average annual ivory exports were around 40 tons; by 1973 they were 213 tons. Of the thirty-four states with elephant populations, all but three (Botswana, South Africa and Zimbabwe) were experiencing declines in numbers.[17] South Africa and Zimbabwe were still engaged in culling to control numbers. Zimbabwe's most influential elephant experts, Rowan Martin and David Cumming, were in favour of a regulated ivory trade, and this position hardened as Martin and others worked on the early plans for the CAMPFIRE scheme. They had good reason to support a continued trade, as they sold ivory from culls to fund conservation and anti-poaching measures.

In the early to mid-1980s, there was fierce debate within the AESG over the southern African pro-trade view and data showing increased poaching and declining numbers in East and Central Africa. Evidence from the Wildlife Trade Monitoring Unit (WTMU), which was compiling trade statistics for CITES, showed that average tusk weight was falling and more elephants were being killed to supply the same weight of ivory.[18] When the IUCN's Species Survival Commission met in Kenya in April 1980, it grappled with the question of the real threat to the continent's elephants—was it minor, with the ivory trade playing only a small part, or were poaching and the legal trade reducing numbers dramatically? *Oryx's* report of the meeting took a pessimistic view, warning that:

> "The elephant must be considered in danger of extinction in the wild before the end of the century if trends that apply to the whole of Africa are not reversed. The root of the trouble is the high price of ivory since the world instability of money following the 1973 oil-price hike. A kilogram of ivory was worth $7.25 in the 1960s, but $74 in 1979. World exports of African ivory… have multiplied ten times to over a million kg a year."[19]

The report said that, on the basis of this material, the IUCN and WWF, while not opposing a regulated, legitimate trade in ivory, planned to work to close loopholes enabling smuggling, to strengthen

CITES regulation and to use Hong Kong and Japan's new membership of CITES to establish greater control at the import end; the latter two members accounted for 80 per cent of global imports.

If this represented an evolution in attitudes and a greater awareness of the threat posed by poaching, there was still little agreement among the experts on the number of elephants being killed to feed the trade. In 1982, Parker and Martin wrote a report concluding that there was evidence that previous estimates of the number of elephants killed had been exaggerated and that import figures were fairly representative of the ivory leaving Africa, as only a small amount of poached ivory was smuggled, and "the most widespread method of getting illegal tusks out of Africa has been to 'legalise' them... so that the tusks arrive at their overseas destinations quite openly and indistinguishable from ivory of legitimate origin."[20] According to their report, the weight of ivory exported was beginning to fall, with 991,000 kg exported in 1976, 816,000 in 1978 and 680,000 kg in 1980.[21] They estimated that, on the basis of the export figures, the number of elephants killed to supply the trade were as follows: 54,625 in 1976; 44,979 in 1978; and 37,482 in 1980. Taking Douglas-Hamilton's minimum figure for elephant numbers of 1,343,340, this meant that even in 1976, the year with the highest rate of exports and therefore of elephants killed, the trade figure was 4.1 per cent, while the lowest figure, in 1980, would be just 2.8 per cent. They concluded that "these proportions are within the theoretical capacity for an elephant population to sustain", and that around 40,000 elephants were most likely being killed to provide the known amount of ivory traded, adding, "We do not claim that the situation *vis-à-vis* elephant conservation is satisfactory—nor that it is unsatisfactory—but our findings give grounds for less pessimism over one aspect—the ivory trade."[22]

However, poaching increased massively during the 1980s, and elephant populations declined faster. Martin came to the conclusion that poaching had become the major threat to elephant survival.[23] In 1982, AESG Chairman David Western wrote that, while export weights had declined, a sharp drop in mean tusk weights from 10.11 kg in 1979 to 6.21 kg in 1982 showed that "increasing numbers of elephants of progressively younger age were being killed" and that the number of elephants killed for ivory traded rose 40 per cent between the late '70s and early '80s, from around 45,000 to 65,000.[24] The weight of expert opinion now began to move towards a more pessimistic view of the trade's effects. In a subsequent study of hunting patterns and the ivory trade, Western and Pilgram disagreed with Parker's thesis that declining elephant numbers could be explained mainly by encroaching human populations and cultivation, arguing that hunting is not random and does not take place in areas of greatest human pressure on habitats. They argued that if the demand for ivory and hunting continued at the pace of the 1980s, elephant populations would drop rapidly.[25]

Western and Pilgram concluded that the decline in numbers and higher rate of shooting of elephants was market-driven, with the market value of ivory increasing 5.9 times between 1969 and 1978. They predicted that, because of the decline in per capita GDP in Africa, economic forces "would encourage increasing numbers of people to engage in elephant hunting as a source of income", supplying demand from East Asia but also from end-use buyers in Europe and North America.[26] The high levels of corruption in many states, the increasing availability of automatic weapons through insurgencies or civil wars in many parts of the elephant range, incentives created by local economic conditions and inadequate law enforcement combined to provide the most viable conditions for the illegal trade in tusks. Pilgram and Western said that if countries in southern Africa with stable or expanding populations were removed from the statistics, the trend of population decline in over-hunted areas would be even more extreme.[27]

There were attempts at this stage to build CITES into a more effective regulatory organisation for the ivory trade. It asked signatory states to register their stockpiles and establish annual export quotas. This was voluntary and CITES did not have the resources to do more than verify a tiny proportion of the trade. Walker was spot on when he wrote, "The frequency with which illegal African shipments managed to piggyback onto legal ones meant not only that many export statistics were suspect but that they were highly unreliable as indications of impact on elephants populations".[28] CITES member-states issued permits for ivory they exported but these did not include worked ivory, and the permits were often forged, corruptly issued to cover poached ivory or simply poorly administered, creating the opportunity for corruption while giving an appearance of regulation. Nor did CITES prevent the

187

cutting of poached ivory to circumvent the permits. Hong Kong dealers set up carving factories in Dubai, where poached tusks could be
worked to be legally imported to Hong Kong (a CITES member) without permits.[29]

The evidence of substantial reductions in elephant populations led
conservation and animal welfare NGOs to adopt ever stronger positions. Many, like the WWF and the US-based African Wildlife
Foundation (AWF), had been increasingly concerned about falling
numbers but did not oppose the ivory trade or sustainable-use policies
being developed in Zimbabwe and Zambia, which were viewed with
sympathy and even financed by some NGOs. There was no suggestion
that these schemes were part of the problem, even though some
involved culling or hunting elephants, sale of meat, hides and ivory.
NGOs became caught between the entrenched positions of the competing experts and their own desire to gain a higher profile and elicit
donations. Compromise was difficult, especially when media coverage
focused on sensation and discord rather than nuance. Influencing public
opinion became a key part of the role of NGOs in the USA and Britain.
Groups like the WWF and AWF were urged by both camps to adopt
their views and support their arguments. The AWF newsletter and the
specialist journals *Oryx* and *Pachyderm* became arenas for fierce debate.

Those who supported Douglas-Hamilton's population estimates and
shared his growing concern about declining numbers in East and
Central Africa began to make their voices heard more strongly. Both
the AWF and the WWF moved towards a more critical view of the
ivory trade, without coming out in full support of a total ban. Those
favouring a tougher approach stressed the evidence of growing poaching in Tanzania as an example of the dangers of ivory trading[30] and
pointed to what Douglas-Hamilton called the "African Arms Race",
which was contributing to the scale of poaching.[31] He identified a toxic
mix of rising ivory prices, the availability of weapons, the growing
incidence of insurgency and a plethora of armed groups wanting to use
ivory and meat from slaughtered animals to fund or feed combatants—
the latter was certainly taking place on an increasing scale, but was not
and is not, in itself, a driver of the ivory trade within Africa. War did,
however, create the opportunity for the corrupt and greedy to act with
ever greater impunity, as we have seen. One should add that wide-

spread corruption in government, the wildlife departments and security forces were at the heart of poaching and smuggling.

In 1985, the biennial CITES conference voted to establish a quota system for ivory exports from member-states. The latter would submit figures for an annual quota for exports and would only be permitted to trade that amount of ivory. At the same time, the British government and, ironically, the Ivory Division of the Japan General Merchandise Importers' Association jointly funded a new CITES unit to help monitor and control the global trade.[32] The certificated tusks traded under the quota would have an official stamp and CITES would be informed of each consignment. But CITES didn't have the resources to make this work, and critics of the ivory trade—NGOs like the EIA—pointed to the monitoring unit's funding by ivory traders[33] and the fact that member-states often set quotas far above what was possible within their own elephant populations; for instance, see the whole Mozambique-Burundi ivory fiasco detailed in the previous chapter. Similarly, in 1986, Somalia submitted a quota of 17,000 tusks in 1986, when its elephant population was only around 6,000.[34] Most of the ivory—expected to bring in $3.72m, but smuggled out before an official sale could take place—was believed to have been poached in Kenya in the early 1980s.[35] Furthermore, CITES certification made ivory more valuable; countries like Singapore, which joined CITES, could immediately increase the value of their stockpiles simply by registering them.

The inadequacy of the quota system was apparent and even proponents of sustainable-use and a regulated ivory trade were becoming alarmed about the continuing decline in elephant populations. Rowan Martin, the proponent of the Zimbabwean CAMPFIRE scheme and openly contemptuous of what he called the "bunny-huggers" of the anti-trade camp,[36] in 1986 drew attention to the decline, suggesting that the minimum population should now be put at 800,000. He accepted that human population growth and encroachment alone didn't explain the falling numbers, suggesting that a combination of the high value of ivory, the greed of poachers but also "fundamental socio-economic problems regarding the ownership of the resource, disparate values of ivory in different countries, and major administrative shortcomings" combined to threaten elephant numbers.[37] This approach began to address issues of political economy and corruption as causes

of the problem, and recommended far more work on "adaptive management strategies" and a "well-designed programme to bring elephant
utilization under the firm control of wildlife authorities in their respective countries".[38] The problem, of course, was that this firm control
would not be exerted in corruption-riddled countries where wildlife
departments were still part of the problem rather than the solution,
such as Kenya, Zambia and Tanzania. Yet, given the problems discussed
above, many concerned with the future of the elephant saw CITES as
no better suited to its task of monitoring the international trade.

The arguments continued, with a growing split between the experts
from southern and East Africa. At the AESG meeting at Victoria Falls in
1985, Douglas-Hamilton said that the quota system wouldn't work, as
it gave CITES's blessing to continued exports of ivory from countries
whose populations had crashed because of poaching. He accepted that
some countries, like Zimbabwe, were managing their elephants effi-
ciently, but felt that "while selling ivory might be a good thing for
Zimbabwe elephants, it was a bad thing for elephants in the rest of
Africa... [as] other African countries didn't have the machinery in
place to regulate a trade which was quite out of control".[39] The conservationists' worries increased when the first annual quotas were submitted to CITES. Sudan put in a quota for 12,971 tusks and Tanzania
16,400, at a time when there was evidence of poaching in both states.[40]
The distrust of a system with quotas set by governments not renowned
for integrity was magnified by growing awareness among leading
experts, including the pro-trade David Cumming of the Zimbabwe
Wildlife Department, that:

> "Patronage of the corrupt businessman and the corrupt officials by corrupt
> politicians can produce formidable triangular alliances which lead to illegal
> and devastating exploitation of natural resources... These corrupt alliances
> are undoubtedly a major driving force in the recent over-exploitation of
> elephant in many parts of Africa... We have been too preoccupied with
> chasing poachers in the field."[41]

One could certainly conclude that this is still the case, with both
poachers and rangers at the sharp end and the middlemen and patrons
generally acting with a great measure of impunity. Tanzania was an example of how the spread of corruption helped facilitate the growth in elephant poaching in Selous, Ruaha, Mikumi and the Serengeti. Thriving

populations had been hit hard in these areas, and there was considerable evidence of the involvement of wildlife, government and police officials. By the late 1980s, growing government concern over the possible effects of poaching on long-term development of a lucrative tourism industry resulted in the promotion of Costa Mlay to head of the wildlife department. He was committed to fighting poaching and corruption and got government support for an increasingly tough approach to corruption within the wildlife department, police and civil service.

With hindsight, though, it is hard to know whether Mlay was as honest and committed to fighting corruption as many thought. By the time of his death in 2004, he had become head of the Tanzania Wildlife Research Institute. There, his reputation for integrity was sullied by clear evidence that he was stealing research fees and embezzling grants from major sponsors. The eminent lion researcher Craig Packer says it is not clear whether Mlay was stealing in order to provide for his family after his death (as he knew he was dying from an AIDS-related condition) or whether "he was just a crook with no fear of the consequences" and had always been on the take.[42] While there is no direct evidence of his involvement in the illicit ivory trade, the corruption he engaged in at TAWIRI should make researchers wary of quite what his motives were all along. This is another example of the way that highest levels in the management of wildlife conservation and anti-poaching have been compromised in Tanzania—where corruption, rather than conflict, has been the enabler of the illicit trade.

The existence of loopholes, the lack of rigorous monitoring of the CITES quota system and the inclusion in quotas of ivory confiscated from poachers and smugglers made many sceptical that the system was enforceable in some states, unable or unwilling to root out dishonest officials and traders laundering illegal ivory.[43] Equally problematic was the willingness of ivory importers to buy illegal ivory without regard for its provenance. Martin highlighted in 1988 that China was a growing market for ivory, with a thriving, government-backed carving industry. He estimated that as much as 88 per cent of the ivory imported into China—all from Africa—could be illegal. He foretold that China could become an increasingly important player in the global trade.[44] Over centuries, the demand structures have evolved; as one state or region became a lesser source of demand, another took its place. Demand reduction could take place periodically, through campaigning by NGOs and even governments, but the structure of demand always seemed to evolve to continue and usually expand the commerce—creating the incentive for legal or illegal hunting to take place, and for corruption to oil the wheels of the trade.

The failure of the CITES system led to the formation of an alliance between a number of eminent elephant specialists, with backing from NGOs and officials like Mlay, who said that a ban on trade was necessary (whatever their actual motives). After an AESG meeting in Nyeri, Kenya in May 1987, Douglas-Hamilton agreed with Cynthia Moss and Joyce Poole that they should fight to get a trade ban, win over the IUCN and WWF and launch a campaign to discourage people from buying ivory.[45] Many of the conservationists were willing to allow exemptions from any ban or moratorium for southern African range states with well-managed populations. As late as November 1988, Douglas-Hamilton was quoted as saying that "a proposition for an all-embracing moratorium would ignore the fact that sustainable yield is a reality in parts of southern Africa" and that a ban on such states' ability to gain funds for conservation from a regulated ivory trade could endanger elephants.[46] Moss, on the other hand, held the view that a ban was necessary until a workable form of regulation could be found for states managing their populations effectively. She wrote in 1988 that "I would ask people not to buy ivory until a time comes when one can be sure that the tusk is either from an elephant killed legally or from one who died of natural causes."[47]

Attitudes hardened and, at a series of meetings leading up to October 1989, the differences and personal animosity between the pro- and anti-trade camps increased, ruling out compromise. Richard Leakey described a meeting of African range states in Gaborone in July 1989 as attended by, "The most fractious group of men and women I've ever dealt with"[48] though he did confess that allies in the pro-ban camp told him that he had been too rough on the southern African delegates and that "some of my remarks had embarrassed people"; he admitted that "I belittled and derided the arguments put forward by the southern African countries describing them as selfish".[49] Such animosity hindered both the establishment of a viable system of regulation and a moratorium that could protect the threatened populations of Central and East Africa without thwarting southern African sustainable-use programmes. In the end, the conservationists like Douglas-Hamilton, Poole and Moss pushed for a total ban that did not provide exemption for southern Africa. Scientific approaches and reasoned debate were overshadowed by the divisive demands of campaigning.

The evidence of extensive poaching in East and Central Africa and Zambia, and the public-domain data showing South African and UNITA poaching on a huge scale in Angola, increased the determination of NGOs eager for public support and donations and others opposed to the trade. Some African governments, notably Tanzania's and later Kenya's, took a harder line on poaching and the illegal trade, even though they knew this would mean a moratorium or complete ban. Although Costa Mlay was an African voice raised in support of much tougher regulation, the public debate even within Africa was domi-nated by the "prima *bwanas*" and western NGOs. As a result of the debate, and of public opposition in Western Europe and North America to killing elephants for ivory, the European Economic Community (EEC), Britain and the USA were pushed into adopting positions sym-pathetic to limits or a complete ban. In February 1989, the US branch of the WWF successfully persuaded the US government to ban ivory imports from Somalia, a CITES member. The WWF-US pointed out that Somalia had a population of about 4,500 elephants but was seeking to export 25,000 tusks under a CITES quota.[50] The WWF identified that the vast majority of Somalia's stock, as in 1986, was ivory poached in Kenya. In May 1989, the EEC announced that it was tightening import procedures and would ban imports from countries that did not have CITES quotas—it also pledged $550,000 to assist the work of the AESG and its rhino counterpart.[51]

One of the factors that pushed governments and conservationists towards favouring a ban rather than regulated trade was the growing evidence that one of the chief factors facilitating poaching in Africa was corruption in government and wildlife departments. This was hardly a revelation, but attention was increasingly being widened from poach-ing and smuggling networks to include corruption. This angle was and still is key to understanding why—despite militarised anti-poaching, regular seizures of smuggled ivory and the ban on the legal trade to drive out the illegal one—so little has been achieved. Corruption had huge implications for attempts to develop a regulated trade. Many traders already operated on both sides of legality, and compromised wildlife and government officials could protect poachers, smugglers and traders from regulations to stop the illicit trade. Poaching continued and increased hugely in the 1970s and 1980s, despite bans on hunting in many range states and NGO and Western aid for anti-poaching operations. At a 1987 meeting of the AESG in Nyeri, Kenya, participants agreed that:

> "Corruption within countries in Africa emerged as a common underlying factor associated with rhino and elephant poaching and the continuing illegal trade in ivory and rhino horn. Poached ivory is entering the international market with legal documents issued by corrupt officials... Conservation action in the field will continue to be compromised as long as corruption within official circles is tolerated."[52]

The Nyeri meeting agreed a new estimate of Africa's elephant population of 764,410, down nearly 600,000 from 1979. This comprised 16,290 elephants in West Africa (down from 17,090 in 1979); 375,800 in Central Africa (down from 497,400); 190,720 in East Africa (down from 546,650); and 181,600 in southern Africa (down from 282,200). The decline in the latter region was almost entirely due to the loss of over 100,000 elephants in Zambia and nearly 35,000 in Mozambique, which outweighed the rise in numbers in Botswana and Zimbabwe.[53] Botswana's population had grown from 21,000 to 50,000 and Zimbabwe's from 21,000 to 50,000 (despite evidence of poaching on a substantial scale in south-east Zimbabwe). The Nyeri report further estimated that in Tanzania the population was declining at 7.5 per cent annually and by at least 10 per cent in eastern Kenya, Somalia and Sudan. It concluded that there were many causes of this, "including a large illegal ivory trade, poverty (including that of wildlife officers), civilian disruption, lack of arms control, antagonism to wildlife (especially elephants causing crop damage), undermanned, underfinanced and undertrained wildlife authorities; [and] lack of liaison between ivory traders and conservation authorities". According to the report, poaching was so serious in Tsavo that the park had only 5,400 elephants but a carrying capacity of over 25,000.[54]

The figures posited a serious decline in numbers, with poaching now identified as the cause. This was disputed by Parker and others, who felt the new estimates were unscientific and manufactured to push a particular agenda—but subsequent, more rigorous surveys suggest that even if there was a significant margin for error there was an accelerated decline requiring prompt action from the range states and CITES. The sense of crisis grew when worrying new estimates emerged between the Nyeri meeting and the 1989 Lausanne CITES ban. The Renewable Resources Assessment Group at Imperial College London said that the continental population could have fallen to 720,000 in 1988 and 637,000 in mid-1989. It also said the decline could be "almost entirely explained by the quantities of ivory exported from Africa", with a rate of decline of 9–18 per cent across East Africa, but only 3–5 per cent in southern Africa.[55] The better performance in southern Africa, with some populations still growing, meant that Rowan Martin, Cumming and the governments of Botswana, Malawi, South Africa, Zambia (despite its fall in numbers) and Zimbabwe still argued for the retention of a legal trade for their countries, even if pressure was increasing for a moratorium across the rest of Africa.

The pro-ban arguments began to prevail when the US-based AWF was won over, and although the WWF didn't entirely abandon its acceptance of the need to cull and utilise elephant products in certain circumstances, publicly it fell in line with the pro-ban camp. The campaign centred on getting the African elephant listed on the CITES Appendix 1 for animals threatened with extinction; trade in products from these animals is allowed only in exceptional circumstances. As the campaign for a re-listing developed, the Ivory Trade Review Group (ITRG) was established by the IUCN, WWF and Wildlife Conservation International to investigate the trade and its effects on elephant populations, with the intention of providing an up-to-date ivory trade report. The group mixed scientists and economists specialising in commodity trade.

The CITES Secretariat commissioned its own report from Parker, paid for by the Kowloon and Hong Kong Ivory Manufacturers' Association.[56] Parker asked Graeme Caughley, an ecologist who had studied the elephant populations in Luangwa, to carry out the research. Caughley concluded that yields of ivory from range states were falling and that "the trade showed every sign of classic over-harvesting", which, if it continued, would see the elephant becoming "commercially extinct" in East Africa within five years and across Africa as a whole in twenty.[57] This report was in line with the study produced by the ITRG, which predicted the virtual extinction of African elephants within twenty to thirty years if current rates of killing continued. It put the 1989 population for the entire continent at 627,410.[58] A later report by the ITRG, in advance of the CITES conference in October, lowered the figure further to 608,000. As Stiles argues, this report, detailing as it did the loss of about half of the elephant population in ten years, led to increased support for a trade ban.[59]

The CITES ban fight

The increasing support for a ban among leading researchers meant that they shed or downplayed their previous willingness to have strict controls in areas hit hardest by poaching along with regulated trading in southern Africa. Douglas-Hamilton had been prepared to support a variable ban with the better managed southern African populations exempt, but he changed his view and supported a total ban, taking a harder line partly because of his horror at the extensive poaching among the elephants he had studied at Lake Manyara in Tanzania.[60] Others had similar experiences which added a very personal element to their views. At first, they didn't win over enough governments to ensure that the CITES conference would vote for a re-listing to Appendix I, which would mean a ban. Nevertheless, they were lobbying strenuously for support from conservation and animal welfare NGOs and called on the public to stop buying or wearing ivory, a campaign that gained the support of the AWF. The AWF held a press conference at the National Zoo in Washington in February 1989 to launch a "Don't Buy Ivory" campaign[61] and later declared 1989 the Year of the Elephant.

The AWF had been prepared to support the idea of sustainable use, but clearly saw immediate advantage in adopting an anti-trade stance, vastly increasing its public profile and raking in the donations—Bonner notes that its Vice-President, Diana McMeekin, had worn ivory bracelets until the AWF's conversion and the start of the anti-ivory campaign.[62] As the AWF and other NGOs entered the fray, the message became simplified to the point of losing sight of the trade's context and the needs of range states. At this time, Bonner asserts, "not a single

African country was in favour of a ban on ivory trading"[63]—a view with which I concur. The pressure for a ban came from non-African experts and NGOs, not African governments. The WWF was wary of jumping on the ban bandwagon; at an April 1988 meeting in Lusaka between the organisation's national groups and African wildlife department representatives, the delegates condemned the AWF warnings of African elephant extinction as an "example of emotional and inaccurate reporting on the elephant situation in Africa".[64] However, the success of the AWF campaign put pressure on the WWF's American wing, which feared losing public support if it stuck to promoting sustainable-use strategies, including the sale of ivory to support conservation. As the emotive public campaign continued and Western governments began to support the idea of a ban, in June 1989, the WWF publicly called for a ban, ditching in public (though not necessarily in private) the backing for sustinable-use.[65]

The anti-ivory campaign became a very effective way for NGOs to raise their profiles and improve fund-raising. As Walker put it, "The simpler—and more gut-wrenching—the message, the more money it raised", with slogans like "African Chainsaw Massacre" accompanying bloody and shocking pictures of dead elephants with their tusks hacked out.[66] The message was stark and uncompromising: if you bought ivory or supported the continuation of a regulated trade and community-based, sustainable-use programmes, you endorsed this carnage. Growing evidence that the campaign was winning over opinion in the USA led the Bush Sr administration to ban all ivory imports in June 1989 and to support a ban at the CITES meeting. The Thatcher government in Britain did the same and British-ruled Hong Kong followed suit, along with Canada, Switzerland, Australia and even Japan adopting similar positions.

At first, though, no African countries were in favour. Perez Olindo, the head of the Kenyan wildlife department—subsequently sacked by President Moi—was opposed to a ban, supporting the positions of Botswana, South Africa and Zimbabwe. Neither was Tanzania calling for a ban or a re-listing of African elephant populations. Rather than a ban, African countries wanted and needed more funding for conservation and anti-poaching patrols—the paucity of funds for wildlife departments meant that while ideally, as set out in studies by Jachmann and

Bell,[67] there should be a ranger for every 23.8 square km of national park, most countries had far fewer. Even at the height of the poaching in the 1970s and 1980s, Zambia had one for every 400 square km.[68] But anti-trade campaigning and Western NGO and government pressure led to changes of heart in both Kenya and Tanzania.

The positions of these two countries—which had suffered massive waves of poaching and the corruption which facilitated it—were to be of crucial importance. In Tanzania, Mlay was more opposed to the ivory trade than his predecessors and publicly said the right things about fighting the corruption and smuggling that had enabled poaching to burgeon. In Kenya, the appointment of Richard Leakey had a huge effect on the policies of the wildlife department, which became the Kenya Wildlife Service (KWS), but also on Kenya's international conservation profile. A leading anthropologist and public speaker, well-known in Europe and the USA and among conservationists through his role as head of the East African Wildlife Society, he was someone who could get the ear of the president and garner international attention. Leakey says that during the late 1980s he'd become increasingly convinced that poaching was driving elephants to the brink of extinction. Leakey knew that his predecessor, Olindo, had commissioned a report identifying senior government and wildlife officials involved in and profiting from poaching, but that this was not going to be made public and the government wouldn't act on it. Leakey, by contrast, held the press conference described in Chapter 4. Months passed with Olindo unable to act against those he knew were corrupt, including senior wardens in his own department—he had identified sixty-seven corrupt wildlife officials but, because many had political protection, he was only able to sack sixteen.[69] In April 1989, Moi replaced Olindo with Leakey to give Kenya a higher profile in the fight against poaching and restore its tarnished image, which was threatening its lucrative tourism industry. By the time Leakey took over, started rooting out corruption and finding funding for the new KWS, he had come round to the view that a comprehensive ban was the only answer, which helped him to get funding from American conservation NGOs.

The PR side of the anti-trade campaign was ratcheted up, with the successful Saatchi and Saatchi advertising company helping the AWF, papers like the *International Herald Tribune* giving it free space for adverts and celebrities like Brigitte Bardot joining in. The use of grue-some images of elephants with hacked-up heads continued, along with slogans like "Dressed to Kill" or "Accessories to Murder" under pic-tures of women wearing ivory.[70] The AWF's membership doubled in one year and it hired Olindo as an African voice on board, though he frequently disagreed with the strident elephant genocide claims and the push for a ban. When the WWF converted to the ban campaign (against the wishes of WWF-International Africa director John Hanks), it worked alongside investigative, militant groups like the EIA to push for support from Western and African countries. It found allies in both Leakey and Mlay. Leakey persuaded President Moi to allow him to support the CITES re-listing on behalf of Kenya.[71] This was opposed by some Kenyan-based conservationists, some of the trade experts like Western, Parker and Esmond Martin and by Olindo, favouring a ban in some range states but not in southern Africa. The hegemony of Western experts in decision-making on conservation was further confirmed when, as Leakey admits, the Kenyan and Tanzanian re-listing proposals were drafted by Western elephant experts like Bill Clark, Joyce Poole and Jorgen Thomsen of WWF/TRAFFIC, rather than by the govern-ments or wildlife departments.

The Kenyans had another trick up their sleeves—though as Leakey says, they nearly missed the chance to play it. Soon after his appoint-ment as KWS head, he was shown huge stocks of confiscated and nat-ural-mortality tusks. In desperate need of funds and with ivory fetching $100 a pound, he felt that it should be sold and the money used to re-equip anti-poaching units and get the department out of its financial difficulties. He even discussed values and the mechanics of holding a sale with Ian Parker. According to Leakey, Parker told him that news of a likely sale had reached Kenya's ivory traders, who had already fixed the price they would pay and who would get the ivory when it was sold—all beyond the control of the Kenyan authorities. The sale went ahead and was stitched up by the traders, but Leakey delayed its finali-sation while he got Douglas-Hamilton to examine the tusks—only to find that there were more tusks and a greater weight than officials had told him or entered on the sale permit. The decision to sell the ivory was then criticised by the independent campaigning paper *Weekly Review*. Leakey changed his mind, deciding that the ivory should be publicly burned at a ceremony in Nairobi National Park.[72] He talked President Moi into attending the ceremony on 18 July 1989 and lighting the pyre. It was a huge PR event, welcomed by the campaign to ban the trade; burnings and crushings of ivory stocks have since become part of the heavily stage-managed tactics of anti-trade countries and campaigners. The ceremony was followed by pledges of funding and of support for the CITES re-listing from Western NGOs and governments. Financial support for conservation and anti-poaching was offered by the US, UK, German, Italian and Japanese governments and the World Bank, the latter pledging $150m for a five-year programme with another $150m available according to progress. Momentum kept building in 1989: the media attention on Kenya increased in August after the killing of George Adamson by an armed Somali gang. In September, poachers killed eleven elephants in Tsavo. Leakey admits that he deliberately held back release of this news until just before the CITES conference in October, to give it greater impact.[73]

If Tanzanian and Kenyan support for an ivory ban began to shift the balance, another major influence was the interim summary of the second ITRG report. The summary released to the media took a much harder line than the full 700-page version. It recommended a total ban as the best solution and ignored the disagreement of several members of the group, notably Edward Barbier and David Pearce, who believed a ban would act as a $50m tax on range states, removing a source of income and conservation funding. The dissenting members of the review group contended that those parts of the report that gained media attention ahead of the CITES conference didn't reflect the views of all members, and that experts from southern Africa had been excluded from the study.[74] The interim version of the report was considered at a July 1989 meeting of the CITES African Elephant Working Group in Gaborone, which tried to come up with a unified African position on the ivory trade. Only Kenya, Tanzania, Ethiopia, Somalia and Zaire favoured a total ban, with southern African states resisting and most of the rest wavering in the middle but susceptible to NGO and Western pressure. The AWF, WWF and EIA were present at the meeting and lobbied hard.[75] Even though it took place in Botswana, which opposed a total ban, it was largely dominated by the East African states and NGOs, with opponents of the ban like Cumming and Hanks missing.

Many participants at both Gaborone and the CITES conference were strongly influenced by the seemingly pro-ban ITRG report, yet an alternative summary published in *Pachyderm* by ITRG coordinator Steven Cobb and AESG chairman David Western showed that the report did not deny that exploitation of elephants could be part of a strategy to cut poaching and conserve populations in the long-run; these sections gained little attention in the media and during the CITES vote on Appendix I. Western and Cobb argued convincingly that the downward trend in elephant populations was caused by the ivory trade and poaching.[76] They pointed out that poaching was heavy in many range states, that elephant loss was happening five times faster than habitat loss and two-and-a-half times faster than human population expansion, and that killing at the current rate could halve the elephant population of Africa every ten years.[77] Noting that legal ivory sales were worth $120m annually to Africa, they said the quota system had "reduced illegal imports into consumer nations" but failed to slow the rate of killing. The inherent weaknesses in a system with few checks and no oversight by a funded international regime left it open to manipulation by ivory traders and corrupt officials in Africa.[78] Cobb and Western's article and the official summary of the ITRG report emphasised that corruption, poaching and smuggling were depriving African governments of most of the revenue from ivory.

The summary of the ITRG report supported a ban, but did warn of possible consequences: "The Group recognizes that a ban, not associated with incentives, will fail to conserve the supply and manage the demand. A ban may provide as much encouragement, through raising prices, to expand the trade as to constrict it…The economic self-interest of states required to limit their ivory trade, must be realistically designed into any programme to accompany a ban."[79] But, as Barbier and his fellow dissenters on the ITRG wrote,[80] this was not done and the complete ban meant the relisting wasn't just a measure for CITES range states "to limit their ivory trade" but to lose it completely until such time as a CITES vote could be held to allow one-off ivory sales in "exceptional circumstances". The official summary of the report admitted that:

> "The long-term aim of elephant conservation in Africa… must be to re-establish substantial and stable populations, as a basis for tourism and,

where appropriate, sustainable harvesting of ivory and other products....
Nobody present believed that Appendix l alone would transform the prospects for the elephant, nor would it halt the illegal trade in ivory. Within
that context, everybody voiced their misgivings on one aspect or another
of the problems associated with an Appendix I listing".[81]

But this equivocation and any misgivings about the ban went by the
board when it came to the voting in Lausanne. The opportunity for a
fine-tuned approach with differing forms of exploitation according to
circumstances and health of populations was lost in the passionate verbal battle and manoeuvring by mutually exclusive camps.

At the Lausanne Conference of the Parties to CITES (October
1989), the debate over the elephant listing proposals lasted four days.
The WWF and other NGOs organised emotive demonstrations outside
the venue supporting a full ban. During the prolonged debate, the
NGOs bitterly and publicly attacked the Botswana and Zimbabwe delegations, which argued for a split listing or the exemption of the southern African states from the ban. The re-listing proposal to put all
African elephants on Appendix I was tabled by Austria, the Gambia,
Hungary, Kenya, Tanzania and the USA, but failed to get enough support. Zimbabwe, with the support of Angola, Botswana, Cameroon,
Congo, Gabon, Malawi, Mozambique, South Africa and Zambia, proposed the split listing of Africa's elephants with southern African populations remaining on Appendix II—this was also defeated. The deadlock
was broken, to the anger of the southern African states, by an amended
proposal put forward by Somalia, for the transfer of all African elephants to Appendix I with the provision that, under circumstances yet
to be defined, the elephant populations of some range states could later
be returned to Appendix II. This was passed, with Botswana, Malawi,
Mozambique and Zimbabwe abstaining and registering reservations,
meaning that they could continue trading with other parties that
entered reservations and with non-CITES countries.[82] CITES set up a
panel of experts to examine the criteria for future transfers of elephant
populations to Appendix II, which Botswana and Zimbabwe had suggested could happen at the next meeting in Buenos Aires in 1991. The
effect of the CITES vote was a ban on trade in ivory in the signatory
states, coming into force on 18 January 1990.

In his report of the CITES meeting as chairman of the AESG, David
Western referred to the result as a "contorted compromise", neither a

complete victory for the abolitionists (of which he counted himself one) nor satisfying the needs and views of southern African states. He said that, while "it went against the grain" of his belief in the need for a ban, "the southern African position must be accommodated in the interests of elephant conservation... The dual listing of African elephants on Appendix 1 and Appendix II is supported but must be accompanied by strong controls to ensure that trading nations do not become a conduit for illegal ivory."[83] Barbier and the ITRG dissenters felt the result at CITES was far from constructive, noting both the failure to provide compensation for loss of ivory earnings as a source of conservation funding and the damage the ban could do to schemes like CAMPFIRE. They said that re-listing made sense for countries like Kenya with declining populations but not for Botswana or Zimbabwe, where funds had been invested to manage the expanding numbers. They said that pushing the trade underground would, in the long term, not end but encourage smuggling and poaching. They were to be proved right.[84]

After the ban: the re-listing and one-off sale controversies

The publicity given to criticism of the ivory trade and the vote to institute a ban had the short-term effect of reducing demand and bringing about a fall in global ivory prices. The ban did not, however, stop poaching.[85] By 18 January 1990, Botswana, China, Malawi, South Africa, the UK, Zambia and Zimbabwe had entered reservations over Appendix I, enabling them to trade in ivory with non-parties or others with reservations. Britain's position was hypocritical, as it had strongly pushed for a ban, but now wanted a reservation to sell Hong Kong's ivory stocks.[86] The British reservation lasted six months, during which several large shipments left Hong Kong; according to the *Traffic Bulletin* of September 1990, most were unlicensed. Leakey was furious and said that British activity was encouraging poaching, which had been declining.[87] There was no proof of a direct link between the British action and any purported rise in poaching, but it became a mantra of the anti-trade groups that any proposal for, or agreement on, limited ivory sales would immediately increase poaching.

Following the conference, Botswana, Malawi, Namibia, Zambia and Zimbabwe formed the Southern African Centre for Ivory Marketing

(SACIM), but said that they would not start exporting ivory without consulting CITES. South Africa, which had announced a one-year moratorium on ivory sales at Lausanne in an attempt to stop the re-listing of its elephants, applied to CITES for the down-listing of its elephants to Appendix II. Interestingly, the US Fish and Wildlife Service drew up proposals for the USA to declare the African elephant endangered, except for the populations in Botswana, South Africa and Zimbabwe. This indicated some willingness to be more flexible on the CITES appendices, and it meant that ivory classed as trophies could be imported into the USA. This suited the American hunting lobby, but it sent a message that Americans could shoot elephants and retain the ivory, while Africans shouldn't be able to decide what to do with their wildlife resources.[88] When a group of range states met seventeen potential Western donors in Paris in early 1990, Costa Mlay said East African wildlife departments needed $84m to implement anti-poaching measures, and countries like Zaire and Gabon even more to train and arm rangers. Despite the expectations raised at Lausanne, the USA only came up with $2.5m, France $1m and Britain $5m. Olindo was said to be furious that, having pushed for a ban, the West was failing to support conservation in practice.[89]

There was also evidence of growing frustration among the small group of African specialists on elephant conservation about the way that bitter personal battles between *prima bwana* factions were damaging attempts to reach a consensus. The AESG acting chairman, C. G. Gakahu, wrote in 1991 that:

> "Members of the African Elephant and Rhino Specialist Group (AERSG) are people selected for their knowledge and technical capabilities... Their responsibility is to identify the problems, needs, and priorities of securing the welfare of pachyderms. To achieve this goal there must be general agreement on activities and methods... If some members feel aggrieved it will be difficult, if not impossible, to reach consensus on a united strategy... Personal convictions coupled with an unbending stand will make our task even more taxing".[90]

The same issue was brought up when Holly Dublin took over as chair of the group. She and an African colleague, Bahini won wa Musti, lamented that the "division and disunity brought about by the issue of the ivory trade will not disappear. We must accept that different opinions exist, and move forward". They urged the members of the group to cooperate in developing the African Elephant Database as a compilation of data to aid conservation, rather than fighting old battles.[91]

Dublin and the elephant researcher Hugo Jachmann took up the issue of poor international response following the CITES vote. In a study for the WWF on the effects of the ban, they pulled no punches, writing that "It is a damning indictment of the donor community that, in general, they have not provided the critically-needed funding promised to these range states at the time of the Appendix I listing".[92] They also noted that those countries that had received foreign funding in the years before the vote, like Tanzania and Zambia, had success in reducing poaching and smuggling levels, whereas poaching continued when funding was not provided as promised. Furthermore, "this perceived failure of donors to follow through on their commitments [was] undeniably viewed with bitterness, anger and scepticism,"[93] and contributed to the lack of long-term success in developing law enforcement and management programmes.

Dublin and Jachmann reported that, for a short period, the ban limited ivory exports, reduced intra-African trade and led to a drop in global prices. The main positive effect was psychological, leading to lower demand in North America, western Europe and even Japan.[94] Yet, over her next few years as AESG chair, Holly Dublin warned of the continuing shortfall in donor funding for conservation and the growing problem of human-elephant conflict. In 1993 she highlighted that "country after country reported an increase in the incidence of human/ elephant conflict outside protected areas... the general consensus was that the increase in conflict has been commensurate with a decrease in poaching activity"; alongside this, she noted an increase in the number of elephants lost to poaching in areas where funds available to address the problem were falling.[95]

In the run up to the 1992 CITES conference in Kyoto, Botswana, South Africa, Namibia, Malawi and Zimbabwe all proposed down-listing their populations from Appendix I to Appendix II. Those against argued, somewhat perversely, that allowing these countries to sell ivory legally would increase the world price and claimed, without credible evidence, that mere talk of a resumption of some legal trade had already increased poaching in East Africa[96]—this in the same year as Dublin and Jachmann's report that poaching in East Africa had declined since 1989.[97] The five SACIM countries then submitted a proposal to CITES for exemption from the ivory trade ban. Again, this was opposed by those favouring a ban on the unsupported basis that it would increase poaching elsewhere by raising demand for ivory and enabling poached ivory from elsewhere to be laundered in SACIM states.[98]

As Kyoto approached, the Fauna Preservation Society in the UK argued that if the CITES-appointed panel of elephant experts found that the southern African elephant populations could be down-listed, "it should be only on the condition that the ban on international trade in ivory remains in place. The Appendix II listing would then mean that only trade in non-ivory elephant products would be permissible."[99] This, like some of the other arguments against re-listing, was based on the assumption that a legalised trade would encourage higher prices and more poaching, rather than increase the ivory available and so keep prices lower, and reduce the incentive to poach by meeting demand legally. The question should have been how a legalised trade would work to ensure that poached ivory was not mixed with legal ivory. Instead of seeking workable solutions, the debates again centred on highly polarized positions

Once again, NGOs and Western elephant specialists opposed to the ban drowned out the African voices. As David Harland wrote at the time, the debate gave "a massively disproportionate weight to the voice of the rich countries and the nongovernmental lobbyists in those countries... The views of the poorer countries.... [were] marginalised".[100] Harland also perceptively identified why the arguments become so simplistic and emotive:

"[they] must be pitched at a level meaningful to the constituencies from which these lobbies draw their support. That means two things. First, there is a hugely disproportionate interest in the 'charismatic megafauna'... Secondly, complicated solutions, however effective, must be abandoned in favour of simpler ones—ones that will have appeal at the bumper-sticker level. Thus it is very much easier to say "Save the Elephant: Ban the Ivory Trade" than it is to say "Save the Elephant: Support a Programme to Make Elephant Habitat Viable Against Human Encroachment".[101]

Some groups and experts, like the WWF and Iain Douglas-Hamilton,[102] did not actively oppose the down-listing, but others, like the EIA, launched expensive and emotive campaigns against down-listing which, as so often, mixed research with campaigning slogans and material unsupported by evidence.[103] As Harland noted, "It seemed not to concern EIA supporters that information in the report was misleading, and in important respects just plain wrong. Apparently the truth was not so important as the funding base. Where the elephant featured in all this was unclear."[104]

The strength of the anti-trade camp and the emotion of the public campaigns was such that there was no chance of enough countries being won over; the southern Africans' down-listing attempt failed. Again, pressure from Western NGOs had been key in disempowering African range states. This was a continuation of a process that had started with the passing of the first colonial game laws disenfranchising Africans when it came to control over wildlife resources,[105] except that now African wildlife was seen as a global concern, rather than a source of colonial sport or enrichment. At a meeting of the Wildlife Society of Zimbabwe in August 1983, John Hanks, who had been head of African projects at WWF-International, had taken up this point, arguing that "Uninformed sentiment and emotion have intruded into what should be essentially an African problem, resolved by African people".[106] Though Hanks's role in Operation Lock and his subsequent published apologia indicated that he had few qualms about sanctioning external intervention in Africa for the sake of Western-inspired conservation policy, he argued forcefully that different elephant populations in Africa and different human-elephant interactions required different management. At the same meeting, Douglas-Hamilton had been in favour of retaining the ivory trade ban, yet had raised no objection to Zimbabwe's sustainable-use approach of selling meat and skin but not ivory,[107] a rather bizarre and illogical argument.

As the debates and arguments continued, there began to be more voices raised drawing attention to the drawbacks of the ban, its possible negative effects and the counter-productive aspects of stunts like burning ivory stocks. The prominent conservationist John Burton attacked the Kenyan ivory burning, warning that "it will not help save any elephants... [but] will have the effect of increasing the demand for, and the value of, other ivory being smuggled from that country... Unless all countries unite and agree to destroy all ivory, for ever, one country doing so is futile, to the point where one must also question the motives."[108] Burton recommended that ivory be stockpiled and released to flood the market, bringing down prices so that poaching was no longer profitable and bribing officials to facilitate it pointless. He also recommended that African and Asian states form "a cartel, controlling the supply at a level where the price is high enough to pay for national conservation measures but not high enough to make poaching for the international markets cost-effective. This will not be easy to achieve, but it will certainly be more effective than burning ivory."[109]

The thrust of this argument was supported in a 1995 report by researchers brought together by the AESG, the WWF and TRAFFIC, who pointed out that in "seven countries for which data were available, budgets for wildlife protection had plummeted: in Tanzania, Zambia and Zimbabwe by more than 90 per cent; in Malawi by 25 per cent… the budget in Cameroon declined by 20 per cent and in Gabon by 33 per cent… Even Kenya, which received more funds from external donors than any other country surveyed, experienced a 13.5 per cent decline for anti-poaching".[110] Budgets were down to 5 per cent of the estimated minimum needed to ensure an acceptable level of protection: $200 per square km. The report also warned that, after a two-year lull, poaching had increased in Kenya, Angola, Mozambique, Chad, Sudan, Nigeria and Zaire.[111] Despite growing questioning of the efficacy of the ban, South Africa was unsuccessful in getting its elephants down-listed at the CITES conference of November 1994, despite a US and EU decision to abstain rather than oppose the proposal.[112]

During the 1990s, considerable work was carried out to refine survey techniques through the African Elephant Database. The statistics produced now split the estimates into definite, probable, possible and speculative categories—for instance, the 1996 figures for Africa were 286,000 definite, with a further 101,000 probable, another 156,000 possible and an additional 36,000 speculative; it was hoped that the new figures would add scientific rigour to debates, reducing their emotive content.[113] TRAFFIC also continued its work of monitoring illegal trade in ivory and assessing ivory stocks, adding to the verifiable data contributing to discussions of future elephant and ivory management. Tom Milliken of TRAFFIC estimated in 1996 that, while overall ivory trade was still down, there was a growth in Asian-run, Africa-based processing operations to turn raw ivory into ivory blanks for making seals and *hankos* (signature stamps) to be sold in Hong Kong, Japan and China.[114]

In 1997, a detailed report on Africa's elephants populations noted the success of Botswana and Zimbabwe in managing their herds, but also pointed out that despite the ban there was evidence of both poached and natural-mortality ivory being channelled through illicit trade rather than adding to government stocks, leading to the conclusion that illegal killing was gradually increasing in the second half of the 1990s, especially in areas where enforcement was poor or under-funded.[115] It was also pointed out that 6 tons of raw ivory had been seized from poacher-smugglers in Tanzania in 1996 and that considerable amounts of carved ivory were openly on sale in many West African countries, most of the raw ivory having being imported from other countries.[116] This indicated continuation of poaching and smuggling in many areas, with little obvious attempt to stop it in some countries that had voted for the ban: "It is incontrovertible that poaching and other illegal killing of elephants continues and represents a serious problem for under-resourced wildlife authorities. The illegal trade is widespread and serves both the Far Eastern market and the Western tourist market more generally."[117] The report further stated that, where poaching had declined, this wasn't only due to the CITES ban, but to improved law enforcement or the ending of civil conflicts which had created conditions for poaching.

In November 1996, ministers and senior officials from thirty-one African range states met in Dakar, Senegal, to discuss the future of the African elephant. According to *Oryx*'s January 1997 report of the meeting, there was growing appreciation that management techniques for elephant populations needed to involve some element of sustainable use. Botswana's delegates told the Dakar meeting that they now had 79,000 elephants. Botswana, Namibia and Zimbabwe outlined proposals to the CITES Panel of Experts[118] for down-listing of their elephant populations and the resumption of legal trade with a one-off shipment to Japan. There was a measured reaction from the delegates, though Kenya fiercely opposed the proposals at the next CITES conference, in Harare in June 1997.

At the tenth CITES conference in Harare, the application by Botswana, Namibia and Zimbabwe for down-listing and a one-off sale of ivory to Japan was approved by the Panel of Experts, who concluded that elephant management in the three countries was good enough to warrant it. The down-listing was approved with immediate effect, but the one-off sale of ivory from certified government stocks was delayed for two years to allow for further monitoring of ivory movements worldwide.[119] In her report of the meeting, Holly Dublin stressed that the one-off ivory sale would only be from existing stock and would involve no new killing of elephants, adding that there was evidence of growth in the market despite the ban; it appeared impossible to suppress demand.[120]

An increasing number of studies on elephant numbers and the future of the ivory trade made the case for sustainable use and a regulated trade. Sas-Rolfes, the expert on the economics of sustainable conservation, argued that destroying stockpiles would not stop poaching: "the reverse is probably true. Trading in old ivory stocks does not in itself pose a threat to living elephants; in fact it is more likely to help conserve them. Consumers who have already decided to acquire ivory will seek the best price… If their only source is from fresh illegal stocks, they are likely to contribute indirectly to further poaching… if they are offered the option of a cheaper alternative source, they will obviously choose that… If ivory from legal stockpiles is offered at competitive prices, poaching and black market trading will be discouraged through competition, not encouraged."[121] The clear message was that destroying legal ivory made poaching and black market trading more lucrative, as scarcity pushed up price.

The EIA came out strongly against the one-off sale to Japan, arguing that it would stimulate poaching, and others reported that dealers in West and Central Africa saw it as a sign that the trade was reviving.[122] Some specialists were highly critical of "the constant dissemination of rumours, anecdotal information and unsubstantiated data on current levels of poaching" by the EIA and others.[123] The EIA kept up its barrage of opposition to the southern African sales, alleging a major upsurge in Kenya as a result of the ivory sales, reporting poaching of thirty elephants in Tsavo in 1999[124]—a figure that in fact indicated no increase, but a continuation of the level of poaching, which had been fluctuating throughout the 1990s between 1929–75. Douglas-Hamilton feared that the resumption of sales would give the wrong signal to traders, while recognising that the southern African states had a case, arguing that they had numerous elephants, little poaching and accumulated stocks of ivory. While admitting that the short-term ivory trading by Botswana, Namibia, Zimbabwe and South Africa "may have little effect on those elephant populations", he expressed concern that it might have wholly unintended consequences for East Africa, where corruption was still a problem and there had been an increase in the availability of firearms. David Cumming of Zimbabwe disagreed with this view, saying the attempts to stop southern African states selling ivory, and thereby preventing a sustainable-use off-take of about 5,000 elephants from a population of 200,000, was "robbing Peter to pay Paul", depriving range states of the income to ensure funding for management and law enforcement.[125]

The NGO campaign and Kenya's opposition to the one-off sales were taken up to full volume at the next CITES conference, in Nairobi in April 2000. Banners screaming "The ivory trade kills elephants" and other slogans adorned the roads near the conference venue at the United Nations Environment Programme (UNEP) headquarters and a crowd of young Kenyans were placed near the entrance holding up photos of dead elephants with their tusks hacked out. This set the scene for President Moi to use his opening speech to push Kenya's proposal to re-list southern African elephants as Appendix I. Ultimately, a backroom deal was struck, whereby Kenya dropped its bid while southern African range states did not press for CITES permission for annual ivory quotas; South Africa's elephants were moved to Appendix II and sales of non-ivory elephant products were allowed.[126]

Over the next two years, the EIA went on the offensive again, with campaigning reports opposing quotas or one-off sales entitled *Lethal Experiment: How the CITES-approved Ivory Sale Led to Increased Elephant Poaching* (2000) and *Back in Business: Elephant Poaching and the Ivory Black Markets of Asia* (2002). These claimed that the increase in poaching was largely due to the down-listing and one-off sales. There was certainly evidence of a continuing illicit trade, with ivory trade experts Stiles and Martin reporting significant illegal movements of ivory within Africa, as well as smuggling to markets in East Asia, especially China and South Korea. They identified a substantial illegal trade in raw ivory between Central and West Africa, with markets thriving in the latter region, and noted the low level of law enforcement in the DRC, the CAR, Cameroon and Mozambique, where ivory could be bought cheaply.[127]

In 2001, European Union funding enabled the launching of the CITES/IUCN-backed Monitoring the Illegal Killing of Elephants (MIKE) programme to track poaching and other illegal killing. Its formation was timely, as in the early 2000s there were indications of expanding demand for ivory in China, a rise in prices and a consequent rise in poaching and ivory seizures. Stiles and Martin wrote that by late 2003 there was a strong resurgence in trade and ivory carving in southern China, Hong Kong, Taiwan, Thailand, Cameroon and Nigeria—all of which was fuelled by poaching, as none of the ivory from the one-off sales had gone to these destinations. They concluded that the increase in trade had nothing to do with the one-off sales, but was the result of a rise in Asian demand, as China's economy produced wealth and drove increasing trade. Stiles and Martin added that one-off sales only muddied the waters of the ivory trade debate and that a clear, consistent policy was needed.[128]

The next CITES conference, in Chile in 2002, fell right in the middle of the one-off sales debate. Botswana, Namibia, South Africa and Zimbabwe applied for permission to trade in ivory from legal stocks. All the African range states agreed, with the exception of Kenya, which continued to blame increases in poaching on the one-off sale. Botswana had also wanted an annual quota, as its steadily increasing elephant population was far in excess of its estimated carrying capacity of 60,000. Kenya and India tried again—but failed—to get all southern African populations re-listed on Appendix I. In the end, the meeting agreed one-off sales for Botswana, Namibia and South Africa amounting to 60 tons, again delayed for two years, pending MIKE investigations.[129] Zimbabwe's bid failed because of the disapprobation with which the Mugabe government was now viewed outside Africa.

Meanwhile, another anti-trade onslaught was underway from NGOs and in the media, warning of an elephant holocaust and a return to the poaching levels of the 1980s.[130] The EIA said that "Unfettered ivory markets are impacting elephant populations in many range states. Poaching is rising in a number of countries, aided by ineffectual enforcement and corruption… To allow further legal sales of ivory… would place intolerable pressure on threatened elephant populations and reward an industry which continues to thrive on illegal sup-plies".[131] This argument seemed to lack a certain logic, as the one-off sales would be legal, tightly controlled and to one buyer—and, if any-thing, would undercut the illegal market. This view is supported by Stiles's conclusions that "There is little evidence to support claims that the 1999 southern African ivory auctions stimulated ivory demand or elephant poaching. Levels of elephant poaching and illegal ivory trading in a country are more likely to be related to wildlife management prac-tices, law enforcement and corruption than to choice of CITES appen-dix listings and consequent extent of trade restrictions".[132]

NGOs need simple, strong messages to convince their audiences and garner donations. Those which had adopted a strong anti-trade position and felt they could dictate to African range states what to do with their elephants couldn't now step back and say legal trade was now accept-able, despite the evidence presented by Stiles and others that a regu-lated trade and sustainable use was the best method of elephant con-servation. But the argument rumbles on, with NGO campaigns, Western public sentiment and the positions of anti-trade states block-ing any advance towards a more viable, nuanced long-term policy. By the 2007 CITES conference in The Hague, the ivory sale agreed at Chile in 2002 had still not taken place, despite the approval of Japan as the buyer—it was held up by protests from NGOs and anti-trade activ-ists about Japan's ivory control system. At The Hague, China emerged as a likely buyer, despite its growing reputation as the major destination for poached ivory. The conference approved the biggest one-off sale since the 1989 ban, of 108 tons: 43,682.91 kg from Botswana, 9,209.68 kg from Namibia, 51,121.8 kg from South Africa and 3,755.55 kg from Zimbabwe.[133] Part of the deal was that there would then be a nine-year moratorium on any further requests for ivory sales, a clause inserted by the EU to ensure majority approval. The CITES Standing Committee approved the sale on 16 July 2008, with China and Japan as the destinations. At the auction that took place in November 2008, 101 tons were sold, with 62 tons going to China and 39 to Japan, earning £15,440,777 for the four exporting countries.[134]

Despite the moratorium agreed in 2007, another bitter row devel-oped at the 2010 conference in Doha, as Tanzania and Zambia sought down-listing of their elephants, legalisation of meat and hide sales and a one-off ivory sale. Both countries had far from spotless records when it came to conservation and corruption and the bids failed. Tanzania was becoming a centre for poaching and smuggling,[135] of both its own and Mozambican ivory. The arguments that developed were as fierce as ever and Holly Dublin, still AESG chair, lamented once more "that I was disheartened to see that the divisiveness over ivory trade is as deep now as it has been at any time I can recall. I worry that the focus on the legal ivory trade within the CITES context is diverting our attention and constructive efforts from the situation we are facing and the urgent steps that must be taken to reduce the impact of illegal killing on some populations of elephants in Africa".[136] A rerun of the same polarised and divisive arguments can be expected if southern African states push again for one-off sales or some form of re-listing at the CITES conference due to be held in South Africa in September–October 2016.

Already by May 2016, battle lines were being drawn. Competing proposals pit bids by Namibia and Zimbabwe to allow new sales of ivory stocks against a bid spearheaded by Kenya for a complete global ban on ivory trading. Those seeking to open up the trade claim that doing so would raise badly needed funds for conservation. Opponents of further sales argue that it would provide cover for poachers. CITES Secretary-General John Scanlon has tried to smooth things over, saying in May that: "In all of these issues we have two competing views. They are all aiming for the same objective which is ensuring the survival of species in the wild."[137]

7

RESURGENT POACHING

SOARING CHINESE DEMAND
AND DEVELOPING INSURGENCY DISCOURSE

The effect of the CITES ban in cutting the volume of ivory traded and reducing demand was short-lived and the promised financial aid for law enforcement by range states did not materialise in most cases. Demand picked up again in the decade after the ban. Illegal ivory from stockpiles and increased poaching were the means by which this demand was satisfied. It was driven largely by China's economic expansion and the growth there of a prosperous business class. The market had declined but not disappeared in Europe and America, where there was still commerce in worked ivory and tusks. Tanzania, Mozambique and central Africa became the focus of a new wave of poaching. The population in southern Africa continued to grow, and there was some recovery of populations in Kenya and Uganda, though both remained important transit points for illicit ivory leaving Africa. While ivory was the main incentive for illegal killing it is worth noting that in some areas of central Africa the bushmeat trade was partly responsible.[1] A detailed study by Wittmeyer et al. estimated that between 2010 and 2012, 100,000 elephants were killed in Africa,[2] and another showed that forest elephants in central Africa had declined by 60 per cent between 2002 and 2011.[3]

IVORY

The resurgence in killing and trafficking after the ban was uneven across range states, but by the start of the second decade of the new millennium was a serious threat. The scale of the problem was set out starkly in a December 2013 report by CITES, the International Union for Conservation of Nature (IUCN) and TRAFFIC to the African Elephant Summit held in Botswana. It confirmed that poaching had risen since the mid-2000s and skyrocketed between 2009 and 2011, levelling off in 2012 but remaining at an unsustainably high level. This corroborated Wittmeyer et al.'s estimate of 100,000. The seizures of ivory monitored by the Elephant Trade Information System (ETIS) in 2013 exceeded any other year since monitoring started in 1990. Over 25,000 kg of ivory were confiscated between August 2005 and August 2006; on Wasser et al.'s calculation that what is seized is about a tenth of the actual illicit trade, the latter could have reached 250,000 kg of ivory, or about 38,000 elephants. The wholesale price of ivory rose from $200 per kg in 2004 to $850 per kg in 2006.[4] Another 2013 report, by the United Nations Environment Programme (UNEP), said that in recent years overall poaching levels had increased threefold, and that there was a real danger of elephants disappearing from most of their remaining refuges in west and central Africa.[5] The total African elephant population was in the range of 420,000 to 650,000—a major drop even from Douglas-Hamilton's conservative estimate of 1.34 million in 1979.

The assertion of NGOs like the Environmental Investigation Agency (EIA) that the rise in demand and poaching was due to one-off legal sales of ivory from Botswana, Namibia, Zimbabwe and South Africa to Japan and later China[6] is very hard to back up—the material put forward to justify conservation groups' opposition to the sales seemed more concerned with campaigning than with supported fact. I would give more weight to the analysis of Stiles, with his experience of studying the ivory trade, that "consumers who have a long-standing desire for worked ivory and the economic means to purchase it drive ivory market activity. The CITES-approved sales are irrelevant to market demand."[7] That is not to say that the one-off sales were in themselves a sensible move, in terms of a regulated trade that served conservation goals, but that there is no clear proof that they were the dynamic driving the huge rise in illicit trade to China, which seems more clearly

216

linked to the expansion of the Chinese economy and the rise of a rich business class.

The re-emergence of long-established ivory trading networks, and the greed of traders, their political patrons and facilitators of trade, were part of the narrative of poaching-smuggling-acquisitiveness, but new discourses also developed and, at times, became dominant. These concerned, primarily, Chinese demand for ivory and the association of increased poaching between 2007 and 2015 with conflicts, rebel movements and insecurity in Africa, especially in a post-9/11 context of Western concern about Africa-based insurgency and Islamist movements. Wildlife trafficking came to be seen as being of wider strategic significance than just the threat to individual states or wildlife. Some of this narrative had a basis in reality, but it was often exaggerated or embellished because of political expediency, the dovetailing of NGO campaigns and government concerns and a very selective—at times misleading—media framing of what was driving the killing of elephants.

Chinese demand drives illicit trade

Demand in Japan, western Europe and America had diminished after the campaigns against buying ivory and the ban, and while it picked up a little and remained a factor in the global demand structure, it was the steep rise in Chinese purchasing that generated the boom in demand and so poaching. Between the ban in 1989 and 1997, there was a gradual increase in Chinese imports, but by 1998 trade expert E. B. Martin identified that the Chinese were becoming the main buyers of African ivory.[8] In Sudan, where the thriving carving and export industry had declined after 1989, Martin said the commerce in ivory had been "saved" by the arrival of Chinese businessmen and workers, who bought ivory in Khartoum and took it back to China. Chinese demand, and the involvement of Chinese traders and middlemen in Africa, increased in the early years of the millennium, with large seizures of ivory bound for China. Despite periodic seizures and arrests of smugglers, the Chinese authorities did not make a concerted attempt to stop illegal imports or regulate the domestic market. As a result, the booming Chinese economy, growing presence of Chinese businessmen and workers across Africa, and close ties between the Chinese and elephant range state governments, facilitated the ivory trade, the establishment of routes utilising Chinese commercial penetration of Africa and the relative impunity with which Chinese smugglers operated. Chinese workers took ivory back to China to sell at a huge profit and Chinese crime syndicates began to utilise business networks to establish themselves in countries like Sudan and Tanzania, taking over much of the illicit trade from the more established traders.

Detailed examination of the ivory trade in China indicates a progressive increase in demand. Vigne and Martin conducted a survey in 2010 and found more ivory than ever on sale in leading centres like Guangzhou: 6,437 items, an increase of 50 per cent since their survey in 2004.[9] The authors reported finding 3,206 illegal ivory items for sale at twenty-five unlicensed outlets. More than two thirds of the illegal ivory objects were judged to have been made after 1990. In 2008, China bought 62 tons of tusks from southern Africa in the CITES-approved sale, but, despite this, smuggling of tusks into China continued, with at least 688 seizures in 2010 of ivory destined for China. Before 2009, there were fewer than 100 seizures per year. There is also evidence in China of a massive growth in online ivory trading, often linked to other illegal commerce.[10]

The demand has encouraged the growth of Chinese crime syndicates dealing in ivory, but has also increasingly involved the million-plus Chinese working in Africa. There is evidence from monitoring groups and conservationists that illicit killing and trading increases in elephant ranges near to construction or mining ventures involving Chinese workers. Evidence gathered by the International Fund for Animal Welfare (IFAW) shows that road building provides a means for Chinese workers to access and bring out ivory from the remote killing areas. In 2011, more than 150 Chinese citizens were arrested in African states for smuggling ivory; 90 per cent of those arrested in possession of ivory at Nairobi airport were Chinese.[11] Mary Rice, the executive director of the EIA, says that Chinese networks have changed the dynamics of smuggling in countries like Tanzania. Instead of Tanzanian nationals and long-established South Asian or Swahili/Shirazi traders running the networks to export tusks, this increasingly "is actually being driven by resident Chinese people who [have] established themselves" in Tanzania and created new networks to serve buyers back in

China.[12] Chinese businesses have the cover of legitimate commerce to disguise smuggling, and smugglers have developed networks of mutual benefit and protection with government officials and politicians. Rice and trade experts like Martin, Vigne and Stiles all agree that it is corruption and networks of politicians, officials, smugglers and businessmen which are at the heart of the modern ivory enterprise.

Vigne and Martin told me that, while researching their 2014 report, they found that the Chinese ivory industry was expanding massively and that Chinese illegal imports were by far the largest in the world, while law enforcement and efforts to tackle corruption were weak, despite Chinese promises to fight the trade.[13] Wholesale prices for ivory in China rose from $900 per kg for tusks of five kilos or more in 2010 to $2,100 per kg in 2014; the number of licensed ivory factories increased from nine in 2004 to thirty-seven in 2013, with three times as many illegal outlets. Whereas, at the start of the 2000s, much of the ivory on sale in China was purchased by foreign visitors, by 2014, the vast majority was bought by Chinese collectors or investors banking on scarcity boosting prices.[14]

The Chinese government responded to criticism of China's role in the illicit trade with pledges to fight illegal activity, while accusing the Western media of picking on China. In March 2014, the Director-General of the Chinese Foreign Ministry's Department of Africa Affairs, Mr Lu Shaye, said that the Western media was blaming increased poaching in Africa on Chinese demand and that this was misleading and aimed at damaging the friendship between China and Africa. On 8 May, during a visit to the African Union headquarters in Addis Ababa, Chinese premier Li Keqiang tried to prove China's commitment to fighting poaching by pledging $10m to assist law enforcement. However, the Chinese ambassador to Tanzania, Dr Lu Youqing, tried to shift responsibility, saying that poaching was a result of poverty in Africa, rather than Chinese demand.[15] The Chinese government took more decisive public action in late February 2015, when it announced a twelve-month ban on imports of carved ivory and tusks. The measure would not affect the legal domestic trade or the sale of ivory from government stockpiles. The ban also excluded Hong Kong, with its extensive legal and illegal trades. Some wildlife organisations and commentators said this would have a marginal effect on incentives to poach in Africa, as it was not accompanied by stronger measures against the illegal trade.[16] Conservationists in Africa welcomed the ban, but said far more needed to be done to stop the slaughter of elephants. Douglas-Hamilton told the author that he didn't put any great faith in it as a measure on its own but hoped it was a signal that China was moving towards more viable tightening of controls.

The government's adoption of a tougher profile in controlling the ivory trade was accompanied by the crushing of 660 kg of seized ivory in Beijing in a joint event organised by China's CITES officials, the Chinese customs agency, WildAid and the Wildlife Conservation Society (WCS). A government statement released to coincide with the ivory destruction said, "We will strictly control ivory processing and trade until the commercial processing and sale of ivory and its products are eventually halted". Peter Knights of WildAid said that while the announcement was significant, he would wait to see whether it was followed up. Scepticism was warranted because, in the past, China had seized 40 tons of illegal ivory and then sold it to licensed carvers, who were able to sell it legally.[17] The crushing event was also used to publicise the launching of an offensive against the importing of ivory by Chinese nationals coming back from abroad, under the slogan "Bring No Ivory Home". But Yannick Kuehl, regional director of TRAFFIC, said that while the Chinese were trying to present a better image globally, little was being done about Hong Kong as a supplier of Chinese buyers.

The role of Hong Kong as the world's largest retail market for ivory and as a major transit hub for illicit ivory was detailed in WildAid's report, *Illusion of Control*, in October 2015. This report said that the Hong Kong authorities' claim to have strict controls in place governing ivory sales did not stand up to scrutiny and that "corruption and obfuscation" were masking the extent of illicit trading by international smuggling syndicates. Elizabeth Qat, a Hong Kong legislative councillor, told WildAid that "Time and again, the illegal ivory trade and ivory laundry in Hong Kong have been exposed… with no effective measures implemented to crack down on illicit sales and exports".[18] Traders admitted to the undercover investigators compiling the report that they imported illegal ivory to replenish ivory sold from the legal inventory; many used faked documents and others means to continue importing and selling illicit ivory. Over 90 per cent of the ivory sold in Hong

Kong is sold to people from mainland China. The evidence suggests that even if efforts were made to close down much of the ivory trade in China and stop imports from Africa, Hong Kong would remain a back door route for illicit ivory.

In September 2015, during President Xi Jinping's official visit to the United States, he and President Obama made a joint pledge to combat the ivory trade and announced what the White House called "nearly complete bans on ivory import and export, including significant and timely restrictions on the import of ivory as hunting trophies, and… significant and timely steps to halt the domestic commercial trade of ivory".[19] China repeated that it would phase out domestic trade, though it fell short of banning all trade and was vague about what "nearly complete" meant. Similarly, when Hong Kong's chief executive, Leung Chun-ying, announced in January 2016 in his annual policy address that he would phase out Hong Kong's "local ivory trade" and impose heavier penalties for smuggling and illicit trading, he didn't give a time-table or say whether this meant a total ban on all trade, including exports to China. The announcement was welcomed by WildAid and Elizabeth Qat, the latter urging the Hong Kong authorities to implement this process without delay.[20] At the time of writing in June 2016, no further details of the timing or extent of the changes have been provided, despite Leung having promised that legislative measures would be enacted "as soon as possible to ban the import and export of elephant hunting trophies and explore other legislation as part of [the] effort to phase out the local ivory trade".[21]

At the end of 2015, Vigne and Martin reported that the market price for ivory was declining, even in China, and had dropped from $2,100 per kg to $1,200, though E.B. Martin cautioned that even at this lower price the incentive for poor people in African range states to engage in poaching to feed demand was still high, and that such poaching would still occur as long as the middlemen and organisers of illicit trade networks still wanted to buy ivory.[22] The fall in price may be linked with China's economic downturn or the moratorium on imports of trophy ivory and more strenuous attempts to enforce anti-smuggling measures. Whether the fall will continue or the new price level be sustained remains to be seen. In late 2015 and early 2016 there were noticeably more reports in the Chinese media and carried by the official Chinese news agency,

Xinhua, about both poaching in Africa and attempts to suppress the illicit trade and conserve elephants and rhinos.[23]

The Chinese government's decision in 2015 to impose a year-long moratorium on the importing of ivory in the form of hunting trophies (the only legal way to import post-1989 unworked ivory) and to move to end the domestic ivory trade has been a major development in attempts to limit the trade, and, as noted, may have affected the price fall. In March 2016, the moratorium on imports was extended to 2020. It is believed that China has sufficient stocks of ivory to supply the domestic market if a long-term ban on imports of ivory follows on from China's pledge in September 2015 to stop ivory trading—though no date or plan has been announced detailing how or giving any sort of timetable for action. China has large stockpiles of legal ivory and private traders hold illegal stocks. The government has released about five tons a year from its stockpile for sale to licensed carving workshops, according to China's top CITES official, Meng Xianlin.[24] In 2009, official stocks were believed to be at 73 tons. If 35 tons have been sold to traders in the last seven years, then China has about 38 tons left, which, without any supplement from illegal imports or illicit stocks held by private traders, would give over seven years' supply to traders before stocks would be exhausted and imports again needed—if the entire trade and domestic demand had not by then been suppressed.[25] If China acts to end imports (beyond the moratorium to 2020 on hunting trophies), even for a limited period, a litmus test of the likely long-term effect on poaching will be whether the price drop continues or goes into reverse. It may be that an extended import moratorium would push up prices as scarcity increases value and so prompts further poaching. Ivory is already believed to be a commodity that traders hold on to, hoping to make huge profits from stocks whose value increases as scarcity pushes up prices. A choke on imports could lead to greater speculation and increasing value for ivory stocks (legal or illegal) and provide the incentive for continued or even increased poaching.

Although China has become the primary driver of illicit trade, the markets and trade in southern Europe and the United States should not be forgotten. That Obama pledged to close down most of the domestic US trade in ivory (a promise already made during a state visit to Kenya) suggested the existence of a sizeable trade. In 2008, in an in-depth report on the ivory trade, Stiles and Martin described the United States as one of the world's major ivory markets, with more worked ivory on sale than anywhere except China.[26] They found that large amounts of worked ivory were smuggled into the country from China by individuals, with internet purchasing a major part of both illicit and legal trades. Despite a total prohibition of trade in post-ban ivory (other than hunting trophies), the authors discovered that at least one third of the ivory on sale was post-1990.[27]

In a study published in 2013, Stiles found sixty licensed retailers operating in New York, which remained the most important trading centre for ivory in the USA. Between 2008 and 2013, there had been a 60 per cent fall in the number of outlets selling ivory and a halving of the number of items for sale, although Stiles believed that New York and San Francisco were still major gateways for the importing of illegal ivory, indicating, as Stiles put it, that "China is not the only culprit promoting elephant poaching through its illegal ivory markets. The USA is right there with them".[28]

Europe, for all its posturing about the ivory trade and criticism of China's role in generating demand, is still an important market for ivory and has a legal domestic trade with lax controls. Even after the CITES ban, antique (pre-1947) ivory could be legally imported into Europe and traded between countries. European Union regulations introduced after the CITES ban allow the sale of ivory objects within the Union as long as the seller can provide proof of legal purchase. In a 2005 survey, Martin and Stiles found that 16,444 ivory items were on sale in Germany; 8,325 in London; and smaller amounts in Spain and Italy, giving a total for the four countries of 27,154 items on sale.[29] A survey by Interpol and IFAW found over 660 adverts on sixty-one online auction sites over a two-week period in 2013, offering a total weight of 4,500 kg of ivory for sale. The report said that regular seizures of ivory were still being made in Europe, with the weight of seizures per year from 2007 to 2011 varying between 125 kg and 450 kg.[30] In February 2014, France became the first European country to destroy stocks of ivory, with a ceremony to crush three tons at the Champ de Mars.

East Africa: a mixed picture of recovery and resurgent poaching

After the 1989 CITES vote, Kenya experienced a decline in poaching as the publicity around the ban reduced demand and there was improved enforcement by the reformed Wildlife Service (KWS). Killings fell from 800–1,000 a year in the late 1980s to just over 100 between 1989 and 1990. KWS head Richard Leakey said this resulted from improved morale, more vehicles for patrolling and the supply of modern weapons to rangers. He was confident that "the poaching, although it will never stop completely, will come down to a point where certainly elephant numbers will begin to increase again in places like Tsavo, where they have had such a hammering for so long".[31] The KWS, however, remained dependent on grants from the AWF, the WCS, Conservation International (CI), the WWF and the Frankfurt Zoological Society. Leakey said this rendered it financially weak and so dependent on donors that they had "considerable influence in some areas" of policy and a large say in the setting of the country's conservation agenda.[32] He lamented that "Kenya had been dependent on foreign donors for so long that we had the mentality of welfare recipients: we were no longer able to determine our own priorities or manage our own affairs without an outsider standing over our shoulder".[33] NGOs had developed a sense of ownership over Kenyan conservation, increasing the alienation of many Kenyans from the whole system.

The KWS's problems increased in the mid-1990s when poaching picked up again and elephants started being killed in Kora, Meru, the north-east and Tsavo. The KWS anti-poaching head, Abdul Bashir, put the blame on Somali *shifta*[34]—not an unreasonable supposition, as the 1991 fall of the Somali dictator Siad Barre had led to the disintegration of the Somali army and internecine warfare between political factions and Somali clans, which had access to the old regime's substantial arsenal. Increasing numbers of refugees crossed into Kenya to escape the fighting, as did armed groups who engaged in livestock raiding and poaching. The ivory that was poached was smuggled out by a variety of routes—to southern Somali ports, Ethiopia or Uganda. This was a difficult and tense period in Kenya, as the Moi government had been forced to give in to demands to end one-party rule and domestic political conflict and violence were increasing.

The negatives were balanced out to an extent by signs of recovery in elephant numbers. Despite some poaching, numbers in Tsavo had increased by nearly 10 per cent by 1991, reaching 6,800. By 1994, herds in the Samburu-Laikipia area, outside national park boundaries, had reached 3,000, and their ranges were expanding, bringing them into greater conflict with farmers and pastoralists. This led to increased local anger over the growth in elephant numbers, a higher rate of control shooting and growing numbers of illegal killings by local people. This was a real dilemma for the government, caught between conservation and tourism objectives on the one hand and, on the other, the need for the government to retain popular support and be seen to be trying to protect people and their livelihoods.

By mid-1994, the main areas of concern as far as poaching was concerned were the Tana River, districts around Isiolo and districts near the Somali and Ethiopian borders. David Western, who became KWS director in 1994, said that fifteen elephants had been poached in these areas in the first six months of 1994, but on the good side, the Tsavo population had grown to 7,600.[35] By 1995, Kenya's elephant population was put at 24,000, up from the 1988 low of 22,000. However, the range of Kenya's elephants had diminished and, with the fast-increasing human population, human-elephant conflict was as much of a problem as poaching. Some rural communities argued that there were too many elephants living in close proximity to arable and livestock farmers, such as in Laikipia, or where pastoralists had switched to arable farming and fenced off land, restricting elephant movement.[36] Between 1990 and 1993, 108 people were killed by elephants in Kenya and 119 elephants were killed in control shootings.[37]

Kenya signalled its intent to fight the ivory trade with a further symbolic ivory burning on 9 February 1995. By 1997, though, there were further reports of a rise in poaching; the KWS convened a meeting in November 1997 to discuss mortality rates. Its figures suggested a consistent level of poaching in the years between 1992 and 1997. The numbers of elephants poached annually between 1992 and 1997 were 35, 75, 61, 34, 29 and 44 respectively; the population was put at 27,000.[38] If poaching was still within limits deemed manageable—if not acceptable—there were worrying signs. Seizures of ivory had risen to a greater extent than known killings of elephants—suggesting either an underestimate of the numbers killed or an increased use of Kenya as a transit point for ivory from neighbouring states. Tom Milliken of TRAFFIC believed poaching was rising in Kenya, as was trafficking, with 319.9 kg of ivory seized in 1998 and 1,803.5 kg in 1999. He said poaching had been increasing since 1994, but disagreed with the KWS view that CITES approval for a one-off sale of southern African ivory in 1997 had sparked the increase.[39]

By 2002, there was clear evidence of a growth in poaching, with ten elephants shot in one raid in Tsavo East in March. The KWS, with support from a helicopter and two light aircraft, pursued the gang responsible, shot dead its leader and seized their weapons, including a rocket-propelled grenade launcher. There were also reports of increasing killing for ivory on the Galana Ranch and in the Laikipia-Samburu area. In October 2002, the KWS said that eighty-two elephants had been killed that year, compared with fifty-seven in the whole of 2001; the main smuggling route for the new wave of poaching was north through Somalia and Sudan, where prices were said to have reached a thirteen-year high.[40]

Writing in 2009, Douglas-Hamilton highlighted reports of "dramatically increased poaching over the last year", which were of serious concern. He said that MIKE sites in Samburu and Laikipia had detected moderate annual increases in numbers killed illegally between 2003 and 2008. But he feared a major spike in killings in 2008 and the first half of 2009 "could be a tipping point", at which the level of poaching increased to where it was once more reducing elephant numbers. Up until then, Kenya's populations in Tsavo, Amboseli and Samburu-Laikipia had been stable or increasing despite a constant—though not high—level of poaching. But this was changing.[41] As the evidence of increased illegal killings multiplied, official comments on the problem concentrated on blaming outsiders. The all-purpose enemy—Somalis—were said to be at the centre of the new upsurge. KWS reports on increased poaching failed to mention the range of poachers (some Kenyan, some Kenyan Somalis and some Somalis coming across the border), the Kenyan middlemen, their official/political patrons or the rise in demand and prices for ivory in China. They concentrated on Somali warlords and *shifta*. Reports of verifiable, single poaching operations by Somalis became the focus of the poaching narrative.

NGOs were often keen to jump on the bandwagon, because tying poaching to Islamist or clan warlords in Somalia, already vilified in the media, provided a powerful fundraising tool, one that avoided addressing the problems of Kenyan gang involvement with political protection and the high level of corruption within Kenya that facilitated the trade. A discourse developed that described Kenyan elephants being poached to fund militias in Somalia.[42]

This was not a total invention, and Somalis were involved in poaching. But Somalis were not the only or necessarily the dominant force in poaching in Kenya. My research across a wide range of sources and interviews with leading Kenyan-based conservationists and ivory trade specialists points to a complex mix of criminal gangs with political patronage, local people like the Waliangulu resuming poaching because of the incentive of booming ivory prices, and, yes, Somalis. But the media likes a simple narrative with impact that needs little complex explanation and this suited the Kenyan authorities and conservation NGOs seeking donations. The failed state of Somalia destabilising the region was a major media frame for reporting East Africa and could be easily adapted to report the new wave of poaching. Martin and Vigne, noting that in 2007 and 2008 146 elephants were poached in Kenya, rising to 150 in the first eight months of 2009, reported that traders based in Isiolo were buying tusks from Samburu poachers. Many of these tusks were smuggled out through Ethiopia via Mandera and Moyale, and not to Somalia.[43]

Large amounts of poached ivory, along with ivory smuggled into Kenya from Tanzania or central Africa, were exported by Asian or Chinese syndicates, using Nairobi's airport and Mombasa. Examples of this included the seizure in 2010 of 2 tons of ivory at Nairobi's international airport, packed in a consignment of avocados bound for Malaysia;[44] the discovery by Thai customs officials in April 2011 of 2,033 kg of ivory from Mombasa packed in boxes of frozen mackerel;[45] and the seizure of 465 tusks in Mombasa packed in a cargo of carved soapstone and bound for Cambodia. Cambodia, Laos, Malaysia, Thailand and Vietnam were used as transit routes to smuggle ivory to China. The effect of Chinese demand on the rate of poaching in Kenya was highlighted by Wittmeyer, who said that the increasing killing of elephants in Samburu-Laikipia was directly related to Chinese demand.

This had led to higher poaching from 2009 through to 2011 and a doubling of prices paid to poachers. A poaching trip could earn a wild-life ranger the equivalent of two and a half years' salary, or an unskilled worker fifteen years' income.[46]

The post-2008 increase in poaching threatened to end the recovery of herds in Kenya; monitoring evidence shows that in the Samburu-Laikipia region the population peaked in 2008 at 7,145 and was reduced by poaching to 6,361 in 2012.[47] There was also increased ille-gal killing in Tsavo,[48] where there had been a gradual recovery, with estimates for the entire Tsavo-Mkomazi ecosystem rising from 8,068 in 1999 to 12,573 in February 2011. Poaching led to a decline by 2014, when it was reported that numbers had dropped to 11,000. The numbers killed across Kenya rose in 2012 and 2013, with an estimated 384 and 304 identified as having been poached in those respective years, out of what the KWS said was a population of 28,000.[49] Esmond Martin told the author in early 2015 that he believed KWS figures were an underestimate and that the total could be two to three times as high, something with which a 2014 study by Born Free USA/C4ADS concurred, noting that between 2011 and 2014, 1,500 ele-phants had been lost in the Tsavo ecosystem. The report said that ordi-nary Kenyans had been lured into poaching by the rising income avail-able from ivory and high levels of poverty in areas where there was human-elephant conflict.[50] Cattle raiding between pastoral communi-ties and low cattle prices also contributed to pastoral communities engaging in poaching, while crop damage in arable farming areas encouraged illegal killing.

The trade in ivory in Kenya is sophisticated and flexible, with mid-dlemen-traders gathering tusks at regional trade hubs and passing them on to the trafficking syndicates, who smuggle them out of the country, usually through Mombasa. Poor law enforcement and corruption enable smuggling to continue with relative impunity. The KWS strug-gles with mismanagement, underfunding and corruption, while the Kenyan Police are viewed as the most egregious institution of a country riddled with official corruption. Leakey believed that this corruption, and not Al Shabab or Somalis, was behind the new poaching problem. In an interview in mid-2013, he expressed regret that, as when he first took over the KWS, "politics, corruption and inertia in the wildlife department, and in the government at large, were all so entrenched that failure almost seemed inevitable" when it came to stamping out poaching and illicit ivory dealing.[51]

One of the major problems in fighting the illicit trade in Kenya is the high level of corruption at Mombasa Port. Despite government pledges to crack down on both poaching and smuggling and the institution of tougher sentences, in 2015 there was still a series of seizures of ivory buried in cargoes of tea, chillies, dried fish and other agricultural exports that have been shipped from Mombasa, notably the 4 tons of ivory found in containers of tea by Singaporean customs in May 2015. Tom Milliken of TRAFFIC says that the problem with Mombasa is the tie-up between international smuggling syndicates and the Kenyan political elite,[52] with the latter benefiting from, and so facilitating, the actions of the latter. The ability of the smuggling networks to bribe port officials undercuts any public rhetoric from the government about stopping the trade. *The Wall Street Journal* reported that Kenyan port authorities had admitted to its staff that "kickbacks and bribes" were a problem at Mombasa and one customs official told the newspaper that he received regular payments of KSh500,000 ($4,900) to smooth the way for ivory shipments hidden in containers. This whistleblower said that it was only when insufficient bribes were paid that customs officials would check and seize containers.[53]

By mid-2015, the Kenyan government had increased penalties for poaching and smuggling and promised to step up efforts to crack down on illicit killing and commerce. There were some signs that the new, more rigorous approach was having an effect. Ian Craig, the head of conservation at the Northern Rangelands Trust (NRT) community-based conservation scheme, told the author in September 2015 that the 2011–13 period was very bad, with increasing illegal killing rates, but that in 2014 things began turn and during 2015 rates had dropped to their lowest in five years. Craig credited the tougher regulations and also greater national awareness and engagement with combating the trade. He said that corruption remained a problem because "just like drugs, just like illegal immigrants moving through, it's high value. You can buy people off. If you want to move ivory into the port you have to buy people off and move it in there, and that's happening. It would be naïve to think that it wasn't and so corruption definitely has a role to play."

229

Alongside the more stringent regulations and better intelligence, and despite the evidence of continuing high-level corruption, there are some optimistic signs that Kenya is finding ways to link local conservation and law enforcement efforts with the interests and livelihoods of local people. Initiatives like the Northern Rangelands Trust in the Samburu-Laikipia region (home to one of the largest surviving elephant populations in the country but with serious poaching problems) and also Payment for Environmental Service (PES) schemes, which involve leasing land for conservation and pay fees to local communities, are encouraging.[54] The Tsavo Trust works particularly with the Orma people on the eastern edge of Tsavo, mentoring and providing advice and some financial assistance in the establishment of conservancies and programmes to reduce human-elephant conflict and poaching—it is dependent on donations and sponsorship and is not self-financing.

The NRT has twenty-seven conservancies, which cover 340,000 square km (the same area covered by national parks in Kenya). It helps communities (chiefly pastoral ones in the Samburu-Laikipia-Marsabit areas) by guaranteeing high prices for livestock to provide steady income, helping mediate in conflicts between pastoralist communities and combating rustling. In return, it elicits community involvement in conservation and anti-poaching, also providing around 1,000 paid jobs in anti-poaching and tourism (based on seven tourist lodges in the conservancies). Income goes to the communities and the NRT assists them in setting up businesses to ensure maximum income generation and management of income. This is aimed at providing direct and obvious benefits to communities involved.[55] The Trust says this has resulted in successful development of intelligence on illegal hunting and the formation of well-trained and, crucially, well-paid anti-poaching units recruited from among local people.[56]

The management of the conservancies by the communities, with the assistance of the NRT, has brought buy-in—something lacking in the Galana scheme set up by Ian Parker to encourage the Waliangulu to end poaching. The Trust's elephant monitoring figures suggest success in bringing down levels of illegal killing—in 2011 and 2012, poaching was unacceptably high in the areas the Trust covered, with 108 elephants killed for their tusks in 2012. In 2013, as anti-poaching operations improved and communities themselves took a more active role in discouraging poaching, the number killed was down to forty-five. The downside of the NRT approach is that it is heavily donor-dependent and doesn't generate substantial income from other sources, despite some tourism earnings, and it remains to be seen whether donor funding will continue to enable the scheme to operate on a large scale.

In February 2016, ahead of both a massive ivory burning ceremony and a summit in Kenya of the Giants Club—an exclusive forum that brings together African heads of state, global business leaders and elephant protection experts to secure Africa's remaining elephant populations and the landscapes they depend on—the Environment and Natural Resources Cabinet Secretary, Judi Wakhungu, said that in the last three years the government had doubled its efforts at combating elephant poaching and illegal trade in ivory within and across its borders. She reported that the government believed that only ninety-three elephants were poached in 2015, compared with 164 the previous year. She said that the government held a stockpile of 135 tons of ivory and that much of this would be destroyed at the burning ceremony in April.[57] It is worth noting that the introduction of sniffer dog teams at Nairobi's airport has resulted in a massive increase in ivory seizures there. The US-based African Wildlife Foundation has supplied trained sniffer dogs, which are being used by teams from the KWS. In the first few weeks of operations, four smugglers were caught trying to get worked ivory out to China, some of it thought to have originated in West and Central Africa.[58] The seizures confirmed Kenya's role as a staging post for ivory trading between other range states and China. Kenya is also receiving funding and technical help from the United States to improve security and ivory detection at Mombasa, according to Wakhungu, who admitted that the port had long been a transit point for poached ivory and other smuggled goods.[59]

If Kenya offered glimmers of hope, with elephant numbers increasing gradually in some areas, Sudan and South Sudan were gloom personified. They split in 2011 following a referendum in which southerners voted overwhelmingly for independence—something provided for in the 2005 Comprehensive Peace Agreement (CPA) between the Khartoum government and the southern Sudan People's Liberation Movement (SPLM and its army, the SPLA), which brought to an end decades of civil war. The war had exacted an appalling human toll, destroying much of the infrastructure in the south and creating conditions in which the country's large elephant herds had been decimated by a variety of forces—the Sudanese army, militias like the Janjaweed, the southern rebel movements and local people seeking to survive amid the violence and disruption of the local economy.

Ivory poached during the conflict was taken out through Khartoum, Ethiopia and Uganda. The population of elephants in the south (there were none left in the north) fell from an estimated 133,000 in 1976 to 40,000 in 1992. The South Sudan Wildlife Conservation and Tourism Ministry and the WCS estimated that by the signing of the CPA there were only 5–10,000 elephants left. Between the CPA and the outbreak of civil war in South Sudan in December 2013, the WCS assisted the southern wildlife authorities in conserving and monitoring the surviving herds, many of which were situated in the Boma National Park near the border with Ethiopia or in the Sudd swamplands near the border with Uganda. In July 2013, radio collars were attached to sixty elephants to enable tracking and locating elephant herds and later another twenty-six were collared, but Paul Elkan of the WCS told the author in August 2014 that at least a third of the collared animals had disappeared, presumed killed.

The surviving southern population was vulnerable. War had shattered the conservation infrastructure and even when the Sudanese army and militias pulled out, there was still a continuous threat from small arms which had flooded the country during the war and a plethora of local rebel groups in conflict with or allied to the SPLA, and local people were often forced to rely on hunting to survive the loss of livestock or displacement by fighting. During the war, the Sudanese army and the northern-backed militias had killed elephants and rhinos. Tusks were sent north in army lorries, with the Khartoum government and the army benefiting from this by-product of conflict. The end of the war and the establishment of the autonomous southern administration under the SPLM, followed by independence, offered some hope of progress. The new government was committed to protecting the remaining wildlife and rehabilitating the national parks with aid from the WCS and the US government. The WCS radio collar programme and funding of anti-poaching units in Boma and other parks was a step forward. But even before the outbreak of the civil war in December

2013, it was clear that the legacies of conflict and division between communities would be hard to overcome and could be disastrous for the remaining elephants. In mid-2013, just as the WCS programme really got off the ground, fighting between the SPLA and a militia from the Murle people spilled over into Boma. Three wildlife rangers and the Park Warden, Brigadier Kolo Pino, were killed by the SPLA when they tried to crush the Murle rebels—the warden and rangers were also Murle.[60]

The outbreak of the civil war put the elephant herds in jeopardy, as anti-poaching operations were rendered impossible and rival armed groups were active in and around Boma and near the Ugandan border, where other herds were situated. In central Equatoria, near the border with the DRC, the head of the Lantoto National Park reported the killing of six elephants in early 2014 and that armed groups were constantly poaching wildlife there. By December 2014, the WCS and South Sudan wildlife authorities were pessimistically putting the surviving population at 2,500, with the WCS's Paul Elkan warning that the elephant could be rendered extinct in the country within five years.[61] The African Elephant Database figure for South Sudan in 2013 was 1,172 definite and a possible maximum figure of 5,882.[62] In April 2016, it was reported that seventeen elephants had been poached in wetland areas of South Sudan, among the safest refuges for the remaining elephants.

The wildlife director for Unity State, Major-General James Gatjiath, said the elephants were killed in a wildlife corridor between Unity State and the Bahr el-Ghazal region. He said this wasn't the first incident of poaching there and that fifteen elephants had been killed several months previously. He said buffalo and antelope were being killed for meat almost daily, and added that he had insufficient staff to protect wildlife.[63] This depressing account backed up reports by the WCS in South Sudan that illegal killing of wildlife for meat and ivory was increasing, with cases involving nineteen SPLA soldiers, members of the Cobra Faction militia, South Sudanese civilians and Darfur-based Sudanese poachers and traders all involved. Many were involved in bushmeat production for sale locally, but some soldiers, militia members and Sudanese were poaching or trafficking ivory to be taken out of the country after being flown to Juba.[64]

The only good news from South Sudan was that camera traps in the south-west of the country had taken pictures of forest elephants, thought to be extinct in South Sudan. Researchers from Bucknell University and Flora and Fauna International (FFI) spotted the critically endangered animals using camera traps set up in South Sudan's western Equatoria, state in an area of densely forested hills near the borders with the DRC and the CAR. The Smithsonian Institute in the United States said that the discovery was "also good news for forest elephants generally. Across Africa, over 60 per cent of the animals disappeared between 2002 and 2011 amid intense poaching pressure".[65]

Elephants were extinct in the rest of Sudan well before the end of the war in the south, but Khartoum-Omdurman remained a major centre for ivory trading, which has developed in the last twenty years as economic relations between Sudan and China have blossomed, with Chinese companies taking a major role in the oil industry, road building and infrastructural projects. The presence of large numbers of Chinese provided a ready market for the large quantities of ivory on sale. Sudan was a major hub on the route for exporting ivory from South Sudan, the DRC, Uganda, the CAR, Chad and Cameroon. The Enough Project, which tracks insurgent groups like Uganda's Lord's Resistance Army (LRA), reported in October 2015 that the Sudanese army, Janjaweed, SPLA soldiers and other South Sudanese armed groups were heavily involved in poaching in Garamba, DRC (see below for greater detail).[66] Ivory was exported via Khartoum to China and to Egypt by road and camel caravan. Despite being banned under Sudanese law, Khartoum's ivory markets have thrived with the numerous Chinese customers. In 2005, Martin said the number of carvers had increased from 100 to 150 since 1997 (after a period of decline following the CITES ban). In a survey he found 11,329 ivory items made from post-1990 ivory on sale in fifty different retail outlets.[67]

It is worth examining the major role played in the current Sudanese ivory trade by the Janjaweed, which shows both evolution of the trade and continuity with the past role of Baggara-Rizeigat Arabs in raiding and trading in tusks and other goods. It should be emphasised that the Janjaweed is not a purely military or insurgent group directly comparable with the LRA, Al Shabab or Boko Haram. It is an irregular militia formed from pastoral/nomadic communities which have been involved for centuries in long-distance trade, whether in ivory, slaves, livestock or weapons, between Sudan, Chad, the CAR and other central African states. The Janjaweed were not fighting or accumulating wealth for a specific political purpose, but as part of a diversified way of life which could include fighting alongside the Sudanese army in the south or Darfur in return for arms, money and licence to loot.

Even though Janjaweed ivory poaching has grabbed headlines because of the militia's involvement in the killing of 300–450 elephants in a raid on Bouba N'Djida National Park in Cameroon in January 2012, it is not believed by those who have studied the militia in detail that ivory is a major part of its income, nor that it funds its military activities.[68] This is not an ivory-insurgency link so much as a criminal organisation-trading network that hires itself out to the Sudanese army. In their written evidence to the US Senate Foreign Relations Committee in May 2012, Ginette Hemley of the WWF and Tom Milliken of TRAFFIC emphasised the Janjaweed's long association with raiding, slaving and ivory trading and the way they have taken advantage of porous borders and conflicts in Darfur, South Sudan, the CAR, Chad and the DRC to carry out their criminal activities.[69] Stiles has also emphasised the militia's history as raiders, noting that the term *Janjaweed* is not the name of a movement but combines words from Darfur languages meaning armed horsemen.

The modern incarnation of the Janjaweed is as groups of mounted gunmen involved in periodic banditry and looting in areas of Sudan's Darfur province, bordering Libya, Chad and the CAR, and also returning at times to trading and pastoralism.[70] They are drawn chiefly from the Abbala Rizeigat, with lineage and linguistic connections to communities in eastern Chad. Their traditional lifestyle involved moving back and forth across the borders of western Darfur in search of water and grazing for their herds. But they had long been involved in trading and in raiding other communities' livestock. They were traditionally armed with long spears and only a few guns. They gained access to large quantities of modern arms in the early 1980s when a combination of drought and the Chadian civil war led to an influx of armed Chadian militias and pastoralists into Darfur seeking grazing and sanctuary from the conflict. Some Rizeigat had been recruited and armed to serve in Gaddafi's Libyan Islamic Legion, which fought in Chad until the late

1980s. The Chadian influx sparked conflict with and between Darfurian communities but also trade for guns. Those who had fought for Gaddafi returned from Chad in 1988, increasing the availability of weapons.

The Janjaweed were utilised by the Sudanese government to fight the SPLA in the south and became part of the complex of communities and insurgent groups involved in the long and brutal Darfur conflict. This provided them with more arms and opportunities for raiding, sanctioned by the Sudanese army. Their mobility, weaponry and experience of cross-border smuggling and raiding equipped them to carry out poaching expeditions into the CAR and Chad, where they harvested ivory and meat.[71] The Janjaweed had links with rebel groups in Chad and carried out poaching in Chadian national parks (for further details, see below). Their raids carried them as far as north-eastern Cameroon. The tusks taken on these expeditions were chiefly sold via the thriving Khartoum-Omdurman ivory market or transported to the Far East from Khartoum with the connivance of the army and Sudanese officials. The Janjaweed, along with Chadian poaching gangs, have operated to devastating effect in the CAR, at times with the cooperation of the Seleka movement while the latter was briefly in power, but even since Seleka lost power they have continued poaching in Seleka-controlled areas near to national parks and concentrations of elephants. Sudanese militias, including Janjaweed elements, are believed to have assisted Seleka into power and to have poached on its behalf. In the 2000s and 2010s, many of the poachers operating in the CAR came from Sudan and Chad and, according to the International Crisis Group, operated in units twenty to eighty strong. They are thought to poach for their own profit but also on behalf of and funded by Sudanese families from the Nyala area in South Darfur with a long history of ivory trading. They buy tusks from poachers in the Sudanese towns of Buram, Tulus and Am Dafok, near the CAR border, and transport them to Nyala, where they are sold to Sudanese and foreign traders who export it to Asia.[72]

The brief lull in poaching in Tanzania, after the CITES ban and an anti-poaching blitz, was followed by a devastating resumption in the new millennium. It involved criminal networks linking poachers, smugglers and foreign buyers with venal politicians and officials, including some in the wildlife department and police force. The close political and ever-expanding commercial relations with China were a key factor, as there were ready buyers and trading networks developing that involved the large Chinese community in Tanzania, as well as the long-standing Indian traders. In their study of the effects of the ban, Dublin and Jachmann said that at first poaching seemed to have declined in Ruaha and Selous, which had been hard hit by poachers with the elephant populations dropping from 43,685 in 1977 to 17,341 in 1990 in Ruaha and, in Selous, from 42,841 in 1986 to 20,400 in 1991.[73]

The ban followed the launch of Operation Uhai, an anti-poaching offensive preceded by a major undercover operation to gather intelligence on poachers and smugglers. The enforcement phase of the operation involved wildlife rangers and the army and was Tanzania's most successful attempt to fight the trade, helped by a short-lived increase in international funding. In two years, Uhai led to the arrest of 2,607 poachers and the recovery of 3,054 tusks, but few reports of action against traders and their patrons. The success in clamping down on killing, if not in rooting out those who organised and profited most from it, led to a recovery in numbers in Selous, with numbers up to 52,000 in 1996. Other populations in Tanzania also began to recover. In the Mkomazi-Tsavo ecosystem, numbers grew by 98 per cent between 1988 and 2008, reaching 12,573. Martin and Vigne described Uhai as like flicking a switch, which stopped poaching almost overnight and sustained the reduction for years.[74] But by the end of 1997, poaching was starting up again, albeit at a lower level than ten years previously. With the rise in demand in China, Tanzania in the 2000s became a major source of ivory. The ivory syndicates targeted Selous and Ruaha, which still had substantial populations.

In 2010, both Tanzania and Zambia petitioned CITES to have their elephant populations down-listed to Appendix II, like the southern African populations. Not only did this not fit well with evidence of increased poaching and trafficking in both countries, but it followed the CITES decision of 2008 to have a nine-year moratorium on ivory sales from southern Africa. The attempts came to nothing, but illustrated the disconnect between the increasing illicit trade and the outlook of some range state governments. Data available at the time of the abortive CITES down-listing bid showed that the largest single ivory seizure since the ivory trade ban (6.5 tons in Singapore in 2002) was proved by DNA analyses to have originated almost entirely from Zambia. Ivory from Tanzania made up 41 per cent of seizures in 2006 (11 of 27 tons). Wasser et al.'s study of the DNA testing of 2,600 kg of ivory seized from Hong Kong and 5,200 kg from Taiwan confirmed origins from Selous (southern Tanzania) and the neighbouring Niassa Game Reserves complex (northern Mozambique).[75] An EIA investigation into Tanzania's ivory trade, part of a campaign to stop the downlisting, suggested widespread availability of illicit ivory in Tanzania and the heavy involvement of Chinese and other Asian nationals in the trade—the Agency said that of 24 tons of ivory seized globally in 2009, 12 tons were from Tanzania.[76] Police and customs seizures in Tanzania implicated networks of indigenous and Chinese businessmen, Tanzanian customs officials and employees of the Tanzania Revenue Authority, six of whom were arrested on smuggling charges in 2009. In January 2011, in one of the few successes for the Lusaka Task Force, an investigation led to the seizure in Vietnam of 769 pieces of tusk weighing 2,005 kg, en route from Zanzibar to buyers in China.[77]

The extent of poaching in Selous and the Niassa Reserve by Tanzanian gangs led to the listing of Selous in 2014 as a World Heritage Site in Danger. Tim Badman, director of the IUCN World Heritage programme, said that poaching was alarmingly high and that the Selous population had dropped from 70,000 in 2005 to 13,000 in 2013.[78] A study by the Selous Elephant Emergency Project, published in 2014, reported that the Selous and surrounding ecosystems had lost two thirds of their elephants in just a few years.[79] Tanzania's Minister for Natural Resources and Tourism, Lazaro Nyalandu, has pledged to improve enforcement, action against smugglers, and customs checks at ports and airports, but given that corruption involves customs and port officials, optimism about turning the situation around is not high.

The general air of pessimism about Tanzania's ability to halt the poaching was increased with the publication of the EIA's sensational 2014 report, *Vanishing Point*. This campaigning document aimed at putting pressure on the Tanzanian and Chinese governments to end the trade. As with previous reports, it was a mixture, as one leading elephant scientist told me, of "pure gold with a lot of dross" that had campaigning at its heart and left the reader to sort out what was accurate and what was there just to have impact. Mary Rice of the EIA defended the report in an interview with me but stressed that the EIA was foremost a campaigning group. She said it was "very frustrating" that the media had seized on the report's accusation that ivory had been smuggled out of Tanzania on the Chinese president's plane at the end of a state visit in March 2013. This part of the report was based on data from informers without other corroboration. It was the weakest part of the report but, of course, got the most press attention and thereby drew attention to the report as a whole and to the EIA's campaigns. It was rejected by the Tanzanian and Chinese governments, the latter issuing press statements denying the allegations and attacking the EIA as "a dodgy organization".[80]

The gold in the report, according to conservationists to whom I spoke, concerned the extent of corruption in the Tanzanian government, customs, police and wildlife departments and the relations between official corruption and criminal syndicates involved in smuggling. The report also gave the latest estimates of elephant losses, confirming the census figures from Tanzania that just 13,084 elephants were left in Selous with 25,000 killed between 2010 and 2013. In the Ruaha-Rungwa region, the population fell from 31,625 in 2009 to 20,900 in 2013 and then to a staggering 8,272 in 2014 before rising to 15,836 in 2015—Dr Trevor Jones of the Southern Tanzania Elephant Programme said that individual years alone do not give an accurate reflection of the population, as a variety of factors may account for rises and falls, but that "the trend in the population—the most important finding from a conservation point of view—is clearly shown. This trend is downwards, at an extremely worrying rate" and poaching is the cause.[81]

The scale of poaching was due to demand and corruption facilitating poaching and smuggling, and the "lack of resources in the wildlife department", which "left the area largely unprotected, largely due to the termination of a scheme under which the majority of earnings from photographic and hunting safaris were retained to fund anti-poaching—funds available dropped from $2.8m to $800,000".[82] During President Kikwete's presidency (2005–15), the elephant population will have dropped from 142,000 to 55,000—figures supported by those of the Elephant Database, which put the minimum numbers in Tanzania in 2013 at 53,833.

Kikwete has been vocally supportive of conservation but has failed to take strong action to dismiss, let alone prosecute, corrupt politicians and officials. One minister for natural resources and tourism, Khamis Kagasheki, "named four CCM [Chama Cha Mapinduzi, ruling party] MPs who were involved in poaching and told parliament that 'This business involves rich people and politicians who have formed a very sophisticated network'". In 2012, a list of people in the government, public service and the business sector allegedly involved in poaching was handed to President Kikwete, but nothing was done.[83] The EIA published Kagasheki's disclosure that senior members of and donors to the ruling CCM were heavily involved in protecting and profiting from the ivory trade. It named, as key members of illicit trade networks, Mohsin Abdallah, who owns hunting blocks near Selous and a transport business, Zantas Air, and CCM Secretary-General and Former Defence Minister Abdulrahman Kinana. A Tanzanian MP, Peter Msigwa, accused Mr Kinana in parliament of involvement in the ivory trade, something which Kinana has repeatedly denied as "unfounded and malicious". He denied knowledge of an ivory shipment of 6.2 tons seized in Vietnam in 2009 from a ship operated by his company, Sharaf Shipping.[84] Far from getting support from Kikwete and the government to investigate these accusations and root out corruption, Kagasheki lost his job as minister.

The failure to pursue the key players in the illicit trade has enabled the very flexible and adaptable networks of Chinese smugglers, corrupt officials, Tanzanian middlemen and poachers to continue to thrive, with only the poachers in serious danger of prosecution or of being shot during anti-poaching operations. The middlemen, traders, officials and politicians act with little risk of arrest or, even if they are caught and prosecuted, of conviction or heavy sentences. But the last months of 2015 and the opening months of 2016 showed some hope that greater efforts were being made to combat poaching and smuggling and to deal with corruption.

In October, an elite Tanzanian organised crime squad arrested Yang Feng Glan, a Chinese national and Dar es Salaam restaurant owner nicknamed the "Ivory Queen", on charges of running an illicit ivory trading network over several years. According to police sources, she ran a smuggling ring that received tusks poached in national parks and then smuggled them out to markets in East Asia and China. It was said she and her network had been under surveillance for a year by Tanzania's National and Transnational Serious Crimes Investigation Unit, which was particularly concerned with ivory trading. The unit's operation was partly funded by donations from the Protected Area Management Solutions Foundation (PAMS), run by the South African conservationist, Wayne Lotter. He was assassinated in Tanzania in August 2017 in an attack suspected of being organised by criminals linked with the ivory trade. Yang was charged with heading a criminal network responsible for smuggling 706 pieces of ivory worth $2.5m between 2000 and 2014. Yang denied the charges but was held on remand.[85] In 2019 she was sentenced to fifteen years in jail for smuggling ivory, which was believed to have involved the killing of 400 elephants. Two Tanzanian men were also found guilty of involvement in the ring. In March 2016, a Dar es Salaam court handed down long terms to two ivory smugglers, indicating a toughening of sentencing policy. Huang Gin and Xu Fujie were both jailed for thirty-five years for illegal possession of tusks from an estimated 210 elephants.

On a broader front, the election of John Magufuli as president of Tanzania in October 2015 offers hope of a serious campaign against government and parastatal corruption. Nicknamed "The Bulldozer" for his energetic and aggressive approach to politics, Magufuli immediately set about sacking hospital administrators found to be corrupt and sent his new Prime Minister, Kassim Majaliwa, to the notoriously mismanaged and corrupt port in Dar es Salaam, where he found that taxes totalling $40 million hadn't been paid and that the port authority and customs authorities were mired in corruption. Magufuli immediately suspended and arrested the Tanzania Revenue Authority's commissioner general and five top officials. He also sacked the head of the port authority and several senior officials in the transport ministry. Dar es Salaam has become one of the major transit points for ivory, precious metals, gems and other illicit goods leaving East Africa for China and other Asian destinations because of the extent of corruption.

Encouragingly, in February 2016, the Tourism and Natural Resources Minister, Jumanne Maghembe, announced that as part of continuing efforts to clamp down on wildlife poaching "once and for all", the government was going to establish a permanent multi-sectoral task force, with members drawn from the police, the army, and all local conserva-

IVORY

tion bodies;[86] though one must hope that, in the process of setting it up, the corrupt police, army and wildlife officials who are an integral part of the illicit trade networks are weeded out and do not become part of the task force. The president himself added to the sense of a new urgency by ordering courts to fast-track all cases relating to smuggling ivory, wildlife trophies and drugs.[87] It remains to be seen if Magufuli's campaign will continue, and whether it will have a profound and lasting effect on the political and public service corruption that is at the heart of the illegal ivory trade in Tanzania.[88]

One other positive development in Tanzania has been in the Ruvuma area between the heavily poached Selous and the equally badly affected Niassa Park across the border in Mozambique. The Ruvuma Elephant Project (REP) has been established to operate in the wildlife corridor connecting Selous and Niassa. Here, where wildlife moves between the two reserves, a strategy has been put in place that allows wildlife to cross unfenced land between them and engages local communities in anti-poaching. Surveys conducted on the ground and then from the air between December 2011 and November 2013 revealed that the number of elephant carcasses recorded in the REP territory dropped from 216 in the first year of the survey to sixty-eight in the second. Wayne Lotter, director of PAMS, which oversees REP, believes cooperation with wildlife and enforcement agencies in Tanzania and Mozambique and, in particular, community involvement have been keys to the project's success, and that intelligence gathering in poachers' communities of origin has been crucial.

Lotter clearly identified the problem of getting local people on board with conservation: "It's a minority of cases where people are actually happy with a game reserve or a national park… The issues are you have a farm. You have elephants and other herbivores that come out and graze your crops… It impacts directly on their livelihood. Generally they don't get compensated by conservation… Villagers get killed by elephants… They're not getting any benefit from the wildlife."[89] The REP has employed 200 local people in conservation and anti-poaching, and helped provide income from wildlife. The results have been a decline in poaching, the recovery of 175 poached tusks and the arrest of 563 poachers with local assistance. The project reduced illegal killing at a time when Selous and Niassa were experiencing major outbreaks that threatened the large elephant populations. In March 2015, the Tanzanian government, the WCS and USAID launched another community-related scheme covering the Southern Highlands and the Ruaha-Katavi region, which is home to 25,000 elephants across an area of 115,000 square km.

It is too early to say what long-term effect such schemes will have, but they offer a glimmer of light in a very gloomy environment for elephant conservation in Tanzania, where 60 per cent of elephants have been killed in five years. Between 2009 and 2014, the estimated population dropped from 109,051 to 43,330. With an annual birth rate of maximum 5 per cent, this suggests that over 85,000 elephants could have been killed in Tanzania in this period, with corruption and the role of international criminal syndicates the chief factors in the decline. The continuing poaching problem was emphasised in January 2016 when huge international media attention focused on the death of Roger Gower, a British pilot working with anti-poaching teams in northern Tanzania. He was shot by poachers armed with AK-47s while he was flying as part of an anti-poaching operation at Maswa, following the poaching of elephants there. His death highlighted the danger to rangers and anti-poaching personnel when dealing with well-armed gangs prepared to kill rather than be captured.[90] In early February, five men were arrested in connection with his killing and with the trafficking of illegal weapons and ivory.

Uganda has experienced a recovery in elephant numbers in recent years, but has had a continuing role as a smuggling hub. There is convincing evidence that the Ugandan army is involved in poaching under the cover of counter-insurgency operations in neighbouring states. At the time of the trade ban and its immediate aftermath, Uganda's elephant population was very low, with about 500 animals in Queen Elizabeth National Park, approximately 280 in Murchison Falls, perhaps 300–400 in Kidepo and smaller populations in Rwenzori and outside protected areas. The African Elephant Database figure for Uganda's population in 1995 was 1,318 definite and 1,848 maximum.[91] The decline was caused by poaching in the 1970s and 1980s, by armies, militias, rebel groups and local people desperate for food and income in a country devastated by war.

Although Uganda was still affected by conflict arising from the insurgency launched by the LRA in the north-west and the Allied

Democratic Forces (ADF) in the west along the border with the DRC, the 1990s and early 2000s saw improvements in law enforcement in protected areas. The result was that the projected maximum for the elephant population was up to 2,722 by 1998, and in 2002 the Database recorded a definite population of 2,064 and a maximum of 2,732.[92] In 2003, the Ugandan Wildlife Authority (UWA), with support from the army, smashed a trafficking and poaching ring operating in Murchison Falls National Park. The joint operation followed the killing of seven elephants. One of the leaders of the poaching gang was an officer in the Ugandan People's Defence Force (UPDF) and its membership included a man from a security detail assigned to protect the Karuma-Pakwach road, who provided automatic rifles in return for four tusks. This was an example of the Ugandan military's involvement in the trade—not as part of a military campaign or to support counter-insurgency, but as part of a criminal enterprise. Evidence of this corruption and official or military engagement in the illicit trade continued to mount, even as elephant numbers recovered and anti-poaching measures inside the country improved. By 2007, the African Elephant Database estimated a minimum of 2,337 and a maximum of 6,559—a substantial increase. By 2013, the estimate had risen to 3,452 definite and a maximum of 7,894. The Great Elephant Census's initial findings for Uganda suggested that, by 2014, the verifiable numbers were up to about 5,000.[93]

Improved enforcement and an end to the conflicts inside Uganda had reduced opportunities for the army to conceal poaching behind a façade of counter-insurgency—but reports grew of Ugandan army units poaching in neighbouring states, particular the DRC's Garamba National Park (see DRC section below). As late as 2014, John Okot Emitchell, the Nairobi-based field officer of the Lusaka Agreement Task Force (a grouping of regional states including Kenya, Uganda, Zambia and Tanzania, pledged to work together to stamp out the ivory trade), reported that 12 tons of ivory from Uganda had been seized in Nairobi over the previous two years. Okot said that intelligence gathering had proved that high-ranking government and military officials were involved in poaching and in the transit of central African ivory through Uganda to be flown out or exported via smuggling syndicates in Mombasa.[94]

Dr Andrew Seguya, the executive director of the UWA, warned at a wildlife conference in Kampala that illegal ivory buyers, particularly well-established traders from West Africa, had relocated to Kampala because of Uganda's porous borders and weak laws, and because civil war in the CAR had obstructed their operations there. They were using Uganda to pass ivory on to East Asian syndicates. The network of corruption in Uganda included senior government and military personnel, customs officers and companies that cleared goods through customs. The extent of the trade and lack of law enforcement meant that Uganda was included in the CITES "Gang of Eight" most heavily involved in the ivory trade; the others were China, Kenya, Thailand, Malaysia, Vietnam, the Philippines and Tanzania. At the same conference, John Makombo, the UWA's director of conservation, said that in the previous couple of years there had been a rise, though not a catastrophic one, in poaching in Uganda. In the previous ten years, 234 elephants had been poached, but in 2011 alone, fifty-six elephants were killed. The WWF representative for Uganda, David Duli, said that laws needed to be tightened along with enforcement, as "At the moment, if you're caught with ivory, you could pay about one million shillings yet a 10 kg tusk goes for between $10–20,000 (approx. Shs54 million)".[95]

At the time of writing, little of great import seems to have been done to tighten law enforcement and stop the illicit transport of poached ivory through Uganda. Continuing corruption and the unwillingness of the judiciary to take wildlife crime seriously remain serious impediments in combating the smugglers and organised crime networks. Even more worrying is that senior UWA staff have been involved in trafficking. In February 2015, the *New Vision* newspaper reported that officers of the UWA, army and police had been caught smuggling rhino horn through Entebbe International Airport. They were said to be part of a well-organised smuggling syndicate involving a number of senior UWA officials, which the newspaper reported had been revealed by a UWA investigation. The investigation showed that UWA personnel were working with the Aviation Police at the airport to get the ivory out. Corrupt soldiers, policemen and UWA staff had also been involved in the theft of confiscated horns and tusks from the UWA high security stores in Kampala. On 4 February 2015, *New Vision* reported that Gerald Tenywa, the journalist who had covered the story, had as a result received death threats and warnings not to delve further into the smuggling operations. The unwillingness of the judiciary to take smuggling seriously and use existing laws to convict those involved came to light at around the same time. In October 2013, the Ugandan Revenue Authority had seized a consignment of 832 pieces of ivory worth several million dollars being smuggled through Uganda from the DRC. Despite the illicit nature of the ivory, high court judge Justice Musalu Musene ruled in the smugglers' favour and ordered the release of the ivory for export. In March 2014, the Ugandan appeal court reversed the court decision and halted the release.

The theft of ivory and rhino horn from the UWA and the court case over the confiscated ivory demonstrated the problems of wildlife law enforcement in Uganda and the extent of corruption in the bodies most closely involved in anti-poaching and anti-smuggling operations. It has also become clear that the lack of serious intent to combat the illegal trade goes to the top. In February 2015, the Save the Elephants group highlighted this when they reported that President Museveni had blocked investigations into two UPDF officers—one who actually sat on the board of the Ugandan Wildlife Authority, and another who helped to coordinate security and law enforcement for the UWA—over the disappearance of two tons of ivory seized by the UWA. Bonaventure Ebayi, director of the Lusaka Agreement Task Force, confirmed that the investigation had been stymied. He added that the illicit trade through Uganda was growing and that 13,000 tons of ivory had passed through the country for export in recent years. Save the Elephants also said that Museveni primarily used the UWA intelligence unit to suppress armed opposition groups and to track the LRA and ADF, and wasn't interested in stopping the unit's role in ivory trading.[96]

Ominously, in late 2015, there were signs of an increase in poaching within Uganda's protected areas, with six elephants killed for their tusks in Queen Elizabeth National Park in September, according to the UWA. The manager of Queen Elizabeth, Nelson Guma, told the *Monitor* newspaper in Kampala that there were signs of increasing levels of poaching in the park, using firearms rather than snares to catch antelope for meat. Guma didn't put a figure on the total number of elephants killed in recent years, but said many had been lost and that this was damaging the attempts to rebuild tourism there. He accused politicians of protecting the poachers, but didn't give names or further details.

Central Africa: Gabon the only sanctuary for elephants amid continued decline

Table 4: Central Africa's elephant population, 1995–2013

1995		1998		2002		2007		2013	
Definite	*Max*	*Definite*	*Max*	*Definite*	*Max*	*Definite*	*Max*	*Definite*	*Max*
7320	25219	7322	125508	16450	195793	10383	127246	9448	147970

Source: African Elephant Database, 2013, http://www.elephantdatabase.org/preview_report/2013_africa_final/Loxodonta_africana/2013/Africa/ accessed 15 June 2016.

The variations in figures from the above database don't relate to poaching alone but to the difficulties in carrying out surveys because of the thick forest canopy and to the effects of conflict in many of the states concerned, which prevent full surveys. The region's elephant population had been falling for decades before the CITES ban because of such conflict, as well as legal and illegal hunting. This has continued despite the banning of the trade. At the time of the ban there were crudely estimated to be between 200,000 and 495,000 forest elephants in central Africa. A third of them were believed to be in central and eastern Zaire/DRC, another third in Gabon and the rest in Cameroon, the CAR, Congo, Equatorial Guinea and Gabon, with savannah elephants in northern DRC, northern Cameroon, the CAR and Chad. Most were under threat from poaching for ivory or meat. By 1993, about half the population was thought to have been poached.[97] The poaching was a mixture of small-scale subsistence hunting for meat and organised ivory poaching. The organised poaching, as detailed in Chapter 5, was linked closely with corruption in government, wildlife authorities and the armed forces or police.

In a report on trends in poaching in 2008, Douglas-Hamilton wrote that in central Africa surveys of elephant numbers and of the ivory trade showed continuous decline in the twenty years since the CITES ban; he drew a close link between weak governance, corruption, crime and conflict as the complex of factors enabling poaching to continue. Forest elephants in the DRC were the hardest hit, with the estimate of the absolute maximum population down to around 22,000 by 2008.[98] Central Africa was experiencing continuing reductions in numbers with no end in sight. In Chad, savannah elephants were in rapid decline, with the population in the key Zakouma National Park dropping from 3,800 in 2006 to about 600 in 2008, as a result of the depredations of Sudanese Janjaweed and other poachers. In his evidence to the US Senate Foreign Relations Committee, Douglas-Hamilton estimated that the rise in Chinese demand for ivory and poor law enforcement in central Africa had led to a 62 per cent drop in the overall regional population between 2002 and 2011—an estimate supported by Maisels.[99] By 2013, Gabon was believed to have half the remaining forest elephants and the DRC just a fifth, despite the high levels of poaching in Gabon between 2004 and 2011. The UNEP/Interpol survey in 2014 estimated that there could be as few as 8,000 forest elephants left outside Gabon and the Republic of the Congo.[100] The most important forest haven was the protected Tri-National Dja-Odzala-Minkébé (TRIDOM) area, comprising northern Gabon, south-eastern Cameroon, and northern Republic of the Congo. What is worrying is that over 85 per cent of the forest elephant ivory seized between 2006 and 2014 was traced to the central African TRIDOM ecosystem.

In 1989, Cameroon was estimated to have around 21,200 elephants, 19,700 of them forest elephants.[101] The CITES ban didn't have a major effect on the moderate level of poaching in the country, but within a couple of years there were signs of an increase with tusks smuggled out to Nigeria, where the fall in prices after the ban had increased local demand. In 1991, twenty-seven elephants were killed in Cameroon's Korup National Park, the ivory destined for Nigeria. The highest elephant densities were in the south-east of the country near the borders with Congo and Gabon, but poaching was common there, with logging opening up forests through the construction of roads and also providing a market for bushmeat.

Cameroon has a domestic ivory market, and possession of raw ivory and the sale of worked ivory is legal. Hunting is permitted, with the necessary licences. Where elephants have been poached it has often been by local people using homemade or old firearms, snares and traps. Between 1991 and 1994, one sanctuary, Banyang-Mbo in the south-west of the country, suffered the loss of 186 out of a maximum of 400 elephants. Poaching was encouraged by the sanctuary's proximity to the major domestic ivory market in Douala and the border with Nigeria. The level of local poaching in many areas of Cameroon, with people using crudely made firearms, showed that most people saw little if any benefit in conservation. In the mid-to-late 2000s, the involvement of more organised poaching gangs linked with smuggling syndicates developed as global demand increased. TRAFFIC reported in 2008 that the country was experiencing a wave of poaching with the use of more sophisticated weapons.[102] It was also reported that there were strong suspicions of Cameroonian law enforcement, military, judicial and government officials' involvement in the illegal timber and wildlife trades in protected areas. This facilitated poaching, as did poor law enforcement and the lack of cooperation between Cameroon, Chad, the CAR and Sudan in securing borders against poachers and smugglers.

The involvement of foreign poachers hit the headlines in February 2012, when as many as 450 elephants were killed by a large gang of poachers in the Bouba N'Djida National Park, near the border with Chad. TRAFFIC said that park rangers believed a large group of Sudanese poachers on horseback to be responsible. Prior to this incident, the park was estimated to have 600 elephants.[103] There was some doubt about the exact number of elephants killed, with TRAFFIC correcting its own version and reporting that 250–300 were killed over a three-week period.[104] The episode gained international media attention and helped launch the ivory-insurgency narrative when Gettleman wrote about the killings in *The New York Times* in September 2012. He reported that "Large groups of Janjaweed… were blamed for killing thousands of civilians in the early 2000s, when Darfur erupted in ethnic conflict. International law enforcement officials say that horseback raiders from Darfur wiped out thousands of elephants in central Africa in the 1980s. Now they suspect that hundreds of Janjaweed militiamen rode more than 600 miles from Sudan and were the ones who slaughtered at least 300 elephants in Bouba Ndjida National Park."[105] Where the figure of hundreds of Janjaweed came from is not clear. The conflating of the Janjaweed's bloody role in the Darfur conflict and the slaughter of elephants introduced the idea of the ivory trade funding terror-ism and genocide. When combined with the evidence of LRA poaching and accusations of Al Shabab involvement in the trade, the whole insurgency discourse took off with a vengeance, helped by simplistic media coverage and headlines such as "Elephants Dying in Epic Frenzy as Ivory Fuels Wars and Profits".

There wasn't a repeat of killing on the scale at Bouba N'Djida but poaching continued to reduce Cameroon's elephant population, with Boko Haram reportedly involved as well as the Janjaweed. The Born Free USA/C4ADS report said that Boko Haram was a threat to Cameroon's elephants, as did the leaked minutes of a meeting of African intelligence chiefs in Harare in July 2014.[106] But WCS and MIKE conservationists told the author that there was no evidence of Boko Haram involvement in poaching or smuggling. It seemed a clear case of NGOs jumping on the ivory-insurgency bandwagon to help raise their profile or, in the case of African governments, shifting blame to cover up official corruption, which enabled poaching. To deter attacks, the Cameroon government deployed a Rapid Intervention battalion near Bouba N'Djida and employed more anti-poaching personnel. In May 2014, the Cameroon government said that soldiers deployed to protect elephants in Waza National Park had killed five poachers, believed to be Sudanese Janjaweed, and seized ten horses, 2,000 bullets and eighty-eight elephant tusks. The park, near the northern border with Nigeria and Chad, is believed to house 1,000 elephants.

The Born Free report in 2014 identified the major poaching threat to Cameroon's elephants, especially those on the borders with Gabon and Congo in the TRIDOM area, as local poaching groups, facilitated by syndicates with political protection and the opening up of forested areas by extensive logging and road projects.[107] In January 2015, despite the military presence around the park and improved anti-poaching capability, twenty elephants were reported to have been killed in Bouba N'Djida. Army officers involved in protection work said that while the poachers could have come from outside Cameroon, they were clearly assisted by local people. They failed to add that Cameroonian officials and army officers were heavily involved in ivory smuggling—ivory poached in the CAR was smuggled across the border with the protection of officials and exported through Douala.[108]

The elephants of the CAR were in an even more precarious situation. A report published in 1989 drew attention to the mix of groups involved in poaching and the varying motives for it. It highlighted local, Sudanese and Chadian poachers, and the demand for ivory internationally and for meat locally. The authors identified the failure to control or prevent the trade in weapons, elephant meat and tusks as major factors in the scale of poaching.[109] In 1989, there were widely varying estimates of the numbers of elephants surviving—one put the total at 19,000 (including savannah elephants)[110] while another said that there were just 6,420 forest elephants remaining.[111] A key elephant refuge was the forested Dzanga-Sangha region, which included the world-famous Dzanga Bai (a clearing where forest elephants and lowland gorillas come out of the forest to feed), situated in the south-west of the country in a salient between Congo and Cameroon. The current population of the Dzanga-Sangha region is hard to estimate, but Andrea Turkalo has identified 4,000 individual elephants that use the Bai.[112]

Forest elephants were concentrated in the more heavily-wooded south of the country, while the north and north-east, bordering Chad and Sudan, had populations of savannah elephants in the Bamingui-Bangoran and Manovo-Gounda St Floris Parks. These areas are highly vulnerable because of the annual influx of Chadian pastoralists seeking grazing. In the mid-1980s, the region had around 4,830 elephants, but poaching by Chadians and Sudanese had by 2005 reduced the numbers to 922 in the parks and the adjacent Vassako Bolo Wildlife Reserve and commercial hunting blocks. A survey carried out in the dry season in 2007 discovered that 553 elephants had been killed by Sudanese Arabs. The Janjaweed had been operating in areas of the CAR for several years, after droughts in Darfur killed many of their livestock.

In the late 2000s and the 2010s, the major threat that developed to both savannah and forest elephants was a combination of increasing market demand for ivory, growing instability culminating in the overthrow of President Bozize in March 2013 and his replacement by a regime led by the Seleka militia group, which was supported by and included Chadian fighters and some armed groups from Darfur. There were increasing incursions by Sudanese, Chadian and LRA poachers. Governments in Bangui had rarely been able to exert control over the whole of the national territory, especially around the borders with Sudan, Chad and the DRC. But the last years of Bozize's rule, the short, bloody period of Seleka's control and then the weak control exerted by an interim government backed by the African Union and UN saw the breakdown of law and order. This enabled increased poaching, with local hunters and foreign gangs taking advantage of the chaos. The LRA rebels, long since ousted from Uganda, had established a base for their leader, Joseph Kony, in an area straddling the CAR-South Sudan-Sudan border known as Kafia Kingi. Other LRA remnants scraped an existence in the northern DRC or near the CAR-DRC border.

Ivory poached during the 2000s was smuggled out using Chadian and Sudanese networks to markets in Khartoum-Omdurman. In the early 2000s, licensed hunters reported finding 200 elephant carcasses from poaching in the legal hunting areas in the north.[113] Poaching also continued in the Dzanga-Sangha area, although its fame as a haven for endangered wildlife led to strenuous efforts to protect it by the WWF, conservation NGOs and USAID. In 2012, Douglas-Hamilton told the US Senate Foreign Relations Committee that some advances had been achieved through strengthening anti-poaching capabilities, and that not a single elephant had been killed illegally in 2011, despite attempted incursions by Sudanese poaching gangs.[114] However, the overthrow of Bozize and consequent civil violence weakened defences, and in May 2013 Sudanese poachers entered the park and killed twenty-six forest elephants at Dzanga.

After the attack, conservationists worked to restore anti-poaching capabilities, and former Israeli soldier Nir Kalron, who runs the military-style wildlife protection consultancy Maisha and works with the Elephant Action League, became involved. Kalron has a long history as a soldier and military advisor to a variety of distasteful African regimes, and has now moved into wildlife protection and anti-poaching.[115] Kalron gathered a team of former Israeli soldiers and helped train local rangers, coming to a deal with the local Seleka commander to stop attacks on the elephants. Andrea Turkalo, who studies the Dzangha Bai elephants, has said that such extreme measures had been necessitated by the need to protect the animals in a war zone.[116] The WWF appointed a former French army officer, Stéphane Crayne, as a technical advisor to improve anti-poaching capabilities. The efforts involved Crayne and the rangers negotiating delicate local agreements with

Seleka and even with a former CAR army sergeant, who had become a virtual warlord in the area and was involved in poaching. The uneasy situation meant that anti-poaching efforts necessarily involved "talking to the enemy", as the military wasn't available to combat the local army warlord. Seleka, Crayne believes, didn't poach animals themselves, but at times got local people to hunt for them. According to him, the militia had the potential to become partners in anti-poaching, but it was pushed out by the interim government formed with African Union and UN backing.

Tusks poached by the variety of groups involved in illegal killing would be taken out through Cameroon with the involvement or protection of Cameroonian officials. Cameroonian traders had moved into towns near Dzanga-Sangha and, according to Crayne, three trading networks were operating along the CAR-Cameroon border. There was also evidence that ministers in the interim CAR government were involved in the illicit trade.[117] Crayne reports that there were clear structures underlying the poaching at Bayanga-Dzanga-Sangha. The area, he points out, is

> "a localized ivory sourcing-point. No more multi-ton ivory source exists in the world, so they hit us methodically. Here, poaching does not start as an organized, well planned out activity on the ground... Multiple hunters, gangs, businessmen and logisticians converge and complement each other organically. Ring-leaders are fewer even, equating to a pyramid-like model where a bottom-up harvesting system is very effective and where the lower levels are hardly relevant to stop the killing. They have the initiative."[118]

The complexity of this situation relates to the political and military context after Seleka were forced from power. Seleka rebels carved out areas of control and came to arrangements with both local poachers and the well-armed groups from Chad and Sudan, some of whose members are suspected of having supported Seleka's seizure of power. These gangs have established smuggling routes to get ivory and other commodities, including diamonds, out to southern Darfur, from where they are taken to Nyala and then Khartoum. The effects of conflict, corruption and criminal activity have reduced the country's elephant population to a fraction of its original size. The African Elephant Database in 2013 estimated the numbers to be a minimum of 464 and an absolute maximum of 1,885. Vira and Ewing suggested a speculative maximum of 3,000 in their 2014 report and said the majority were now concentrated in the Dzanga-Sangha region.[119] These, according to Crayne, are still at risk in a region suffering from weak government, poor institutional penetration, little law enforcement, a porous border with Cameroon, the periodic presence of Sudanese and Chadian poachers and the prevalence of corruption. On paper, neighbouring states, like Cameroon, are stronger, with functioning institutions, but in border areas law enforcement is poor and corruption greater, facilitating movement of poachers, traffickers and contraband.

War, insecurity and the role of armed groups in a variety of criminal and illicit trading activities have been deadly for Chad's elephant herds. The long, poorly policed and porous borders with Sudan and the CAR rendered Chad as vulnerable as its neighbours to incursions by Sudanese poachers. The use of Darfur as a rear base by Chadian armed factions and the linguistic, lineage and trading links between Chadian and western Sudanese communities meant that cross-border poaching and trade was carried out to the mutual advantage of communities in both states. The Chadian elephant population was around 3,000 by 1989 and in 1995 the African Elephant Database reported 1,040 definite sightings and a possible maximum of 3,140. Poaching continued during the 1990s, despite the end of Chad's civil war. By 1998, the database maximum figure was down to 1,900—the definite category stood at zero. CITES said in 2000 that frequent reports of poaching in Chad by local hunters and those from neighbouring countries, using automatic rifles and spears, were taking a toll on the remaining population, especially in Zakouma National Park. The hunters were said to be a mix of local people, Chadian soldiers or militiamen and nomadic pastoralists-hunters.[120] But despite this, the database figure for 2002, perhaps indicating changes due to improved survey methods or migration of animals, showed a higher figure, with 1,989 definite and a possible maximum of 4,539. By 2009, Douglas-Hamilton reported a drop in numbers from a possible 3,800 in 2006 to 600 in 2009[121]—the most recent database figures give 912 definite and a maximum of 1,114.

Zakouma has not only suffered poaching but also the theft of gathered tusks and confiscated ivory from the park headquarters. In 2008, well-armed and organised raiders stole 1.5m tons of ivory worth $1.3m from a strongroom, killing three rangers in the process. The raiders, who arrived on horseback, were said to have been Janjaweed who, according to Chadian authorities, had killed hundreds of elephants in Zakouma in recent years. One uncorroborated report said that a Janjaweed gang of more than thirty had killed 100 elephants in a single attack.[122] On a more positive note, Douglas-Hamilton believes that MIKE figures show that the assumption of administration of the park by the Western-funded African Parks organisation has enabled anti-poaching operations to improve, with the annual death toll, which had been in the high hundreds up to 2010, cut to eleven in 2011,[123] although in 2012 six rangers were killed in an attack by a well-armed group of Sudanese poachers. African Parks, which is a non-profit organisation funded through donations and sponsorship, runs ten national parks spread across Rwanda, Chad, the DRC, the Republic of the Congo, the CAR, Malawi and Zambia and has plans to increase this number to twenty by 2020. It enters into twenty-year agreements with governments to take over management, training and deployment of anti-poaching teams and reintroduction of species that have become locally extinct.

African Parks says that it is committed to developing community schemes to make sure that local people benefit from conservation programmes and so support them—though this is usually in the form of employing rangers and other staff and providing jobs through ecotourism development.[124] This represents a further out-sourcing of responsibility for conservation and the distancing of local communities from a sense of ownership and control, though it has to be said that in many of the countries where it operates, African Parks brings management expertise and experience to parks that have been starved of resources and skilled manpower. Most funding is received through the EU, the Dutch national lottery, the WWF, the Walton Family Foundation and the US Fish and Wildlife Service.

To emphasise his government's commitment to fighting poaching, in February 2014 President Idriss Déby burned the country's 1.1-ton ivory stockpile and pledged to protect the remaining elephants, of which it was said there were now 450 in Zakouma, including remnants that had fled from Manovo-Gounda St Floris National Park in the CAR to escape poaching by the Sudanese, according to Ruggiero, who reported that in 2013 no illegal killings had been monitored and that Chadian government backing for the African Parks conservation and anti-poaching operations was bearing fruit.[125] In April 2014, as part of its wider programme of support for security in the region, the US government sent a team of US Marines to Chad to train 100 rangers from the environment ministry's mobile brigade, used to track down poachers.

African Parks has also taken over administration and anti-poaching in the Republic of the Congo's Odzala-Kokoua Park, which, along with Congo's other two main parks Nouabalé-Ndoki and Conkouti-Douli (run by the WCS), are home to about 12–13,000 elephants. Odzala-Kokoua had been badly affected by poaching, facilitated by rampant corruption at all levels of the Congolese government and security forces and frequent bouts of warfare between rival armed factions. This killed off about half the country's elephants in a decade. To try to get local people on their side and turn poachers into gamekeepers, African Parks has run a programme of training captured hunters as rangers, as an alternative to purely militarised anti-poaching, which, with Western NGO and government backing, has become the dominant—though not always efficacious—response across Africa in the 2000s and 2010s.

Gabon has, for many years, been the most important refuge for central Africa's forest elephants, despite bouts of heavy killing in protected areas. A rich state with a small population and massive oil earnings, it devoted few resources to conservation and, despite its wealth and high per capita income, was marked by huge inequalities in rural areas. It didn't suffer the conflicts which marked its larger neighbours and oil wealth meant that forest resources hadn't been uniformly overexploited. There were large areas of untouched forest, home to tens of thousands of elephants. These factors have made Gabon "one of the few countries in the world that still offer exceptional potential for conservation".[126] But where extensive logging does occur, it is locally significant in terms of habitat loss and often increases poaching, as roads are cut to haul out timber and there is a greater demand for bushmeat.

The key elephant range is in the north of the country where the Minkébé National Park borders Congo and Cameroon in a large area of rainforest that includes the Cameroonian Mengam Protected Area and Nki National Park, the Congolese Odzala-Kokoua National Park and the Nouabalé-Ndoki National Park. The Congolese areas were heavily poached in the 1980s and 1990s, causing elephants to move increasingly into Minkébé. Congo's population had fallen to about 32,000 by 1995. By contrast, Gabon had between 61,000 and 82,000 elephants, according to the 1995 African Elephant Database. Over the next eighteen years, the database indicates a fluctuation in the maximum estimate of between 61,000 and 81,000—this suggested that the loss of elephants matched or exceeded natural growth rates, indicating a sustained level of poaching. Barnes et al. confirmed this and asserted that poaching in the 1990s was localised and not highly organised, although there were periodic reports of West African ivory smugglers being caught trying to get tusks out of the country.[127]

In December 2012, Gettleman reported that Gabon wildlife officials had told him that hunters had killed 10,000 elephants in Minkébé in recent years—which would explain the failure of the population to increase. Much of the hunting was by poor rural dwellers seeking income from ivory and meat for local consumption, but there was also evidence of well-armed gangs killing large numbers.[128] The police and wildlife authorities were trying to take action against poaching. Gettleman observed that the local jails were "filling up with small-time poachers and ivory traffickers…many of them destitute rural dwellers". A much more detailed scientific report published in 2013 corroborated what Gettleman said and estimated that Gabon had lost 11,000 elephants by 2013; this amounted to about half of Minkébé's population.[129] One of the causes of the massive increase in poaching was the establishment of informal gold mining camps on the edge of the park, which rapidly expanded from 300 miners to 5,000. Many took up poaching for bushmeat and ivory. The Minkébé Park authorities estimated that 50–100 elephants were being killed daily at the height of the poaching. The ease with which ivory could be smuggled out through Cameroon and on to China encouraged extensive illegal hunting.

The Gabon government responded to the evident upsurge with pledges of greater support for anti-poaching measures and said that it would tighten wildlife laws and sentences for poaching and smuggling. In June 2012, Gabon's president, Ali Bongo, followed the usual path of those trying to appear to be doing something: lighting a pyre of 10,000 lbs of ivory. But a February 2014 report to a Zoological Society of London symposium by Lee White of Gabon's Agence Nationale des Parcs Nationaux noted the poor anti-poaching and conservation infrastructure in Gabon and the low level of investment in national parks.[130] White, who is reputedly close to President Bongo and a supporter of his conservation policies,[131] said the increase in the size of the gold mining camps had led to an influx not just of miners but of traders, drug dealers, prostitutes and illegal arms dealers, many of whom became involved in the ivory and bushmeat trades. Ivory and other contraband was smuggled from the area to Djoum in Cameroon.

White believed as many as 14,000 elephants to have been killed in and around Minkébé between 2004 and 2012. Overall, he estimated that 20,000 elephants had been killed in Gabon in a decade[132] and that the nature of poaching had changed, with organised foreign poaching gangs taking over from locals, though not completely pushing them out. The total Gabon population had been reduced from a maximum of around 70,000 in 2007 to 40–45,000 in 2014. Bongo did increase funding for a specialised, 240-strong anti-poaching unit, to be trained through the US Africom military command, but given the country's oil wealth and Bongo's personal fortune the funds committed were insignificant given the scale of the problem. Africom is the headquarters group for US military involvement in Africa, from training, provision of advisors and surveillance and communications support to "military operations to disrupt, degrade and neutralize violent extremist organizations that present a transnational threat...[and continue] partnering to help African partner nations build the capacity they need to secure the region."[133]

In late 2015, it was announced that a small group of British military advisors from the Royal Scottish Borderers would work in Gabon with security and anti-poaching forces to improve capabilities to fight well-organised poaching gangs. The government was clearly coming to terms with the fact that poaching was a growing, serious threat to its forest elephants population, which wildlife sources in Gabon put at a maximum of 45,000 in 2015, thought to be half the entire African forest elephant population. Rangers, however, were quoted in reports as saying that they were outgunned by gangs, who were killing elephants at "an alarming rate".[134]

The DRC (formerly Zaire) once had Africa's largest forest elephant population, but years of endemic corruption, conflict and weak governance had facilitated poaching, reducing the population of 377,700 in

1979 to 84,500 in 1989. The database figures for 1995 show an absolute maximum of 83,618, dropping to just over 45,000 in 2002 and 13,917 in 2013—these included both forest and savannah elephants. Forest elephants were found in scattered populations across the Congo Basin forests, while the savannah herds were located in and around Garamba National Park, where numbers had fallen from 7,700 in the early 1980s to 6,000 in the 1990s as a result of poaching by Sudanese gangs, rebel groups and the army. The illicit trade was carried out by a constantly shifting array of groups—local hunters after bushmeat, the same hunters commissioned by businessmen or corrupt officials to obtain ivory for them, rebel groups, the Zairean/DRC army and foreign groups or military units who intervened in the civil wars that brought about and then followed the fall of Mobutu. These wars saw not only external intervention and the plundering of mineral and wildlife resources, but also the fragmentation of the fighting into localised conflicts over resources between communities. Over five million people died directly or indirectly as a result of the years of war from 1996 to the mid-2000s and millions more were rendered destitute or displaced. This horrendous conflict had a hugely destructive effect on wildlife and conservation, rendering law enforcement almost impossible and creating insecurity across the elephant ranges, which combined with endemic corruption to provide the ideal opportunity for poachers, traders and their patrons.

The surviving forest elephants had their major havens in the Okapi Wildlife Reserve, Virunga, Salonga, Maiko and Kahuzi-Biega National Parks and the surrounding forest areas. But they were vulnerable in these theoretically protected regions because of the effects of conflict, corruption, the lack of resources for conservation and rangers' vulnerability to attack by large armed groups. Reserves were repeatedly invaded by rival armies, local militias like the Mai Mai and the Ugandan and Rwandan armies, as well as illegal miners and locals seeking food. In the aftermath of the Rwandan genocide of 1994 and at the start of the civil war in late 1996 and early 1997, Kahuzi-Biega was overrun by refugees, Hutu militias and Rwandan army units, who killed hippos and elephants on a huge scale for meat and ivory. Garamba was also overrun and the ranger headquarters looted. Poaching was particularly heavy in Kahuzi-Biega in the period around 1999, with seventeen elephants and twenty gorillas killed in a short space of time. The park's elephant population was estimated at 3,600–3,720 in 1997 but was down to 771 by 2000. In the lowland areas of the park, the 1,900 counted in 1997 had disappeared by 2001.[135]

In 2000, a survey of forest elephants in Virunga indicated 486–535 animals, compared with over about 630 in the mid-1980s. However, there was some evidence by 2000[136] of a slow recovery in numbers as the focus of conflict moved away from the park. In Salonga in central DRC, a survey showed considerable reduction, with swamp areas once frequented by large herds showing little or no sign of activity. Poachers captured by rangers in July 2000 said that they had recently shot a small elephant and sold it at Mbandaka, but that they were having increasing difficulty in finding elephants. These were local poachers, but the main threat to the timid herds remaining was heavily armed groups of professional poachers, who could outgun the rangers, a number of whom had been killed. As a result, there had been no patrols along the park's rivers—the main transport routes in the heavily forested area—for seven years.

The DRC's savannah elephant population was concentrated in Garamba National Park in the north, on the border with South Sudan. The population had been regularly raided by Congolese, Sudanese and Ugandan poachers—some part of commercial poaching gangs, others from militias, rebel groups or the Sudanese and Ugandan armies. Kes Hillman-Smith, a veteran Congo wildlife researcher, found in 2001 that 70–80 per cent of the poachers operating in the park were Sudanese, many of them SPLA fighters or deserters from the SPLA. They poached rhino and elephant both as a commercial operation and for meat.[137] Anti-poaching operations suffered during the occupation of the park in 1997 during the first phase of the civil war and there was considerable poaching of elephants and buffalo as a result. The second phase of the civil war after 1998 also affected the park, with the park headquarters looted and occupied by Ugandan-backed Congolese rebels. They seemed to take little part in the poaching, however, and some anti-poaching operations were able to continue.

The poaching gangs operated throughout the conflict and were a more or less permanent presence in the park. Surveys between 1995 and 2000 showed that the elephant population had fallen from 11,175 to 5,874 in 1998, rising a little to 6,022 in 2000.[138] The park was more affected by the war in southern Sudan and then the civil war in newly-independent South Sudan than even the Congo conflicts, given the major role of Sudanese in killing elephants. In the 2000s poaching resumed, but almost solely for ivory and rhino horn. By 2004, there were no elephants north of the Garamba River and a count showed just 2,000 in the park as a whole. The poachers were varied—SPLA, SPLA deserters, Janjaweed and locals hunting with the connivance of government and security officials. An increasing poaching problem was posed by the arrival in the 2000s of several hundred members of the LRA, who had no other means of subsistence than stealing from local people and killing animals for food and ivory. The deployment of Congolese army units in the park to combat the LRA led to increased poaching, as the soldiers took an active part, too.

A survey in 2007 estimated that there were 1,202 elephants in Garamba's southern sector. During the survey twenty-eight elephant carcasses were discovered, along with thirteen poaching camps. Rangers told the researchers that there had been significant poaching in the previous eighteen months by highly organised, heavily armed Arabic groups, including the Janjaweed, who had entered from the CAR, Chad and Sudan.[139] Despite the reduced numbers, poaching continued into the 2010s with Janjaweed, southern Sudanese, the LRA and the Ugandan army involved. On one occasion, a Russian Mi17 helicopter operated by the Ugandan army was seen taking off from the scene of an ambush in which twenty-two elephants were killed and their tusks taken.[140] Gettleman was told by Garamba staff that some of the elephants killed had been shot from the air.[141] The specialist on conflict in the DRC, Kristof Titeca, reported in 2013 that the combination of the LRA, former SPLA personnel and Janjaweed are responsible for the majority of poaching in the park, operating in small groups and abducting or robbing local people.[142] Much of the ivory from the non-LRA gangs is taken out to Uganda and sold to traders in Kampala who export it to Asia. The towns of Arua in Uganda and Ariwara in the DRC, both important trading areas for ivory in the nineteenth century, are today important hubs for the transport of ivory from Garamba into Uganda.

African Parks took over management of Garamba in April 2014. The Park Manager, Jean-Marc Froment, said the park was under attack on all fronts from southern Sudanese, LRA and Janjaweed, as well as local poachers and members of the Congolese army. Rangers were frequently outgunned and, in October 2015, four rangers were killed by poachers;[143] another two were killed in February 2016. The Garamba deaths in 2015 brought to the number of game rangers killed in Africa that year to twenty-seven, and the number killed in the last decade to over 1,000—showing the human cost of conservation. There has been increased emphasis on anti-poaching, with park rangers augmented by Congolese security forces, assisted by members of the US Africom. Nevertheless, sixty-eight elephants were poached in April and May 2014, about 4 per cent of the remaining population in the park. The slaughter continued into 2015, with thirty killed in March by northern Sudanese raiders. This dire situation was highlighted in 2015 in a report on the LRA by the Enough Project. It estimated, on the basis of interviews with parks staff, LRA defectors and elephant conservation experts, that 130–150 elephants were being poached each year, 80 per cent of them by South Sudanese, though the park staff couldn't say whether they were SPLA, soldiers, deserters or members of South Sudan's myriad armed factions and rebel groups. The park was believed by late 2015 to have about 1,000 elephants remaining. In November 2015, it was announced that UNESCO's Rapid Response Facility had granted emergency funding to Garamba to help tackle the continuing elephant poaching crisis. Reporting the grant, Flora and Fauna International have said that 215 elephants have been killed in the past eighteen months and that there has been a heavy human toll, with four rangers and a soldier killed in November 2015 during an anti-poaching operation.[144]

Southern Africa: Botswana booming but a mixed picture across the region

Table 5: Southern Africa's elephant population, 1995–2013

1995		1998		2002		2007		2013	
Definite	Max	Definite	Max	Definite	Max	Definite	Max	Definite	Max
170,837	229,682	196,845	236,725	246,592	303,920	297,718	355,391	278,520	354,312

The 1989 trade ban had been opposed vigorously by the range states of southern Africa, which had better managed herds and growing numbers of elephants—exceptions being Angola and Mozambique, which were still plagued by illegal hunting linked to South Africa's wars of destabilisation, and Zambia, where corruption played a major role in facilitating illicit killing. Botswana's herds were the big success story. Elephant numbers in South Africa and Namibia were increasing and culling was still going on in Kruger National Park to limit the increase in the population. Zimbabwe had a growing population but continuing problems with poaching in the south-east around Gonarezhou and from Zambian poachers crossing into the Zambezi Valley.

A couple of years after the ban, arguments over southern African states' desire to sell ivory to support conservation were still raging in the specialist journals. *Oryx* reported in January 1992 that there was a growing campaign by the pro-trade groups to highlight the growth in elephant numbers, something the journal criticised, having generally adopted a pro-ban position. The countries of East Africa, led by Kenya, and leading conservationists like Douglas-Hamilton, backed by vociferous and sensationalist campaigning by the EIA and other NGOs, opposed any relaxation of the ban. On the other hand, southern African conservationists, like Rowan Martin, believed that the better management in southern Africa, the use of funds from selling legal ivory and the development of community-based utilisation schemes like CAMPFIRE and LIRDP showed that southern Africa had a viable, alternative strategy. By 2000, *Oryx* contributors admitted that southern African herds were increasing steadily, to the point that in some areas they were destroying vegetation and endangering bio-diversity—Kruger, for example, was said to have 9,000 elephants, which represented 2,000 above its notional carrying capacity.[145]

In their 2005 survey of the region for the WWF, Cumming and Jones reported that elephant conservation had been remarkably successful and that there were now 250–300,000 elephants, compared with 6,000 south of the Zambezi in 1900. They warned of growing human-elephant conflict and the compression or fragmentation of ranges in some areas due to expanding human populations.[146] Culling, even in overcrowded Kruger, had been stopped in 1994 and further growth was inevitable at about 3–7 per cent a year—but with little chance of major expansion in the range available. Attempts were made through the development of transfrontier projects, like the Great Limpopo Transfrontier Park, which linked Limpopo National Park in Mozambique, Kruger, and Gonarezhou, and KAZA (Kavango Zambezi Transfrontier Conservation Area), which linked Botswana, Angola, Namibia, Zambia and Zimbabwe. These schemes, often labelled peace parks, aimed at creating larger ecosystems to enable migration and avoiding the damage caused by concentration of populations. They achieved some success, but often involved the expulsion of local farmers and creation of new areas of conflict. They exacerbated the problems of "marginalization and exclusion" and the criminalisation of local subsistence hunting in areas that had not previously been protected areas.[147]

As Büscher has argued, the peace parks and transfrontier ideas have biodiversity as their watchword but are based on the support of global business elites that see massive tourism opportunities beckoning and, through support from groups like the Peace Parks Foundation, have come to exert ever greater influence over conservation policies and land use in the transfrontier regions concerned.[148] The transfrontier parks may open up wider areas for wildlife and create corridors that permit migration, but they also open opportunities for investment and privatisation of wildlife and perpetuate the disempowerment of local people—as the Tsonga people around the Kruger Park have found. As business groups and political leaders involved in the projects gain in control and influence, with access to national governments, the local people are further distanced and marginalised from control or even any stake in what happens to the land and its resources.[149]

By 2013, the regional elephant population was put at a definite 297,718 with a possible maximum of 354,312. Most populations were growing, though there were severe poaching problems in Mozambique's Niassa Park and surrounding regions, continued poaching by Zambian gangs in their own country but also in Zimbabwe and Botswana, a small but worrying increase in poaching in Botswana and repeated mass poisonings of elephants in Zimbabwe's Hwange National Park. Angola remained an area where there was limited data but some indication of subsistence hunting and other illegal killing in the remote and poor south-east.[150]

Angola was at war from 1960 to 2002, with a few unstable ceasefires providing breathing space for its suffering people. There was no breathing space for elephants. The early phases of the liberation war (1960–74) had little known effect, but the period from independence in 1975 to 2002 was disastrous, mainly through cooperation between the UNITA movement and the South African Defence Force in killing elephants and rhino to help fund the insurgency against the government, to feather the nests of senior soldiers and to provide funds for covert anti-ANC activities inside South Africa. In the 1970s, rough estimates of elephant numbers suggested 70,000 in the south alone[151]—but this seems to have been an underestimate if the figure of 100,000 elephants killed in UNITA-SADF ivory operations is accurate. In any case, it is clear that the depletion of Angola's elephants was substantial. By 1987, there were said to be 40,426 at most in the whole of Angola, but continued war and South African depredations reduced this to 18,000 in 1989.[152] Fewer were killed between 1990 and 1992 as South Africa's involvement ended, but UNITA is still believed to have harvested and sold ivory to supplement diamond income. The UNITA threat declined with the ceasefire and the holding of elections in 1992, but the failure of the peace deal led to renewed war until the defeat of UNITA in 2002. After the end of the war, the MPLA government failed to provide for demobilised UNITA fighters or to recover the large quantities of arms in circulation. This meant that poaching continued in remote areas as a means of subsistence rather than as a military-related activity. Elephants are also frequently victims of the hundreds of thousands of landmines sown indiscriminately across central and south-eastern Angola.

Some researchers believed that Angola's elephant populations were slowly recovering after 1992, though systematic monitoring or conservation remained unrealisable.[153] It was clear that some elephants were being killed for their ivory and Angola was a transit route for illicit ivory from the DRC. It was openly sold in markets in Luanda. In 2006, raw ivory was fetching between $35 and $100 per kg locally—a fortune for an impoverished peasant or demobilised soldier. The elephant population was at an all-time low; in 2003, Julian Blanc had estimated 36 definite, 0 probable, 150 possible and 60 speculative.[154] In 2007, the African Elephant Database put the definite figure at 818, with an absolute maximum of 2,537. In 2013, the same source gave the same definite figure and a maximum of 2,530, showing a small decrease, but clearly no growth through reproduction or migration from the overcrowded regions of Botswana across the Caprivi Strip.

There was no clear, verifiable evidence of the level of poaching, but the ready availability of ivory in Luanda and other towns suggested that poaching as well as illegal imports were supplying the market. TRAFFIC estimated in 2006 that 1.5 tons of ivory, equivalent to 300 elephants, were sold annually in Angola's markets, mainly to Chinese workers.[155] Angola did not have laws against ivory trading and did not become a signatory to CITES until December 2013. A year after joining, the illegal ivory trade was reported by Martin and Vigne to be booming in Luanda, especially the Benfica market, with Chinese the main customers. Luanda had become the single biggest ivory retail market in southern Africa, with 10,888 recently carved ivory items available without proper documentation and whole tusks on sale at $150–250 per kg.[156] The increase in trade and the size of the market was a direct result of the presence of Chinese nationals—the prices were a tenth of those in China and so workers could take ivory back and make a huge profit. Although some ivory poached in Angola was on sale, the Angolan herds couldn't supply demand; most of it came from central Africa.

The majority of elephants in Angola were concentrated in the south-east along the Kwando River or within 12 km of Jamba (UNITA's old headquarters, where protection had been given to elephants to try to demonstrate the existence of a conservation policy). Other herds were in adjacent areas about 35 km from the border with Namibia. As the above estimates indicate, there was a gradual increase in numbers after 2002, partly through breeding but also with the gradual recolonisation of areas of south-eastern Angola by elephants from the Caprivi Strip and northern Botswana, something that the KAZA transfrontier conservation zone aimed at encouraging. Chase and Griffin tracked elephants with radio collars moving from the Kwando area of northern Botswana, across Caprivi and into southern Angola; others were tracked from the Okavango Delta.[157] They had to run the gauntlet of small-scale poaching and landmines, though in 2015 José Agostinho of the HALO Trust demining group cited evidence that elephants were increasingly able to avoid mines by sniffing them out. There were other small elephant populations scattered across southern and east-central Angola, and a small population of forest elephants moved between the Republic of the Congo and Angola's Cabinda Enclave on the Atlantic Coast, where they came into regular conflict with local farmers.

In March 2016, the Angolan government issued a decree banning all domestic trade in ivory and providing for the deployment of a crime unit both at Luanda's Quatro de Fevereiro International Airport and in the localities of Maria Teresa (Cuanza Norte) and Bengo province, in an attempt to crack down on trading and smuggling in and out of the country. Few informed observers of Angola believe this will have the slightest effect; it is generally considered a cosmetic measure to please CITES and win a few brownie points internationally at a time when the oil price fall has been severely damaging the Angolan economy.

Human-elephant conflict was a periodic problem in Botswana, though not to the extent one might have expected given the constantly growing elephant population. There were clear signs that such conflict was growing after January 2014, when all hunting was banned in Botswana, and there was evidence that local communities were less willing to live alongside wildlife if they were deprived of the means of benefiting from it. The hunting ban represents a major shift in policy, as before that Botswana had a thriving hunting industry and had been lobbying to have its elephants downlisted and be allowed to sell ivory stocks.

In the 1990s, the government and the wildlife department had been aware of implications of the growth in the elephant population, with the danger of environmental damage and human-elephant conflict. In November 1993, Seeyiso Diphuko, the executive secretary of the National Conservation Strategy Board, told the author that Botswana had an approximate carrying capacity of 60,000 elephants and was already exceeding that.[158] He and senior officials of the wildlife department believed that culling and other forms of management would have to be used to prevent overstocking. They considered it vital that these measures include sustainable-use programmes to compensate local communities for elephant damage to crops. Foreign Minister Gaositwe Chiepe and Vice-President Festus Mogae both told the author that Botswana would continue working to gain CITES permission to sell stocks and ivory from control measures to provide funding for conservation.

Private game concession owners said that trophy and other high-cost hunting was necessary to bring in money for local communities and to provide employment in areas where people were affected by elephants, or where it was necessary for farming and livestock rearing to be limited because of wildlife. Local people could sell hunting quotas to foreign hunters willing to pay tens of thousands of dollars to shoot an elephant and to pay for local guides, skinners, drivers, food and accommodation. The government set out to combine conservation, utilisation and rural development to provide a better standard of living for people while protecting the environment.[159] This did not please many conservationists but brought in income for local people, provided employment and helped build acceptance for conservation strategies, avoiding widespread subsistence or commercial poaching. Local communities generally supported rather than obstructed anti-poaching operations, including those conducted by the Botswana Defence Force (BDF). As discussed in Chapter 6, international NGOs—from the EIA to the AWF and the WWF—opposed attempts to re-legalise ivory trading for southern African states and the use of trophy hunting and other forms of commercial hunting as part of a strategy to generate income and protect wildlife. Nevertheless, Botswana, until its change of heart in 2014, used hunting and private safari concessions to provide extra layers of protection against poachers intruding into protected areas and to generate income for local people.

Both the role of communities in conservation projects and the attempts to get support from rural populations were very important and the Botswana government had attempted to give communities a sense of ownership over wildlife and responsibility for it. Annual quotas for hunting were set by the Department of Wildlife for controlled hunting areas in order to allow hunting while ensuring sustainable yields and working to control elephant numbers.[160] In 1993, communities within each controlled hunting area were given the right to apply to manage their own quotas. In one area with large numbers of elephants in the Chobe Enclave, five villages were the first to exercise this option and were given control of their community quota. Village committees chose representatives to serve on a board that managed the utilisation of the quotas. Early on, they decided to contract a safari company to manage the hunting and ensure fewer animals were shot than the quota allowed, in order to conserve wildlife in the hope of getting a larger quota the following year. To maximise local incomes and generate support, the board decided to hold on to just 10 per cent of the revenue and distribute 90 per cent to the participating villages. The example is one that demonstrates the mutual benefit derived from the projects and explains why for many years there was reduced conflict between rural communities, conservationists and the wildlife.

The development of community involvement was managed by the Department of Wildlife and National Parks (DWNP) and supported by USAID through a natural resources management programme. It reduced resentment of wildlife and developed acceptance of coexistence, but failed to give all local people a clear sense of ownership. Surveys of community projects show they still thought ownership resided with the government.[161] The decision of the Khama government to ban trophy and commercial hunting from January 2014 engendered a feeling of deprivation and anger in communities receiving income from hunting. There are signs that it may have resulted in increased poaching by local people in protected areas and local cooperation in the Chobe and Linyanti regions with Zambian elephant poachers.[162]

Successful conservation strategies and strong anti-poaching capabilities provided by the DWNP and the BDF had helped enable sustained expansion in elephant numbers—estimated at 62,998–80,174 in 1995, 76,664–103,3472 by 1998, 100,000–143,103 by 2002, and 133,829–174,487 by 2007.[163] Population growth has increased densities of animals in the Okavango and Chobe, and the range over which they can be found. In 2006, while camping in the Central Kalahari Game Reserve, I had seen no evidence of elephants and DWNP rangers said that you just didn't see them there. During a visit to the same area in July 2015, I saw significant amounts of elephant dung along well-used game trails in the centre and north of the reserve. Game guides told me that small but regular numbers of elephants were to be found moving through the reserve.

While the national parks and reserves provide safe havens for elephants, only 23 per cent of Botswana's elephants are found inside the parks, a percentage which increases to 32 per cent in the dry season. Even though large numbers of elephants are present outside the parks and reserves, illegal killings were low in Botswana during the 1990s and 2000s—forty-two in 2001 and only eight in 2002. There has been an increase, though it doesn't yet affect population growth. Michael Flyman, who is in charge of the DWNP's elephant surveys, told me that 30–50 elephants a year are now being killed in the Chobe-Linyanti area. Illegal killing has been increasing over the last three to four years and there is evidence of local people helping the poachers, which was not happening much before the hunting ban.

According to Flyman and Steve Johnson of SAREP (Southern Africa Regional Environment Program), the poaching is carried out by sophisticated gangs based in Zambia, using silenced hunting rifles. They pay Namibian fishermen in the Caprivi to take them to Botswana, where local people help them find the elephants and extricate the tusks. According to the Maun regional wildlife officer, Amos Ramokati, local people are clearly involved, and some of the poached tusks are trafficked through Maun to Zambia. The government has clearly registered the growth in poaching and the involvement of local people both in facilitating it and in trafficking tusks. In 2014–15, the government provided funds and received assistance from the Chinese government to strengthen the wildlife anti-poaching units and increased manpower by 175.[164] In January 2016, the Save the Elephants News Service carried a report from Botswana that a councillor of the opposition Botswana Congress Party from Nata and three other Batswana were being held in prison awaiting trial after being caught with two elephant tusks. They were said to have been working with Zimbabwean ivory dealers to smuggle the tusks to Zambia.

Since the 2014 hunting ban, there has been an increase in poaching-related poisoning, with animal carcasses poisoned to kill predators and scavengers, especially vultures, and so reduce the chance of fresh elephant carcasses being discovered by anti-poaching patrols (this has also been identified as a growing problem in Kruger, South Africa, where a small but worrying increase in elephant poaching has been accompanied by the poisoning of elephant carcasses, which has led to the deaths of several lions, jackals and well over 100 vultures; it is also a growing habit of poachers in Mozambique and Zimbabwe). Lions killed by poison or by other forms of poaching are often used to supply the demand for lion bones to be used in Chinese medicine.[165] Some Batswana MPs have started lobbying to have the hunting ban lifted, arguing that it damages rural peoples' livelihoods. Ronald Shamukuni, MP for the northern Chobe region, said that elephants were too numerous in the Chobe area and were forcing people to abandon their farms, as the people couldn't kill them to protect crops or reduce numbers. In March 2015, he announced, "I am pleading with the [wildlife] minister to find ways to reduce the number of elephants in our area". Two other MPs backed his appeal.[166] Steve Johnson of SAREP said he feared the hunting ban had been put in place with insufficient understanding of the vital importance of hunting income for small, remote communities with no other viable form of subsistence. This, he said, could endanger CBNRM (Community-Based Natural Resource Management) schemes in the region, which are vital to developing and maintaining both local incomes and support for sustainable conservation.[167]

Botswana's elephant population is the largest in Africa, but is not static in the sense of residing permanently in Botswana. The DWNP-Elephants Without Borders surveys in recent years have demonstrated variations that reflect migration to and from Zimbabwe in the north-east, across the Caprivi Strip into Zambia and Angola, and west into Namibia. The regular and well-organised aerial and ground surveys show a steady growth in numbers in the wider ecosystem and a consistently high population in Botswana, concentrated in the Okavango-Chobe-Savuti-Linyanti area. The 2012 dry season survey showed the highest population numbers ever recorded, with 207,545 estimated and a maximum of 212,914, and numbers significantly higher than ever in Moremi, Makgadikgadi and Nxai Pans National Parks.[168] The 2013 survey was more conservative with an estimate of 156,401 and a maximum of 166,882.[169]

Michael Flyman told the author that these fluctuations did not suggest a sudden fall in population and that the lack of significant numbers of carcasses pointed to migration rather than death or killing as the explanation. The 2014 survey estimated the population at 129,939 with a maximum of 142,453 and again there was no increase or unusually high number of carcasses. The most, though still not substantial, numbers of carcasses were seen in the Okavango Panhandle and Chobe Enclave, near areas with arable farming, perhaps indicating some increase in conflict combined with the gradual increase in poaching. Elephant numbers in Chobe have been falling, reducing density in what was an overcrowded area. Those I spoke to in Botswana in 2015 believed that the change in elephant populations is mostly due to movements by elephants across international borders and district boundaries within Botswana, rather than illegal killing.

The movement of elephants could also be the key to the problem of overcrowding, though it won't necessarily alleviate human-elephant conflict or the loss of locals' income from wildlife utilisation. The continuing work to establish wildlife corridors that link Botswana, Angola, Namibia, Zambia and Zimbabwe is particularly important. With between 150,000 and 212,000 elephants in the wider ecosystem, which has Botswana's north at its centre, the creation of wildlife corridors could facilitate dispersal, avoid over-concentration and reduce elephant stress and ecological damage. If carried out in consultation with local people and alongside efforts to enhance their incomes, it could also alleviate some of the problems of conflict with elephants. At the heart of this project is KAZA's objective of a transfrontier conservation system spanning a huge area north to south from Kafue in Zambia to the south of the Okavango Delta and west to east from Rundu (Namibia) and Cuito Cuanavale (Angola) to Hwange and Chizarira (Zimbabwe).

KAZA was formally signed into existence on 18 August 2011. One of its aims is for elephants and other wildlife to disperse and repopulate areas denuded by poaching in Zambia and Angola, which could enable growth in numbers while avoiding over-concentration of elephants in Chobe, Savuti and Linyanti. Baboloki Autlwetse, head of Botswana's Kalahari Conservation Society, believes KAZA is vital to long-term conservation of species and habitats but is currently a paper entity and needs each member to establish clear national plans and implement viable anti-poaching and law enforcement regimes, while working to develop community support and benefits. He admitted that Zambia and Angola had a long way to go in addressing these issues.[170] Southeastern Angola is geographically, economically and politically peripheral and wildlife conservation is not a priority for the notoriously corrupt Dos Santos government. There is evidence of significant poaching of buffalo, eland and hippo for meat, as local people impoverished by decades of war and current government neglect use civil war-era weapons to hunt for survival. KAZA is a great plan on paper but is yet to really develop into a fully viable long-term operation—it will have to work hard to avoid the problems—top-down conservation and exclusion and further alienation of local people—that other transfrontier projects have resulted in.

Another problem for KAZA is that the areas of the Caprivi Strip that were to become elephant corridors cut across existing legal hunting areas. Trophy hunting is still sanctioned by the Namibian government. The hunting wouldn't damage overall elephant numbers but could prove an obstacle to migration, as elephants avoid hunting blocks.[171] Since the days of the SADF/UNITA decimation of wildlife, the Caprivi Strip has been poorly policed in terms of conservation and regulation governing where and when to hunt. One of the KAZA areas that would be repopulated under the scheme is Sioma-Ngwezi National Park in southern Zambia. Recent surveys by Mike Chase of Elephants Without Borders have indicated a high rate of poaching of the remaining elephants there, which doesn't bode well for elephants moving back in. A survey of the park in 2014 showed thirty-three live and an estimated 218 dead elephants.[172]

Chase also found the highest level of illicit killing of elephants in the Caprivi for twelve years. The Caprivi is the entry point for Namibian and Zambian poachers infiltrating northern Botswana (while Zimbabweans use points further east). Over the last twenty years, the BDF and game rangers have adopted a tough policy towards poachers entering the country and about thirty Namibians, twenty-two Zimbabweans and an unknown number of Zambians have been shot dead by the BDF in anti-poaching operations, to the anger of the communities from which they come.[173] Botswana vigorously defends its right to use maximum force against poachers armed with firearms who enter the country. But the militarised approach doesn't always sit well with attempts to develop cross-border cooperation and community buy-in through KAZA. Namibian civic groups have protested about killings and suggested that BDF units have crossed the border into Namibia to shoot suspected poachers, leading to a cooling of relations between the two governments at times. Namibia's Deputy Prime Minister, Netumbo Nandi-Ndaitwah, held talks with Botswana in May 2014 and sought assurances that Botswana wasn't shooting Namibian trespassers on sight.

What is clear, as I was told in Botswana in July 2015, is that KAZA lacks the level of inter-governmental cooperation, alignment of conservation and sustainable-use policies, anti-poaching capabilities and comparable levels of integrity and competence in managing wildlife. Botswana is generally succeeding because it has remained largely corruption-free. Angola and Zambia are two of the most corrupt or incompetent governments when it comes to wildlife management and integrity in public life, while Zimbabwe is showing signs of a growth in unregulated killing and illicit utilisation of wildlife.

The killing of elephants to harvest ivory in Malawi continued after the trade ban at a slightly increased level, despite the past depletion of herds and a 20 per cent increase in spending on enforcement.[174] The population was down to 2,400 in 1989, with the main concentration in Kasungu National Park in steady decline. It was reduced from 672 in 1992 to fifty-eight by 2005—about thirty elephants were being killed in Kasungu annually in the early 1990s.[175] Zambian poachers were the main culprits, with local Malawian tobacco farmers only poaching when economic necessity drove them to it. There were smuggling networks operating in the country, involving members of the police and military. In January 1992, an army major, Austen Kambota, was arrested along with a known smuggler, Wakisa Masoka, at Lilongwe Airport trying to smuggle 200 kg of ivory to South Africa—experts believed the ivory had come from seventy-eight small tusks and indicated that immature animals had been killed to provide it.[176] The poaching was threatening to wipe out the scattered herds and in 1994 it was reported that the small population in Majete National Park, near the border with Mozambique's Tete province, had been exterminated or driven out. One reason for the disappearance was that a huge refugee camp for Mozambicans fleeing the civil war there had been built in an area used by elephants in the dry season. The combination of poaching by gangs crossing into Malawi from Mozambique and the presence of 60,000 refugees led to the population demise. In 2007, after park management was handed to African Parks, seventy elephants from Liwonde were relocated to Majete to try to establish a herd there, as the refugee camp was long gone and the Mozambican civil war had ended, reducing opportunities for infiltration.

By the early 2000s, overall numbers had fallen further. The African Elephant Database figure for the country was 647 definite (down from 1,111 in 1995) and a speculative maximum of 3,885. In 2014, the number of elephants in Kasungu was estimated to be around 100, almost double the 2005 figure, as poaching had declined, purely because of the lack of elephants.[177] To prevent further poaching, the government not only allowed African Parks to take over management of the Majete and Liwonde Parks and the Nkhotakota Reserve, but also moved down the more militarised anti-poaching route, with the familiar consequences of shoot-to-kill policies, harassment of local people, beatings and further alienation of communities near protected areas. South African mercenaries were brought in to train anti-poaching units in Liwonde. The operations were funded by international NGOs. Within a short period of time, the rangers were implicated in 300 murders, 325 disappearances and 250 rapes, as well as allegations of torture and intimidation.[178]

In 2016, it was reported that African Parks was moving 500 elephants from Majete and Liwonde to Nkhotakota to relieve signs of over-crowding in the two reserves and establish a larger herd in the latter—this will be the largest translocation exercise ever undertaken in Africa.[179] Yet the danger for Malawi's elephants is still real, as poaching continues with the involvement of senior government officials and members of the intelligence and law enforcement agencies, who run poaching networks that supply ivory to Chinese traders. Unconfirmed reports in February 2016 suggested that the organisation of poaching was directed from the top of the Malawian National Intelligence Bureau and that officials from State House were aware of what was going on but had taken no action.[180]

Mozambique has a much larger elephant population because of its size and less dense human population. In the new millennium it became one of the major sources of ivory. In 1992, the elephant population had been put at between 15,000 and 20,000—down from 59,000 in 1978.[181] The African Elephant Database put the maximum possible population in 1995 at 15,410, with only 717 definite; in 1998 the definite figure rose to 6,898 but the maximum fell to 13,340; in 2002, ten years after the end of the civil war, the database definite total was 11,647, with the absolute maximum up to 17,506; 2007's figures showed major growth, perhaps through more sophisticated surveying techniques, with 14,079 definite and a maximum of 26,088. By 2013, the estimates had jumped again, with 16,422 and a maximum of 32,976.[182] The largest population was in the Niassa ecosystem on the border with Tanzania. There were an estimated 12,000 elephants there, an increase on the 9,000 in the region in 1988, but evidence of a fall of at least 1,600 between 2002 and 2013 indicated that recovery had stopped and numbers were falling, with illicit killing the only viable explanation—if elephants hadn't been poached, one would have expected the Niassa population to have risen to 25,000–34,000 on a 4–5 per cent annual reproduction rate.

The Niassa poaching problem was a result of the increasing demand from China, the massive price increases on the global ivory market and the consequent incentive for a resumption of large-scale killing. The willingness of local people to hunt, help organised gangs or fail to support anti-poaching efforts was linked closely with extensive human-elephant conflict around Niassa and official corruption and incompetence. Crop damage by elephants was being raised regularly by local people at village-, district- and provincial-level meetings between community representatives and government or Frelimo party officials and had led to rioting and attacks on government administrative centres in one district. This conflict, combined with incentives for poaching, does not bode well for Mozambique's elephants. The population in the Niassa National Reserve in northern Mozambique is relatively large and is part of a widely distributed regional population, with movement to and from range areas in Tanzania. While this is something transfrontier parks try to encourage, in areas with poor law enforcement and local resentment of elephants this can lead to increased vulnerability to the influx of poachers working with disgruntled local communities. The Selous-Niassa-Rovuma area is example of the importance of large dispersal areas for elephants but also of the vulnerability to poaching where corruption is rife and enforcement poor. Much of the ivory seized in recent years en route to China has been proved by DNA analysis to come from herds in the region, where poverty, weak governance, corruption and a high unemployment rate mean that poaching or helping organised poaching syndicates can seem to be a way out of impoverishment.

In 2013, the United Nations Development Programme's Human Development Index ranked Mozambique 185th out of 187 countries surveyed and noted that the areas around the Niassa and Limpopo transfrontier elephant ranges were among the most deprived. Vira and Ewing noted that wildlife rangers were extremely poorly paid and that thirty out of 100 rangers in the Limpopo National Park were under investigation for assisting poachers, and a number of Niassa rangers had been arrested for the same reason.[183] Criminal syndicates were active on the Tanzanian and South Africa borders with Mozambique and few of the small arms that flooded the country during years of civil war had been decommissioned or confiscated. Illicit ivory trading went side by side with the recruitment of young Mozambicans to hunt rhinos for South African-based syndicates and the illegal timber trade, which supplied rosewood and other valuable and endangered woods to China.[184]

In 2012, the WWF found that Niassa was experiencing a huge increase in poaching, with 2,667 carcasses found in 2009–2012, a four-fold increase on previous years.[185] The ivory taken from the park is chiefly sent north through Tanzania's Chinese-dominated smuggling network. Poaching is facilitated by government and Frelimo corruption, with the latter involving not just low-level officials but a chain stretching up to senior party members and members of the armed forces, the latter suspected of using heavy military weapons and helicopters in poaching in Quirimbas National Park. Frelimo party officials were linked to the killing of fifty elephants in the Niassa region in September 2012.[186] The WWF estimated that 480–900 elephants were killed in Quirimbas between 2011 and 2013.[187] Government ministers call almost ritually for greater law enforcement and blame the poaching increase on international organised crime syndicates, but ignore the vital facilitating role of government and party corruption—though Tourism Minister Carvalho Muária, speaking at a WWF workshop in Maputo in June 2014, did admit corruption among poorly paid rangers. He told the workshop that he believed Mozambique had a population of 22,000 elephants.

In September 2014, Carlos Lopes Pereira, of the Wildlife Conservation Society, said that as a result of continued poaching, estimates were now suggesting a population of only 19,600.[188] In May 2015, the WCS and the Mozambican government gave an even more apocalyptic estimate of the decline in numbers, concluding after extensive surveys that there had been a 48 per cent decline in elephant numbers, from just over 20,000 to an estimated 10,300, as a result of "rampant elephant poaching" over the previous five years. Northern Mozambique, including the Niassa National Reserve, was the hardest hit, accounting for 95 per cent of elephant deaths. They estimated that by 2015 the population there had fallen to an estimated 6,100. Aerial surveys found as many carcasses as live elephants in some areas of Niassa, which was where 95 per cent of the animals were poached—according to the WCS, the Niassa region's population had dropped from 15,400 to 6,100, with only 4,440 in the Niassa Reserve; 43% of the elephants spotted there were dead.[189]

At the time of writing, Mozambique is bracketed with Tanzania and areas of central Africa as the major source of illicit ivory coming onto the world market, with little sign that the corruption facilitating its supply will be tackled in the foreseeable future. The WWF's international policy expert on wildlife trade, Colman O'Criodain, stated in June 2014 that "Mozambique has emerged as one of the main places of the slaughter of elephants and ivory transit in Africa and as a profitable warehouse for transit and export of rhino horn for the Asian markets. We need to see urgent action and ongoing commitment to combat these illegal activities."[190] Support was forthcoming from the international community, with the London *Sunday Times* reporting on 27 May 2015 that the World Bank's International Development Association arm had granted $40m to Mozambique to fund conservation efforts, which will includ support for hunting programmes aimed at generating funds for local development and conservation and so combating local support for poaching through sustainable-use projects. Mozambique has hunting blocks in close proximity to protected areas. This could be a sign that more realistic policies are beginning to be considered, but they will not flourish until the ruling Frelimo party gets to grips with corruption throughout government institutions, the wildlife service, the military and the body politic. Nor is it encouraging that conflict has re-emerged on a small scale in 2015 and early 2016 between the government and the former rebel movement Renamo, with attacks by the latter on police patrols and posts in Renamo's home area.

Namibia's independence in 1990, following the withdrawal of the South African army and the end of the use of the north as a rearbase for support for UNITA and attacks in to Angola, enabled the new SWAPO government to redevelop conservation programmes and market the country as a safari destination. SWAPO's policy, utilising the wildlife tourism infrastructure developed by the South Africans, was of conservation with community involvement to protect species like black rhino and elephant, but also develop income generation for poor, rural communities. Projects in Damaraland and Kaokoveld employing 300 locally recruited game guards enabled poaching to be restricted and the elephant population in the region to grow from 250 in 1990 to 350 in 1992. The programmes in those areas built on the work of Garth Owen-Smith and his creation of a system of community guards among the Himba and Herero people funded by the Endangered Wildlife Trust, an NGO based in Johannesburg. Owen-Smith recruited volunteer rangers, who were paid the equivalent of $25 per month plus food and household supplies, which was an important boost to income in an area where frequent droughts destroyed the livestock on which the communities depended.[191]

These improvements in conservation implementation led Namibia's elephant population to increase. Estimated at 5,000 in 1989, it rose to a minimum of 5,843 but a possible maximum of 11,599 by 1995 and then, by 2002, a minimum of 7,769 but about the same projected maximum, according to the African Elephant Database. Cumming and Jones were more optimistic and put the probable population at 15,000 in 2005, concentrated in the Kaokoveld-Damaraland-Kunene, Etosha, Khaudom (on the border with Botswana) and the Caprivi Strip[192]— Namibia also had a share in the large herds that moved across the region stretching from Hwange in Zimbabwe through southern Zambia, northern Botswana and Angola and the Caprivi Strip. Migration into Namibia was encouraged by the low rate of poaching and small numbers killed as a result of human-elephant conflict.

Namibia's Ministry of Environment and Tourism established a management plan, which included the provision for culling, though it hasn't yet been used to reduce numbers. The government, like its southern African neighbours, wanted to be able to trade in elephant products to enable local communities to benefit from sustainable use by cropping in areas of high concentration. But even without ivory income, community conservancies were an important conservation and development tool, alongside the national parks. According to the Integrated Rural Development and Nature Conservation project in Namibia, there were seventy-nine community conservancies operating by 2014, employing local people as game guards and generating income through tourism and sustainable use, which included some trophy hunting; 45 per cent of the projects were in the Kunene region. In northern

Namibia and the Caprivi, it was estimated that N$23.5m ($1.65m) was earned in 2013 from selling quotas for trophy and other hunting to safari operators catering for foreign hunters, according to Pohamba Shifeta, the deputy minister for environment and tourism.

There were some signs of a slight increase in poaching after the ivory boom took off in 2009 and there was increasing Chinese commercial and construction activity in Namibia. In April 2014, it was reported that since 2012 there had been a substantial rise in poaching in the Caprivi, with illegal killings up from single figures to seventy-eight in 2012 and in the twenties in 2013, in which year thirty-five smugglers had been arrested. A smuggling ring involving Guo Yunhui, a Chinese guesthouse owner in Katima Mulilo in the Caprivi, had been uncovered. Using other members of the Chinese communities in Katima and Rundu (both hubs of the SADF/UNITA ivory trade), Guo Yunhui ran a wildlife-trafficking business in cooperation with poachers from Zambia. Katima has a thriving Chinese commercial area and many of the shop-owners are believed to be involved in ivory trading, obtaining tusks from Zambians poaching in Botswana, Namibia and Zambia.[193] Guo was said to be buying ivory for $300 per kg and trucking it to other centres of Chinese economic activity in the region, from where it was taken to China by returning workers.

In November 2015, Colgar Sikopo, the head of the Directorate of Parks and Wildlife Management, said that in the previous four years poaching of elephants had increased, with 230 killed, along with 100 rhinos. According to Sikopo, it was clear from intelligence and from arrests of Chinese traders that China was the final destination of ivory poached in Namibia, though he tried to soften the criticism by adding that the Chinese government was helping Namibia in fighting the trade.[194]

There was controversy in June 2014, when it was reported that up to a third of the desert-dwelling elephants in north-western Kunene were going to be offered up for trophy hunting to provide income for local people. Concern was expressed that killing these elephants would endanger future reproduction and was not warranted by the numbers concerning evidence of human-elephant conflict.[195] The Ministry of the Environment and Tourism reacted angrily, denying the figures, but not the plans to set a quota for trophy hunting. A press release said that there were at least 391 elephants in the region and the population was growing steadily, noting that the overall Namibian population had risen to 20,000 animals. It asserted that trophy hunting brought in much-needed income and provided meat, adding that communal conservancies now accounted for 19 per cent of communal lands and were bringing in N$40m ($40m) a year through sustainable utilisation of wildlife, while serving to conserve it.[196] According to this statement, the elephant population was growing at 3.3 per cent a year and the quotas were well below sustainable off-take levels, and crop damage and human-elephant conflict had increased with growing elephant numbers; it further stated that local communities had to be protected along with wildlife.

In South Africa, the period after the CITES ban encompassed the constitutional transition and advent of government by the African National Congress (ANC). The new government started an investigation into ivory and other wildlife trafficking by the SADF during the conflicts in Angola and Mozambique. But there were no major changes in wildlife or elephant management policy. The main elephant population in the country was still concentrated in Kruger and surrounding private reserves. By the mid-1990s, the population there exceeded the planned level of 8,000, even though 16,000 elephants had been culled in the twenty-seven years preceding 1994. In 1995, it was decided that no more elephants would be culled until at least 2005 and that other strategies would be tried, such as using water supplies to affect concentrations in the park, contraception and relocation to other areas of South Africa. So far, despite ever increasing numbers, there has been no resumption of culling. But relocation has been used to reduce numbers. In 1994, 145 elephants were relocated as whole family units and ninety-five juveniles were sold to unidentified buyers who did not want adult elephants.[197]

The decision to suspend culling went alongside the announcement that South Africa would not support attempts to lift the ivory trade ban at the CITES conference of parties in 1997, following failures to overturn it at two previous meetings. This position may have helped improve South Africa's standing with influential wildlife NGOs and in October 1996 it was announced that IFAW, which was totally opposed to culling, had given the South African National Parks (SANP) Board a grant of

$2.5m to assist with conservation of elephants, notably a plan to enlarge Addo National Park to allow relocation of elephants from Kruger.[198]

In 1999, the Parks Board approved a new Kruger elephant plan, which again ruled out culling for the time being and concentrated on zoning and withdrawing pumped water sources to prevent the concentration of elephants in particular areas.[199] A census in 2004 in the park indicated that the population had reached 13,000, with 800 elephants relocated to smaller parks and reserves. The steady growth was facilitated by the very low level of poaching in the park, something which has been maintained despite the catastrophic rise in rhino poaching in Kruger. The 2002 African Elephant Database figure for 2002 showed South Africa as having a maximum of 14,926 elephants—the vast majority in Kruger and surrounding private reserves, with 337 in Addo, 310 in Hluhluwe-Umfolozi and 318 in Madikwe. A scientific study in 2006 supported the decision not to resume culling on a large scale but did warn that what it called "localised management of numbers to protect biodiversity" might have to be used, though it wasn't clear exactly what this would entail.[200] One measure to prevent vegetation damage in woodland areas was the taking down of fences between Kruger and Limpopo National Park in Mozambique as part of the transfrontier park project and also between Kruger and private reserves to the west.

By 2010, the park's population was estimated at 11,672, with a growth rate of 7 per cent a year, according to SANP chief executive David Mahanda. He said that despite the healthy growth rate, culling was still not being considered.[201] In 2012, in a detailed elephant management plan for Kruger, Sam Ferreira put the population at 13,750 and said that while culling, contraception, relocation and "range manipulation" were all management approaches being considered, there were no immediate plans for a cull; between 2000 and 2005, seventy-nine elephants had been killed in crop protection operations and to remove elephants that were a danger to local communities.[202] Ferreira said the need to cull was reduced by the removal of fences that had allowed Kruger's elephants to migrate across a wider area.[203] He could have added that poaching in Mozambique's Limpopo Park was more of a problem and served to keep down the overall population numbers in the transfrontier area.

In May 2014, SANP reported clear evidence, for the first time in years, that a bull elephant had been poached in Kruger and its tusks removed, in the northern Pafuri area of the park near the border with Mozambique. In May 2015, SANP had announced that nineteen elephants had been poached in the park since January 2015, which led Hector Magome of conservation services at SANP to warn that Kruger could be in danger of being hit by an avalanche of poaching.[204] Most of the elephants were killed in the north near the Mozambican border— two at the beginning of the year, three in July, two in August, seven in September and five in the first three weeks of October. Kruger communications head William Mabasa expressed confidence that they could cope, but the inability of the wildlife and security enforcement bodies to prevent the escalating killing of rhino (4,635 between 2007 and 2015) does not inspire confidence. One distinct possibility is that with fewer rhino available and with demand for tusks still high, poachers who were after horn are now switching to ivory.

In 2013, the African Elephant Database estimate for South Africa's population was a minimum of 20,260 and a maximum of 25,027— 16,571 in Kruger, 596 in Addo, 600 in Hluhluwe and 800 in Madikwe.

At the time of the trade ban, Zambia had an estimated 41,000 elephants, just over a quarter of the population of ten years before. In their study of illegal hunting following the ban, Dublin and Jachmann noted signs of recovery in some areas and the effect of the community-based programmes like ADMADE and LIRDP in recruiting village scouts to combat poaching. They also, however, pointed to increased poaching in Kafue National Park, resulting from the stationing of army units in the region, which could poach with impunity and also supplied weapons and ammunition to local hunters to poach on their behalf.[205] In Luangwa, the area worst affected by poaching before the ban, the initial successes of the integrated-resource programme LIRDP cut illegal hunting from the 1988 level of 160 elephants killed to twenty-seven in 1989 and twelve in 1991. Dublin and Jachmann said this was not caused directly by the ban but resulted from the community involvement and increase in the number of game scouts. By 1991 no fresh carcasses were being found by scouts in Luangwa—and yet there was evidence of large quantities of ivory leaving the country by air to Swaziland or by road to South Africa and Burundi. They concluded that the ban had not in itself played a major role in reducing poaching as the killing of elephants had not stopped, but "In areas where poaching has increased beyond expected levels it can be attributed to additional factors such as corruption in the military and illegal activity from neighbouring countries such as Zaire and Angola".

The LIRDP was having a positive effect because it increased local intelligence gathering, recruited local men as rangers and provided financial benefit to the local community. Better enforcement, a sentencing policy for poachers and smugglers related to the severity of their crimes and the offering in the LIRDP area of cash rewards for information leading to arrests all had more obvious effects than the trade ban, at least in Luangwa. But there was strong evidence that corruption in the government, police, army and wildlife service was sustaining illicit killing and trading, reinforced by regular seizures of ivory, such as that in August 1994, when wildlife rangers confiscated 216 elephant tusks and arrested several army officers who had transported the ivory from the west of the country to the capital, Lusaka, under a cargo of beef. Some of the ivory was believed to have originated in Angola.

Estimates of the overall Zambian elephant population continued falling, with the African Elephant Database giving the 1995 figures as 19,702 definite and an absolute maximum of 33,003; in 1998, it was down to 15,873 definite and a maximum of 29,016; in 2002, 12,457 definite and a maximum of 27,049. While movements between ranges and seasonal fluctuations can affect surveys, the continued decline was chiefly due to continuing poaching, mainly outside areas with community-based programmes—though these were of declining efficacy as local control was gradually eaten away by the wildlife department and central government, leading to less buy-in by local people.

In 1998, the old National Parks and Wildlife Service was changed into the Zambia Wildlife Authority (ZAWA) in a messy process in which LIRDP and ADMADE lost some of their autonomy. At the same time, there was conflict between the communities taking part in the projects and local chiefs, who wanted more of the project income to be paid to them in order to play a role in setting priorities and resented their loss of control over local resources as local people were empowered. Nevertheless, at first there were still important achievements, with local people the accepting that they had a role in and could attach value to conservation. Communities received tangible benefits and were devolved responsibility for managing wildlife to develop sustainable-use programmes through a regulated off-take of wildlife for meat and hides (under the LIRDP there had been no culling of elephants for commercial purposes).[206] Dalal-Clayton and Child believed that when it was working well with community involvement, the LIRDP was "as advanced as any in Africa… and the rapid progress made in the past four years, validate the claims of the community wildlife movement that such community-based approaches are the way forward in wildlife management".[207] About 40–50 per cent of project income was distributed to local communities as a dividend or to fund local projects of direct benefit. Income fell after President Chiluba banned hunting in 2001 and 2002, reducing income for community projects that made money from selling quotas or from the meat produced. By that time, LIRDP had been converted into the South Luangwa Area Management Unit (SLAMU) and was under closer ZAWA control.

One drawback of the Luangwa project was that while it improved community income and funding for conservation, and increased local involvement in restricting poaching (because elephants weren't hunted and so were not of direct economic benefit to local people), there was still anger when elephants damaged crops and there were regular demands that crop raiders be killed. Overall, though, LIRDP and then SLAMU did boost conservation capabilities in South Luangwa and reduce the pace of illegal killing of elephants.[208] Between 1988 and 1996, the elephant population of South Luangwa increased from 2,400 to 9,600 and fewer carcasses of illegally killed elephants were discovered during surveys. Ironically, this success led to increased human-elephant conflict and more aggressive community reactions and complaints, reducing support for the community-based projects and even resulting in local people helping poachers in return for meat.

After ZAWA assumed greater control, the authority retained 50 per cent of the income from the project, which undermined the level of income control by the community boards and led to further disenchantment. Whereas in CBNRM schemes in Chobe, Botswana 100 per cent of the income was retained by communities, in Zambia 55 per cent went directly to ZAWA and local chiefs. Support ebbed and Musumali et al. found that "local communities don't really identify with the initiatives and few understand their purpose and roles. Inadequacies in transparency and accountability have led to loss of credibility and erosion of confidence: the state continues in its reluctance to legitimize local jurisdictions and thus leaves communities confused over their position".[209] In northern Luangwa, not part of the community project, elephant numbers had fallen from 17,000 in 1973 to 1,800 in 1991. By 1997, while poaching had been reduced it was still prevalent enough to stop any growth in numbers of elephants and the estimate remained as same as six years earlier.

Poaching began to increase across Zambia in the 2000s, in line with rising Chinese demand and higher prices. There was evidence that corruption within ZAWA was one of the factors enabling illicit networks to meet demand. The EIA reported that a notorious poacher, Benson Nkunika, had been caught at Mfuwe, near South Luangwa, and revealed widespread corruption within ZAWA, to the extent that he claimed to have been commissioned to poach 100 elephants by the Park Warden, Rodgers Nkhoma. Nkhoma was transferred from the park but not prosecuted.[210] Investigations by ZAWA personnel from outside the area revealed extensive corruption and links between poachers, rangers and smuggling networks in Chipata, on the border with Malawi. According to the information given to the EIA, ivory would be harvested in the park and trucked to Chipata and across the border to Lilongwe, where there was a carving factory. The factory was raided by Malawian anti-corruption agents in February 2002. Documents seized in the raid revealed an extensive and long-standing trade network.[211]

By 2005, estimates put the number of elephants in Zambia at just above 21,500, with 14,000 in the two Luangwa parks, 5,000 in Kafue, 1,500 in the Lower Zambezi Valley, 1,000 in Sioma-Ngwezi and smaller, scattered populations in the north-east and north-west. The increase in Sioma-Ngwezi was due mainly to migration from Botswana and Zimbabwe's densely populated elephant ranges. Poaching was still rife in the park and it remains a problem today for the KAZA transfrontier plans to allow the spread of concentrated elephant populations.[212] Preliminary reports from the Great Elephant Census suggested Zambia's population was 21,000 in 2015.[213]

In 1989, Zimbabwe's elephant population was estimated at 43,000, but with significant numbers migrating seasonally between Zimbabwe and Botswana and some movement between Gonarezhou, Kruger and the Limpopo National Park—later to be linked in a transfrontier project. The CITES ban had an effect on the legal and well-regulated ivory carving business in Zimbabwe and on the long-term financing of CAMPFIRE projects. There were about 200 legal carving businesses in the country and their trade declined by 75 per cent when the ban was introduced, as the European, American and Japanese tourists who had bought ivory no longer did so. Under the CITES regulations, the national parks and wildlife department was still allowed to sell legal ivory to carvers, which it did at $74 per kg. But within two years of the ban there were reports of increased poaching and a rise in prices. *Oryx* reported that in some areas poaching had increased by 300 per cent since the ban. The Zimbabwean wildlife authorities blamed the ban for the rise in poaching. Despite the rise in illegal killing, the elephant population was still thought to be increasing by five per cent annually.

One important initiative at this time was the move by major landowners in the south-eastern Lowveld to band together to form the Savé Valley Conservancy—a block of land north-east of Gonarezhou, where fifteen landowners pulled down the fences between their properties to form a large unfenced area, which already had a large wildlife population, including elephants migrating back and forth to Gonarezhou. The organisers planned to restock the area with surplus animals from the national park, where despite the poaching it was decided that 2,000 elephants had to be removed. The wealthy ranchers intended to set up their own anti-poaching units and develop sustainable use through cropping abundant species and through tourism as means of generating income.[214] The national parks department, coping with a severe drought in the Lowveld, was having to combine translocation of 1,000 elephants with culling and feeding programmes. The meat from the culling was distributed to local people whose crops or livestock had been destroyed by drought, according to the Zimbabwe Wildlife Authority in August 1992. By April 1994, Gonarezhou had moved 650 elephants to Savé Valley. Another 200 had been sent to Madikwe Game Reserve in South Africa. In 1995, the wildlife department announced that it was to conduct a survey of wildlife populations in Hwange, where elephant numbers were increasing, and there were suggestions that 8,600 elephants would need to be removed by one means or another. The population of the park was put at 30,000. The African Elephant Database put the national population in 1995 at a minimum of 56,297 and a maximum of 81,855.

Against this background, the development of CAMPFIRE proceeded, though without the ability to maximise income from the export of natural-mortality or culled ivory. Those managing CAMPFIRE schemes locally could sell hunting quotas for elephants and, depending on the destination country, trophies could be exported; but tusks or worked ivory from the projects could not. Rowan Martin, who had been one of the masterminds behind the scheme, had opposed the CITES ban and worked for relisting of Zimbabwe's elephants. Others directly connected with the programme also viewed the CITES vote negatively. Simbarashe Hove, the executive officer of the CAMPFIRE scheme in the Nyaminyami district, near Matusadona National Park, said that the CITES ban "was, let me put it bluntly, irresponsible. All these organizations, if they really wanted to come up with something, they should have talked with us. You know what this ban means to local people? There will be too many elephants. The elephant population is growing. You don't need surveys, you can just see it. It means the people are exposed to more danger than they are now."[215] Hove said that in areas with too many elephants, sustainable use was the only answer to offset losses to local people from elephants raiding their fields—one farmer alone lost 264 bags of maize, twenty-four bags of groundnuts and four bales of cotton when elephants stripped his fields, rendering him destitute.[216] In such situations, farmers would kill elephants or put pressure on local and national government to cull rather than conserve them.

Without income from the sale of elephant meat, hides and ivory, income for schemes would be reduced and the incentive to protect wildlife diminished, although the projects still generated enough income to survive through culling impala, buffalo and other abundant species, and selling hunting quotas to wealthy foreign hunters. Under CAMPFIRE, at least 50 per cent of the income from sport hunting in project areas went to the local population. In the twelve districts with programmes, home to over 400,000 people, 90 per cent of the Z$11,538,508 income in 1990 came from sport hunting.[217] The inability to sell ivory from sustainable off-take had cost Nyaminyami

Z$40,000 (about US$20,000) during the first eight months of 1990, according to Russell Taylor, a WWF scientist working in the area who supported sustainable use.[218] The annual income of farming families in the areas was Z$200, so the benefits of selling ivory were obvious. CAMPFIRE survived the initial loss of ivory income and it was reported that the scheme had led to an increase in the area of land given over to wildlife from 12 per cent of the national area to 35 per cent over the first five years of the scheme. At the same time, Rowan Martin, its architect and chief supporter, lost his job with the national parks and wildlife department due to in-fighting within the department and the influence of the World Bank, which funded a restructuring exercise in 1993. There was less emphasis on sustainable use and more on protection, leading to the suspension of culling to reduce numbers in 1993. The change in policy was welcomed by Western NGOs and a few local animal welfare groups but not the majority of conservation NGOs in Zimbabwe, which saw culling and sustainable-use as the correct, pragmatic approach to conservation.[219]

In 1996, CAMPFIRE continued to expand despite the loss of ivory income due to the trade ban, and brought income to 600,000 people in seventy to eighty wards in the poorest districts of Zimbabwe.[220] The projects were helping both conservation and local income generation, but were plagued by conflicts over use of the income between traditional chiefs and communities and between varying levels of local government; mismanagement was a severe problem in some areas. It was also a concern that while over 50 per cent of income was reserved for communities, most went to projects run by the district councils, and "for most CAMPFIRE communities, the small size of the payments at a household level probably does not provide much incentive to forego other, more immediately and individually rewarding land-use practices", which threatened buy-in to the schemes in the long-term. In some areas, there was also conflict between communities opting for CAMPFIRE approaches and local cattle ranchers, who feared the knocking down of fences and predation of stock.[221] The patronage aspect and competition between councils and other state bodies for access to income exacerbated alienation of local people in some of the schemes and were an almost inevitable result in a country riven by political factionalism and rival patronage networks, and one where

CAMPFIRE itself could be seen a top-down programme used by local government administration as an alternative to its meagre funding from central government.

However, the WWF scientist, Russell Taylor, who worked with the Nyaminyami CAMPFIRE scheme, wrote that in his area the scheme was working to overcome the problems caused by elephants for local farmers through crop damage, destruction of water supply systems and human deaths or injury. There were an estimated 2,000 elephants in this area on the edge of Matusadona National Park. Before CAMPFIRE, local people had shot elephants in an unregulated and potentially unsustainable way to protect themselves and their crops. But under CAMPFIRE, they generated income through selling hunting quotas and had come to tolerate elephant presence more—combined safari hunting and organised crop protection killing was taking out twenty elephants, or 1 per cent of the population, annually, which wasn't reducing numbers given a higher natural reproduction rate. Taylor concluded that in the long-term elephant conservation depended on local people and on policies that recognised the productive role of wildlife utilisation and put power in local hands, providing obvious material benefit to individual householders and farmers.[222]

Despite problems with CAMPFIRE and some evidence of continued poachings, Zimbabwe's elephant population was growing in the 1990s, with more land becoming available through community schemes and private conservancies. In 1995, the African Elephant Database estimated the definite population at 56,297, which rose to 63,070 by 1998, with the absolute maximum for both years being above 81,000. The information officer for the CAMPFIRE Association, Tawona Tavengwa, wrote that the association could sell quotas totalling 276 elephants a year to trophy hunters, which would provide about 60 per cent of CAMPFIRE income.[223] By 2000, however, concerns were growing again over poaching. An aerial survey of elephants in the Zambezi Valley in late 1999, carried out by the WWF's Southern African Regional Programme Office (WWF-SARPO) which broadly supports Zimbabwe's pro-trade position, found 1,378 carcasses in the area, which was 11.25 per cent of the elephants seen in the survey— five times the normal ratio of carcasses to live animals. Press reports in 1999 indicated that at least 350 elephants had been illegally killed that year in Zimbabwe.[224]

One reason for increased poaching, of game generally and not just elephants, was the government-inspired land occupation programme that started in 2000. The seizure of farms by war veterans, unemployed youths from urban areas and supporters of the ruling ZANU-PF party was violent and made many black farm workers destitute, while bringing people unskilled in farming into rural areas. Poaching assumed critical proportions and many game ranches were seized. The Savé Valley Conservancy was badly affected by land occupations, with 6,000 squatters taking up residence. Many of the CAMPFIRE schemes were also badly affected and the ability of communities to protect and regulate the off-take of wildlife declined. Parts of Gonarezhou National Park were invaded by those involved in land seizures. Wolmer et al. noted the contradiction between the land distribution programme, which stressed distributing land to poor, black Zimbabweans (though many of the political elite benefited disproportionately) for cultivation, and the regulated, conservation-minded, community-state partnerships involved in schemes like CAMPFIRE and some of the conservancies.[225]

Game ranching, commercial hunting operations and ecotourism would not easily live side-by-side with chaotic and violent land redistribution. Many ZANU-PF members and government ministers criticised the conservancies and other schemes as ways of "privatising" wildlife resources and saw CAMPFIRE as a means of preserving unpopular conservation policies originated by the old white ruling elite and perpetuated through support from foreign NGOs. The situation eased somewhat after the 2002 presidential election, which Mugabe contrived to win through violence, harassment and control of the majority of the media. The land programme was a highly political one, as much about defeating political opponents as about achieving equitable distribution of land. As the spate of seizures petered out and ownership or control was consolidated, community-based schemes and some conservancies were able to recover and offer alternative models of development, with many conservancies adopting community-sensitive schemes to benefit local communities, including offering them land inside the conservancies as long as the fences stayed down.

Amid the social, economic and political turmoil of Mugabe's Zimbabwe, the elephant population continued to grow. Cumming and Jones estimate that by 2001 the numbers had reached 89,000, with an annual growth rate of 5 per cent.[226] There was growing human-elephant conflict in communal lands bordering parks, reserves and conservancies, with about 9 per cent of the elephant population residing outside protected areas. Crop raiding and human deaths led to a regular programme of control shooting, which accounted for 579 elephants killed between 2001 and the end of 2003. The continuation of CAMPFIRE schemes did help mitigate community anger over damage and limited illegal killing to protect crops. But Rowan Martin lamented that government attitudes towards CAMPFIRE were not consistent, that there was a tendency to view local empowerment as a weakening of central control and that periodic efforts to expropriate local resources or prevent district councils from distributing revenues to communities, despite the role of wildlife income in alleviating poverty, were damaging to the schemes.[227]

In the 2000s and 2010s, there was both a growth in the elephant population but also in poaching, facilitated by corruption in government and the security forces. The Elephant Database put the population at a minimum of 81,555 and maximum of 96,258 in 2002, at 84,416–99,407 in 2005 and 67,954–96,632 in 2013, the latter figure showing a small decrease in the maximum figure but a major fall in definite numbers, partly due to poaching. The ivory price boom of the 2009–2015 period and consequent rise in poaching in range states impinged on Zimbabwe's elephants, with increases in reported ivory seizures over the period—over fifty tusks were confiscated in just one week in May 2012. The propensity to poach, incentivised by high prices and the existence of political patrons willing to protect poachers and smuggling syndicates, was worsened by extreme statements by some ministers when there was conflict over land ownership on conservancies or on the margins of protected areas. In 2011, during a dispute in the Lowveld, the Indigenisation Minister Saviour Kasukuwere stepped up the rhetoric, saying he would "drive all the animals on the conservancies into Gonarezhou National Park and… *braai* [barbecue] whatever remained behind".[228] Groups of landless people resettled in conservancies under the land reform were, according to the government, to be treated as new partners in the conservancies, but they were generally uninterested in the conservation and utilisation strategies being pursued and often reverted land to cattle-rearing.

In 2011–12, land seizures continued, particularly in the Chiredzi River Conservancy, as people who had not secured land as part of the fast-track programme started in 2000 sought to benefit with support from ZANU-PF politicians like Kasukuwere, who gained political leverage from this stance as he engaged in factional struggles within the party. Conflict over land ownership, conservancy partnerships and the unhelpful intervention of unscrupulous politicians provided opportunities for poaching syndicates to move in and operate with impunity. Even though Mugabe backed the formation of the transfrontier park incorporating Gonarezhou, Kruger and Limpopo, along with linking corridors to Savé Valley, the presence of the new communities within the area meant anti-poaching operations were made more difficulty and illicit killing for ivory increased with the suspected involvement of senior political and military leaders.[229]

In 2013, a new form of poaching developed in Hwange National Park that continues to be used at the time of writing: cyanide poisoning. In the first incidents, at least 100 elephants died when industrial-grade cyanide was put in watering holes along well-used elephant trails. There were reports from Gonarezhou, Mana Pools, Zambezi and Matusadona National Parks of similar, if more limited, uses of poison to kill elephants. There were further deaths by poisoning in Hwange in late 2013 and nine poachers were arrested, but no one higher up the ivory chain. Researchers estimated that between 105 and 115 elephants were killed with cyanide in 2013.[230] In late October 2015, it was being reported that twenty-two elephants had been poisoned and had their tusks hacked off in Hwange. By early November, the number had risen to sixty and Zimbabwean newspapers reported that a senior policeman and corrupt officials were involved in the killing. The journalists who broke the story, *Sunday Mail* editor Mabasa Sas and reporters Tinashe Farawo and Brian Chitemba, were promptly arrested. The police denied that an assistant commissioner, a lower-ranking officer, a local Asian businessman and corrupt rangers from the park were involved in a poaching and smuggling ring, adding that the reporters would be charged with spreading false stories.[231]

Periodic arrests of low-level poachers kept the poisoning stories in the Zimbabwean press and police sources said that a criminal syndicate run by Busani Moyo and Lukas Nhliziyo supplied the cyanide to the poachers and received the ivory.[232] But the two were not arrested despite informants in the police telling journalists that the two were believed to be part of a "well-known" and organised criminal syndicate operating in Hwange and the Victoria Falls, terrorising wildlife with impunity. According to these sources, the Moyo-Nhliziyo "syndicate has National Parks and ZRP [police] details working within their ranks, and we strongly suspect they have corrupted the prosecutors".[233] Syndicates operating in the Hwange and Victoria Falls area were said by the sources to be of long standing and to be operating with the knowledge of the police and presumably the protection of senior officers and/or politicians. Moyo had already been convicted once for possession of 237kg of ivory and sentenced to nine years imprisonment with labour, but was still free, ostensibly on bail pending appeal.

Interestingly, the publicity in Zimbabwe around the poisonings and the potential damage to hard currency earnings from tourism in Hwange led the newly-appointed Minister for Environment, Water and Climate, Saviour Kasukuwere, to stop his "*braai* the animals" approach and call for stiffer penalties for wildlife offenders, calling on the Wildlife Authority to strengthen its "foot soldier" in affected areas and work more closely with the police. This sounds fine enough, but of course the authorities are riddled with corruption, and many rangers and policemen are connected with criminal and patronage networks that block effective action against all but those poachers at the bottom of the chain. In February 2016, it was reported that the managing director of a Zimbabwean mining company, Godfrey Nyakudya, had been arrested and accused of being the organiser behind the cyanide poisoning of more than 300 elephants in Hwange and another 100 in other protected areas between 2013 and the end of 2015.[234] At the time of writing, he was in prison in Bulawayo, still awaiting trial. The government had previously blamed the poisonings on disgruntled villagers and wildlife department employees, but the evidence suggests an organised criminal network, which may involve wildlife officials. The new environment minister, Oppah Muchinguri, had said in November 2015 that low staff morale among rangers and resentment of national parks on the part of local villagers were behind the poisonings. What is much more likely is that poorly paid rangers and poor villagers were drawn into the poisoning and ivory smuggling operation run by businessmen.

Despite the denials, cover-ups and harassment of journalists and whistleblowers, Zimbabwean wildlife officials had to admit that about 1,000 elephants were illegally killed between 2008 and 2012. The causal factors in the poaching resurgence were a combination of the land seizures, falling viability of CAMPFIRE schemes as income had dropped for the local communities involved, political corruption and the ever greater importance of patronage networks. The small independent Zimbabwean press frequently accuses national and provincial ZANU-PF leaders and government officials of being godfathers of poaching and of plundering conservancies.[235] When the influential ZANU-PF governor of Masvingo Province, Titus Maluleke, was given land in Savé Valley under the land reform programme, he said openly that "We are not interested in wildlife, we do not want to learn about the business. We want cash".[236] Political leaders, including senior ZANU-PF and government figures in Mugabe's inner circle, are regularly accused of involvement in poaching and smuggling syndicates, but they and the authorities in Harare always deny having any connection with the trade.[237] When suspicion of profiting from poaching goes right to the top of the political system, illicit hunting and trafficking can proceed with impunity.

Another elephant scandal to hit Zimbabwe was the capture of baby elephants in Hwange for sale to China. NGOs and other wildlife activists accused government officials, among them cabinet ministers, of colluding with wildlife dealers in the covert export of elephants to China. The environment minister at the time, Kasukuwere, defended the export deal, saying that Zimbabwe needed the funds that would be raised. His successor, Oppah Muchinguri, confirmed in January 2016 that the exporting of young elephants would be continued despite criticism. This brought international NGO criticism down on the government and wildlife authorities just as they were fighting a rearguard action against a US government decision in February 2014 to ban the import of trophy ivory from sport hunting in Zimbabwe into the United States. The ban represented the heightened US opposition to wildlife trafficking as part of the broad linking of ivory and insurgency or organised crime. The combination of the elephant poisonings and baby elephant exports meant that the Western media and public opinion were becoming highly critical of Zimbabwe's policies. The Zimbabwean government announced that it would lobby the US Congress to reverse the decision and Edson Chidziya, director of Zimbabwe's Parks and Wildlife Management Department, went to Washington to speak before a congressional panel, though to no great effect.

Rowan Martin joined the fray and argued, with some justification, that despite the poisonings Zimbabwe's elephant population was increasing, not falling, and that the poisonings and other examples of poaching had only a marginal effect. CAMPFIRE and other community-based schemes, he argued, would be further damaged by the loss of trophy income and the deterrent effect this would have on hunters spending hard currency in Zimbabwe, much of which would aid conservation. He also claimed, somewhat disingenuously, that Zimbabwe was having a measure of success in catching poachers,[238] neglecting to mention the high-level corruption that maintained, facilitated and profited from the illicit trade and which showed no signs of diminishing. A year after the ivory trophy ban was imposed, the Safari Operators Association of Zimbabwe reported that Zimbabwe's earnings from safari hunting had dropped by 30 per cent, and that in areas with community-based schemes some 800,000 families had experienced substantial drops in their income as a result. The national CAMPFIRE managing director, Charles Jonga, wrote to the US Congress that the trophy ban was damaging the programme, which benefited conservation and poor rural communities by providing about $2 million in income that could not be replaced from other sources.[239]

West Africa: continued decline and fear about viability of scattered populations

The depredations of ivory hunters, massive increases in population, development of cash crops like cocoa and palm oil and human-elephant conflict had over two centuries reduced the population to scattered groups spread thinly across West Africa, with most populations isolated and vulnerable. The country-by-country database figures show very low figures in the definite columns, with only Burkina Faso (4,203), Ghana (857), Benin (838) and Mali (344) having anything like sustainable populations by 2013.[240] Even the maximum numbers possible for the regional range states were indicative of a lack of growth between 1989

Table 6: Estimates for West Africa's elephant populations, 1979 and 1989

	1979	*1989*
Benin	900	2,100
Burkina Faso	1,700	3,900
Ghana	3,500	1,100
Guinea	300	300
Guinea-Bissau	–	20
Ivory Coast	4,000	3,300
Liberia	900	650
Mali	1,000	600
Mauritania	160	20
Niger	1,500	800
Nigeria	2,300	3,100
Senegal	450	50
Sierra Leone	300	250
Togo	80	100
Regional total	17,090	16,290

Source: David Western, 'The Ecological Role of Elephants in Africa', *Pachyderm*, 12, 1989.

Table 7: West Africa's elephant population, 1995–2013

1995		1998		2002		2007		2013	
Definite	Max	Definite	Max	Definite	Max	Definite	Max	Definite	Max
2,760	14,725	2,489	12,803	5,458	13,183	7,487	12,290	7,543	17,487

Source: African Elephant Database.

and 2013 and in some areas (like Sierra Leone and Senegal) elephants had largely disappeared. Conservation measures, cross-border corridors and transfrontier arrangements had helped Burkinabe, Ghanaian and Beninois herds recover a little, but for the region as a whole, the picture was bleak.

Elephants are found in about fifty-four separate ranges in West Africa—thirty-five in forest areas and nineteen in savannah or Sahel scrub. Only three populations are listed in the database as having more than 1,000 individuals: W du Burkina National Park (2,161), the Konkombouri and Pama Hunting Zone (2,111) and the Aires de l'Est

Hunting Areas (897), all in Burkina Faso, and Pendjari Biosphere Reserve in Benin (1,291). Mali's small population of savannah elephants in the Gourma region (344) tended to get the most media coverage, partly due to the Malian civil war and suggestions that the conflict had led to poaching by armed militias, but also because it was the last surviving population of the once widespread Sahel savannah elephants.

In Burkina Faso, despite the growing problem of desertification and resulting shortage of grazing and cultivable land, the elephant population has been growing and is the most viable population in the region. Elephants are concentrated in the south-west of the country adjacent to Benin's elephant range. The law still permits hunting and elephants survive in areas that include hunting blocks and game ranches, where wildlife cropping is permitted. Poaching in the main ranges in Burkina Faso has been at a consistently low level for decades. This is despite regular complaints from villagers about elephant damage to crops. In January 2015, for example, the inhabitants of villages around Niangokolo in south-western Burkina protested over crop destruction by the local herds as they searched for food at a time of poor rains.[241] There was little reaction from national or local authorities and there has been little control shooting or illicit killing registered by conservationists or the government. An increase in poaching was, however, reported in W du Burkina National Park in 2013, according to Shelley Waterland, programmes manager for Born Free. She went to the park and talked with the wildlife authorities and anti-poaching teams, concluding that the soaring demand in China had finally hit the Burkinabe herds, with alarming levels of elephant poaching inside the park, but no numbers were given to enable an assessment of the scale of the poaching.[242]

In many areas, like Mole National Park in Ghana, the problem is less poaching than the shrinking of elephant ranges and the lack of protected or viable corridors between protected areas, which keeps populations isolated. Those that stray out of protected areas may be poached or killed to protect crops. Poaching is generally low in Ghana, partly because of a successful anti-poaching programme funded by Dutch development organisations and overseen by the expert on enforcement and conservation, Hugo Jachmann. Control shooting is continuing in non-protected areas, however. In other areas of West Africa, such as Guinea and Guinea-Bissau, populations are so fragmented and threatened by habit loss that long-term survival is deemed unlikely.[243]

While Ivory Coast's elephants are not as threatened in the immediate future, the elephant database estimate shows the population falling from 551–2,196 in 1995 to 137–1,139 in 2013, through human-elephant conflict, habitat loss and poaching, especially during the civil wars in 2002–4 and 2011, when anti-poaching operations weren't possible in many areas and guns became more widely available. Local people hunt for meat and ivory and, with an expanding rural population, there is ever greater pressure on cultivable land for cash crops like cocoa. In 2014, IFAW funded a programme in cooperation with the Ivorian government to relocate some of the remaining herds from areas where they were in constant conflict with local farmers.[244] Poaching is hard to assess in scale but in October 2013, 189 tusks weighing 769 kg were discovered by Malaysian customs in a shipment of soya beans bound for China from Ivory Coast.

Mali's savannah elephant population in the Gourma region has been extensively studied and has received more press coverage than most populations in West Africa. Often referred to as desert elephants, they inhabit areas of the Sahel in the Gourma region, bordering northern Burkina Faso. In the 1980s, the Malian population fell from around 1,000 spread across five or six main areas. Heavy poaching more or less wiped it out in the Boucle du Baoulé Park in the west; the small population south-east of Bamako was reduced to less than twenty by the mid-1980s, and today has disappeared completely. Gourma now has the only surviving population of Sahel elephants, which were once numerous across the whole Sahel region before being wiped out in the 1980s by poaching, and is the last refuge for elephants in the whole of Mali. The population was put at 344 in 2013, having fallen from double that number at the start of the new millennium. It has suffered poaching attacks since then and is probably hovering around the 300 mark.

Despite the shortage of grazing and water in the Gourma region, a surprising level of tolerance has been exhibited by the Tamasheq (Tuareg) and Peulh (Fulani, Fulbé) pastoralists, and the more settled Souraih and Dogon, who are not generally thought to be responsible for poaching when it occurs. Researchers have reported seeing pastoralists and their flocks sharing grazing areas without conflict and elephants avoid waterholes when the herders water their livestock.[245] Gangs of poachers from urban areas using vehicles and automatic weapons are generally blamed for poaching, while local pastoralist communities have cooperated with conservationists and continued to do so after the outbreak of the Tuareg and then Islamist rebellions in 2012.

Between 2013 and 2014 only eight elephants were killed, despite the conflict and the loss of government control over areas remote from Bamako. The researcher and conservationist Susan Canney has been working with the Gourma elephants for several years and she says that, when she sought the help of the local people, "We found that a common attitude was 'we don't want the elephants to disappear, because if the elephants disappear, it means the environment is no longer good for us'". She says the local community set up a management committee, instigated enforcement patrols, and set aside a massive area of land for the elephants. When the war started, local community leaders appealed to the rebel groups to respect the relationship between the communities and elephants. The protection measures were helped by a conservation group, the Mali Elephant Project, providing food to local communities, which helped persuade them to stay with their communities rather than join the Tuareg separatist movement, the MNLA, or Islamist groups like Ansar Dine.[246]

In May 2014, though, gunmen on motorbikes killed five elephants at Indamane in the Gourma elephant range. In February 2015, the worst attack took place, with the killing of nineteen elephants; Canney said the elephants had been killed over a two-week period.[247] This dangerous level of poaching continued for the rest of the year, taking advantage of the government's concentration on security in the north, with frequent attacks there by Islamist groups and Tuareg insurgents. Susan Canney said in late January 2016 that eighty-three elephants were killed during 2015 and sixteen had already been killed in the first four weeks of 2016. This could have brought the population down to little more than 200—the last aerial census was in 2007.[248]

Following news of the increase in poaching, the Malian Ministry of Water and Forestry asked the UN force in Mali, MINUSMA, to help the anti-poaching units combat the poachers. MINUSMA was said to have agreed and the Malian government also approved the Malian Elephant Project's deployment and arming of fifty extra rangers to increase the manpower of the anti-poaching units. The increased efforts to stem the killing of elephants had the support of the Douentza and

Hourma local communities, who wrote to the Malian president in December 2015, appealing for help—two local mayors said in the letter that increased security was vital, as the people of Gourma knew who the poachers were but feared reprisals if they reported them because of the prevailing insecurity in the region.[249]

There is no proof that the Islamist or Tuareg insurgent groups are mainly responsible for the poaching, but it can certainly be said that the insecurity their revolt has given rise to has created the conditions for an upsurge in poaching and it would not be surprising if some of the members of the armed groups are themselves taking advantage of this to generate funds or just to make some money on the side. Sophie Ravier, the UN's environment representative in Mali, has said that the insurgent groups are involved in a range of trafficking, including drugs and people, and so it would be surprising if they had not included ivory in their illicit commerce.[250]

Nigeria, with its large land area and mix of forest and savannah habitats would be expected to have a substantial population of elephants, but long-term harvesting for ivory, human-elephant conflict and the clearing of forest habitats for settlement and cultivation have all reduced the population to probably fewer than 1,000 animals. The Elephant Database figures for 2013 put the national estimate at a maximum of 741, down from the possible maximum of 1,615 in 1995. The main forest area that had provided a protected haven, the Yankari National Park, saw its population drop from 600 in 1995 to between eighty-two and 250 in 2013. The lower figures was given by the elephant database, though the WCS, which was involved in conservation work with the park authorities, put the population at about 350 in 2014—Andrew Dunn, the Nigeria country director for the WCS, had put the population at 348 in 2011.[251] The fall in numbers is mainly due to poachers but their origin is unclear, though there has been considerable human-elephant conflict on the borders of the park. In communication with the author, Andrew Dunn ridiculed the idea that the Boko Haram insurgent group was involved in poaching in Nigeria and Cameroon.

Ivory poached in Nigeria and brought in from central Africa passes through the thriving ivory market in Lagos, where TRAFFIC investigators found 14,349 ivory items on sale in thirty-six retail outlets in

2012,[252] three times the amount found during a survey ten years before. Five large carving workshops were operating in the city, most of the carvers coming from Guinea or Mali. Martin and Vigne's survey in Nigeria found that most of the ivory being carved or sold was from central Africa, with little or no attempt at enforcement by the government.[253] A small amount of the ivory comes from poaching in Yankari, estimated at twenty animals a year.[254]

The new ivory discourse: insurgency, insecurity and the war on terror

Conflict has clearly played a role in facilitating or exacerbating illicit killing for ivory in range states. The SADF/UNITA operation and then poaching by Renamo, the Zimbabwean army and criminal gangs in Gonarezhou are obvious examples. The wars in the Congo/Zaire/DRC and Sudan also demonstrated the catastrophic effect that conflict could have on elephant populations. These aspects of conservation and the international trade in ivory were known and periodically reported, but were not a dominant part of the discourse on the ivory trade. This changed in the late 2000s and 2010s, partly as a result of international revulsion at the murderous activities of the Janjaweed in Darfur and the LRA in northern Uganda, the CAR and the DRC, and horror at the thought that these groups could be funding their military forces by killing elephants. This was exacerbated by the growing concern of Western countries about the danger of regional conflicts in Africa, Asia and the Middle East becoming threats to their security or breeding grounds for insurgencies that could destabilise regional allies or ally themselves with groups like Al Qaeda, seen as a permanent threat to Western interests.

Western security policy towards regional conflicts developed rapidly after the euphoria of the post-Cold War period and combined prevention of the spread of conflicts with a veneer of humanitarian concern. It led to interventions by the UN and USA in Somalia in 1992–5 and British intervention in the civil war in Sierra Leone in 2000. Interventions were justified on the grounds of humanitarian action but this often cloaked national or strategic interests. What were termed the "new wars" were a threat to world security because, though often low-intensity conflicts, they involved regional or international connections that made them more of a perceived threat to the West than purely localised conflicts[255] or those, like the bloody DRC war, that were viewed as being just too complex and intangible to allow attempts at intervention, other than by sending a few thousand UN peacekeepers.

Alarm over and intervention in these conflicts increased after the 9/11 attacks and the invasions of Afghanistan and Iraq. Al Qaeda's survival as a global organisation encouraging anti-Western Islamist movements kept Western governments in a state of continual vigilance over conflicts that could feed into what was portrayed as the Islamist threat to the West. In 2006, this led to Ethiopia's US-backed intervention in Somalia to destroy the Union of Islamic Courts movement (not openly affiliated to Al Qaeda or other jihadi groups, just suspiciously Islamist), which led to the formation of the more militant Islamist Al Shabab movement—Al Shabab had a more overtly anti-Western stance and in 2012 declared its allegiance to Al Qaeda.

Although the LRA was not Islamist, it became a concern through its ability to further destabilise already insecure areas of Central Africa and one of the US's key military allies in the region, Uganda. While not seen as a direct security threat, there was Western distaste for the activities of the Janjaweed in Darfur's conflict and its potential for destabilisation and weakening border security and stability in Central Africa. When evidence emerged of the involvement of the LRA, Janjaweed and Al Shabab in poaching and smuggling of illicit ivory, this became the "collusion of two evils", as Maguire and Haenlein described it, and fed fears that wildlife trafficking could have global security implications in "a growing crime-conflict-terror nexus".[256]

Suddenly, the illicit ivory was centre stage in international politics rather than a side issue of concern to conservation NGOs. It grabbed the attention of world leaders and the mainstream Western media and became a dominant theme in coverage of wildlife trafficking—for a while, the insurgency-crime-ivory narrative seemed the only game in town. It was also very influential, having a very rapid effect on Western policy and leading to a targeted but not particularly well-researched dovetailing of counter-insurgency and anti-poaching strategies.

The early reports of the ivory-insurgency link were persuasive and my early writings on the phenomenon reflected the growing interest in the role that insurgency could play in the ivory trade, though as part of a wider poaching and trafficking problem.[257] But the interest of politicians in using the poaching of elephants as another means of demonising opponents and the opportunistic use by NGOs of the insurgency link to focus security concerns of governments on ivory trafficking meant that the collusion of two evils created the collusion of two interests. This created a misleading picture and led to skewed policies, with an increasingly heavy emphasis on militarisation, and coordination of counter-insurgency and wildlife law enforcement. Newspaper articles typified the new media approach with the unnecessary sensationalising of what were hideous incidents. They used the tried and tested approach of feeding on emotions of compassion and pity, adding the fear element, namely that insurgent-poachers pose a security threat, and hinting that ultimately it is the reader who is threatened.

For many African states which took up this theme—notably Kenya, Uganda and Zimbabwe—it was a very useful way of deflecting attention from the corruption, patronage networks, crime syndicates, poor law enforcement and weak judicial systems that facilitated poaching and smuggling with impunity for those higher up the chain than the poor poacher in the bush, who was more likely to be shot or imprisoned. African governments could also play up the ivory-insurgency connection to try to get more Western funding and logistical or surveillance support for their own fights against domestic or regional opponents. The new millennium has seen increased US, British and French support for anti-poaching operations from Chad and Gabon to Kenya, and increased financial, surveillance and logistical help for the fight against the LRA, Boko Haram and Al Shabab, including the use of drones for monitoring, and to physically eliminate Al Shabab commanders.

There was evidence that environmental crime as a whole was rising and that insurgent, rebel and criminal groups were taking huge amounts of money from it—UNEP and Interpol put the figure at $70–123 billion a year[258]—and that the activities of a mix of military and criminal groups threaten "the security and sustainable development of many nations".[259] But the very direct connections made between elephant poaching, the ivory trade and insurgency are open to question. In March 2012, the Senate Foreign Relations Committee held hearings on the security implications of the ivory trade, globally and for the USA. In his opening statement John Kerry, chairman of the committee and later US secretary of state, stressed the security threat by poaching operations that could fund insurgency and "terror". Kerry emphasised the human cost of poaching in Africa and that revenue from illicit ivory could fund rebels and terrorists.[260] His words were echoed by Tom Cardamone of Global Financial Integrity, a think tank monitoring illicit financial dealings. Caradmone said that illegal wildlife trading involved crime syndicates and groups like Al Qaeda, often working together, and that these posed "serious national security concerns for the United States and our partners".[261] He emphasised the role of groups like the SPLA, DRC rebels and the LRA in ivory poaching, though he couldn't make a convincing link between these groups, ivory and Al Qaeda.

In early 2013, US Secretary of State Hillary Clinton held a meeting with the Washington diplomatic community and repeated the message of the Senate hearings that ivory poaching was a threat to African states and global security.[262] She picked out the Janjaweed and the LRA as particular problems. When the Elephant Action League produced its report on Al Shabab and ivory,[263] the level of official concern heightened as the Somali Islamist group was affiliated with Al Qaeda, though, as will be seen, the evidence of ivory playing a major role in the group's funding is thin. The report purported to show that Al Shabab was financing a significant part of its military activities through ivory poaching and trading. It had a huge effect out of all proportion to its content and the supporting evidence, and helped lead to the conversion of Western political leaders into wildlife warriors as part of their war on terror. The effect was enhanced by assertions, with no supporting evidence, that Boko Haram was a threat to Cameroon's elephants and involved in selling ivory,[264] and the growing evidence, far more supportable, that the LRA and Janjaweed were involved in the ivory trade. Despite the massive differences between the movements, their aims, the scale of their role in ivory dealing and the varying strength of the evidence for each case, it all became part of a new narrative. The simplistic linking of two evils was convenient for the media and for Western leaders keen to grab attention and generate greater public support for unpopular military interventions, or support for distasteful regimes fighting equally distasteful rebel groups.

In 2013–14, a further series of reports came out from IFAW, UNEP, UNEP/Interpol and Born Free/C4ADS[265] highlighting the role of rebel and insurgent groups in poaching and ivory trading and the security, human and conservation threats they posed. The UNEP and UNEP/Interpol reports were the most meticulously researched and gave prominence to corruption and criminal activity, too, making clear that "the value of ivory is not enough alone to fund a war".[266] The joint report with Interpol stressed that the entire value of the ivory trade to sub-Saharan rebel or insurgent groups was only $4–12.2m a year. But the overall effect of the reports, and the reiteration in some of them of the Al Shabab-ivory link, was to increase the stress put on the insurgent/security aspect in political and media discourse on wildlife trafficking. This led to Western pledges of greater financial support for anti-poaching and the dispatch of military advisers by the USA and Britain to give military training to anti-poaching units. These policies had serious effects on the nature of wildlife protection measures. As Humphreys and Smith point out, "The intensification of the counter-poaching strategy is clearly part of a trend that has witnessed the increasing militarization of wildlife management, the physical manifestation of this approach also bears resemblance to some notable developments in late-modern warfare… The combative language suggests that a policy of enhanced confrontation with the poachers is being ramped up".[267] Part of this ramping up was the involvement of groups like Nir Kalron's Maisha Consulting, C4ADS and the deployment of drones and sophisticated military surveillance techniques in anti-poaching operations.

In September 2013, it was announced that the Clinton Foundation, Western governments and conservation groups were pledging $80m to "stop the slaughter of Africa's elephants" by countering poaching, interdicting trafficking and working to reduce demand. The Foundation stressed the need to increase the number of anti-poaching units and improve intelligence gathering, adding that the commitment to fighting the ivory trade would focus attention on the national and global security implications of wildlife trafficking by terrorist groups and criminal syndicates. The announcement utilised the usual and simplistic bracketing of the Janjaweed, the LRA and Al Shabab.[268] The move was welcomed enthusiastically by groups like the AWF, Conservation International and IFAW, who were keen to harness global campaigns against perceived security threats to the conservation movement in order to access the funding, despite the questionable linking of the security and conservation threats. Closer investigation of the Clinton Foundation announcement revealed that much of it was hype—most of the funding pledged was money previously promised and there was little new injection of new funds. In addition, as Edge identified, the new warnings of an elephant apocalypse in the security-poaching discourse ignored the expansion in numbers in some areas and the fact that serious poaching threats applied only to specific areas and not Africa in general. Edge, adding that NGOs benefit from alarmist talk and that every poaching outrage ensures an influx of funds into their coffers, concluded that responsible conservation should "present considered facts and opinion; genuine action and accountability".[269]

The facts didn't get in the way of a US National Strategy for Combating Wildlife Trafficking being launched, which highlighted the security consequences of trafficking and stressed aid for enforcement and the strengthening of partnerships with NGOs and private industry in implementing this. The strategy included a pledge to restrict domestic ivory trading, something which President Obama would announce twice in 2015 as though it were new policy.[270] In February 2014, the London conference on the illegal wildlife trade reiterated the security concerns and issued the London Declaration, signed by forty-six participating governments including most of the African range states, indicating an unprecedentedly high-level political commitment to fighting wildlife and ivory trafficking on a global basis. A report by the influential think tank, Chatham House, timed to coincide with the conference advised that in the past threats to endangered species had been stressed but now the implications for global security and "the stability of government" needed to be brought to the fore,[271] though the report offered no convincing evidence that the ivory trade was being harnessed by rebel or "terrorist" groups to such an extent that it constituted a serious threat to international or national security and stability.

As the combination of the security threat discourse and the militarisation of conservation became a dominant strand in discussion of the illicit ivory trade, voices were raised warning that militarisation and the use of drones and other military technology could backfire and further alienate local people, making the illicit hunting and trading harder to root out and increasing the conflict between conservationists, NGOs and local communities.[272] As the example from Malawi demonstrated, there is also a real danger that militarisation not only alienates key local communities but carries the risk of human rights abuses.[273] By late 2015, studies by Haenlein and Maguire, Duffy, Humphreys and Smith and an analysis by Vanda Felbab-Brown of the Brookings Institution had begun to deconstruct and criticise the ivory-insurgency-global security discourse and to caution against accepting the myths and misperceptions of the discourse, warning of the perils of militarisation and reminding people that corruption and criminal activity lay at the heart of the illicit ivory trade.[274] The latter report, written as Obama headed to Kenya with measures against the ivory trade on his agenda in July 2015, stressed that

> "the thrust of his engagement should not be principally on the misdirected over-securitization of wildlife conservation, which has involved a skewed and narrow focus on the role of militant groups in wildlife… Instead, he should focus on issues of corruption among rangers, ecolodges, and often high-government officials and the participation of local communities in poaching. Without routing out this pervasive corruption and breaking the economic incentives of local communities to participate in or tolerate poaching, the bush wars will be lost, no matter how heavy the rangers' equipment".[275]

Ivory and insurgency: Al Shabab and the LRA

The release of the Elephant Action League (EAL)'s *Africa's White Gold of Jihad: al-Shabaab and Conflict Ivory* was to have an effect out of all proportion to the strength of its story or the verifiability of the information it contained—particularly the undercover monitoring of cell phone calls between ivory traders in Nairobi, poachers and alleged contacts in Al Shabab trading in ivory. The report would probably have been interesting but treated as just one more account of poaching had Al Shabab's Kenyan wing not carried out its attack on Nairobi's Westgate Mall shopping complex on 21 September 2013, killing sixty-seven people. Soon after the attack, the media in Kenya, the UK and the USA seized on the EAL report and produced headlines, like this one from the London *Independent* on 5 October 2013: *Illegal ivory trade funds Al-Shabab terrorist attacks*.[276] This story and others like it across the world recounted uncritically the EAL version of Al Shabab's role in the illicit ivory trade and made the direct connection to the Westgate attack, with no evidence whatsoever. A day later, again with no supporting evidence, President Kenyatta of Kenya wrote a piece in the *Wall Street Journal* stating, that Al Shabab

> "is well-financed. Kenya and our international partners have identified three routes of funding: the illegal trade in ivory, the diversion of international remittances intended for others, and the theft of money intended for mainstream Muslim organizations. Only weeks before the attack on Westgate, the government of Kenya launched a campaign calling for a global moratorium on ivory trading. While we are already investing more in anti-poaching measures, this illegal trade—for which al-Shabaab acts as a facilitator and broker—cannot be curtailed without an offensive against overseas buyers."[277]

From then on, the EAL report was quoted widely and often uncritically in reports by NGOs like IFAW and Born Free and by think tanks like Chatham House as proof of the ivory-terrorism link, and was reported with misleading sensationalism by the media, as the *Independent* story quoted above indicates.

It is worth looking critically at the report, written for the EAL by Nir Kalron of Maisha Consulting and Andrea Crosta of the EAL.[278] Said to be the product of eighteen months of investigations, at its centre was the claim that Al Shabab could be receiving as much as 40 per cent of the funds to pay its fighters from the illicit ivory trade. Referring briefly but simplistically to the role of Somalis in poaching in Kenya in the 1970s and 1980s, the report's authors relate one particular story—which may be based on truth, or could be an invented narrative to demonstrate how Somali poachers are supplying the illicit trade via Al Shabab—of Somali poachers with military training and automatic weapons killing elephants in Meru National Park in Kenya and then texting a Somali ivory trader in Nairobi to say, "brother we have some goods to deliver, around 40 kilos, contact our cousins and let's make the deal". That trader, according to the unverifiable undercover investigation by the EAL, then used a satphone to contact "a man sitting in an office in Kismayo", guarded by Al Shabab militiamen, to arrange transport and export of the poached tusks.[279] The account is full of tiny and often inconsequential detail intended to convey accuracy and larded with images of Al Shabab's black flags and AK-47s, to give it the racy feel of a spy thriller—one question that springs to mind is this: how would the investigator in Nairobi know that the Kismayo office was guarded at that time by Al Shabab militiamen? These sorts of questions hang over much of the detail utilised in the EAL narrative, which tries to make the point that stories like the Meru poaching incident and subsequent phone calls are regular occurrences.

The story then conflates the high ivory price, widespread poaching in Central and parts of East Africa, the KWS fight against poaching (leaving out the rampant corruption in Kenya) and the international smuggling networks to produce a narrative whereby Al Shabab has become an important part of "a sophisticated network of poachers, small and big-time brokers, and informants, all linked to the trade in ivory and rhino horn". The account relies on the network's alleged infiltration by investigators and their supposed presence when phone calls are made by Somali middlemen in Nairobi to poachers around Isiolo and to major illicit ivory brokers in Asia. When poachers in Kenya cannot fulfil orders for the brokers, then the middlemen approach poachers and other middlemen in the DRC or the CAR to obtain tusks.[280] How the tusks from these countries are smuggled in is not detailed, nor is it ever explained why traders who have been using the existing trade networks for decades to smuggle ivory from Central Africa through Khartoum, Uganda and Mombasa would ditch these routes in order to supply Al Shabab traders in Kismayo and allow Al Shabab to take a major cut of the profits to fund their insurgency. Great detail, with no corroboration, is given of the route to get ivory from Isiolo to Kismayo, but again no supporting evidence of why this route is chosen by the Kenyan brokers who sell the ivory.

The report goes on to give exact figures for how much Al Shabab fighters earn and how much ivory contributes to supporting the Islamist group's armed struggle. The conclusion is that,

"In effect, ivory serves as one of the lifelines of al-Shabaab, enabling it to maintain its grip over young soldiers, most of whom are not radically motivated. According to a source within the militant group, between one to three tons of ivory, fetching a price of roughly US$200 per kilo, pass through the ports in southern Somalia every month. A quick calculation puts Shabaab's monthly income from ivory at between US$200,000 and US$600,000. Maintaining an army of roughly 5,000 men, each earning

US$300 USD, demands at least US$1,500,000 a month, of which the ivory trade could supply a big chunk of it [sic]."[281]

The EAL does detail other sources of income for the movement, but stresses the role of ivory as a key source of funding and gives these definite figures with no supporting material from international enforcement organisations or ivory trade experts. The EAL report says that ivory is of great importance to Al Shabab and is a result of clear and strategic financial planning, not opportunistic access to ivory or just part of the general Al Shabab revenue stream from taxing legal and illegal goods traded within its territory. The authors claim Al Shabab is involved in poaching, brokerage and trading "enabling them to reap huge profits from the mark-up in the trade"[282]—a mark-up presumably at the expense of the existing ivory trade brokers and middlemen who, for some unaccountable reason, have decided to forego much of their profit from existing trade to work with Al Shabab.

The Al Shabab-ivory discourse was taken up keenly by Western media and influential publications like *National Geographic, Voice of America* and the *Los Angeles Times*, which repeated the EAL account as though it were proven fact; some of the pieces were even co-authored by Kalron and Crosta—the authors of the report. The effect of this on public and even government opinion became more pronounced and significant after the Westgate Mall attack.[283] But there are big holes in the account, a lack of verifiable and corroborated evidence and a clear gap between the quantities of ivory the EAL says is traded by Al Shabab and the likely availability from the sources supposedly used by Al Shabab. Specialists with the international ivory trade and poaching monitoring organisations TRAFFIC and MIKE have questioned both the funding of the Westgate attack and the extent of Al Shabab involvement in poaching and the ivory trade, warning that the evidence is far from solid and that care needs to be taken in assessing the movement's earnings from ivory.[284]

This demonstrates the problems of identifying insurgent movements' involvement in poaching and trading and the tendency for the media and campaigning groups to seize on rumour, partial information or small-scale ivory finds to create a narrative that utilises the "War on Terror" framing of conflicts like Somalia to highlight the threat posed by poachers and uses a movement's notoriety to publicise the threat to elephants. In e-mail correspondence with Andreas Crosta, I asked about the difference between MIKE figures for poaching in Kenya and the quantities he quoted. His answer was to try to move the goalposts, play down the whole Kenyan poaching narrative in his original piece and say instead that large amounts were collected from neighbouring countries. That is not beyond the bounds of possibility, as I have established earlier in this chapter that large amounts of ivory from Central Africa, Tanzania, Uganda and South Sudan pass through Kenya to be exported from Mombasa. But Crosta claims that Al Shabab has been able to access this ivory, without providing an explanation of why Africa-based middlemen and Indian or Chinese international syndicates using Dar es Salaam, Khartoum and Mombasa would drop long-standing, existing trade routes to risk exporting through conflict areas of Somalia.[285] Furthermore, as ivory trade specialist Dan Stiles told me, why were Tanzania and Sudan not mentioned in the original report if they are part of the story, and how is it that the EAL's price calculations work, as Al Shabab would have to be receiving ivory absolutely free to make the profits claimed by the report?[286]

Crosta, in his replies to me, writes off MIKE figures and the research-based ivory trade studies of experts like Stiles, simply because they don't fit with the EAL narrative, which has its own internal logic but little verifiable evidence, while being largely at odds with the known facts about the nature of the illicit trade and the role of corruption, crime syndicates and Asian networks. Crosta also tried in our correspondence to roll back on the role of Nairobi-based traders in the ivory-Al Shabab chain, stating that "no Kenya-based trader ever went to Somalia delivering ivory". This in itself may be true, but here it is an attempt to side-step the awkward fact that the whole chain built in the EAL narrative starts with the texts and phone calls involving the Nairobi trader and Somali poachers. Just why Somali poachers would have used a Nairobi middleman to get tusks out through Somalia is also not clear.

The whole narrative is confused and based solely on accepting at face value the unsupported evidence of an investigator being present when texts are received and satphone calls made. There is no other supporting evidence and all the elephant experts and trade specialists to whom I spoke in Kenya played down the Al Shabab link and said that at most the group may poach opportunistically in northern Kenya, get hold of small amounts of ivory from Somali poachers in Kenya or tax ivory passing through territory it controls. It is true that ivory is not important as a source of funding for Al Shabab and therefore not a significant part of a regional or global security threat. As Stiles and Maguire and Haenlein[287] have pointed out, Al Shabab gets most of its finances from taxing businesses operating in areas under its control, from charging traders for transporting goods through its territory and from the illegal charcoal trade, not ivory. The major studies of Al Shabab and of wildlife crime all omit to mention ivory as a major source of funding.[288] The weight of evidence and the EAL report's lack of corroboration have led to a growing questioning of the latter's value and of the harmful effect it may have had in creating a myth about the nature of links between African insurgencies and ivory.[289]

The LRA's role in ivory poaching and trading, already referred to in the sections on the DRC and the CAR, is far better established, though the amounts of ivory are relatively small and the effects on elephant populations localised. The LRA, formed out of a bizarre Ugandan insurgent group known as the Holy Spirit Movement, fought the Ugandan army in a brutal bush war in northern Uganda from 1988 until 2008, when it was pushed out of Uganda. It now ekes out a precarious existence in border areas of South Sudan, the CAR and the DRC, relying on robbery, abductions and poaching to survive,[290] killing the elephants in the CAR and the DRC then selling the ivory through contacts in Sudan. The LRA leader, Joseph Kony, is based in the Sudanese-controlled Kafia Kingi enclave (claimed by South Sudan as its territory) but has small groups in or near Garamba in the DRC, in the CAR's Haut-Mbomou region and along the CAR-DRC border.[291]

The LRA now only has about 120 fighters and probably an equal number of dependents and is constantly being weakened by defections. It retains links with the Sudanese army and elements of Seleka in the CAR, and all have a mutual interest in the ivory trade and supply Kony with food and ammunition in return for ivory and other illicitly obtained goods. The LRA obtains its ivory from poaching in Garamba (where it is a minor player in comparison with the Janjaweed and SPLA or other groups from South Sudan). The ivory is then carried by LRA members or abducted villagers up through the DRC and the CAR border areas to Kafia Kingi, from where it is traded in the town of

Songo to Sudanese merchants or the Sudanese army. According to the Enough Project's well-researched report in October 2015, based on testimony from LRA defectors or prisoners, thirty-eight tusks were poached and sold in 2012 and about twenty to thirty tusks each year in 2013 and 2014, or approximately 100 pieces in total; there may be more traded than that, of which the informants were not aware. The Songo traders supply Kony with food, AK-47 ammunition and grenades for rocket-propelled grenade launchers.[292]

The LRA will clearly continue, as long as it is able to survive, to use ivory as a means of obtaining food and ammunition, though it does not pose a major, rather than localised, threat to elephant numbers. It is a brutal, local irritant rather than a serious security problem—hated and feared by many of the people in whose vicinity it operates but not likely to destabilise governments on its own. Despite this, the ivory narrative, horror at the atrocities the LRA committed in Uganda, its continued use of violence, and its tactic of preying on local people (as well as wildlife) have given it a prominence beyond its actual strength. This led the USA to give military assistance to Ugandan, DRC and, until the civil war in the CAR, Central African forces to destroy the group and capture or kill Kony. Ivory helps keep the LRA alive and helps ensure continued support from Sudan, but it is not a big player in the ivory trade, even in Garamba. The region would be a better place without it, but its threat to African security and elephants should not be overestimated.

8

CONCLUSION

Why do people hunt elephants?

From the historical narrative I've constructed it is clear that people have hunted elephants for as long as they've had the organisation and weapons with which to do so. It started as hunting for food and hides, which a slain elephant could supply in abundance. The ivory produced was of little value until communities started carving it for use as tools, weapons or ornamentation. At first ivory was a by-product of subsistence hunting but as human societies became more sophisticated and produced a surplus that could support the production of items purely for decoration, their aesthetic or symbolic value or for trade grew, so ivory became a commodity that could be traded and had a value in itself, especially when skilfully carved, taking on societal and even religious significance in some communities.

The expansion of human communities and the development of settled, arable agriculture required the use of more and more land and the clearing of forest and bush and the use of grasslands for grazing livestock. This gave rise to human-elephant conflict over use of land, resulting from elephants deprived of food sources or cultivation in areas through which they moved, raiding farms and destroying crops. In the process they came into violent conflict with farming communities and both people and elephants were killed.

Progressive economic development and the ability to produce a surplus that could support the manufacturing or trading of luxury goods, as well as the establishment of ever more hierarchical and sophisticated societies in which the wealthy and powerful could buy luxury goods and use those goods as symbols of their riches and power, increased the value of ivory and was the dynamo for the development of a global ivory trade. With the increasing ability to trade over great distances by land and sea, ivory became a commodity that helped develop and maintain long-distance commerce. It encouraged those communities that specialised in hunting or mixed hunting with pastoralism and settled cultivation to become hunters. In the process, many hunters became traders or middlemen in the lengthening commercial chain between the hunter in sub-Saharan Africa and the buyer in Egypt, India, China, Rome, Greece or later in western Europe and North America.

Hunters killed elephants for many reasons—for meat, hides or ivory to trade, or to protect crops and people. In times of drought or economic hardship, hunting became more important as a means of survival. The development of trade meant that hunting and gathering natural-mortality ivory could become a source of wealth for hunters, traders and coastal peoples, but one that was reliant on external demand and created gatekeepers who benefited—the hunter-traders and middlemen rather than the existing specialist hunting communities (like the Waliangulu). But the wealth created for the gatekeepers could be transitory, and often political power lay with those at the end of the train. The rich merchants commissioned and controlled the trade, reacting to external demand and the price that could be commanded by ivory.

In times of conflict, ivory could become a resource worth fighting for and one that could increase the strength of combatants. The ability of communities to trade ivory for guns and ammunition could alter local and regional power balances and give middlemen and gatekeepers the ability to exercise hegemony over other communities—this could be used to create larger, hierarchical communities or to project power to access more resources (be it ivory, slaves, cattle etc). The expansion of the ivory trade helped create extraverted economies in parts of Africa, where reliance on selling commodities to buyers external to the continent represented a limited form of economic wealth creation.

CONCLUSION

This economy, lacking domestic development of any breadth or depth or any expansion of productive capacity, enriched the gatekeepers of the trade and enabled them to maintain political power, but on very shallow foundations.

This broad system of extraverted economic activity and gatekeeping has evolved and persisted in a variety of forms to the present day. Across African elephant range states, a variety of gatekeepers have significant control and gather substantial benefits from the ivory trade. This is true for both the legal trade when it has operated and the illegal trade, where the wealth and resources to commission illicit hunting, the networks of patronage and criminal syndicates that facilitate smuggling and the ability to protect the illicit trading chain from arrest, prosecution and imprisonment have taken varying and evolving forms between range states and over time.

Who poaches, who smuggles and who is in control?

Corruption, political power and wealth accumulation and utilisation are at the heart of the ivory trade, but it also feeds off impoverishment of communities, resentment over alienation from control of wildlife sources, and conflict leading to availability of weapons and opportunities to poach with impunity, whether by local people, criminal gangs, militias, rebel groups and national armies or a combination of them all. There is no single dominant supply driver of illicit hunting. External demand creates a market and an incentive, but the specific local circumstances in range states determine the mix of factors that turn incentive into poaching and smuggling—so supply and demand are linked, but not always in an obvious and directly causal fashion, with different dynamics operating in different places and at different times. Insurgency and conflict have a role, but not a decisive one for the trade as a whole—the funding of insurgent groups may be one factor, but is not a dominant one. Illicit hunting and trading in conflict zones are an opportunistic response to existing demand for ivory; a means to an end but not an end in itself.

Poverty may lead local peoples to hunt, as may drought, which destroys crops and kills livestock. But many of those who are at the hunting end of the chain may come from traditional hunting communi-

317

ties deprived of the right to hunt under colonialism; they may be local people angry at the loss of land, at crop damage or at the loss of local control over wildlife resources that they could utilise to improve income and living standards. Groups like the LRA may now poach just to survive. Others, like the Janjaweed, may have a history of trading, raiding and hunting for ivory, by which they have maintained the way of life, which has evolved in the communities from which they are drawn or conflict has provided them with the means and opportunity to exploit wildlife for gain. There is no single reason why people hunt and no single identity for the hunter. Weak governance, rampant corruption and utilisation by informal patron-client networks by the powerful provide the space in which illicit trading networks thrive, whether for ivory, rhino horn, diamonds, timber, narcotics or people trafficking.[1] Ultimately, forms of political and economic corruption are key.

The criminalisation of indigenous hunting under colonialism enabled corruption to become the core of the illicit hunting and trading networks; it oils the wheels of the machine that feeds external demand. Criminalisation and loss of community control over resources explain why local people often show resistance to wildlife laws, acceptance of or support for subsistence and commercial poaching and a willingness to engage with the corrupt gatekeepers who control the trade—this is true also for the prevalence of illicit hunting in conflict zones.[2]

Human-elephant conflict, community-based conservation and the international ivory trade

The effects of human-elephant conflict on local communities and on elephant populations are a serious and growing problem. In many ways, this problem is linked to the disempowerment of local communities and their loss of ownership of and control over local resources. Criminalisation stopped legal hunting, reduced the ability of people to protect crops and livestock and encouraged the acceptance and even encouragement of illicit killing, which easily morphed from illegal crop protection into subsistence and commercial poaching. The effects, for example, of banning hunting in Botswana in January 2014 were rapidly seen: a rise in poaching and signs of growing willingness to cooperate with poaching gangs rather than support law enforcement, as communities lost the right to utilise wildlife, derive income from it and limit elephant numbers in areas of cultivation—the same is true with poisoning of predators in livestock-raising areas. Once you disempower people and threaten their livelihoods, you effectively encourage acceptance of poaching or even push people into involvement in the practice.

Criminalisation, loss of local empowerment and the consequent alienation from conservation or from regulated and sustainable use of wildlife resources then help the growth of corruption and the weakening of enforcement. To reiterate Russell Taylor's powerful argument, elephant conservation

> "lies in the hands of local people who will make the ultimate decision as to how they finally use their land. That decision will be strongly influenced by what benefits from wildlife, and elephants in particular, perceived and actual, accrue to individual householders and farmers. Only when perceived as an asset will the conservation of elephants truly become part of a locally developed and integrated approach to land use, and part of an economy that makes wise and sustainable use of natural resources".[3]

Community-based conservation and sustainable-use schemes have not been universally successful. They have not always been able to sustain short-term advances in local attitudes towards regulated use of wildlife resources and long-term conservation—in other words, to gain community support for arrangements that limit conflict with elephants, provide income for local communities and persuade local people to co-exist with elephants and see a benefit in doing so. LIRDP in Zambia, schemes in Chobe in Botswana, CAMPFIRE in Zimbabwe, community conservancies in Namibia and NRT in Kenya have all had or still have strongly positive aspects. Yet all are either dependent on external (usually foreign NGO) funding, subject to wildlife authorities' reluctance to relinquish power to local communities, and the similar desire of local chiefs or political gatekeepers to want to exert control and derive rents from the schemes, or confronting the problems of maintaining autonomy and management in political and economic systems that are patrimonial and corrupt. But the community and sustainable-use models, to me, still offer the best way forward.

Prior to the hunting ban, local support for or acceptance of conservation measures was an important part of Botswana's success in limiting elephant poaching and enabling the population's substantial expansion in numbers. People who derived benefit through incomes from selling hunting quotas, could themselves choose to hunt within the quotas and could also benefit from tourism income. The absence of extensive corruption in government and public service was a major factor in making the system work—whether the successful conservation of elephants survives the hunting ban remains to be seen.

In many parts of Africa, the handing over of national parks and reserves to groups like African Parks has had some success in the short term, but perpetuates the long-term alienation of local people from wildlife and exclusion from protected areas, and builds a fortress of conservation that keeps people out.[4] This doesn't mean that such solutions can't succeed, but that success will be dependent on developing buy-in from local communities through the provision or income and a sense of control, rather than further removing their agency and handing it to NGOs or private, externally based organisations. Similarly, militarised anti-poaching may have short-term successes in stopping outbreaks of poaching and deterring poaching gangs, but alienates local people by creating resentment, ensuring that they see anti-poaching operations as aimed against whole communities. Again, the community approach—a hearts and minds approach that wins the trust and cooperation of local communities—seems to offer greater benefits than militarisation and an even greater use of technology such as drones. Control of wildlife was taken from communities and must in some way be returned.

As Otekat observed, governments need to do something for the local communities to stop them poaching, other than just punishment and law enforcement. Local people need to benefit from wildlife or be compensated for damage caused through conservation of species in close proximity to farms and villages.[5] If people benefit from conservation through enhanced income and living standards, they will see poachers as stealing from them. This is not easy to achieve, particularly in countries beset by poverty, corruption, rule through patronage and informal networks, weak governance and inadequate law enforcement. Ultimately, the development of better governance, devolution of power and empowerment of those living in close proximity to wildlife is the only solution to the democratic deficit, the conflict over conservation and the thriving of illicit trade—the government and patronage gate-

CONCLUSION

keepers need to be weaned off their "what's in it for me" mentality. Better governance, empowerment of communities and conflict resolution are also the long-term way to cut the ivory-insurgency link. Weak institutional penetration, systems in which informal networks are more powerful than the established enforcement and regulatory authorities, and competition for control over the "gate" create the conditions for conflict, facilitating illicit trade in all its forms. In a curious way, the general concentration of NGO activity on working through governments has increased the power of government gatekeepers, as they "keep the gate" for funding and other assistance from NGOs.

If those are the effective pre-requisites for stopping illicit hunting and trading at the African end of the ivory supply chain, what about the future of the international trade in ivory, which is the driver of demand and so of poaching? Clearly, reduction in demand is key but has not been successfully achieved on a global basis, despite the ban and campaigning by NGOs, increasingly supported by governments worried by the ivory-insurgency-organised crime discourse at a time of proliferating forms of non-state violence and global linkages between regional conflicts and Western states' vulnerability to political violence—from 9/11 through to the November 2015 attacks in Paris.

The 1989 CITES ban led to a short-term fall in demand and to a similarly short-lived reduction in the amount of ivory traded. That effect is long gone and the ban now seems impotent in the face of high demand in China and signs that it could grow in Vietnam and other developing East Asian economies, coupled with the existence of flexible but sophisticated illicit trade networks and high ivory prices that incentivise hunting and feed the corrupt networks in Africa—be they criminal, civilian or military—that facilitate it. There was hope that Chinese rhetoric about fighting the trade would dampen demand there and lead to greater action to end the illicit importing of tusks, while closing down the domestic, legal trade that also utilises illegal ivory laundered through trade with Hong Kong and substituted for legal stocks by traders. But the rhetoric has been matched by few actions and no concerted plan or timetable to end the trade. As CITES head John Scanlon noted in January 2016, China has taken minor measures to reduce the legal trade and has been more energetic in stopping illegal imports, but has yet to put in place a total ban on imports, purchases from Hong Kong or the domestic trade.[6] Hong Kong has said it will end its ivory trade but is yet to come up with concrete measures or a timetable.

One small glimmer of light at the end of the tunnel is that at the time of writing, ivory prices in China have fallen by nearly 50 per cent, though it remains to be seen whether this will be sustained or whether it relates to the 2015 downturn in Chinese economic performance and growth and a temporary dampening of demand resulting from Chinese government rhetoric on ending the trade at some time in the future.[7] John Scanlon expressed the hope that the fall in prices would continue and would reduce not only the incentive to poach but also the profits for middlemen and the practice of buyers in China purchasing ivory as an investment and awaiting increases in prices that would bring a handsome profit. Scanlon has further said that while the gangs behind the illicit trade could still make a profit, he hopes a continued decline, combined with stronger anti-poaching and anti-smuggling efforts, would send a clear message that poaching and trading ivory is shifting from a "low risk, high profit to high risk, low profit" occupation.[8] That is, perhaps, rather optimistic, given the way the ivory trade has reacted to bans, enforcement and demand over the last fifty years, but it was the expression of a wish shared by most conservationists, researchers and trade experts. If a steady drop in price could reduce incentives to poach, then the level of poaching could fall, though there would be a danger of poaching increasing to ensure income despite lower prices, and demand could increase in new markets as the price increased the likely pool of buyers—as happened in Nigeria after the 1989 ban, when falling prices helped to kick-start a stronger demand.

The London wildlife crime conference in February 2014, the statements and policy initiatives on ivory by Obama and Kerry and involvement of other leading politicians like Hillary Clinton, and the continuing campaigns by NGOs against any legal trade in ivory, combined with opposition to legalisation or one-off sales from African ranges states like Kenya, Tanzania and now even Botswana, indicate that any change to CITES trade regulations is unlikely in the near future. While it has been suggested that the September 2016 CITES Conference of Parties in South Africa might see a southern African push for legalised ivory sales,[9] with Namibia keen to sell ivory stocks, Botswana (which once lobbied for legal sales) announced in February 2014 along with Tanzania, Gabon and Chad that it wanted a ten-year moratorium on any ivory sales, making any vote in favour of even limited sales at the CITES meeting very unlikely.

The existing moratorium agreed by CITES signatories ends in 2017. Botswana, along with South Africa, Namibia, Tanzania and Zimbabwe, oppose the burning or crushing of stockpiles of ivory and each holds substantial stockpiles that they may seek to sell at the end of any moratorium period. In November 2015, a declaration was signed in Cotonou, Benin by twenty-five range states belonging to the African Elephant Coalition[10] (excluding all the southern African range states, Zambia and Tanzania—the latter attending but not signing or making public comment on the declaration). This declaration called for a rigid application of the trade ban, without exceptions, and for all African elephants (including the southern African populations, which currently have Appendix II status) to be categorised as critically endangered, by promoting them to Appendix I on the CITES list.[11]

While a change in the status of southern African elephants is a distant possibility, it is clear that any bid to get agreement for further legal ivory sales from southern African or Tanzanian stocks is also unlikely to get far at the September 2016 conference, because a majority of range states—along with European and North American signatories—would oppose it. This was reinforced by the results of the sixty-sixth CITES Standing Committee in January 2016, at which the US, the European Union, Kenya, Uganda and a majority of other countries represented argued that "given the current poaching crisis it would be unproductive and dangerous to proceed with discussions about legalizing the ivory trade".[12] South Africa wanted CITES to discuss the legal ivory trade, proceeding from the position that legalising trade would force prices down by increasing the supply of ivory. A majority of Standing Committee members voted to suspend discussions of a mechanism to legalise the trade. The South Africans, supported by Zimbabwe and Botswana, spoke strongly against the destruction of ivory stocks, but again a majority of committee members were in favour. The Standing Committee also called for Angola, Laos and Nigeria to be suspended from any trading in CITES-listed species because of their failures to act to stop the illegal trade in ivory and rhino horn through their territories. It further called on

IVORY

Tanzania and Mozambique to take urgent steps to bring the high level of elephant poaching in those states under control.

Since 2011, there have been thirteen ivory burning or crushing ceremonies in eleven territories: Kenya, Gabon, the Philippines, India, the United States, China, Hong Kong, France, Chad, Belgium, Portugal and Sri Lanka. Malawi, New Zealand, and Vietnam have said they are considering destroying their stocks and Kenya carried out another highly publicised and substantial tusk burning event at the end of April 2016, to coincide with a Giants Club summit on elephant conservation—a gathering of political and business leaders, TV and film celebrities to publicise the cause of elephant conservation.[13] At the 2014 CITES Standing Committee meeting, the organisation had encouraged signatories to destroy ivory stocks.

Despite the strong bloc of African range states and non-African countries opposing any legalised trade, one has to ask whether, in the long term, there is any realistic alternative to developing a regulated legal trade in ivory that rewards those range states and communities that can protect elephants. If you don't develop long-term sustainable-use programmes that reduce human-elephant conflict, ensure community support for both conservation and realistic and accepted forms of wildlife law enforcement, then what is the answer? It is absolutely clear that twenty-seven years of banning the ivory trade and promoting militarised anti-poaching has not worked, and that demand reduction strategies have only shifted the focus of market demand rather than drastically reducing it. John Scanlon said in March 2016 that, for the fourth year running, data gathered by CITES/MIKE showed that as a result of poaching, more elephants were being killed than being born each year—figures indicated 14,606 elephant deaths in 2015. The statistics showed that 60 per cent of elephant deaths were due to poaching, and that in West and Central Africa the threat to the long-term survival of elephants was severe. Scanlon did express the hope that encouraging signs of a decline in poaching in parts of East Africa, especially Kenya, would be sustained.[14]

Top-down conservation, backed up by external domination of the debate over elephants and externally funded militarisation of conservation, are not the answers. As Dan Stiles has pointed out, the trade ban, combined with a growth in demand, has led to "a free-for-all for illegal raw ivory in the absence of any hope for legal ivory". Globally the only realistic and viable long-term solution would be a regulated and strictly limited trade system "supplying humane legal raw ivory to traders obtained from natural mortality and problem elephant control to replace poached ivory"[15], in combination with community-based conservation projects empowering people in the areas where elephants survive in substantial numbers, and continuing efforts to drive down demand by attaching a stigma to buying ivory. Demand is unlikely to ever disappear completely. It was reduced by the ivory ban and then emerged again, even more strongly. Demand reduction may help, but ultimately, aligning survival of elephants with workable, locally-acceptable forms of sustainable use is likely to be the only answer that combines conservation of the elephant population with the needs and interests of the human populations in range states.

NOTES

INTRODUCTION

1. Keith Somerville, 'The Ivory Wars: how poaching in Central Africa fuels the LRA and Janjaweed', *African Arguments*, 14 January 2013, http://africanarguments.org/2013/01/14/the-ivory-wars-how-poaching-in-central-africa-fuels-the-lra-and-janjaweed-%E2%80%93-by-keith-somerville/ accessed 28 October 2015; Keith Somerville, 'African Wars and the Politics of Ivory', http://www.e-ir.info/2013/04/09/african-wars-and-the-politics-of-ivory/ accessed 28 October 2015.
2. Keith Somerville, *Africa's Long Road Since Independence: The Many Histories of a Continent*, London: Hurst and Co., 2015.
3. Frederick Cooper, *Africa since 1940: The Past of the Present*, Cambridge: CUP, 2002; see also discussion of the application of the concept in Somerville, 2015.
4. Ibid. pp. 4–5.
5. Frederick Cooper, 'From Colonial State to Gatekeeper State in Africa', Working Paper Series, The Mario Einaudi Center for International Studies, Paper 04–05, October 2005, p. 8.
6. See Somerville, 2015, pp. 11–12, 114–5 and 327–31.
7. Personal communication.
8. Raymond Bonner, *At the Hand of Man: Peril and Hope for Africa's Wildlife*, London: Simon and Schuster, 1993, p. 122.
9. Particularly Rosaleen Duffy, whose works are referenced throughout the book and who has spoken to the author of the use of the term.

1. AFRICA AND IVORY: AN ANCIENT BUT BLOODY AND BRUTAL TRADE

1. John Frederick Walker, *Ivory's Ghosts: The White Gold of History and the Fate of Elephants*, New York: Grove Press, 2009, pp. 1–3. This work has

been invaluable in guiding the present narrative through the early history of the trade and in finding a wide range of sources on that history; see also N. J. Conard, 'Paleolithic Ivory Sculptures from Southwestern Germany and the Origins of Figurative Art', *Nature*, 426, 2003, pp. 830–2.

2. Doran H. Ross, 'Imagining Elephants: An overview', in Doran H. Ross (ed.), *Elephant: The Animal and Its Ivory in African Culture*, Los Angeles, CA: Fowler Museum of Cultural History, University of California, 1992, pp. 1–39, 6–7.

3. Jeheskel Shoshani, 'The African Elephant and Its Environment', in Ross, 1992, pp. 43–59, 45.

4. Keith Somerville, 'W African elephants a "separate" species', *BBC News*, 26 September 2002, http://news.bbc.co.uk/1/hi/sci/tech/2282801.stm/ accessed 27 November 2014.

5. The IUCN Red List of Threatened Species, 'Loxodonta Africana', http://www.iucnredlist.org/details/12392/0/ accessed 11 February 2015.

6. Shoshani, 1992, p. 57.

7. Bryan Shorrocks, *The Biology of African Savannahs*, Oxford: Oxford University Press, 2007, pp. 161–4.

8. Robin S. Reid, *Savannas of Our Birth: People, Wildlife and Change in East Africa*, Berkeley, CA: University of California Press, 2012, p. 14.

9. William Beinart and Lotte Hughes, *Environment and Empire*, Oxford: Oxford University Press, 2007, pp. 60–1.

10. See Jean-François Bayart, 'Africa in the world: a history of extraversion', *African Affairs*, 99, 395, 2000, pp. 217–67; and Frederick Cooper, 'From Colonial State to Gatekeeper State in Africa', Working Paper Series, The Mario Einaudi Centre for International Studies, Paper 04–05, October 2005.

11. See, for example, H. S. Daannaa, 'The Acephalous Society and the Indirect Rule System in Africa', *Journal of Legal Pluralism And Unofficial Law*, 34, 1994, p. 62, http://www.jlp.bham.ac.uk/volumes/34/daannaa-art.pdf/ accessed 23 May 2016.

12. Alex Thomson, *An Introduction to African Politics*, London: Routledge, 3rd edn 2010, p. 11.

13. Richard Gray and David Birmingham, 'Some Economic and Political Consequences of Trade in Central and Eastern Africa in the Pre-Colonial Period', in Richard Gray and David Birmingham (eds), *Pre-Colonial African Trade Essays on Trade in Central and Eastern Africa Before 1900*, London: Oxford University Press, 1970, pp. 1–23, p. 5.

14. J. Vansina, 'Long-distance trade-routes in Central Africa', *Journal of African History*, 1962 III, pp. 375–90, pp. 376–7.

15. Edward A. Alpers, 'The Ivory Trade in Africa: An Historical Overview', in Ross, 1992, pp. 349–63.
16. Ian Parker and Mohamed Amin, *Ivory Crisis*, London: The Hogarth Press, 1983, pp. 33–51.
17. Edward I. Steinhart, *Black Poachers, White Hunters: A Social History of Hunting in Colonial Kenya*, Oxford: James Currey, 2006, p. 21.
18. Mark Elvin, *The Retreat of the Elephants: An Environmental History of China*, New Haven, CT: Yale University Press, 2004, p. 9.
19. Walker, 2009, p. 25.
20. Alpers, 1992, p. 349.
21. Walker, 2009, p. 27.
22. Reid, 2012, p. 103.
23. *Chryselephantine Statue of Athena*, http://ancient-greece.org/art/athena-statue.html/ accessed 1 December 2014.
24. Abdul Sheriff, *Slaves, Spices and Ivory in Zanzibar: Integration of an East African Commercial Empire into the World Economy, 1770–1873*, Oxford: James Currey, 1987, p. 12.
25. John Iliffe, *Africans: The History of a Continent*, Cambridge: Cambridge University Press, 2nd edn 2007, p. 50.
26. Alpers, 1992, p. 352.
27. Sidney Littlefield Kasfir, 'Ivory from Zariba Country to the Land of Zinj', in Ross, 1992, pp. 309–327; see also Iliffe, 2007, pp. 53–4; Walker, 2009, pp. 49–50.
28. David Birmingham, 'Society and economy before A.D. 1400', in David Birmingham and Phyllis Martin (eds), *History of Central Africa Volume One*, London: Longman, 1983, pp. 1–29, p. 24.
29. D. N. Beach, 'The Zimbabwe plateau and its peoples', in Birmingham and Martin, 1983, pp. 245–77, pp. 258–9.
30. Basil Davidson, *West Africa Before the Colonial Era: A History to 1850*, London: Pearson Education, 1998, p. 19.
31. Philip Snow, *The Star Raft: China's Encounter with Africa*, London: Weidenfeld and Nicholson, 1988, pp. 12–14.
32. T. Hakansson, 'The human ecology of world systems in East Africa: the impact of the ivory trade', *Human Ecology*, 32, 5, October 2004, pp. 561–91, p. 565.
33. David Birmingham, *Portugal and Africa*, Athens, OH: Ohio University Press, 1999, pp. 2–3.
34. Barbara Winston Blackmun, 'The Elephant and Its Ivory in Benin', in Ross, 1992, pp. 162–86, p. 163; Meredith, 2001, pp. 49–50.
35. Ross, 1992, p. 32 and Alpers, 1992, p. 353.
36. Davidson, 1998, p. 183.

37. J. Vansina, 'Long-distance trade-routes in Central Africa', *Journal of African History*, 1962 III, pp. 375–90, p. 379.

38. Phyllis Martin, 'The Trade of the Loango in the Seventeenth and Eighteenth Centuries', in Gray and Birmingham, 1970, pp. 138–61, p. 139.

39. Ibid., p. 145.

40. Marion Johnson, 'The West African Ivory Trade During the Eighteenth Century', *International Journal of African Historical Studies*, 15, 3, 1982, pp. 435–53, p. 452.

41. Edward A. Alpers, *Ivory and Slaves: Changing Patterns of International Trade in East Central Africa to the Later Nineteenth Century*, Berkeley, CA: University of California Press, 1975, pp. 58 and 63.

42. Martin Meredith, *Africa's Elephant*, London: Hodder and Stoughton, 2001, pp. 51–2.

43. Alpers, 1992, p. 349.

44. Derek Wilson and Peter Ayerst, *White Gold: The Story of African Ivory*, New York: Taplinger Publishing Company, 1976, p. 27.

45. Alpers, 1975, p. 57.

46. Ian Parker and Mohamed Amin, *Ivory Crisis*, London: The Hogarth Press, 1983, p. 33.

47. Alpers, 1975, p. 82.

48. Monica Wilson, 'Reflections of the Early History of North Malawi', in Bridglal Pachai (ed.), *The Early History of Malawi*, London: Longman, 1972, pp. 136–47, p. 143.

49. H. Leroy Vail, 'Suggestions towards a reinterpreted Tumbuka history', in Pachai, 1972, pp. 148–67, p. 154.

50. Bridglal Pachai, *Malawi: The History of the Nation*, London: Longman, 1973, p. 10.

51. Mungo Park, *Travels in the Interior of Africa*, Ware, Herts: Wordsworth Editions, 2002, p. 11.

52. Meredith, 2001, p. 61.

53. Ibid., p. 62.

2. THE NINETEENTH CENTURY: ONE HUNDRED YEARS OF EXPLOITATION AND EXTERMINATION

1. John M. Mackenzie, *The Empire of Nature*, Manchester: Manchester University Press, 1988, p. 149.

2. Elspeth Huxley in Thomas P. Ofcansky, *Paradise Lost: A History of Game Preservation in East Africa*, Morganstown, WV: West Virginia University Press, 2002, p. xi.

3. John Frederick Walker, *Ivory's Ghosts: The White Gold of History and the Fate of Elephants*, New York: Grove Press, 2009, p. 83.
4. Abdul Sheriff, *Slaves, Spices and Ivory in Zanzibar: Integration of an East African Commercial Empire into the World Economy, 1770–1873*, Oxford & Nairobi: James Currey & EAEP, 1987, pp. 87–90.
5. Ibid., p. 87.
6. Personal communication.
7. E. D. Moore, *Ivory Scourge of Africa*, New Yorker: Harper, 1931, p. 165.
8. Keith Somerville, *Africa's Long Road Since Independence: The Many Histories of a Continent*, London: Hurst and Co, 2015, pp. 4–5.
9. Pier M. Larson, 'African Slave Trade in Global Perspective', John and Richard Reid, *The Oxford Handbook of Modern African History*, Oxford: Oxford University Press, 2013, pp. 56–76, p. 61.
10. Derek Wilson and Peter Ayerst, *White Gold: The Story of African Ivory*, New York: Taplinger Publishing Company, 1976, p. 29.
11. David and Charles Livingstone, *Narrative of an Expedition to the Zambesi and Its Tributaries*, Stroud, Glos: Nonsuch, 2005, p. 111.
12. Sir Richard Burton, *The Lake Regions of Central Africa: From Zanzibar to Lake Tanganyika, Volume I*, Santa Barbara, CA: The Narrative Press, 2001. Starts from Zanzibar 16 June 1857, p. 26.
13. Sir Richard Burton, *The Lake Regions of Central Africa: From Zanzibar to Lake Tanganyika, Volume II*, Santa Barbara, CA: The Narrative Press, 2001, pp. 188–9.
14. Henry Morton Stanley, *How I Found Livingstone*, Ware, Herts: Wordsworth Classics of World Literature, 2010, p. 13.
15. Adam Hochschild, King Leopold's Ghost: *A Story of Greed, Terror and Heroism in Colonial Africa*, London: Pan, 2006, pp. 63–4 and 70.
16. Alfred Sharpe, 'Big Game Shooting in Africa', *Journal of the African Society*, 22, 85, October 1922, pp. 1–4.
17. Moore, 1931, p. 167.
18. Cited by Raymond Bonner, *At the Hand of Man: Peril and Hope for Africa's Wildlife*, London: Simon and Schuster, 1993, p. 48.
19. Joseph Thomson, *To the Central African Lakes and Back, Volume 2*, London: Sampson, Low, Marston, Searle & Rivington, 1881, digitised version https://archive.org/details/tocentralafrica02thomgoog/ accessed 29 December 2014.
20. Mackenzie, 1988, p. 151.
21. John Tosh, 'The Northern Interlacustrine Region', in Richard Gray and David Birmingham (eds), *Pre-Colonial Trade: Essays on Trade in Central and Eastern Africa before 1900*, London: Oxford University Press, 1970, pp. 103–18, p. 113.
22. Mackenzie, 1988, p. 152.

23. Lord Frederick Lugard, *The Rise of Our East African Empire (1893): Early Efforts in Nyasaland and Uganda (volume 2, of 2 vols)*, Google eBook, https://books.google.co.uk/books?id=9dPGBQAAQBAJ&dq=Kilonga-Longa+Congo+Stanely&source=gbs_navlinks_s/ accessed 2 January 2015.

24. Henry M. Stanley, *In Darkest Africa. Or, the Quest, Rescue, and Retreat of Emin Pasha, Governor of Equatoria, Vol. II*, Santa Barabara, CA: The Narrative Press, 2001, p. 82.

25. Henry M. Stanley, *In Darkest Africa. Or, the Quest, Rescue, and Retreat of Emin Pasha, Governor of Equatoria, Vol. I*, Santa Barbara, CA: The Narrative Press, 2001, p. 60.

26. John Hanning Speke, *The Discovery of the Source of the Nile*, Teddington: The Echo Library, 2006, pp. 325–6; see also P.M. Holt, *The Mahdist State in the Sudan 1881–1898: A Study of Its Origins, Development and Overthrow*, Oxford: Clarendon Press, 1970, p. 11.

27. Fergus Nicoll, *The Mahdi of Sudan and the Death of General Gordon*, Stroud, Glous: Sutton Publishing, 2005, pp. 31 and 51.

28. William Beinart, 'Production and the Material Basis of Chieftainship in Pondoland, c. 1830–1880', in Shula Marks and Anthony Atmore (eds), *Economy and Society in Pre-Industrial South Africa*, London: Longman, 1980, pp. 120–47, p. 129.

29. R. G. Gordon-Cumming, *Five Years' Adventures in the Far Interior of South Africa*, London: John Murray, 1856, p. 193.

30. F. C. Selous, 'Big Game in South Africa and its relation to the Tse-Tse Fly', *Journal of the African Society*, 8, 30, January 1909, pp. 113–29, pp. 115–17.

31. Mackenzie, 1988, p. 67.

32. Ibid., p. 68.

33. H. A. Bryden (ed.), *Great and Small Game of Africa*, London: Rowland Hill, 1899, pp. 5–7.

34. Selous, Tsetse 1909.

35. Marion Johnson, *By Ship or by Camel: The Struggle for the Cameroons Ivory Trade in the Nineteenth Century*, London: School of Oriental and African Studies/Institute of Commonwealth Studies, June 1978, p. 1.

36. Samuel Crowther, *Journal of an Expedition up the Niger and Tshadda Rovers Undertaken*, New Delhi: Isha Books, 1855, 2013 reprint, pp. 50–4.

3. THE IVORY TRADE AND CRIMINALISATION OF AFRICAN HUNTERS UNDER COLONIAL RULE

1. David M. Anderson, *The Eroding Commons: The Politics of Ecology in Baringo, Kenya 1890–1963*, Oxford: James Currey, 2002, p. 6.

2. John Mackenzie, 'Chivalry, Social Darwinism and Ritualised Killing: The

hunting ethos in Central Africa up to 1914', in David Anderson and Richard Grove (eds), *Conservation in Africa: People, Policies and Practice*, Cambridge: Cambridge University Press, 1987, pp. 41–61, p. 56.

3. See the work of Igoe and Brockington for a detailed analysis of the processes of exclusion up to the present and the link between exclusionary conservation and companies or governments profiting from wildlife, often in collaboration with conservation NGOs: Jim Igoe and Dan Brockington, 'Neoliberal Conservation: A Brief Introduction', *Conservation and Society*, 5, 4, 2007, pp. 432–49.

4. Personal communication.

5. Ibid.

6. See Edward I. Steinhart, *Black Poachers, White Hunters: A Social History of Hunting in Colonial Kenya*, Oxford: James Currey, 2006.

7. Ibid., p. 106.

8. Cited by John Frederick Walker, *Ivory's Ghosts: The White Gold of History and the Fate of Elephants*, New York: Grove Press, 2009, pp. 133–4.

9. E. D. Moore, *Ivory Scourge of Africa*, New Yorker: Harper, 1931, pp. 213–15.

10. E. B. Martin, 'The Great White Gold Rush', *BBC History*, August 2001, pp. 30–2.

11. Derek Wilson and Peter Ayerst, *White Gold: The Story of African Ivory*, New York: Taplinger Publishing Company, 1976, p. 108.

12. Ibid.

13. Johnston to Sclater, 6 March 1900, Foreign Office, A7/6. See also Steinhart, 2006, pp. 95–6.

14. Errol Trzebinski, *The Kenya Pioneers*, London: Heinemann, 1985.

15. John M. Mackenzie, *The Empire of Nature*, Manchester: Manchester University Press, 1988, p. 206.

16. Raymond Bonner, *At the Hand of Man: Peril and Hope for Africa's Wildlife*, London: Simon and Schuster, 1993, pp. 39–40.

17. *Journal of the Society for the Preservation of the Wild Fauna of the Empire* (henceforth referred to in these footnotes as *Journal*), 2, 1905.

18. *Journal*, 27, 1936.

19. William Beinart and Lotte Hughes, *Environment and Empire*, Oxford: Oxford University Press, 2007, pp. 26–70.

20. Ibid., p. 271.

21. C. W. Hobley, 'The Preservation of Wild Life in the Empire', *Journal of the African Society*, 24, 137, 1935, pp. 403–7, pp. 405–6.

22. C. W. Hobley, C.M.G., 'The Conservation of Wildlife: Retrospect and Prospect', *Journal*, 37, 32, p. 39.

23. Ibid.

24. Richard Fitter and Sir Peter Scott, *The Penitent Butchers: 75 Years of Wildlife Conservation*, London: Collins, 1978, p. 8.

25. Dr P. Chalmers Mitchell, C.B.E., F.R.S., F.Z.S., 'The Preservation of the African Elephant', *Journal*, 1, 1921, p. 45.

26. *Journal*, 1, 1921, p. 34.

27. Ibid., p. 36.

28. Mackenzie, 1988, pp. 152–3.

29. Ibid.

30. R. E. Drake-Brockman, 'The Preservation of the African Elephant', *Journal*, 1, 1921, p. 31.

31. C. W. Hobley, 'Ivory Trade, Africa', *Journal*, 28, 1936, p. 74.

32. *Journal*, 21, 1934, 'International Conference for the Protection of the Fauna and Flora of Africa: Final Act of the Conference, London, 8th November, 1933', p. 34.

33. Michael L. Stone, 'Organized Poaching in Kitui District: A Failure in District Authority, 1900 to 1960', *International Journal of African Historical Studies*, 5, 3, 1972, pp. 436–52, pp. 438 and 440.

34. Anthony Cullen and Sydney Downey, *Saving the Game*, London: Jarrolds, 1960, pp. 56–7.

35. Steinhart, 2006, p. 150.

36. Ian Parker, *EBUR*, 1974, Ian Parker Collection of East African Wildlife Conservation: The Ivory Trade, p. 3, University of Florida Digital Collections, http://ufdc.ufl.edu//AA00020117/00011/ accessed 13 February 2015.

37. Thomas P. Ofcansky, *Paradise Lost: A History of Game Preservation in East Africa*, Morganstown, WV: West Virginia University Press, 2002, p. 15.

38. Interestingly, Lord Hindlip of the Fauna Preservation Society supported Delamere's views and reported them with sympathy: *Journal*, 2, 1905.

39. Ibid., p. 73.

40. W. Robert Foran, *A Breath of the Wilds*, London: Robert Hale, 1958, pp. 18–9. Ian Parker warned the author that he knew Foran personally and there may have been an element of boasting in the numbers he claimed to have shot.

41. Robin Brown, *Bloody Ivory: The Massacre of the African Elephant*, Stroud, Glos.: History Press, 2008, pp. 65–8.

42. Mackenzie, 1988, p. 153.

43. Wilson and Ayerst, 1976, p. 112.

44. *Journal*, 4, 1914, no page number.

45. Ian Parker, *What I Tell You Three Times Is True: Conservation, Ivory, History and Politics*, Kinloss, Moray: Librario Publishing, 2004, p. 47.

46. Mackenzie, 1988, pp. 1516.

47. Reported in *Journal*, 3, 1907.

48. Ibid.
49. *Journal*, 5, 1909, p. 47.
50. Ibid.
51. Roosevelt himself gave a glowing account of his exploits, even though at times he admits to his poor shooting and willingness to wound animals. Theodore Roosevelt, *African Game Trails: An Account of the African Wanderings of an American Hunter-Naturalist*, New York: Charles Scribner's Sons, 1910.
52. Mackenzie, 1988, p. 162.
53. Steinhart, 2006, pp. 156–7.
54. 'Kenya protectorate game ordinance', *Journal*, 2, 1922, p. 58.
55. Stone, 1972, p. 445.
56. Peter T. Dalleo, 'The Somali Role in Organized Poaching in Northeastern Kenya, c. 1909–1939', *International Journal of African Historical Studies*, 3, 22, 1979, pp. 472–82, p. 472.
57. Steinhart, 2006, p. 165.
58. George Adamson, *Bwana Game*, London: Fontana, 1969, p. 66.
59. Ibid., p. 97.
60. Ofcansky, 2002, p. 26.
61. Parker, 2004, p. 63.
62. George Adamson, *My Pride and Joy: An Autobiography*, London: Collins, Harvill, 1986, pp. 43–4 and 47.
63. Lawrence E. Y. Mbogoni, *Aspects of Colonial Tanzania History*, Dar es Salaam: Mkukina Nyota Publishers, 2013, p. 35.
64. Ibid.
65. R. W. Beachey, 'The East African Ivory Trade in the Nineteenth Century', *Journal of African History*, 8, 2, 1967, pp. 269–90, p. 283.
66. Ibid., p. 287.
67. John Iliffe, *A Modern History of Tanganyika*, Cambridge: Cambridge University Press, 1979, p. 130.
68. Ofcansky, 2002, p. 50.
69. Moore, 1931, p. 175.
70. Mbogoni, 2013, p. 35; and E. I. Steinhart, 'Hunters, Poachers and Gamekeepers: Towards a Social History of Hunting in Colonial Kenya', *Journal of African History*, 30, 2, 1989, pp. 247–64, p. 251.
71. This detailed account is provided by Mbogoni, 2013, pp. 37–8.
72. C.F.M. Swynnerton, 'The Working of the Game Ordinance Tanganyika Territory', *Journal*, 6, 1926, p. 32.
73. Ibid., p. 33.
74. 'Report by T. H. Henfrey', *Journal*, 10, 1929.
75. Major Hingston, 'Report on a mission to east Africa for the purpose

of investigating the most suitable methods of ensuring the preservation of its indigenous fauna', *Journal*, 12, 1930, pp. 28 and 36–7.

76. See the annual game reports in editions of the *Journal* from 1936 to 1941.
77. Ibid., pp. 29–30.
78. *Journal*, 1, 1904.
79. *Journal*, 2, 1905, p. 58.
80. George Wilson, 'The Progress of Uganda', *Journal of the African Society*, 6, 22, January 1907, pp. 113–35, p. 129.
81. *Journal*, 5, 1909.
82. Uganda Protectorate, *Report on the Control of Elephants in Uganda*, Entebbe: Government Press, 1923, p. 11.
83. *Journal*, 1921, 1, R.T. Coryndon, Elephants in Uganda, p. 30.
84. Parker, 1974, p. 9.
85. 'Uganda Protectorate: Extracts from the Annual Report of the Game Warden for 1925', *Journal*, 27, 7, p. 26.
86. Ofcansky, 2002, p. 42.
87. Peter P. Garretson, 'Vicious Cycles: Ivory, Slaves and Arms on the New Maji Frontier', in Donald Donham and Wendy James (eds), *The Southern Marches of Imperial Ethiopia: Essays in History and Social Anthropology*, Cambridge: Cambridge University Press, 1986, pp. 196–218, p. 218.
88. Ibid., p. 207.
89. *Journal*, 1, 1904.
90. *Journal*, 5, 1909.
91. 'The Fauna of the Empire', *Journal*, 2, 1922, p. 39.
92. Douglas H. Johnson, 'On the Nilotic Frontier: Imperial Ethiopia in the Southern Sudan, 1898–1936', in Donham and James, 1986, pp. 219–245, p. 228.
93. Ibid., pp. 244–5.
94. M. W. Daly, *Empire on the Nile: The Anglo-Egyptian Sudan, 1898–1934*, Cambridge: Cambridge University Press, 2004, p. 225.
95. Garretson, 1986, p. 210.
96. Major Henry Darley, *Slaves and Ivory: A Record of Adventure and Exploration Among the Abyssinian Slave-Raiders*, London: H.F. and G. Witherby, 1935, p. 52.
97. Beachey, 1967, p. 283.
98. Harold Reynolds, 'Notes on the Azande Tribe of the Congo', *Journal of the African Society*, 1904, 3, 11, pp. 238–46, p. 242.
99. Walter D. M. Bell, *Bell of Africa: The Greatest Elephant Hunter of Them All*, Suffolk: Neville Spearman, 1960, p. 100.
100. Wilson and Ayerst, 1976, p. 119.

101. R. Foran, 'Edwardian Ivory Poachers over the Nile', African Affairs, 57, 227, 1958, pp. 125–34, p. 125.

102. Ibid., p. 133.

103. T. Alexander Barns, 'A Trans-African Expedition', Journal of the African Society, 24, 96, 1925, pp. 272–86, pp. 275–6.

104. John Frederick Walker, Ivory's Ghosts: The White Gold of History and the Fate of Elephants, New York: Grove Press, 2009, p. 137.

105. Journal, 1, 1904.

106. G. Grey, 'Notes on Game in Northern Rhodesia', Journal, 4, 1908, p. 39.

107. Martin Meredith, Africa's Elephant, London: Hodder and Stoughton, 2001, pp. 123–4.

108. Jane Carruthers, Wildlife and Warfare: The Life of James Stevenson-Hamilton, Pietermaritzburg: University of Natal Press, 2001, p. 81.

109. Sabi, 'Fauna of the Empire', Journal, 2, 1922, p. 42.

110. Journal, 20, 1933, p. 43.

111. Colonel A. H. Haywood, 'Gold Coast. Preservation of Wildlife', Journal, 18, 1933, p. 34.

112. Richard Oakley, 'Game Preservation in Nigeria', Journal, 14, 1931, pp. 33–4.

113. Colonel A. H. Haywood, 'Nigeria: Preservation of Wildlife, April 1932', Journal, 17, 1933, p. 33.

114. Steinhart, 2006, p. 174.

115. For a well-developed account of the capitalist, neo-liberal conservation project and discourse, see Dan Brockington, Rosaleen Duffy and Jim Igoe, Nature Unbound: Conservation, Capitalism and the Future of Protected Areas: The Past, Present and Future of Protected Areas, London: Routledge, 2008.

116. Journal, 58, 1948, 'International Union for the Protection of Nature', pp. 12–15.

117. Fitter and Scott, 1978, pp. 9–10.

118. Brockington, Duffy and Igoe, 2008, p. 9.

119. Ibid., pp. 152 and 165.

120. Wilson and Ayerst, 1976, p. 154.

121. Peter T. Dalleo, 'The Somali Role in Organized Poaching in Northeastern Kenya, c. 1909–1939', International Journal of African Historical Studies, 3, 22, 1979, pp. 472–82, p. 472.

122. Parker, 2004, pp. 102–3.

123. Ofcansky, 2002, p. 65.

124. M. H. Cowie, 'National Parks and Reserves in Kenya', Journal, 60, 1949, p. 16.

125. Parker, 2004, p. 52.

126. Steinhart, 2006, p. 168.
127. Parker, 2004, p. 103.
128. Daphne Sheldrick, *The Tsavo Story*, London: Collins and Harvill, 1973, pp. 22–5.
129. Steinhart, 2006, p. 194.
130. Captain Keith Caldwell, 'Report on a visit to East Africa', *Oryx*, 4, December 1951, p. 178.
131. Ofcansky, 2002, p. 146.
132. Ian Parker and Mohamed Amin, *Ivory Crisis*, London: The Hogarth Press, 1983, pp. 48–50.
133. Steinhart, 2006, p. 196.
134. Daphne Sheldrick, *The Tsavo Story*, London: Collins and Harvill, 1973, pp. 44–5.
135. Daphne Sheldrick, *An African Love Story: Life, Love and Elephants*, London: Penguin, 2013, pp. 82–9.
136. Anthony Cullen and Sydney Downey, *Saving the Game*, London: Jarrolds, 1960, pp. 39 and 42.
137. Ibid., pp. 168–9.
138. Sheldrick, 2013, p. 101.
139. Edward Steinhart, 'National parks and anti-poaching in Kenya, 1947–1957', *The International Journal of African Historical Studies*, 27, 1, 1994, pp. 59–76, p. 73.
140. Sheldrick, 2013, p. 103.
141. Ian Parker and Mohamed Amin, *Ivory Crisis*, London: The Hogarth Press, 1983, p. 22.
142. Parker, 2004, pp. 115–16.
143. Ibid., p. 83.
144. Parker and Amin, 1983, p. 20.
145. Personal correspondence.
146. Sheldrick, 1973, p. 92.
147. Ibid.
148. Sheldrick, 1973, p. 93.
149. Parker and Amin, 1983, pp. 55–6.
150. Sheldrick, 1973, p. 113.
151. Ibid., p. 115.
152. Caldwell, 1951, p. 183.
153. 'Report by the Uganda Game Department', *Oryx*, 6, August 1952, pp. 295–7.
154. 'The Secretary's African Tour', *Oryx*, 4, April 1958, p. 242.
155. See Mbogoni, 2013, pp. 39–42.
156. 'Extracts from the Recommendations of the Tanganyika Fauna Conference', *Oryx*, 61, 1950, p. 23.

157. See Myles Turner, *My Serengeti Years: The Memoirs of an African Game Warden*, London: Elm Tree Books, 1987, pp. 156–98.

158. Communicated to the author, during the making of a BBC World Service documentary on conservation in 1993, by members of the Kalahari Conservation Society, honorary game warden for the Okavango Tim Liversedge and Karen Ross of Conservation International. See also Beinart and Hughes, 2007, pp. 292–3.

159. U. de V. Pienaar (Biologist, Skukuza, Kruger National Park) and J. W. van Niekerk (State Veterinarian, Skukuza, Kruger National Park), 'Elephant Control in National Parks: A New Approach', *Oryx*, 1, April 1963, 1, p. 36.

4. CONSERVATION, CORRUPTION, CRIME AND CONFLICT IN EAST AFRICA

1. Ian Parker, *What I Tell You Three Times Is True: Conservation, Ivory, History and Politics*, Kinloss, Moray: Librario Publishing, 2004, p. 251.

2. Clark C. Gibson, *Politicians and Poachers: The Political Economy of Wildlife Policy in Africa*, Cambridge: Cambridge University Press, 1999, p. 4.

3. Ibid., pp. 4–5.

4. David Western, 'Chairman's Report for AERSG' *Pachyderm*, 2, November 1983, p. 2.

5. This is evident in Ian Parker's report on the ivory trade: *EBUR*, Nairobi, October 1974, typescript from Ian Parker Collection of East African Wildlife Conservation: The Ivory Trade, University of Florida, http://ufdc.edu/AA00020117/00011/ accessed 19 March 2015; see also Michela Wrong, *It's Our Turn to East. The Story of a Kenyan Whistle-blower*, London: Fourth Estate, p. 209.

6. Steinhart, 2006, p. 204.

7. Parker, 2004, p. 126.

8. Parker, 2004, pp. 132–3.

9. *Oryx*, 13,2, October 1975, notes section, 'Elephant Deaths in Tsavo East', pp. 121–2.

10. Sheldrick, 1973, p. 272.

11. Cited in Martin Meredith, *Africa's Elephant*, London: Hodder and Stoughton, 2001, p. 201.

12. John Frederick Walker, *Ivory's Ghosts: The White Gold of History and the Fate of Elephants*, New York: Grove Press, 2009, p. 172.

13. Richard Hogg, 'The New Pastoralism: Poverty and Dependency in Northern Kenya', *Africa: Journal of the International African Institute*, 56, 3, 1986, pp. 319–33, p. 322.

14. Hannah Whittaker, 'Pursuing Pastoralists: the Stigma of *Shifta* during the *"Shifta War"* in Kenya, 1963–68', *Eras*, 10, November 2008, p. 3, http://www.arts.monash.edu.au/publications/eras/ accessed 11 March 2015.

15. Ibid., p. 240.

16. *Oryx*, 14, 1, July 1977, pp. 17–18.

17. *Africa Contemporary Record, 1977–78*, vol. 10, p. B269.

18. Iain and Oria Douglas-Hamilton, *Battle for the Elephants*, London: Doubleday, 1992, p. 106.

19. Ibid.

20. Parker, 1974, p. 37.

21. Parker, 2004, pp. 221–3.

22. Douglas-Hamilton and Douglas-Hamilton, 1992, pp. 41–2.

23. Parker, 2004, pp. 242–5.

24. Parker, 2004, p. 244.

25. Parker gives a detailed account of the trade, his investigations and the anger of the Kenyan authorities in his 2004 work, pp. 221–8, 237–50.

26. Parker, 2004, p. 227.

27. Parker, 2004, p. 246.

28. Douglas-Hamilton and Douglas-Hamilton, 1992, p. 128.

29. Richard Leakey and Virginia Morell, *Wildlife Wars: My Battle to Save Kenya's Elephants*, London: Macmillan, 2001, p. 33.

30. Ibid., pp. 40–1.

31. Douglas-Hamilton and Douglas-Hamilton, 1992, p. 309.

32. *New African*, 'Scandal of the Ivory Smugglers', November 1988, pp. 36–7.

33. Raymond Bonner, *At the Hand of Man: Peril and Hope for Africa's Wildlife*, London: Simon and Schuster, 1993, p. 15.

34. Leakey and Morell, 2001, p. 6.

35. Ibid., p. 7.

36. Ibid., pp. 60–3.

37. These figures for the decline are supported by a survey by Iain Douglas-Hamilton and Holly Dublin—see Douglas-Hamilton and Douglas-Hamilton, 1992, p. 270.

38. Parker, 1974, p. 11.

39. Iain Douglas-Hamilton, 'African Elephants: Population Trends and Their Causes', *Oryx*, 21, 1, January 1987, p. 15.

40. *Oryx*, 13, 3, February 1976, notes, p. 227.

41. *Oryx*, 20, 4, October 1986, p. 256.

42. Dan Brockington, Rosaleen Duffy and Jim Igoe, *Nature Unbound:*

Conservation, Capitalism and the Future of Protected Areas: The Past, Present and Future of Protected Areas, London: Routledge, 2008,.p. 154.

43. Douglas-Hamilton and Douglas-Hamilton, 1992, pp. 27–9.
44. *TRAFFIC Bulletin*, 8, 2, 1986.
45. *Washington Post*, 16 December 1986.
46. Edward A. Alpers, 'The Ivory Trade in Africa: An Historical Overview', in Doran H. Ross (ed.), *Elephant: The Animal and Its Ivory in African Culture*, Los Angeles, CA: Fowler Museum of Cultural History, University of California, 1992, p. 362.
47. Akiiki B. Mujaju, 'The Gold Allegations Motion and Political Development in Uganda', *African Affairs*, 86, 345, 1987, pp. 479–504, p. 483, http://afraf.oxfordjournals.org/ accessed 30 March 2015.
48. Parker, 2004, p. 122.
49. Ibid., p. 124.
50. Parker, 1974, p. 9.
51. Parker, 2004, p. 125.
52. 'Poaching in Uganda', *Oryx*, 12, 3, February 1974, p. 316.
53. E. L. Edroma, 'Wildlife Count in a Uganda National Park', *Oryx*, 13, 2, October 1975, p. 176.
54. Douglas-Hamilton and Douglas-Hamilton, 1992, p. 89—he was one of those who saw the carcasses from the air.
55. S. K. Eltringham and R. C. Malpas, 'Elephant Slaughter in Uganda', *Oryx*, 13, 4, July 1976, p. 344.
56. Ibid., p. 345.
57. Ibid., p. 96.
58. Thomas Hakansson, 'The human ecology of world systems in East Africa: the impact of the ivory trade', *Human Ecology*, 32, 5, October 2004, p. 571.
59. 'Destruction in Uganda's Parks', *Oryx*, 15, 2, November 1979, p. 105.
60. Meredith, 2001, p. 210.
61. David Mitchell (of the WWF), 'Uganda's Elephants Near Extinction', *Environmental Conservation*, 7, 3, September 1980, p. 212.
62. E. L. Edroma, 'Road to Extermination in Uganda', *Oryx*, 15, 5, December 1980, p. 451.
63. Douglas-Hamilton and Douglas-Hamilton, 1992, pp. 191–2.
64. Ibid., pp. 235–6.
65. *Oryx*, 20, 4, October 1986, p. 255.
66. Jok Madut Jok, *Sudan: Race, Religion and Violence*, Oxford: Oneworld, 2007, p. 54.
67. Ian Parker, *World Ivory Trade*, 1979, p. 43, http://www.library.ufl.edu/spec/manuscript/guides/parker.htm/ accessed 20 June 2016.
68. Parker, 2004, p. 211.

69. Parker, 1979, p. 64.
70. I.S.C. Parker and E. B. Martin, 'Further Insight into the International Ivory Trade', *Oryx*, 17, 4, December 1983, pp. 198–200.
71. *Oryx*, 17, 4, October 1983, p. 193.
72. Iain Douglas-Hamilton, report in *Pachyderm*, 4, December 1984, p. 8.
73. David Western, 'Chairman's Report for AERSG', *Pachyderm*, 2, November 1983, pp. 2–3.
74. *Pachyderm*, 4, December 1984, p. 8.
75. Ibid., p. 18.
76. Ibid., pp. 264–5.

5. THE KILLING FIELDS OF CENTRAL AND SOUTHERN AFRICA

1. Personal communication.
2. R. B. Martin, J. R. Caldwell and J. G. Barzdo, *African Elephants, CITES and the Ivory Trade*, Lausanne: CITES, 1986, no page numbers.
3. Ian Parker, *World Ivory Trade*, 1979, p. 54, http://www.library.ufl.edu/spec/manuscript/guides/parker.htm/ accessed 20 June 2016. Parker's estimate of considerable hidden poaching was backed up by Iain Douglas-Hamilton's 1979 study, much of which was critical of Parker's interpretations. The consensus on this between two people bitterly divided on most issues regarding elephant numbers and the ivory trade suggests that the accounts are broadly accurate in positing a large hidden trade.
4. Douglas-Hamilton, 1992, p. 171.
5. Martin et al., 1986.
6. 'Encouraging Report on the Congo National Parks', *Oryx*, 5, August 1966, pp. 293–4.
7. *Oryx*, 10, 4, May 1970, p. 208.
8. Parker, 1979, p. 52.
9. Jacques Verschuren, 'Wildlife in Zaire', *Oryx*, 13, 2, October 1975, p. 152.
10. Iain Douglas-Hamilton and Oria Douglas-Hamilton, *Battle for the Elephants*, London: Doubleday, 1992, p. 170.
11. Janet McGaffey, 'How to survive and become rich amidst devastation: the second economy in Zaire', *African Affairs*, 1983, 82, 35, pp. 1–66, p. 6.
12. *Pachyderm*, 4, December 1984, p. 8.
13. Iain Douglas-Hamilton, 'African elephant population: trends and their causes', *Oryx*, 21, 1, January 1987, p. 15.
14. M. P. T. Alers, A. Blom, C. Sikubwabo Kiyengo, T. Masunda and R. F. W. Barnes, 'Preliminary assessment of the status of the forest

elephant in Zaire', *African Journal of Ecology*, 30, 1992, pp. 279–91, p. 280.

15. Ibid., p. 285.
16. 'Trends in Key African Elephant Populations', *Pachyderm*, 4, December 1984, p. 8.
17. Parker, 1979, p. 53.
18. Ibid.
19. *Oryx*, 15, 4, August 1980.
20. *TRAFFIC Bulletin*, 3, 2, March/April 1981.
21. Ibid.
22. *TRAFFIC Bulletin*, 5, 1, May 1983.
23. Douglas-Hamilton and Douglas-Hamilton, 1992, p. 278.
24. *Pachyderm*, 4, December 1984, p. 8.
25. Ian Parker, *What I Tell You Three Times Is True: Conservation, Ivory, History and Politics*, Kinloss, Moray: Librario Publishing, 2004, pp. 308–9.
26. Allan Thornton and Dave Currey, *To Save an Elephant: The Undercover Investigation into the Illegal Ivory Trade*, London: Doubleday, 1991, pp. 82–3.
27. Parker, 2004, pp. 287–8 and 301–3.
28. Personal communication with former South African national Intelligence agent Anthony Turton.
29. Parker, 2004, p. 333.
30. Parker gives a full—if complicated—account of this highly intricate deal in ibid., pp. 333—8.
31. David Cumming and Brian Jones, 'Elephants in Southern Africa: Management Issues and Options', Harare: WWF-SARPO occasional paper no. 11, 2005, pp. i–ii.
32. Chief Wildlife Officer, *Aerial Census of Animals in Botswana, Dry Season 2012*, Gaborone: Department of Wildlife and National Parks, 2013; and Chief Wildlife Officer, *Aerial Census of Animals in Botswana, Dry Season 2013*, Gaborone: Department of Wildlife and National Parks, 2014.
33. Personal communication.
34. Lesley P. Boggs, *Community Power, Participation, Conflict and Development Choice: Community Wildlife Conservation in the Okavango Region of Northern Botswana*, 'Evaulating Eden' Series Discussion Paper No. 17, London: IIED, June 2000, p. 26.
35. Ibid.
36. Robert and June Kay, 'Preservation in N'Gamiland', *Oryx*, 5, October 1962, pp. 285–6.
37. J. J. Mallinson, 'Dangers involved in the exploitation of game in N'Gamiland', *Oryx*, 5, October 1962, p. 288.

38. June Kay, 'Moremi Wildlife Reserve, Okavango', *Oryx*, August 1963, p. 2.
39. William Beinart and Lotte Hughes, *Environment and Empire*, Oxford: Oxford University Press, 2007, p. 293.
40. Parker, 2004, p. 49.
41. E. B. Martin, 'The Ivory Industry in Botswana', *Pachyderm*, 3, June 1984, p. 5.
42. Dan Henk, *The Botswana Defense Force in the Struggle for an African Environment*, Basingstoke: Palgrave Macmillan, 2007, p. 29.
43. Personal communication with Botswana's foreign minister, Gaositwe Chiepe, in 1993 and with Seeyiso Diphuko, head of the National Conservation Strategy Board.
44. Glen Martin, *Game Changer: Animal Rights and the Fate of Africa's Wildlife*, Berkeley, CA: University of California Press, 2012, p. 44.
45. Rosaleen Duffy, *Killing for Conservation*, Oxford: James Currey/The International African Institute, 2000, pp. 10–11.
46. Parker, 2004, p. 263.
47. Personal communication with Steve Johnson, director of the Southern Africa Regional Environment Program, Gaborone, 2 July 2015.
48. *Oryx*, 16, 2, October 1981.
49. Personal communications with wardens in Hwange and wildlife officials in Harare during a research trip to Zimbabwe in March 1982.
50. Katy Payne, *Silent Thunder: In the Presence of Elephants*, Harmondsworth, Middx: Penguin, 1998, p. 198.
51. Chilo Gorge Safari Lodge, http://chilogorge.com/about/ accessed 2 June 2015.
52. E. B. Martin, 'Zimbabwe's Ivory Carving Industry', *TRAFFIC Bulletin*, 6, 2, June 1984.
53. Duffy, 2000, p. 56.
54. Stephen Ellis, 'Of Elephants and Men: Politics and Nature Conservation in South Africa', *Journal of Southern African Studies*, 20, 1, March 1994, pp. 53–69.
55. Environmental Investigation Agency (EIA), *Under Fire: Elephants in the Front Line*, London: EIA, 1992, p. 17.
56. Ibid., p. 18.
57. Ibid., p. 19.
58. EIA, *A System of Extinction: The African Elephant Disaster*, London, EIA, 1989, p. 21.
59. This account is given in detail in the 1992 EIA report, pp. 20–2; it is corroborated by information supplied to the author by former South African National Intelligence agent Anthony Turton and Steve Johnson of SAREP.

60. Duffy, 2000, p. 63.
61. Rosaleen Duffy, 'The role and limitations of state coercion: Anti-poaching policies in Zimbabwe', *Journal of Contemporary African Studies*, 1999, 17, 1, pp. 97–121, p. 109.
62. Rowan Martin, 'Communal Area Management Plan for Indigenous Resources (Project Campfire)', in R. H. V. Bell and E. McShane-Caluzi (eds), *Conservation and Wildlife Management in Africa*, pp. 281–95, p. 281; these were the proceedings of a workshop organized by the US Peace Corps at Kasungu National Park, Malawi, October 1984.
63. Rowan Martin, *The Influence of Governance on Conservation and Wildlife Utilization: Alternative Approaches to Sustainable Use*, Harare: DNPWLM, 1992, pp. 3–8.
64. Clark C. Gibson, *Politicians and Poachers: The Political Economy of Wildlife Policy in Africa*, Cambridge: Cambridge University Press, 1999, p. 27.
65. Douglas-Hamilton and Douglas-Hamilton, 1992, p. 175.
66. Gibson, 1999, pp. 36–7.
67. Department of Game and Fisheries, *Annual Report, 1968*, Lusaka: Government of Zambia, 1970, p. 43.
68. Parker, 1979, p. 45.
69. Richard Bell, interview with the author in Maun, Botswana, November 1993.
70. Martin Meredith, *Africa's Elephant*, London: Hodder and Stoughton, 2001, p. 205.
71. Douglas-Hamilton and Douglas-Hamilton, 1992, p. 175.
72. Ibid., p. 57.
73. Gibson, 1999, p. 54.
74. Personal communication with Richard Bell.
75. Barry Dalal-Clayton and Brian Child, *Lessons from Luangwa: The Story of the Luangwa Integrated Resource Development Project, Zambia*, London: International Institute for Environment and Development, Wildlife and Development Series No. 13, March 2003, p. 53, p. 1.
76. Personal communication with Richard Bell, Gaborone, November 1993.
77. Personal communication with Hugo Jachmann, 13 July 2015.
78. Personal observation and Parker, 1979, p. 47.
79. E. B. Martin, 'Malawi's Ivory Carving Industry', *Pachyderm*, 5, July 1985, p. 9.
80. Personal communication with Hugo Jachmann.
81. R. H. V. Bell, 'Traditional Use of Wildlife Resources in Protected Areas', in Bell and McShane-Caluzi (eds), 1984, pp. 299–315, p. 303.
82. Ibid., p. 311.
83. South African National Parks, *Elephant Management Plan: Kruger National*

Park, 2013–2022, Skukuza: South Africa National Parks, November 2012, p. 19.
84. Iain Douglas-Hamilton, 'Trends in Key African Elephant Populations', *Pachyderm*, 4, December 1984, p. 9.
85. Douglas-Hamilton and Douglas-Hamilton, 1992, p. 73.
86. Personal communication with wildlife officials in Namibia, April 1990.
87. Mr Justice M. B. Kumleben, *Commission of Inquiry into the alleged smuggling of and illegal trade in ivory and rhinoceros horn in South Africa: Report of the Chairman, Mr Justice M B Kumleben*, Pretoria, January 1996.
88. Parker, 1979, p. 138.
89. Ellis, 1994, p. 56.
90. Jan Breytenbach, *Eden's Exiles: One Soldier's Fight For Paradise*, Cape Town, Quellerie, 1997, p. 28.
91. Ibid., p. 57.
92. Ibid., pp. 70–1.
93. Kumleben, p. 111.
94. Personal communication from Breytenbach and Stephen Ellis.
95. Cited by Kumleben, 1996, p. 56.
96. Breytenbach, 1997, pp. 246–7; Fred Bridgland, *Jonas Savimbi: A Key to Africa*, Edinburgh: Mainstream Publishing, 1986.
97. *Sunday Star* (Johannesburg), 10 December 1989.
98. Interview with Reeve and Ellis, 1995, p. 254.
99. David Moore, 'Progress, power, and violent accumulation in Zimbabwe', Journal of Contemporary African Studies, 2012, 30, 1, pp. 1–9, p. 5.
100. Peter Stiff, *Selous Scouts: Top Secret War*, Alberton, South Africa: Galago, 1982, pp. 737–8.
101. Ibid., p. 9.
102. Ron Reid-Daly and Peter Stiff, *Selous Scouts: Top Secret War*, Alberton, South Africa: Galago, 1982, pp. 737–8.
103. Ellis, 1994, p. 59.
104. EIA, 1992, p. 32.
105. *Weekly Mail*, 12 March 1992.
106. Kumleben, 1996, pp. 21–22.
107. Parker, 2004, pp. 344–6.
108. Julian Rademeyer, *Killing for Profit*, Johannesburg: Struik, 2012, Kindle edn, loc. 75.
109. Kumleben, 1996, p. 139.
110. John Hanks, *Operation Lock and the War on Rhino Poaching*, Cape Town: Penguin Books, 2015, pp. 189–91.
111. Ibid., p. 194.

6. THE CITES SAGA

1. Raymond Bonner, *At the Hands of Man: Peril and Hope for Africa's Wildlife*, London: Simon and Schuster, 1993, p. 122.
2. *Oryx*, 12, 4, June 1974, p. 404.
3. Much of the following account draws heavily on private conversations with many of the leading players in the elephant dramas played out at CITES and specialist meetings. Where possible, I will directly quote from those to whom I've spoken, but some have discussed aspects of the debate on condition that their words are not quoted directly, but used to give context. I will also draw extensively on published works and accounts of meetings that are in the public domain.
4. Personal communication.
5. Iain Douglas-Hamilton and Oria Douglas-Hamilton, *Battle for the Elephants*, London: Doubleday, 1992, p. 126.
6. Ibid., 1992, pp. 172–3.
7. Ian Parker, *What I Tell You Three Times Is True: Conservation, Ivory, History and Politics*, Kinloss, Moray: Librario Publishing, 2004, pp. 256–7.
8. Ian Parker, 'The Ivory Trade Volume 1: Commerce in Ivory', in *World Ivory Trade Study*, 1979, p. 209, http://ufdc.ufl.edu/AA00020117/00001/3j/ accessed 5 March 2015.
8. Martin Meredith, *Africa's Elephant*, London: Hodder and Stoughton, 2001, p. 132.
9. WWF estimate, http://wwf.panda.org/what_we_do/endangered_species/elephants/african_elephants/afelephants_threats/ accessed 31 May 2016.
10. Personal communication.
11. Parker, 1979, p. 209.
12. Meredith, 2001, p. 207.
13. Douglas-Hamilton and Douglas-Hamilton, 1992, p. 174.
14. Ibid. This view was expressed in my interviews with a wide range of conservationists, ivory trade specialists and scientists, some of whom felt that Parker and others arguing for a regulated trade believed estimates by their conservationist critics were dishonest, presenting a gloomier picture to enhance their campaign against the ivory trade. The conservationists, and later their allies in the Western-based NGOs, saw those advocating a regulated trade as apologists for the traders, many of whom dealt in a mixture of legal and illegal ivory. Parker seemed unable to perceive the possible conflict of interest between his position as a trader and a representative of traders and his wish to be seen as an objective voice supporting retention of the trade.
15. Edward B. Barbier et al., *Elephants, Economics and Ivory*, London: Earthscan Publications Ltd, 1990, Kindle edn, loc. 1175.

16. Douglas-Hamilton and Douglas-Hamilton, 1992, p. 125; and personal communication with the author.
17. *Oryx*, 14, 4, November 1978, p. 293.
18. Meredith, 2001, p. 208.
19. *Oryx*, 15, 4, August 1980, p. 321.
20. I. S. C. Parker and E. B. Martin, 'How Many Elephants Are Killed for the Ivory Trade?', *Oryx*, 16, 3, February 1982, p. 235.
21. Ibid.
22. Ibid., p. 238.
23. Personal communication.
24. David Western, 'AESG Chairman's Report', *Pachyderm*, 2, November 1983, p. 3.
25. Tim Pilgram and David Western, 'Inferring Hunting Patterns on African Elephants from Tusks in the International Ivory Trade', *Journal of Applied Ecology*, 23, 1986, pp. 503–14, p. 511.
26. Ibid., p. 512.
27. Ibid.
28. John Frederick Walker, *Ivory's Ghosts: The White Gold of History and the Fate of Elephants*, New York: Grove Press, 2009, p. 176.
29. Ibid.
30. Douglas-Hamilton and Douglas-Hamilton, 1992, p. 270.
31. Iain Douglas-Hamilton, 'Elephants Hit by African Arms Race: Recent Factors Affecting Elephant Populations', *Pachyderm*, 2, November 1983, p. 11.
32. *TRAFFIC Bulletin*, 7, 2, June 1985.
33. Allan Thornton and Dave Currey, *To Save an Elephant: The Undercover Investigation into the Illegal Ivory Trade*, London: Doubleday, 1991, p. 159.
34. J. Caldwell, 'Somalia's Ivory Sale', *TRAFFIC Bulletin*, 8, 3–4, April 1986.
35. Douglas-Hamilton and Douglas-Hamilton, 1992, pp. 297–8.
36. Ibid., p. 90; Parker, 2004, p. 399.
37. R. B. Martin, J. R. Caldwell and J. G. Barzdo, *African Elephants, CITES and the Ivory Trade*, Lausanne: CITES, 1986, no page numbers.
38. Ibid.
39. Douglas-Hamilton and Douglas-Hamilton, 1992, p. 295.
40. *Pachyderm*, 6, February 1986, p. 18.
41. David Cumming, 'Chairman's Report, AESG', *Pachyderm*, 7, December 1986.
42. Craig Packer, *Lions in the Balance: Man-Eaters, Manes, and Men with Guns*, Chicago, IL: University of Chicago Press, 2015, p. 95.
43. Iain Douglas-Hamilton, 'African Elephants: Population Trends and Their Causes', *Oryx*, 21, 1, January 1987, p. 13.

44. E. B. Martin, 'China's Ivory Carving Industry', *TRAFFIC Bulletin*, 1–2, November 1988.
45. Douglas-Hamilton and Douglas-Hamilton, 1992, p. 302.
46. Cited by Bonner, 1993, p. 116.
47. Cynthia Moss, *Elephant Memories: Thirteen Years in the Life of an Elephant Family*, New York: William Morrow, 1988, p. 297.
48. Ibid., p. 144.
49. Leakey and Morell, 2001, pp. 233–4.
50. *TRAFFIC Bulletin*, 10, 3–4, May 1989.
51. *TRAFFIC Bulletin*, 10, 3–4, May 1989.
52. D. H. M. Cumming and R. F. du Toit, 'The African Elephant and Rhino Group Nyeri Meeting', *Pachyderm*, 11, 1989, p. 4.
53. Figures from D. H. M. Cumming, R. F. du Toit and S. N. Stuart, *African Elephants and Rhinos: Status Survey and Conservation Action Plan*, Gland, Switzerland: IUCN, 1990.
54. Ibid., p. 18.
55. Cited by Barbier et al., 1990, loc 2471.
56. Meredith, 2001, p. 218.
57. Cited in ibid.
58. See David Western and Stephen Cobb, 'The Ivory Trade Review', *Pachyderm*, 11, 1989, p. 11; and David Western, 'The Ecological Role of Elephants in Africa', *Pachyderm*, 12, 1989.
59. Daniel Stiles, 'The Ivory Trade and Elephant Conservation', *Environmental Conservation*, 31, 4, 2004, pp. 309–21, p. 312.
60. Douglas-Hamilton and Douglas-Hamilton, 1992, pp. 30–1.
61. Walker, 2009, p. 178.
62. Bonner, 1993, pp. 53–4.
63. Ibid., p. 114.
64. Cited by Bonner, 1993, p. 90.
65. Based on confidential personal communications with a number of leading elephant conservationists and scientists.
66. Walker, 2009, p. 179.
67. Personal communication.
68. H. Jachmann and M. Billiouw, 'Elephant poaching and law enforcement in the central Luangwa Valley, Zambia', *Journal of Applied Ecology*, 34, 1997, pp. 233–44; Bell, 1984, pp. 317–325.
69. Bonner, 1993, p. 131.
70. Bonner, 1993, pp. 117–18.
71. Leakey and Morell, 2001, p. 87.
72. Leakey and Morell, 2001, pp. 44–5.
73. Ibid., p. 117.
74. This is most strenuously argued in the work by Barbier et al., 1990—

written by economists and other specialists involved in the ITGR report but arguing that a ban should not necessarily be comprehensive, and that any bans had to be accompanied by funding for conservation in the affected states. See also Bonner, 1993, p. 142.

75. See Bonner, 1993, pp. 144–8, for greater detail on the manoeuvring going on at Gaborone.

76. Western and Cobb, 1989. This was a collaborative study, initiated by AERSG, involving CITES/AEWG,TRAFFIC, WTMU and the funding agencies WCI, WWF, EEC and AWF. Its findings and recommendations were submitted to the African Elephant Working Group's July 1989 meeting in preparation for its recommendations to the CITES conference that October.

77. Ibid.

78. Ibid.

79. ITRG, 'The Ivory Trade and the Future of the African Elephant: SUMMARY OF THE INTERIM REPORT OF THE IVORY TRADE REVIEW GROUP', *Pachyderm*, 12, 1989.

80. Barbier et al., 1990, loc. 238.

81. ITRG, 1989.

82. For a full report of the CITES meeting, see *Oryx*, 21, 1, January 1990.

83. David Western, 'Is the Tide Turning for Elephants and Rhinos? AERSG Chairman's Report', *Pachyderm*, 13, 1990.

84. Barbier, 1990, loc 3091 and 238.

85. Ibid., loc 1021.

86. TRAFFIC Bulletin, 11, 2–3, March 1990.

87. Bonner, 1993, p. 157.

88. TRAFFIC Bulletin, 12, 1–2, 1991.

89. Bonner, 1993, p. 158.

90. C. G. Gakahu, 'AERSG Chairman's Report', *Pachyderm*, 14, 1991.

91. Holly Dublin and Bihini won wa Musti, 'AESG Chairmen's Report', *Pachyderm*, 15, 1992.

92. Holly Dublin and Hugo Jachmann, *The Impact of the Ivory Ban on Illegal Hunting of Elephants in Six Range States in Africa*, Godalming, Surrey: World Wide Fund for Nature (WWF), February 1992, p. 2.

93. Ibid.

94. Ibid., p. 3.

95. Holly Dublin, 'Chairman's Report for AESG', *Pachyderm*, 16, 1993 and 17, 1994.

96. Ibid.

97. Dublin and Jachmann, 1992, p. 2.

98. Oryx, 26, 1, January 1992.

99. Oryx, 26, 2, April 1992.

100. David Harland, 'CITES: '92 and Beyond', *Pachyderm*, 15, 1992, pp. 19–24, p. 20.
101. Ibid.
102. Iain Douglas-Hamilton, *Financial Times*, 29 February–1 March 1992.
103. Environmental Investigation Agency (EIA), *Under Fire: Elephants in the Front Line*, London: EIA, 1992.
104. Harland, 1992, p. 20.
105. Nigel Leader-Williams, 'The Cost of Conserving Elephants', *Pachyderm*, 18, 1994, p. 30.
106. Cited in *Oryx*, 28, 2, April 1994.
107. Ibid.
108. John Burton, 'Disposal of Confiscated Ivory', *Oryx*, 28, 4, October 1994.
109. Ibid.
110. Holly Dublin, T. Milliken, and R. F. W. Barnes, *Four Years After the CITES Ban: Illegal Killing of Elephants, Ivory Trade and Stockpiles*, Cambridge: TRAFFIC International, 1995; see report in 'Elephants: four years after the ivory trade ban', *Oryx*, 29, 2, April 1995.
111. Ibid.
112. *TRAFFIC Bulletin*, 15, 2, 1995.
113. *Oryx*, 30, 2, April 1996.
114. Tom Milliken, 'Monitoring the Ivory Trade and Ivory Stocks in the Post-CITES Ban Period', *Pachyderm*, 22, 1996, p. 77.
115. Robin Sharp, 'The African Elephant, Conservation and CITES', *Oryx*, 31, 2, April 1997.
116. Ibid.
117. Ibid.
118. 'African elephant range states meet in Senegal', *Oryx*, 31, 1 January 1997.
119. *TRAFFIC Bulletin*, 17, 1, 1997.
120. Holly Dublin, 'The Chairman's Report: African Elephant Specialist Group', *Pachyderm*, 24, Jul–Dec 1997, p. 1.
121. Michael 't Sas-Rolfes, 'Elephants, rhinos and the economics of the illegal trade', *Pachyderm*, 24, Jul–Dec 1997, p. 25.
122. EIA, *Proceedings of the African Elephant Conference*, London: EIA, 1997; Ronald Orenstein, *Ivory, Horn and Blood: Behind the Elephant and Rhino Poaching Crisis*, Buffalo, NY: Firefly, 2013, p. 81; 'Elephants facing new slaughter', *Sunday Telegraph*, 5 October 1997, p. 23; 'Poachers profit from easing of trade ban', *Daily Telegraph*, 31 October 1997; 'Illegal ivory trade resumes', *BBC Wildlife*, October 1997, p. 23.
123. Juan Ovejero, 'Africa Resources Trust', *Oryx*, 32, 2, April 1998.
124. *SWARA*, 23, 4, October–December 2000, p. 24.

125. David Cumming, 'Ivory Trading: The Southern African View', *SWARA*, 23, 4, October–December 2000, p. 29.
126. *TRAFFIC Bulletin*, 18, 3, 2000, p. 97.
127. Daniel Stiles and E. B. Martin, 'Status and trends of the ivory trade in Africa, 1989–1999', *Pachyderm*, 30, January–June 2001, p. 24.
128. E. B. Martin and Daniel Stiles, 'Enter "China's Ivory Triangle"', *SWARA*, 26, 1, July–December 2003, pp. 64–5.
129. *Oryx*, 37, 2, April 2003.
130. EIA, *Back in Business: Elephant Poaching and the Ivory Black Markets of Asia*, London: EIA, 2004, p. 1.
131. Ibid., p. 24.
132. Daniel Stiles, 'The ivory trade and elephant conservation', *Environmental Conservation* 31, 4, 2004, pp. 309–21, p. 309.
133. *TRAFFIC Bulletin*, 22, 1, 2008, p. 3.
134. Orenstein, 2013, p. 84.
135. Mary Rice, 'Legal ivory trading severely undermines elephant conservation', *The Ecologist*, 8 November 2012, http://www.theecologist.org/News/news_analysis/1669938/legal_ivory_trading_severely_undermines_elephant_conservation.html/ accessed 18 August 2015; Samuel Wasser, Joyce Poole et al., 'Elephants, Ivory and Trade', *Science*, 327, 12 March 2010, p. 1331.
136. Holly Dublin, 'African Elephant Specialist Group Report', *Pachyderm*, 47, January–June 2010, pp. 1–2.
137. Ed Stoddard, 'African countries still sharply divided over ivory trade', *Daily Nation* (Kenya), 13 May 2016, http://mg.co.za/article/2016–05–13–00-african-countries-still-sharply-divided-over-ivory-trade/ accessed 8 June 2016.

7. RESURGENT POACHING, SOARING CHINESE DEMAND AND DEVELOPING INSURGENCY DISCOURSE

1. BBC Wildlife, April 1997, p. 53.
2. G. Wittmeyer et al., 'Illegal killing for ivory drives global decline in elephants', *Proceedings of the National Academy of Sciences of the United States of America*, 111, 36, 2014, www.pnas.org/cgi/doi/10.1073/pnas.1403984111/ accessed 9 September 2015.
3. F. Maisels et al., 'Devastating decline of Forest Elephants in Central Africa', *PLOS ONE*, 8, 3, 2014, http://journals.plos.org/plosone/article?id=10.1371/journal.pone.0059469/ accessed 9 September 2015.
4. Samuel K. Wasser et al., 'Combating the Illegal Trade in African

Elephant Ivory with DNA Forensics', *Conservation Biology*, 22, 4, August 2008, pp. 1065–71, p. 1065.

5. United Nations Environment Programme (UNEP), *Elephants in the Dust: The African Elephant Crisis*, UNEP/CITES/IUCN/TRAFFIC, 2013, www.unep.org/pdf/RRAivory_draft7.pdf/ accessed 2 June 2016, p. 4.

6. See, for example, Jo Hastie, Julian Newman and Mary Rice, *Back in Business: Elephant Poaching and the Ivory Black Markets of Asia*, London: EIA, 2002.

7. Daniel Stiles, 'CITES-Approved Ivory Sales and Elephant Poaching', *Pachyderm*, 45, July 2008–June 2009, p. 150.

8. See E. B. Martin on new markets for ivory in *Oryx*, 32, 3, July 1998.

9. E. B. Martin and Lucy Vigne, *The Ivory Dynasty: A report on the soaring demand for elephant and mammoth ivory in southern China*, London: Elephant Family, The Aspinall Foundation and Columbus Zoo and Aquarium, 2011.

10. International Fund for Animal Welfare (IFAW), *The Global Security Implications of the Illegal Wildlife Trade*, London: International Fund for Animal Welfare, June 2013, www.ifaw-criminal-nature-uk,pdf/ accessed 14 September 2015.

11. Ibid., p. 17.

12. Personal communication.

13. Ibid.

14. Ibid.

15. Apolinari Tairo, 'China is a good friend for Africa, ready to support elephant conservation', eTN, 21 May 2014, http://www.eturbonews.com/46018/china-good-friend-africa-ready-support-elephant-conservation/ accessed 13 October 2015.

16. Kevin Heath, 'China bans ivory imports—what will happen next month?', *Wildlife News*, 26 February 2015, http://wildlifenews.co.uk/2015/02/china-bans-ivory-imports-what-will-happen-next-month/ accessed 13 October 2015.

17. *Guardian*, 29 May 2015.

18. WildAid, 'Undercover Report Unmasks Corrupt Hong Kong Ivory Trade', www.wildaid.org/news/illusion-control-hong-kongs-legal-ivory-trade/ accessed 26 October 2015.

19. The White House, 'Fact Sheet: President Xi Jinping's State Visit to the United States', https://www.whitehouse.gov/the-press-office/2015/09/25/fact-sheet-president-xi-jinpings-state-visit-united-states/ accessed 28 September 2015.

20. CNN, 13 January 2016, in Save The Elephants News Service, ste-news@elephantnews.org/ accessed 5 April 2016.

21. Associated Press, 14 January 2016.

22. Heidi Voigt, 'How Kenya's Port of Mombasa Became the World's Hub for Ivory Smuggling', *Wall Street Journal*, 16 November 2015, http://www.wsj.com/articles/kenyan-port-is-hub-for-illicit-ivory-trade-1447720944?mod=e2fb/ accessed 4 April 2016.

23. This can be seen in the reports appearing in Save the Elephant's news service, stenews@elephantnews.org.

24. Rachel Bale, 'With Ivory Ban Imminent, What Will Happen to China's Legal Stockpile?', *National Geographic*, 12 November 2015, http://news.nationalgeographic.com/2015/11/151112-ivory-china-elephants-poaching-wildlife-trafficking-conservation/ accessed 1 April 2016.

25. Ibid.

26. E. B. Martin and Daniel Stiles, 'Ivory Markets in the USA', Care for the Wild, 2008, http://savetheelephants.org/wp-content/uploads/2014/03/2008IvoryMarketsUSA.pdf/ accessed 20 June 2016.

27. Ibid.

28. Dan Stiles, 'It's Not Just China: New York is a Gateway for Illegal Ivory', *SWARA*, July–September 2013, pp. 38–40.

29. E. B. Martin and Daniel Stiles, *Ivory Markets of Europe*, Kingsfold, West Sussex: Care for the Wild International and Save the Elephants, 2005, pp. 18, 30 and 56.

30. Interpol/IFAW, 'An investigation into the ivory trade over the internet within the European Union', Interpol, February 2013, www.interpol.int/content/download/18681/166715/version/2/Project%20%Web%20-%PUBLIC.pdf/ accessed 11 September 2015.

31. Richard Leakey, interview in *SWARA*, 2, 1990, p. 16.

32. Ibid. pp. 124–5.

33. Ibid., p. 125.

34. Richard Leakey and Virginia Morell, *Wildlife Wars: My Battle to Save Kenya's Elephants*, London: Macmillan, 2001, p. 142.

35. David Western, interview in *SWARA*, 17, 4, July–August 1994.

36. Winnie Kiiru, 'The current status of human-elephant conflict in Kenya', *Pachyderm*, 19, 1995, p. 15; see also David Western in *SWARA*, 18, 2, March–April 1995, p. 229.

37. Ibid., pp. 13 and 18.

38. *Pachyderm*, 24, July–December 1997, p. 66.

39. Ibid.

40. Ibid.

41. Iain Douglas-Hamilton, 'The current elephant poaching trend', *Pachyderm*, 45, July 2008–June 2009, p. 154.

42. Steve Bloomfield, 'Warlords Turn to Ivory Trade to Fund Slaughter of Humans', *Independent*, 18 March 2008.

43. E.B. Martin and Lucy Vigne, 'The Status of the Retail Ivory Trade in Addis Ababa in 2009', *TRAFFIC Bulletin*, 22, 3, 2010, p. 141.

44. BBC News, 'Kenya makes massive seizure of ivory and rhino horns', 23 August 2010, http://www.bbc. co.uk/news/world-africa-11062 726/ accessed 21 October 2015.

45. Capital FM, Nairobi—http://www.capitalfm.co.ke/news/Kenyanews/ Thaicustoms-seize-two-tonnes-of-ivory-12263.html#i xzz1RsILuNBu/ accessed 21 October 2015.

46. George Wittmeyer, David Daballen and Iain Douglas-Hamilton, 'Rising Ivory Prices Threaten Elephants', *Nature*, 476, 18 August 2011.

47. *Oryx*, 47, 2, 2013, pp. 162–3.

48. UNEP, 2013, p. 36.

49. Varun Vira and Thomas Ewing for Born Free USA/C4ADS, *Ivory's Curse: The Militarization and Professionalization of Poaching in Africa*, New York: Born Free/C4DS, April 2014, www.bornfreeusa.org/downloads/pdf/Ivorys-Curse-2014.pdf/ accessed 21 October 2015.

50. Ibid., p. 58.

51. 'Ivory and Corruption: An Interview with Dr Richard Leakey', *SWARA*, July–September 2013, p. 41.

52. Voigt, 2015.

53. Ibid.

54. The author is grateful to Calvin Cottar for details of these schemes; personal communication.

55. NRT, *The Story of the Northern Rangelands Trust*, 2013, p. 6, http://charliepyesmith.com/wp-content/uploads/2014/01/CPS-story-northern-rangelands-trust.pdf/ accessed 21 June 2016.

56. Personal communication with Ian Craig.

57. *Capital FM* (Nairobi), 26 February 2016.

58. *Mail and Guardian*, 'Four ivory seizures at Kenya's international airport in just one week—so what changed?', 18 January 2016, http:// mgafrica.com/article/2016–01–18-four-ivory-seizures-at-kenyas-international-airport-in-one-week-and-the-dogs-that-make-it-happen/ accessed 7 April 2016.

59. *Star* (Kenya), 27 January 2016.

60. Personal communication with Paul Elkan; Vira and Ewing, 2014, p. 27.

61. Personal communication.

62. African Elephant Database, 2013, http://www.elephantdatabase.org/ preview_report/2013_africa_final/Loxodonta_africana/2013/Africa/ accessed 29 October 2015.

63. Radio Tamazuj, 'Poachers kill 17 more elephants in South Sudan's Sudd wetland', 1 April 2016, https://radiotamazuj.org/en/article/poach-

ers-kill-17-more-elephants-south-sudans-sudd-wetland/ accessed 6 April 2016.

64. Radio Tamazuj, 'War brings devastating assault on South Sudan's wildlife', 4 March 2016, https://radiotamazuj.org/en/article/war-brings-devastating-assault-south-sudans-wildlife/ accessed 6 April 2016.

65. Jason Patinkin, 'Rare Forest Elephants Seen for the First Time in South Sudan', Smithsonian Institute, 11 December 2015, http://www.smithsonianmag.com/science-nature/rare-forest-elephants-seen-first-time-south-sudan-180957526/?no-ist/ accessed 6 April 2016.

66. Ledio Cakaj/Enough Project, *Tusk Wars: Inside the LRA and the Bloody Business of Ivory*, Washington DC: Enough Project, October 2015.

67. E. B. Martin, 'Northern Sudan ivory market flourishes', *Pachyderm*, 39, July–December 2005, p. 67.

68. See Gérard Prunier, *Darfur: The Ambiguous Genocide*, London: Hurst, 2005, pp. 97–100; Julie Flint and Alex de Waal, *Darfur: A New History of a Long War*, London: Zed/African Arguments, 2008, pp. 33–70.

69. Prepared statement of Ginette Hemley, Senior Vice President, Conservation Strategy and Science, World Wildlife Fund, and Tom Milliken, Elephant and Rhino Leader, TRAFFIC: Senate Foreign Relations Committee, 24 May 2012, *Ivory and Insecurity: The Implications of Poaching in Africa*, Hearing May 24, 2012, loc. 1633.

70. Daniel Stiles, *Ivory Trade, Terrorism and U.S. National Security*, ©Daniel Stiles 2014, p. 15.

71. Stiles, 2014, p. 16.

72. International Crisis Group, *The Central African Crisis: From Predation to Stabilisation*, Africa Report no. 219, 17 June 2014, http://www.crisisgroup.org/~/media/Files/africa/central-africa/central-african-republic/219-la-crise-centrafricaine-de-la-predation-a-la-stabilisation-english.pdf/ accessed 27 October 2015.

73. Holly Dublin and Hugo Jachmann, *The Impact of the Ivory Ban on Illegal Hunting of Elephants in Six Range States in Africa*, Godalming, Surrey: World Wide Fund for Nature (WWF), February 1992, p. 18.

74. E. B. Martin and Lucy Vigne report from Selous, 'Under Operation Uhai', *SWARA*, 20/21, 6/1, 1998, p. 9.

75. Samuel Wasser et al., 'Elephants, Ivory and Trade', *Science*, 327, 12 March 2010, p. 1331.

76. EIA, *Open Season: The Burgeoning Illegal Ivory Trade in Tanzania and Zambia*, London: Environmental Investigation Agency, March 2010, p. 1.

77. *TRAFFIC Bulletin*, 23, 2, 2011, p. 68.

78. IUCN, 'Illegal trade puts more World Heritage sites in danger',

18 June 2014, http://www.iucn.org/fr/node/16376/ accessed 7 September 2015.

79. Selous Elephant Emergency Project launched by Federal Republic of Germany, Selous Game Reserve/Ministry of Natural Resources and Tourism, Frankfurt Zoological Society and the International Council for Game and Wildlife Conservation, August 2014.

80. Dan Levin, 'Chinese President's Delegation Tied to Illegal Ivory Purchases During Africa Visit', *The New York Times* Sinosphere blog, 5 November 2014, http://sinosphere.blogs.nytimes.com/2014/11/05/chinese-presidents-delegation-tied-to-illegal-ivory-purchases-during-africa-visit/?_r=0/ accessed 27 October 2015.

81. Dr Trevor Jones, 'New Census Results Confirm Elephant Declines in Ruaha-Rungwa', Southern Tanzania Elephant Program, 10 December 2015, http://www.stzelephants.org/census-results-ruaha-rungwa/ accessed 7 April 2016.

82. EIA, *Vanishing Point: Criminality, Corruption and the Devastation of Tanzania's Elephants*, London: Environmental Investigation Agency, November 2014, p. 13.

83. Ibid., p. 10.

84. EIA, 2014; *The Economist*, 'Big game poachers: Claims of links between politicans and poachers merit further investigation', 8 November 2014, http://www.economist.com/news/middle-east-and-africa/21631202-claims-links-between-politicians-and-poachers-merit-further-investigation-big/ accessed 27 October 2015.

85. Reuters, 10 February 2016.

86. Felister Peter, IPP Media, 10 February 2016, http://www.ippmedia.com/ accessed 7 April 2016.

87. *Daily News* (Tanzania), 24 February 2016.

88. Keith Somerville, 'Africa's Long Road and Current Developments', *Commonwealth Opinion*, 3 January 2016, http://commonwealth-opinion.blogs.sas.ac.uk/2016/africas-long-road-and-current-developments/ accessed 7 April 2016.

89. *Saturday Star*, 'Ruvuma's Success Points Way to Battle the Poaching Scourge (Tanzania/Mozambique), 31 May 2014, http://savetheelephants.org/about-elephants/elephant-news/?detail=1077/ accessed 28 October 2015.

90. Nicola Harley, 'British pilot shot dead by elephant poachers', *Daily Telegraph*, 30 January 2016, http://www.telegraph.co.uk/news/uknews/crime/12131864/British-pilot-shot-dead-by-elephant-poachers.html/ accessed 6 April 2016.

91. African Elephant Database 1995, http://www.elephantdatabase.org/report/1995/Africa/Eastern_Africa/ accessed 21 June 2016.

92. Ibid.

93. Brian Clark Howard, 'Why Elephants Are Recovering in Uganda as They Decline Overall', *National Geographic*, 22 June 2015.

94. Save the Elephants, *Elephant News*, 10 November 2014.

95. Ibid.

96. *The Indian Ocean Newsletter*, 'Museveni Doesn't Make Tracking Ivory Traffic Any Easier (Uganda), 27 Feburary 2015, http://savetheelephants.org/about-elephants/elephant-news/?detail=2219/ accessed 29 October 2015.

97. R. F. W. Barnes et al., 'Elephants and ivory poaching in the forests of equatorial Africa', *Oryx, 27*, 1, January 1993.

98. Iain Douglas-Hamilton, 'The current elephant poaching trend', *Pachyderm*, 45, July 2008–June 2009, p. 154.

99. Iain Douglas-Hamilton, Senate Foreign Relations Committee, 2012, loc. 286; F. Maisels et al., 'Devastating Decline of Forest Elephants in Central Africa', *PLOS One*, 4 March 2013, http://journals/plosone/article?id=10.1371/journal.pone.0059469/ accessed 22 September 2015.

100. C. Nellemann et al. (eds), *The Environmental Crime Crisis: Threats to Sustainable Development from Illegal Exploitation and Trade in Wildlife and Forest Resources, A UNEP Rapid Response Assessment*, United Nations Environment Programme and GRID-Arendal, Nairobi: UNEP/Interpol, 2014, p. 24.

101. David Western, 'The Ecological Role of Elephants in Africa', *Pachyderm*, 12, 1989; D. H. M. Cumming, R. F. du Toit and S. N. Stuart, *African Elephants and Rhinos: Status Survey and Conservation Action Plan*, Gland, Switzerland: IUCN, 1990.

102. *TRAFFIC Bulletin*, 22, 1, 2008, p. 34.

103. TRAFFIC, 'Cameroon elephant poaching crisis spreads', http://www.traffic.org/home/2012/3/29/cameroon-elephant-poaching-crisis-spreads.html/ accessed 2 November 2015.

104. *TRAFFIC Bulletin*, 24, 1, 2012, p. 31.

105. Jeffrey Gettleman, 'Elephants Dying in Epic Frenzy as Ivory Fuels Wars and Profits', *The New York Times*, 3 September 2012, http://www.nytimes.com/2012/09/04/world/africa/africas-elephants-are-being-slaughtered-in-poaching-frenzy.html?_r=0/ accessed 3 November 2015.

106. Vira and Ewing, 2014, p. 82; *Mail and Guardian*, 'African spy chiefs warn of poaching link to terror groups', 8 August 2014, www.mg.co.za/article/2014-08-08-spy-chiefs-warn-of-poaching-link-to-terror-groups/ accessed 7 September 2014.

107. Vira and Ewing, 2014.

108. Personal communication from Stéphane Crayne, a former French army officer who organised anti-poaching units in the CAR's Dzangha-Sanga National Park from 2013 to 2015.

109. J. Michael Fay and Marcellin Agnagna, 'Forest Elephant Populations in the Central African Republic and Congo', *Pachyderm*, 14, 1991, pp. 3–19.

110. David Western, 'The Ecological Role of Elephants in Africa', *Pachyderm*, 12, 1989, pp. 42–5.

111. *Pachyderm*, 12, 1989; and Fay and Agnagna, 1991.

112. Personal communication from Stéphane Crayne.

113. Philippe Bouche et al., 'Has the final countdown to wildlife extinction in Northern Central African Republic begun?', *African Journal of Ecology*, 48, 2009, pp. 994–1003, p. 996.

114. Douglas-Hamilton, 2012, loc. 385.

115. *Haaretz Magazine*, 4 September 2013.

116. Bill McQuay and Christopher Joyce, 'Former Commando Turns Conservationist To Save Elephants of Dzanga Bai', NPR, 9 May 2014, http://www.npr.org/2014/05/09/310259368/former-commando-turns-conservationist-to-save-elephants-of-dzanga-bai/ accessed 3 November 2015.

117. Personal communication; and Stéphane Crayne, *The Professionalization and Militarization of Conservation in the Dzanga-Sangha Protected Area*, paper presented at a workshop on the illegal wildlife trade in conflict areas, Marjan Centre for the Study of Conflict and Conservation, Department of War Studies, King's College, London, 4 November 2015.

118. Stéphane Crayne, 'Counter-Poaching: 6 Degrees of Impunity', *Bio Web*, 3 December 2015, http://bioweb.ie/counter-poaching/ accessed 6 April 2016.

119. Vira and Ewing, 2014, p. 31.

120. *Oryx*, 34, 2, April 2000.

121. Douglas-Hamilton, 2008–9, p. 154.

122. Steve Bloomfield, 'Warlords Turn to Ivory Trade to Fund Slaughter of Humans', *Independent*, 18 March 2008, http://www.commondreams.org/news/2008/03/18/warlords-turn-ivory-trade-fund-slaughter-humans/ accessed 11 September 2008.

123. Douglas-Hamilton, 2012, loc. 385.

124. African Parks, 'African Parks Model', https://www.african-parks.org/african-parks/the-african-parks-model/ accessed 6 April 2016.

125. *National Geographic*, 'Chad Takes Action, and the Elephants Hear It', 27 February 2014/ accessed 5 November 2015.

126. Thomas O. McShane, 'Conservation before the crisis: an opportunity in Gabon', *Oryx*, 24, 1, January 1990, p. 9.

127. R. F. W. Barnes et al., 'Elephants and ivory poaching in the forests of equatorial Africa', *Oryx*, 27, 1, January 1993, p. 32.

128. Jeffrey Gettleman, 'In Gabon, Lure of Ivory Is Hard for Many to Resist', *The New York Times*, 26 December 2012.

129. Maisels et al., 2013.

130. Zoological Society of London (ZSL), International Wildlife Trafficking: Solutions to a Global Crisis', Symposium 11–12 February 2014, London: Zoological Society of London, 2014, p. 13,www.zsl.org/sites/default/files/media/2014–04/Wildlife%20trade%20symposium%20-%20abstracts.pdf/ accessed 9 September 2015.

131. Personal correspondence with a participant in the ZSL conference, who wants to remain anonymous.

132. ZSL, 2014.

133. Africom, 'About the Command', http://www.africom.mil/ accessed 6 April 2016.

134. *Africa News*, 'Gabon to deploy more rangers to counter ivory poachers', 21 January 2016; Save The Elephants News Service, stenews@elephantnews.org/ accessed 6 April 2016.

135. Leonard Mubalama and Eulalie Bashige, 'Caught in the Crossfire', *Pachyderm*, 40, January–June 2006, p. 73.

136. Leonard Mubalama, 'Population and Distribution of Elephants (Loxodonta africana) in the Central Sector of the Virunga National Park, Eastern DRC', *Pachyderm*, 28, January–June 2000, p. 43.

137. Kes Hillman Smith,'Status of northern white rhinos and elephants in Garamba National Park, Democratic Republic of Congo, during the wars', *Pachyderm*, 31, July–December 2001, p 79.

138. Ibid.

139. Emmanuel de Merode, Bila-Isia Inogwabini, José Telo and Ginengayo Panziama, 'Status of elephant populations in Garamba National Park, Democratic Republic of Congo, late 2005', *Pachyderm*, 42, January–June 2007, p. 55.

140. International Fund for Animal Welfare (IFAW), *Criminal Nature: The Global Security Implications of the Illegal Wildlife Trade*, London: International Fund for Animal Welfare, June 2013, p. 14, http://www.ifaw.org/sites/default/files/ifaw-criminal-nature-UK.pdf/ accessed 16 June 2016.

141. Gettleman, September 2012.

142. Kristof Titeca 'Out of Garamba, into Uganda: Poaching and Trade of Ivory in Garamba National Park and LRA-affected Areas in Congo',

Institute of Analysis and Development, Policy and Management, University of Antwerp, Analysis and Policy Briefs, No. 5, 2013.

143. Makini Brice, 'Four rangers killed trying to stop elephant poachers in Congo park', *Independent*, 10 October 2015, http://www.independent.co.uk/news/world/africa/four-rangers-killed-trying-to-stop-elephant-poachers-in-congo-park-a6688871.html/ accessed 20 June 2016.

144. Flora and Fauna International (FFI), 'Emergency support for elephant crisis in Democratic Republic of Congo', 16 November 2015, http://www.fauna-flora.org/news/emergency-support-for-elephant-crisis-in-drc/ accessed 17 November 2015.

145. *Oryx*, 34, 2, April 2000.

146. David Cumming and Brian Jones, *Elephants in Southern Africa: Management Issues and Options*, WWF-SARPO Occasional Paper Number 11, Harare: WWF-SARPO, May 2005, p. i.

147. Rosaleen Duffy, *Nature Crime: How We're Getting Conservation Wrong*, New Haven, CT: Yale University Press, 2010, p. 62.

148. Bram Büscher, *Transforming the Frontier: Peace Parks and the Politics of Neoliberal Conservation in Southern Africa*, Durham, NC and London: Duke University Press, 2013, pp. 6–7.

149. Ibid., p. 53.

150. This was confirmed in conversation with Michael Flyman of the Botswana wildlife department, Baboloki Autletswe of the Kalahari Conservation Society and Steve Johnson of the Southern African Regional Environment Programme (SAREP) in Gaborone in July 2015.

151. S. Anstey, *Angola: Elephants, People and Conservation. A Preliminary Assessment of the Status and Conservation of Elephants in Angola*, Harare: IUCN Regional Office for Southern Africa, 1993, p. 10.

152. Ibid.

153. T. Milliken, A. Pole, and A. Huongo, 'No Peace for Elephants: Unregulated Domestic Ivory Markets in Angola and Mozambique', Cambridge: TRAFFIC International, 2006, p. 5.

154. Cited in ibid., p. 5.

155. TRAFFIC and WWF, 'Illegal ivory trade burgeoning in Angola', *Oryx*, 2006, 40, 3, p. 250.

156. E. B. Martin and Lucy Vigne, 'Luanda—the largest illegal ivory market in southern Africa', *Pachyderm* 55, January–June 2014, p. 30.

157. Michael Chase and Curtice R. Griffin, 'Elephants of south-east Angola in war and peace', *African Journal of Ecology*, 2011, 49, pp. 353–61, 354.

158. Personal communication—this and other statements from Botswana

officials and conservationists were gathered on a BBC World Service programme-making trip in November 1993.

159. This was stressed to me by Diphuko and Vice-President Mogae during the making of the documentary.

160. *Oryx*, 28, 3, July 1994.

161. Lesley P. Boggs, *Community Power, Participation, Conflict and Development Choice: Community Wildlife Conservation in the Okavango Region of Northern Botswana*, London: IED, Evaluating Eden Series Discussion Paper No. 17, June 2000, p. 7.

162. Keith Somerville, 'No longer at ease: clouds on the horizon for Botswana's conservation success story', *African Arguments*, 23 July 2015, http://africanarguments.org/2015/07/23/no-longer-at-ease-clouds-on-the-horizon-for-botswanas-conservation-success-story-by-keith-somerville/ accessed 20 June 2016. Steve Johnson of SAREP and DWNP officials in Maun and Gaborone believe there has been a slow but perceptible increase in poaching and a drop-off in cooperation with the wildlife authorities since the hunting ban.

163. African Elephant Database, 2002, http://www.elephantdatabase.org/report/Loxodonta_africana/2002/Africa/Southern_Africa.

164. Kabo Keaketswe, 'Botswana Intensifies Anti-Poaching Efforts', *Daily News*, 28 January 2016.

165. Personal communications from Flyman, Johnson and Autlwetse.

166. News 24, 'Botswana MPs want wildlife hunting ban lifted', 17 March 2015, http://www.news24.com/Green/News/Botswana-MPs-want-wildlife-hunting-ban-lifted-20150317/ accessed 10 November 2015.

167. Personal communication.

168. Department of Wildlife and National Parks, *Aerial Census of Animals in Northern Botswana, Dry Season 2012*, Gaborone, Chief Wildlife Officer Research and Statistics Division, 2012, p. v.

169. Department of Wildlife and National Parks, *Aerial Census of Animals in Northern Botswana, Dry Season 2013*, Gaborone, Chief Wildlife Officer Research and Statistics Division, 2013, p. 2.

170. Personal communication.

171. Don Pinnock, 'Southern African elephant corridors blocked by poachers', *Daily Maverick*, http://www.dailymaverick.co.za/article/2014–01–09-southern-african-elephant-corridors-blocked-by-poachers/#.V2PbOoTKllJ/ accessed 17 June 2016.

172. Ibid.

173. *The Namibian*, 9 March 2016.

174. Francis X. Mkanda, 'Status of Elephants and Poaching for Ivory in Malawi: A Case Study in Liwonde and Kasungu National Parks', *Pachyderm*, 16, 1993, p. 59.

175. Dublin and Jachmann, 1992, p. 31.

176. *TRAFFIC Bulletin*, 11, 3, 1992.

177. Personal communication with Hugo Jachmann.

178. Duffy, 2010, p. 82.

179. african-elephant@elephantnews.org, Save The Elephants News Service stenews@elephantnews.org/ accessed 6 April 2016.

180. Pius Nyondo, 'Malawi: Dausi in "Ivory-Gate" At Nyika National Park, *Nyasa Times*, 24 February 2016, http://allafrica.com/stories/201602240925.html/ accessed 7 April 2016.

181. Mateus Chambal, 'Current Elephant Range and Status in Mozambique', *Pachyderm*, 16, 1993, p. 48.

182. African Elephant Database, 2013, http://www.elephantdatabase.org/preview_report/2013_africa_final/Loxodonta_africana/2013/Africa/Southern_Africa/ accessed 17 November 2015.

183. Vira and Ewing, 2014, p. 70.

184. Information from Steve Johnson of SAREP.

185. WWF, 'Joint Statement on the Status of Elephant Population in Selous-Niassa Ecosystem', 17 July 2012, http://wwf.panda.org/wwf_news/?205666/JOINT-STATEMENT-ON-THE-STATUS-OF-ELEPHANT-POPULATION-IN-SELOUS-NIASSA-ECOSYSTEM/ accessed 17 November 2015.

186. Vira and Ewing, 2014, p. 77.

187. WWF, 'Urgent international action needed following elephant poaching statistics in Mozambique', 19 June 2014, http://wwf.panda.org/wwf_news/?223851/Urgent-international-action-needed-following-elephant-poaching-statistics-in-Mozambique/ accessed 12 September 2015.

188. AllAfrica.com, 'Mozambique: Elephant Poaching "a National Disaster"', 22 September 2014, http://allafrica.com/stories/201409222278.html/ accessed 12 September 2015.

189. WCS, 'Govt of Mozambique announces major decline in national elephant population', 26 May 2015, http://newsroom.wcs.org/News-Releases/articleType/ArticleView/articleId/6760/Govt-of-Mozambique-announces-major-decline-in-national-elephant-population.aspx/ accessed 23 September 2015.

190. Cited by WWF, 'Urgent international action needed following elephant poaching statistics in Mozambique', 19 June 2014, http://www.wwf.org.za/?11261/WWF-Mozambique-survey/ accessed 20 June 2016.

191. D. Lowenburg, 'The Ivory Bandwagon: International Transmission of Interest-Group Politics', *The Independent Review*, 4, 2, Fall 1999, pp. 217–39, p. 223.

192. Cumming and Jones, 2005, p. 30.
193. Hongxiang Huang and Oxpeckers, 'Chinese merchant gateways for ivory and rhino horns', *Pambazuka*, 10 April 2014, http://pambazuka.org/en/category/features/91299/ accessed 25 September 2015.
194. Oxpeckers Investigative Environmental Journalism, 16 November 2015, *Save The Elephants News Service* stenews@elephantnews.org/ accessed 7 April 2016.
195. Don Pinnock, 'Hunting desert elephants for meat raises a storm—and denials', *Daily Maverick*, 9 June 2014, http://www.dailymaverick.co.za/article/2014-06-09-hunting-desert-elephants-for-meat-raises-a-storm-and-denials/#.U5WgVi9mWhM/ accessed 17 November 2015.
196. http://www.met.gov.na/Documents/Desert%20elephant%20%20press%20release.pdf/ accessed 17 November 2015.
197. *Oryx*, 28, 4, October 1994.
198. *African Wildlife Update*, June 1996, 5.
199. *Oryx*, 34, 1, January 2000.
200. N. Owen-Smith et al., 'A scientific perspective on the management of elephants in the Kruger National Park and elsewhere', *South African Journal of Science*, 102, September–October 2006, pp. 389–94, p. 389.
201. Kruger National Park, 'Culling: Elephant Population Control Discussed', 10 November 2010, www.krugerpark.com/blog/index.php/culling-elephant-population-control-discussed/ accessed 23 September 2015.
202. Sam Ferreira, *Elephant Management Plan: Kruger National Park, 2013–2022*, South African National Parks, Scientific Services, November 2012, pp. 8–9 and p. 32.
203. Ibid., p. 42.
204. South African National Parks, 'Media Release: 19 Elephants killed by poachers in the KNP', 23 October 2015, http://www.sanparks.org/about/news/?id=56511/ accessed 18 November 2015.
205. Dublin and Jachmann, 1992, p. 7.
206. Personal communication from Hugo Jachmann, who was involved in the project with Richard Bell.
207. Barry Dalal-Clayton and Brian Child, *Lessons from Luangwa: The Story of the Luangwa Integrated Resource Development Project, Zambia*, London: International Institute for Environment and Development, Wildlife and Development Series No. 13, March 2003, pp. 2–3.
208. Ibid., p. 38. Jachmann confirmed this in personal communications and his work with Billiouw on poaching and enforcement in Luanga: Hugo Jachmann and M. Billiouw (1997), 'Elephant Poaching and Law-Enforcement in the Central Luangwa Valley, Zambia', *Journal of Applied Ecology*, 34, pp. 233–44.

209. Musole M. Musumali, Thor S. Larsen and Bjorn P. Kaltenborn, 'An impasse in community based natural resource management implementation: the case of Zambia and Botswana', *Oryx*, 41, 3, 2007, p. 311.
210. Jo Hastie, Julian Newman and Mary Rice, *Back in Business*, London: EIA, 2002, p. 4
211. Ibid.
212. Personal communication from Steve Johnson of SAREP, the Kalahari Conservation Society and Michael Flyman of the Botswana wildlife department.
213. Save The Elephants News Service, 28 March 2016, stenews@elephantnews.org/ accessed 7 April 2016.
214. Savé Valley Conservancy, 'Ecological Sustainability', http://savevalleyconservancy.org/about/sustainability/ accessed 19 November 2015.
215. Raymond Bonner, *At the Hands of Man: Peril and Hope for Africa's Wildlife*, London: Simon and Schuster, 1993, p. 253.
216. Ibid., p. 256.
217. Ivan Bond, 'The importance of sport-hunted African elephants to CAMPFIRE in Zimbabwe', *TRAFFIC Bulletin*, 14, 3, 1994, pp. 117–19, p. 117.
218. Bonner, 1993, p. 253.
219. *New Scientist*, 12 June 1993.
220. Brian Child, 'The practice and principles of community-based wildlife management in Zimbabwe: the CAMPFIRE programme', *Biodiversity and Conservation*, 5, 1996, pp. 369–98, p. 370.
221. V. Dzingirai and E. Madzudzo, 'Big Men and CAMPFIRE: A comparative study of the role of external actors in conflicts over local resources', *Zambezia*, 1999, 26, 1, Centre for Applied Social Science (CASS), University of Zimbabwe, pp. 77–8.
222. R. D. Taylor, 'Elephant management in Nyaminyami District, Zimbabwe: turning a liability into an asset', *Pachyderm*, 17, 1993, pp. 19–29, pp. 22–3.
223. *SWARA*, 20, 3, May–June 1997.
224. *SWARA*, 23, 4, October–December 2000, pp. 24–5.
225. W. Wolmer, J. Chaumba and I. Scoones, 'Wildlife management and land reform in Southeastern Zimbabwe: a compatible pairing or a contradiction in terms?', *Sustainable Livelihoods in Southern Africa Research Paper 1*, Brighton: Institute of Development Studies, 2003, p. 1.
226. Cumming and Jones, 2005, p. 58.
227. Rowan B. Martin, *Conditions for effective, stable and equitable conserva-*

tion at the national level in southern Africa: A paper prepared for Theme 4 at a Workshop titled Local Communities, Equity and Protected Areas, to be held from 24–26th October in Durban, South Africa, 2002, p. 16—cms-data.iucn.org/downloads/cca_rmartin.pdf/ accessed 28 September 2015.

228. Ian Scoones, Joseph Chaumba, Mavedzenge Blasio and William Wolmer, 'The New Politics of Zimbabwe's Lowveld: The Struggles over Land at the Margins', *African Affairs*, 111, 445, 2012, pp. 527–50, p. 540.

229. Ibid., p. 542.

230. N. Muboko, V. Muposhi, T. Tarakini, E. Gandiwa, S. Vengesayi and E. Makuwe, 'Cyanide poisoning and African elephant mortality in Hwange National Park, Zimbabwe: a preliminary assessment', *Pachyderm* 55, January–June 2014, p. 92.

231. Reuters, 'Zimbabwe arrests editor, reporters over elephant poaching story', 3 November 2015, http://uk.reuters.com/article/uk-zimbabwe-press-arrest-idUKKCN0SS11C20151103/ accessed 20 June 2016.

232. *The Herald*, 'Zimbabwe: Anti-Poaching Efforts Under Pressure From Corruption', 10 November 2014, http://allafrica.com/stories/20141 1100762.html/ accessed 24 November 2015.

233. Ibid.

234. Adam Cruise, 'Mining Director Busted for Elephant Poisonings', *National Geographic*, 27 February 2016, http://news.nationalgeographic.com/2016/02/160228-wildlife-trafficking-elephants-wildlife-crime/ accessed 7 April 2016.

235. Ibid., p. 51.

236. Ibid.

237. Thulani Mpofu, 'Zimbabwe's wildlife threatened by poachers', *The National*, 8 September 2009, http://www.thenational.ae/news/world/africa/zimbabwes-wildlife-threatened-by-poachers/ accessed 19 November 2015; Vira and Ewing, 2014, p. 51.; Council on Foreign Relations, 'Zimbabwe: The "Crocodile" Who Would Be King', 22 January 2015, http://blogs.cfr.org/campbell/2015/01/22/zimbabwe-the-crocodile-who-would-be-king/ accessed 19 November 2015; MISA, 'Mnangagwa behind ivory rhino smuggling … says British newspaper', *The Zimbabwean*, 3 August 2009, http://www.thezimbabwean.co/2009/08/mnangagwa-behind-ivory-rhino-smuggling-says-british-newspaper/ accessed 17 June 2016.

238. Rowan Martin, *Comment Opposing the Interim Suspension of Imports of Elephant Trophies from Zimbabwe, 79 F.R. 26986 (May 12, 2014)*, 6 June 2014.

239. *Southern Times* (Harare), 23 March 2015.

240. African Elephant Database, 2013, http://www.elephantdatabase.org/preview_report/2013_africa_final/Loxodonta_africana/2013/Africa/West_Africa/ accessed 24 November 2014.

241. http://www.aib.bf/m-2342-niangoloko-des-paysans-manifestent-contre-les-degats-d-elephants.html/ accessed 24 November 2015.

242. http://www.bornfree.org.uk/news/news-article/?no_cache=1&tx_ttnews%5Btt_news%5D=1353 accessed 24 November 2014.

243. David Brugière, Iacouba Badjinca, Cristina Silva, Abubacar Serra and Mamadou Barry, On the road to extinction? The status of elephant Loxodonta africana in Guinea Bissau and western Guinea, West Africa, Oryx, 2006, 40, 4, p 442.

244. http://www.ifaw.org/united-states/news/cote-divoire-african-forest-elephant-move-news-round accessed 24 November 2015.

245. Stephen Blake, Philippe Bouché, Henrik Rasmussen, Anne Orlando and Iain Douglas-Hamilton, *The Last Sahelian Elephants Ranging Behavior, Population Status and Recent History of the Desert Elephants of Mali*, Nairobi: Save the Elephants, August 2003, p. 7.

246. http://news.mongabay.com/2014/0402-hance-canney-lephants.html#xJr3CVb9kScqrRJA.99 accessed 24 September 2015.

247. Susan Canney and Nomba Ganamé, The Mali Elephant Project in IIED, *Conservation, Crime and Communities*, London: International Institute for Environment and Development, Febnruary 2015, p. 20, http://pubs.iied.org/pdfs/14648IIED.pdf? Accessed 30 September 2015.

248. Reuters, 28 January 2016.

249. Mali Web, 3 December 2015, http://www.maliweb.net/contributions/des-representants-des-collectivites-du-gourma/ accessed 6 April 2016.

250. VICE, 3 February 2016, *Save The Elephants News Service* stenews@elephantnews.org accessed 6 April 2016.

251. Andrew Dunn, WCS Nigeria Country Director, and Gilbert Nyanganji, Yankari Project Manager, Improving Protection for Nigeria's Largest Elephant Population in Yankari Game Reserve. Final Report to the International Elephant Foundation from the Wildlife Conservation Society (WCS), New York, May 2011, p. 2.

252. *Traffic, Bulletin*, 24, 2, 2012, p. 43.

253. Esmond Martin and Lucy Vigne, Lagos, Nigeria: One of the Largest Retail Centres for Illegal Ivory Surveyed to Date, *TRAFFIC Bulletin*, 25,1, 2013, p. 35.

254. Ibid., p. 38.

255. See Mary Kaldor, *New and Old wars. Organized Violence in a Global Era*, Stanford, Calif.: Stanford University Press, 2007.
256. Tom Maguire and Cathy Haenlein, *An Illusion of Complicity Terrorism and the Illegal Ivory Trade in East Africa*, Occasional Paper, London: Royal United Services Institute, September 2015, p. 6.https://www.rusi.org/downloads/assets/201509_An_Illusion_of_Complicity.pdf accessed 24 September 2015.
257. Keith Somerville, The Ivory Wars: how poaching in Central Africa fuels the LRA and Janjaweed, *African Arguments*, 14 January 2013 and African wars and the Politics of Ivory, 9 April 2013, http://www.e-ir.info/2013/04/09/african-wars-and-the-politics-of-ivory/.
258. UNEP/Interpol: C. Nellemann, R. Henriksen, P. Raxter, N. Ash, E. Mrema (Eds). 2014. *The Environmental Crime Crisis—Threats to Sustainable Development from Illegal Exploitation and Trade in Wildlife and Forest Resources*. A UNEP Rapid Response Assessment. United Nations Environment Programme and GRID-Arendal, Nairobi and Arendal, www.grida.no accessed 16ᵗʰ September 2015.
259. Ibid.
260. Douglas-Hamilton, 2012, loc. 67.
261. Tom Cardamone, *Ivory and Insecurity: The Global Implications of Poaching in Africa*. Written testimony Before the United States Senate Committee on Foreign Relations, May 2012, www.foreign.senate.gov/imo/media/doc/Tom_Cardamone Testimony.pdf, p. 2, accessed 1ˢᵗ September 2015
262. *SWARA*, January–March 2013, p. 21.
263. Elephant Action league, Africa's White Gold of Jihad: Al-Shabaab and Conflict Ivory, January 2013, http://elephantleague.org/project/africas-white-gold-of-jihad-al-shabaab-and-conflict-ivory/ accessed 30 November 2015.
264. Vira and Ewing, 2014, pp. 11–12.
265. See IFAW, 2013, Vira and Ewing, 2014, and UNEP, 2013; UNEP/Interpol, 2014.
266. UNEP, 2013, p. 57.
267. Jasper Humphreys and M. L. R. Smith, The 'rhinofication' of South African security', *International Affairs*, 2014, 90, 4, pp. 795–8181, p. 795.
268. Save the Elephants, *Elephant News*, 26 September 2013; and, https://www.clintonfoundation.org/clinton-global-initiative/commitments/partnership-save-elephants accessed 30 November 2015; http://blog.conservation.org/2013/10/one-way-to-fight-terrorism-end-the-ivory-trade/#sthash.ykUZE1WE.dpuf accessed 26 September 2015.

269. Jane Edge, What are NGOs doing to stop the slaughter of Africa's elephants? *Africa Geographic*, 17 April 2015.

270. http://allafrica.com/stories/201402121055.html accessed 30 November 2015.

271. Katherine Lawson and Alex Vines, *Global Impacts of the Illegal Wildlife Trade, The Costs of Crime, Insecurity and Institutional Erosion*, London: Chatham House, February 2014, p. 3.

272. Dr Bob Smith, Using Drones to Save Elephants and Rhinos Could Backfire, *Guardian*, 26 June 2014, http://www.theguardian.com/environment/blog/2014/jun/26/using-drones-save-elephants-rhinos-backfire accessed 30 November 2015.

273. Rosaleen Duffy, Waging a war to save diversity: the rise of militarized conservation, *International Affairs*, 90, 4, 2014, pp. 819–34, p. 819.

274. Maguire and Haenlein, 2015; Duffy 2014; Humprheys and Smith, 2014; and, Vanda Felbab-Brown, It's corruption, stupid: Terrorism, wildlife trafficking, and Obama's Africa trip, Brookings, 22 July 2015—http://www.brookings.edu/blogs/up-front/posts/2015/07/22-obama-africa-wildlife-felbabbrown accessed 30 November 2015.

275. Felbab-Brown, 2015.

276. http://www.independent.co.uk/news/world/africa/illegal-ivory-trade-funds-al-shabaabs-terrorist-attacks-8861315.html accessed 1 December 2015.

277. http://www.wsj.com/articles/SB10001424052702304626104579119123262765740 accessed 1 December 2015.

278. Nir Kalron and Andrea Crosta, *Africas White Gold of Al Shabaab and Conflict Ivory*, Jaznuary 2013, http://elephantleague.org/project/africas-white-gold-of-jihad-al-shabaab-and-conflict-ivory/ accessed 1 December 2015.

279. Ibid.

280. Ibid.

281. Ibid. Bold type in original.

282. Ibid.

283. See, for example, Laurel Neme, Andrea Crosta and Nir Kalron, Al Shabaab and the Human Toll of the Illegal Ivory Trade, National Geographic, 3 October 2013 accessed 1 September 2015; Laurel Neme, Andreas Crosta and Nir Kalron, Terrorism and the ivory trade, *LA Times*, 14 October 2013; William Eagle, Somalia's Insurgents Turn Ivory into Big Export Business, *VoA News*, 12 June 2014, http://www.voanews.com/content/somalias-insurgents-turn-ivory-into-big-business/1935/423.html accessed 1 December 2015.

284. Keith Somerville, 'What is driving the demise of the African elephant?', 11 December 2014, http://www.politicsweb.co.za/news-and-analysis/what-is-driving-the-demise-of-the-african-elephant/ accessed 28 November 2015.

285. Personal communication.

286. Personal communication.

287. Daniel Stiles, *Ivory Trade, terrorism and US national security: How connected are they*, Daniel Stiles, 2014. P. 10 (copy supplied by the author), and personal communication; and Maguire and Haenlein, 2015, p.

288. See Mary Harper, *Getting Somalia Wrong? Faith, War and Hope in a Shattered State*, London: Zed, 2012; Stig Jarle Hansen, *Al Shabaab in Somalia*, London: Hurst and Co, 2013; UNEP 2013 and Interpol, *Analytical Report: Ivory Crime and Conflict*, Lyon: Interpol, 2013; UNEP/Interpol, 2014.

289. I'm very grateful to Dan Stiles for advice and critical analysis of the Al Shabab discourse. Esmond Martin, Mary Rice and Ian Douglas-Hamilton all gave advice and information that casts doubt on the thrust of the EAL report. See, also, Maguire and Haelein's 2015 excellent report for RUSI which emphasis the myths and mispreceptions about Al Shabab.

290. See Somerville, Africa's Long Road Since Independence, 2015, pp. 260–3; and Enough Project, 2015.

291. Ledio Cakaj/Enough Project, 'Tusk Wars: Inside the LRA and the Bloody Busines of Ivory', Enough Project, October 2015, pp. 6–7.

292. Ibid., pp. 12–3.

8. CONCLUSION

1. This argument follows the approach to elites and informal networks of patrimonialism benefiting from disorder or weak governance set out by Patrick Chabal and Jean-Pascal Daloz in *Africa Works: Disorder as Political instrument*, Oxford: James Currey, 1999, p. xix; this model also dovetails with the role of gatekeepers and extraversion set out in earlier referenced works of Fred Cooper and Jean-François Bayart.

2. Rosaleen Duffy, Freya A. V. St John, Bram Büscher and Dan Brockington, 'Towards a new understanding of the links between poverty and illegal wildlife hunting', *Conservation Biology*, 29, 4, August 2015, pp. 4 and 6.

3. R. D. Taylor, 'Elephant management in Nyaminyami District, Zimbabwe: turning a liability into an asset', *Pachyderm*, 17, 1993, pp. 19–29.

4. I'm indebted to ivory trade expert Daniel Stiles for this point and for his constructive criticism of sections of this book.

5. John Emilly Otekat, 'The role of local communities in wildlife conservation', *SWARA*, 16, 3, May–June 1993, p. 7.

6. Agence France Presse, 13 January 2016.

7. Thanks to Dan Stiles for this information.

8. Agence France Presse, 13 January 2016.

9. Sifelani Tsiko, 'SADSC faces tough battle at CITES 17', *Southern Times*, 23 March 2016, http://southernafrican.news/2016/03/23/sadc-faces-tough-battle-at-cites-17/ accessed 5 April 2016.

10. Coalition members are Benin, Burkina Faso, Cameroon, Central African Republic, Chad, Côte d'Ivoire, the Democratic Republic of the Congo, the Republic of the Congo, Equatorial Guinea, Eritrea, Ethiopia, Gabon, Ghana, Guinea, Guinea-Bissau, Kenya, Liberia, Mali, Niger, Nigeria, Rwanda, Senegal, Sierra Leone, South Sudan, Togo and Rwanda. Mauritania and the Comoros are non-range state members.

11. Daisy Fletcher, *The Independent*, 10 November 2015.

12. Adam Cruise, 'South Africa an Outlier on Ivory Policies', *National Geographic*, 13 January 2016, http://news.nationalgeographic.com/2016/01/160113-South-Africa-ivory-destruction-legalization-CITES/ accessed 6 April 2016.

13. Ibid.

14. Damian Carrington, 'African elephants "killed faster than they are being born"', *The Guardian*, 3 March 2016, http://www.theguardian.com/environment/2016/mar/03/african-elephants-killed-faster-than-they-are-being-born/ accessed 7 April 2016; see also CITES, 'African Elephants Still in Decline Due to High levels of Poaching', press release, 3 March 2016, https://cites.org/eng/news/pr/african_elephants_still_in_decline_due_to_high_levels_of_poaching_03032016/ accessed 7 April 2016.

15. Dan Stiles, 'Aunt Mildred's Teeth, CITES and the Ivory Trade', *SWARA*, April–June 2013, p. 18.

INDEX

INDEX

INDEX

INDEX

INDEX

INDEX

INDEX

INDEX

INDEX

INDEX